CHRISTIANITY

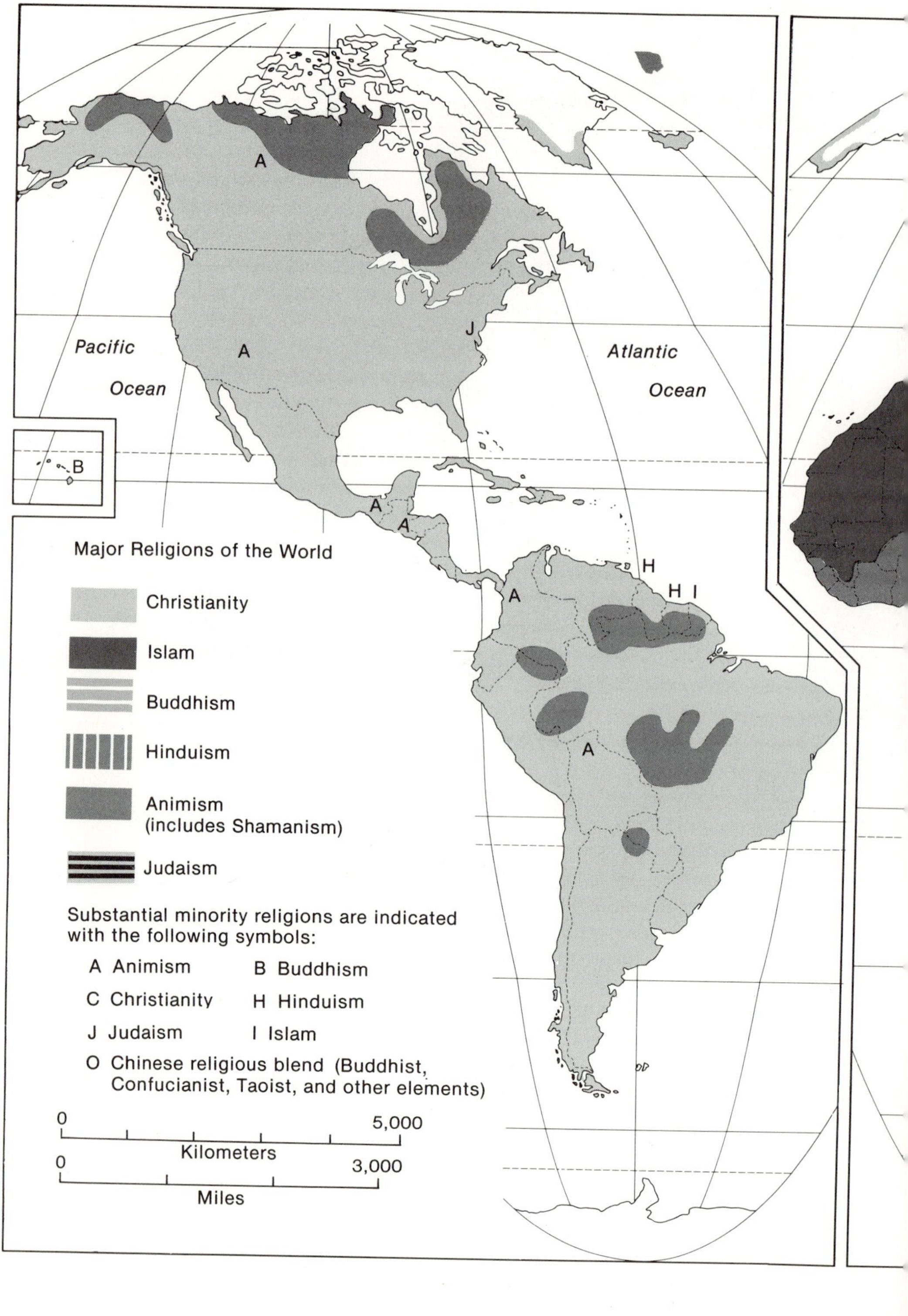

Pacific
Ocean
Atlantic
Ocean
A
A
J
B
A
A
H
H I
A
A
Major Religions of the World
Christianity
Islam
Buddhism
Hinduism
Animism
(includes Shamanism)
Judaism
Substantial minority religions are indicated with the following symbols:
A Animism
B Buddhism
C Christianity
H Hinduism
J Judaism
I Islam
O Chinese religious blend (Buddhist, Confucianist, Taoist, and other elements)
0
5,000
Kilometers
0
3,000
Miles

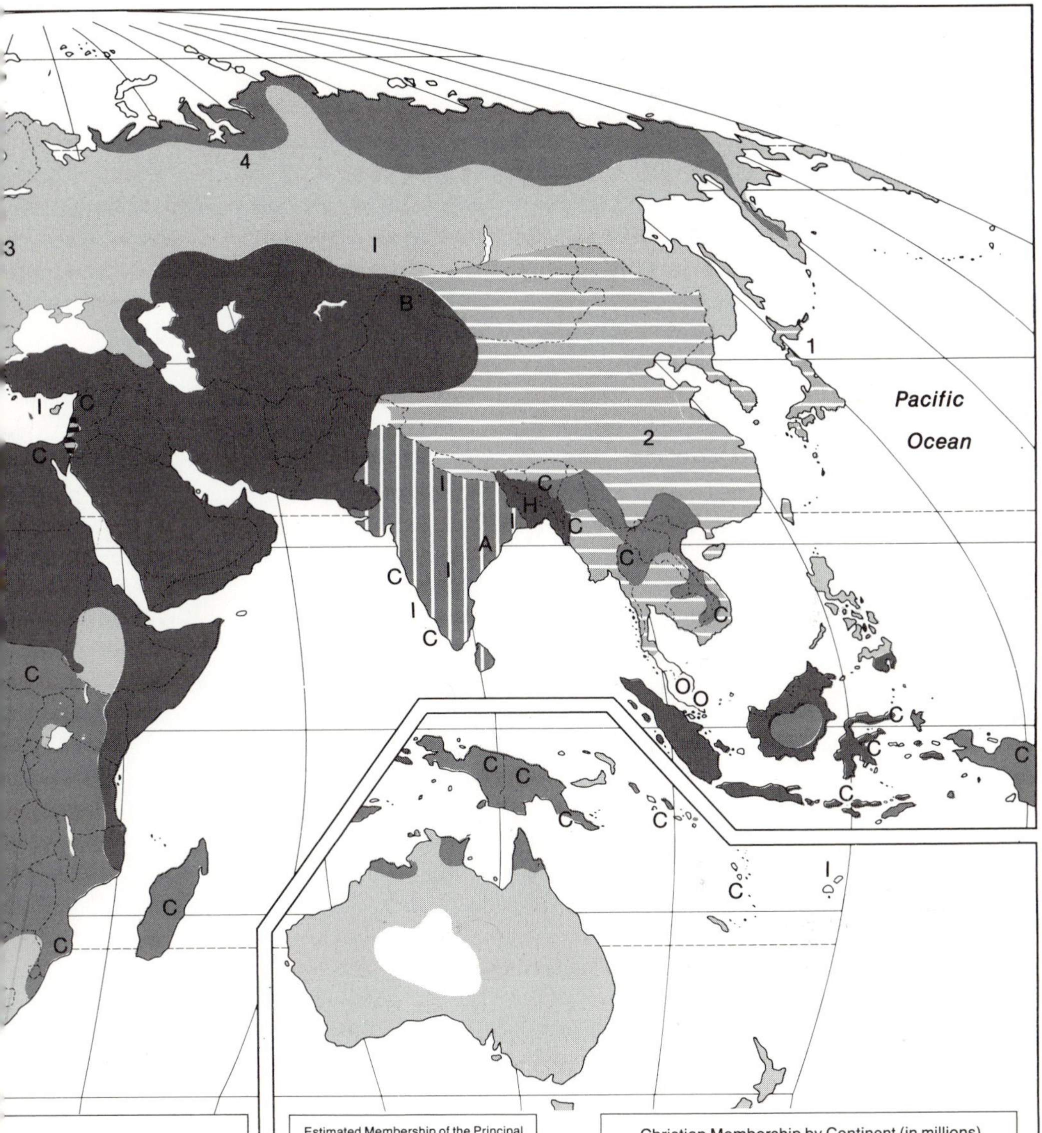

n mixes Buddhism and Shinto.

a mixes Buddhism, Confucianism,
sm, Islam, and Marxism.

ern Europe mixes Marxism and
odox Christianity.

R mixes Marxism, Orthodox Christianity,
Islam.

Estimated Membership of the Principal Religions of the World

Christian	1 billion
Roman Catholic	580 million
Protestant	345 million
Orthodox	75 million
Jewish	15 million
Muslim	590 million
Zoroastrian	270 thousand
Shinto	57 million
Taoist	31 million
Confucian	156 million
Buddhist	255 million
Hindu	478 million

(Source: 1981 Encyclopaedia Brittanica Book of the Year)

Christian Membership by Continent (in millions)

	Roman Catholic	Protestant	Orthodox
North America	133	99	4.75
South America	162	12	0.52
Europe	177	111	55.00
Asia	55	38	2.50
Africa	47	68	13.00
Oceania	4	13	0.41

(Source: 1981 Encyclopaedia Brittanica Book of the Year)

CHRISTIANITY
An Introduction

Denise Lardner Carmody
John Tully Carmody
Wichita State University

Wadsworth Publishing Company
Belmont, California
A Division of Wadsworth, Inc.

Religion editor: Sheryl Fullerton
Production editor: Judith McKibben
Managing designer: Patricia Dunbar
Interior and cover designer: Richard Kharibian
Copy editor: Lorraine Anderson

Printed in the United States of America

1 2 3 4 5 6 7 8 9 10—87 86 85 84 83

Library of Congress Cataloging in Publication Data

Carmody, Denise Lardner, 1935–
Christianity, an introduction.

Bibliography: p.
Includes index.
1. Christianity. I. Carmody, John, 1939–
II. Title.
BR121.2.C29 200 82-4854
AACR2

ISBN 0–534–01181–0

For Paul Magelli,
Dean extraordinary

Contents

Preface

We conceive of this book as a comprehensive introduction to the Christian religion. It derives from courses that we have taught, both together and singly, at state institutions and also at church-affiliated schools. Keeping in mind the special needs of today's undergraduates, we have stressed a well-defined pedagogical format, concrete prose, and numerous contemporary examples. For each chapter we provide an outline, a summary, and study questions. A moderate number of references show some of the major sources for each chapter, and a rather full glossary at the end of the text offers help with technical terms that appear in boldface in the text. Finally, a fairly extensive annotated bibliography offers the more industrious reader many further resources.

We have been moved to write this book because none of the texts we used in teaching the Christianity course proved sufficiently comprehensive. Specifically, none met the need we felt to present the Christian worldview, and the Christian history, and present-day Christian religious experiences. The hallmark of our text, then, is its threefold, comprehensive format of worldview, history, and description of current religious experience. Insofar as students need to know all three, we hope our text will prove especially apt to meet students' needs.

Special thanks go to Karl Kraft, secretary of the religion department at Wichita State University, who typed the text very efficiently and cheerfully; to Sheryl Fullerton of Wadsworth Publishing Company, who was especially diplomatic in editorial negotiations; and to the following scholars who reviewed the manuscript and offered valuable suggestions: John V. Apczynski, Saint Bonaventure University; Frederick M. Denny, University of Colorado; Walter L. Moore, Florida State University; and Joseph B. Tyson, Southern Methodist University.

CHAPTER 1

Introduction

Religion

The correlation of ordinary reality, "the way things are," with mystery marks a religious approach to understanding worldly affairs, for religion finds mystery at the core of human life. Contrary to science, which limits its sure pronouncements to what the senses can verify, religion opens onto realities beyond the senses. Contrary to **secularism**,* which takes the world bounded by space and time as its full horizon, religion recognizes portions of human experience that exceed the world of space and time. T. S. Eliot expressed a part of this religious attitude when he spoke of "the still point of the turning world."[1] There are moments when human beings experience more than what science can measure, and spill over the containers of secularism. Times of love, creativity, deep prayer, and bedrock suffering all give insistent evidence that human beings are *more*.

Mystery is closest in such moments when human beings are *more*. At those times another dimension seems to fill out. Who would deny that the space between two people who are in love is fuller, more energetic, richer than the space between two straphangers on the subway? The time when the artist or scientist enjoys the flame of creativity is qualitatively different from the time when she takes coffee or reads her mail. If you have ever come upon an old person lost in prayer at the back of a chapel, you know that deep prayer has something unworldly about it. If you have ever been forced down to your bedrock by suffering, you know that you have scraped away many false portions to get to your true self.

There is a qualitative intensity or richness in these experiences that human instinct refuses to dismiss. If science or secularism has no place for them, then so much the worse for science or secularism. Our loves, creative works, deep times of prayer, and bedrock sufferings are some of the most important things about us. Certainly they say more about who we are than does our body chemistry or our stock portfolio. And a major reason why these qualitatively intense experiences say more about who we are is that they evoke mystery. Each and all, they reveal that the

*Terms in boldface appear in the glossary.

human person lives out into a fullness, an at least potential *All*, that holds the key to his vocation. When we are struck down by suffering or raised up by beauty, we step outside the bounds of science or secularism and ask questions more personal, more compelling, more directly tied to what being human entails. We ask questions about why we are here on this earth, why we have been given this lifetime, why we so often have to suffer evil and see the defeat of good.

The significance of these questions lies not only in the answers they evoke but in the orientation they give. By raising questions about her origin or destiny, a person confronts the mystery at the core of human existence. Human beings are the only animals who can ask where they came from, where they are going. We are the only animals who have a reflective consciousness interested in grasping our full situation. From this reflective consciousness come the **cultural** developments that distance us from other highly developed animals. However bright, chimpanzees and dolphins have not generated art, science, architecture, drama, or economics. Whatever rudimentary similarities zoologists can find in higher animals' work or play, a chasm remains between humans and other animals. Because of our orientation toward the whole, the full horizon of **being**, the human species has added another layer to evolution. Over the physical layer of life, the biosphere, we have spread a layer of thought, the **noosphere**.

It would take us astray to describe the contemporary advances of the noosphere that communications are making today. It might also distract from this section's main point. For most aspects of today's communications are quantitative, whereas the main point in this section is qualitative. At the heart of human experience there is a still point, a quiet center, where the reflective personality finds life mysterious. When challenged, this personality realizes that life is more than a problem. A problem is something we think we can solve. It is a matter of acquiring more or better information, of applying new or better analytical techniques. A genuine mystery occurs in another order. It is too rich for our minds to grasp, too full of meaning or being or implication. The human person is a genuine mystery. None of us has ever understood ourself or another human person utterly, in the way we can understand a theorem of Euclid's. The universe is a genuine mystery. No matter how far scientists probe into space, or how deeply they descend into subatomic matter, there is present a richness of organization, an immensity of power, that boggles their minds.

The religions turn on mystery. Calling it God, Brahman, Tao, and other names, they have organized all human life by reference to mystery. This is true for traditional Christianity, so we try to keep the mystery before us as we explore Christianity in this introductory text.

The Format of This Book

*Let us now describe how this book is organized. In brief, it proceeds in three parts: the Christian worldview, Christian history, and contemporary faces that Christianity shows.

The main reason for beginning with the Christian worldview is the likelihood that readers will pick this book up assuming they know what Christianity entails. Readers who live in lands that many call Christian may well expect to find familiar notions between these covers. But chances are this will not wholly be the case. The original message of Jesus and the fullest development of Christian culture clash with modern Western belief and practice. Sören Kierkegaard, a nineteenth-century Danish **existentialist** noted for his penetrating thought, encountered a similar situation in his day. In trying to explain the implications of radical Christian faith to his fellow Danish burghers, he found that their "official" Christianity had innoculated them against virtually all the strong strains of Jesus's message. Anything that upset their personal comfort or civic peace they considered "un-Christian."

To confront this problem, we begin by discussing the Christian worldview. In fact, we start the confrontation in the next section of this introduction, by attending to the criticisms that Aleksandr Solzhenitsyn, a **prophetic** Christian and Nobel-Prize-winning Russian writer, has made of American capitalist society. From there, the entire first part of the book will attend to the challenging ideas that lie at the heart of Christian thought.

The second part of our text traces the historical origins of the Christian worldview. How has it developed from Jesus to the present? Where has the Christian faith spread to, how has it fared when it has come into secular power, why has it greeted warmly some forms of **pagan** culture (like philosophy) and opposed bitterly other forms (like modern science)? In a limited space, we describe the major events that spread the Christian influence from the first band of Jesus's followers to a major portion of the Western world and beyond.

The third part of our text presents scenes from diverse dramas of Christian faith being enacted in different parts of the world today. As the history will have made clear, Jesus's followers split into three basic groups. For the sake of convenience, we now separate Christians into great sub-families called Catholic, Protestant, or Orthodox. Catholic Christianity is especially vital today in Latin America, so we shall describe recent events there. Protestant faith and theology have been especially sensitive to the implications of modern science and politics, so we shall examine these implications as discussed at a recent conference of the World Council of Churches on Faith and Science in an Unjust World. Orthodoxy takes an especially intriguing form in Greek and Russian **monasticism**, so we shall describe the strong impact monasticism continues to make on the Orthodox. Finally, to introduce two other members of the Christian family that do not fit any of the above categories but are especially dynamic today, we have included chapters on black American Christianity and current feminist theology. The book concludes with a summary of the heart of the Christian matter.

Our format, then, moves from discussion of the Christian worldview through Christian history to some of Christianity's current faces. To get our discussion of the Christian worldview off to a provocative start, let us consider the impact that Aleksandr Solzhenitsyn caused when he brought his Christian philosophy to Harvard University.

Solzhenitsyn at Harvard

In June 1978, Aleksandr Solzhenitsyn delivered the principal address at Harvard University's 327th commencement. He had been forcibly deported from the Soviet Union in 1974, for a long series of prophetic attacks on that country's leaders and policies. Coming to Vermont, where he continued to document the horrors of the Soviet regime and especially of its infamous prison camps in the Gulag Archipelago, Solzhenitsyn soon made his American hosts realize that their culture also was far from passing muster. The address at Harvard impressed this realization on a broad segment of the academic community.

A prophet is one who speaks a word of judgment that he thinks comes from God. In the biblical tradition, the prophet is a vehicle of the Word of the Lord, which calls human beings to repent of their evils. Solzhenitsyn does not describe himself as hearing speeches from God or witnessing divine visions; nevertheless, he works at the core of the prophetic task, which is warning human beings that they are failing to meet divine standards.

Where did Solzhenitsyn get his sense of having such a mission? From a dramatic happening in his own life. Having been released from the Gulag, he found himself struck down by cancer. In December 1953, he was given only three weeks to live. But, miraculously, he did not die. His cancer, actively malignant and long neglected, went into remission and then was cured. Considering this "act of God" with his experience of the prison camp, Solzhenitsyn developed the conviction that his life was no longer his own. Thenceforth it belonged to the special work God had in store for him.

> "Like the *starsy*, the wandering 'God folk' of Old Russia, Solzhenitsyn made of himself a living witness, an incarnate testimony against the secular legions of evil. He would bestride the land, harried, persecuted, a leprous beggar if need be, to cry out the truth against the black wind of lies—above all, against oblivion, that obscene amnesia whereby the indifferent or numbed generations of the present-day Soviet state have forgotten the millions and millions of victims."[2]

Thus the great spokesman of truth, thickset and bearded, strode onto th Harvard stage and declaimed to the West. His message was no collection of com forts. The same combination of personal suffering and **Orthodox** faith that ha made Solzhenitsyn the enemy of Marxism-Leninism gave him a perspective o American culture that upset many in the Harvard audience. Happy when he ha championed the truth against Soviet Communism, applauding when he had wo the Nobel Prize for Literature, many Americans—especially academicians—turned to stone when they heard his Harvard address. In it many of them m vigorous Christian faith for the first time.

To begin, Solzhenitsyn remarked on Western cowardice: "A decline in courag may be the most striking feature that an outside observer notices in the We today."[3] Second, he said the West has lowered its cultural goals to concentra essentially on its own material well-being. Third, he claimed Western societies ha become legalistic, with results more noxious than they realize: "Whenever the tissue of life is woven of legalistic relationships, this creates an atmosphere of spiritual mediocrity that paralyzes man's noblest impulses."[4]

Solzhenitsyn went on to say that by an abuse, or a misunderstanding, of freedom, the West has sanctioned the rise of overt criminality, sometimes to the point of bending over backwards to protect terrorists' rights. "This tilt of freedom toward evil has come about gradually, but it evidently stems from a humanistic and benevolent concept according to which man—the master of the world—does not bear any evil within himself, and all the defects of life are caused by misguided social systems, which must therefore be corrected. Yet strangely enough, though the best social conditions have been achieved in the West, there still remains a great deal of crime; there is even considerably more of it than in the destitute and lawless Soviet society."[5]

The attack went on, blistering the press, the superficial fashions in Western intellectual circles, socialism, capitalism, power-politics, and more. Nonetheless, it was not simply a scathing indictment. Strong as Solzhenitsyn's criticisms were, little inclined as he was to sugarcoat his medicine, there was a palpable strain of compassion in his words. He said he was not surprised to find weakness in his land of exile: anyone reading the signs of the times would have expected it. But the degree of Western sickness that Solzhenitsyn diagnosed, and the cause he assigned blame to, surprised many of his hearers. He said the sickness was near to crisis, and he pinpointed its cause as the rejection of Christianity, with its "great reserves of mercy and sacrifice." He alleged that in modern times Western states have turned away from Christianity to materialism. They have achieved many human rights, but at the price of dimming a sense of responsibility to God and society. "All the celebrated technological achievements of progress . . . do not redeem the twentieth century's moral poverty. . . ." Thus spake the prophet Aleksandr, as a multitude grumbled in Harvard Yard.[6]

The Challenge of Traditional Christianity

Let's briefly look at some of the tenets of Solzhenitsyn's traditional Christian faith that he feels have been forgotten in the West. In traditional Christianity, technological riches cannot compensate for moral poverty. Traditional Christianity sees as its real treasure the **holy** God. With right relation to the holy God, a person is full of riches. Without right relation to the holy God, a person is inconsolably deprived. Christians have long confessed that the first commandment is to love God with one's whole mind, heart, soul, and strength. The second commandment is like the first: To love one's neighbor as oneself. Solzhenitsyn makes these views the cornerstone of his ethical construction. Unless we understand this, his opinions are likely to seem self-consciously virtuous or antiquated.

In the mainstream of Christian tradition, love of God and love of neighbor are at the heart of being human. God is the creative mystery that makes all things be.

One's neighbor is an image of God, just as one's self is. Nothing is more essential to good order, both personal and social, than acting on these two truths. For Christian thinkers, both the individual personality and society unravel when the first commandment is disobeyed. Human beings start to think of creation as a matter of happenstance. Before long they regard it as a tissue of evolutionary accidents having no rhyme or reason. Neglecting the second commandment brings parallel disasters. If human beings are not reflections of God, they easily become dispensable, abusable. At first hand, Solzhenitsyn has seen a society that disposes of human beings when they protest its murders. To his mind, the Gulag Archipelago results directly from Marxist-Leninist atheism. These are judgments typical of traditional Christian thought.

Traditional Christian thought regards the center of human existence as a mystery beyond our control. *God* names a reality, a power, that is not at our beck and call. Rather, we should be at the beck and call of God, because we derive completely from God's creative love. Modern Western culture has largely cast off these Christian convictions, Solzhenitsyn notes. From the Renaissance, the West has exalted human autonomy. With the rise of modern science, we have gained impressive control over nature. Discoveries in astronomy, biology, and psychology have demolished the centuries-old view that the earth is the center of the universe. No longer can one believe that creation occurred as depicted in the first chapters of Genesis. No longer does the wisdom of the Church seem equal to the problems of our times. Solzhenitsyn does not do justice to these causes of the modern revolt against traditional faith, and he fails to mention the religious wars, bigotries, corruptions, and dishonesties that fed the fires of revolt. When the final accounting is made, religious institutions will have to pay dearly for the damages to humanity that have occurred in modern times. They made faith all too easy to despise.

On the other hand, orthodox Christianity will not absolve modern human beings of guilt, any more than it will absolve the churches. In the Christian view, human beings are more than ignorant; they are also sinful, freely choosing to do evil. East and west, north and south, we can avert our faces from God, refusing to grant our neighbors justice. There is nothing inevitable in a Gulag Archipelago, any more than in a Dachau, Auschwitz, or torture chamber in Brazil. Like the genocides in Cambodia, Nigeria, and Armenia, they tell a shocking story of human malice.

Out of personal experience, Solzhenitsyn tells the West that its quarrel with traditional Christianity is superficial. Line up all the legitimate grievances against Christian religion, he says, and they will not overbalance the need human beings have for a God and a strong moral code. For Solzhenitsyn agrees with his predecessor Dostoevski: If God does not exist, everything is permitted. Negatively, if God does not exist, there is no ultimate judge who will punish the wicked and reward the good. Positively, if God does not exist, we are drowning in moral chaos, unable to find deep joy or peace. In traditional Christianity, God the judge is finally less significant than God the treasure on whom our hearts have been set. Without fullness of being, light, and love, human existence is hellish.

The orthodox way is more positive than negative. Show people the beauty of God, it says, and you will solve half the problem of making a just society. The other half of the problem will remain. Bad will and selfishness will continue to cause awful suffering. But people will no longer live in a madhouse—a society denying itself the one source of its health. Walk the orthodox way and you will leave the company of fools. Solzhenitsyn insists that life is deeper, better, sharper than what godless fools can fathom. It is more exciting and more demanding. Where Wall Street and Madison Avenue lead to spiritual mediocrity, orthodox wisdom leads to the traditional dictum: "God's glory is human beings fully alive."

Faith as a Horizon

A religious faith like Christianity is a horizon against which the believer sets his or her experience. Just as relativity theory or quantum mechanics serves physicists as an interpretational framework, so a religious faith serves believers as an interpretational framework. We establish deep convictions and make choices about nature, society, the self, and ultimate reality based on our interpretational framework or horizon. Part of Solzhenitsyn's quarrel with Western culture is with its unwillingness to make explicit the interpretational framework behind its spiritual lethargy. If it were made explicit, a **dialectic** could be established.

A dialectic is a juxtaposition of differing interpretational frameworks. Lining up the two points of view, one compares them on pivotal questions and attempts to clarify their respective truths. In the first part of our book we pave the way for such a comparison. By explaining the Christian worldview, we provide the understanding necessary for the reader to compare Christianity dialectically with other faiths. Behind our work is the assumption that a liberal education encourages dialectics. We assume that encouraging a clash of faiths is part of a college's or a university's commitment to pursuing truth. It is not our task here to compare Christianity with all other faiths. It is our place to explain the Christian worldview clearly enough, and make enough comparisons, to get the process going.

Perhaps an example of conflicting worldviews will make the idea of establishing a dialectic easier to understand. The main characters in Margaret Atwood's novel *Life Before Man*[7] stand in marked contrast to Aleksandr Solzhenitsyn. Where he is quite certain of his central values, they are centerless. All three of these main characters—Elizabeth, Nate, and Lesje—contemplate suicide, because all three feel empty and depressed. Whatever faith they had, religious or secular, has slipped away. As a result, they stand naked against the winds of aging, loneliness, and failure. The novel depends on our identifying with Elizabeth, Nate, and Lesje. Were they not typical contemporary Westerners, we would put the book down after a few pages. But they *are* typical, so we study them as we would study people who live in our own apartment building, or people we see each morning in the mirror. By and large, contemporary Western society has lost a coherent faith. Elizabeth, Nate, and Lesje are representative in having work that usually bores them and love affairs that fail to satisfy them. The horizon against which they set their daily experiences is murky and minimalist. They expect only enough light to make it through the day, make it to the grave.

Of course, not all contemporary Westerners are faithless, any more than all contemporary Westerners are Christians like Solzhenitsyn. It is also true that not all irreligious contemporary Westerners contemplate suicide, and that many contemporary Christians disagree with Solzhenitsyn significantly. But all contemporary Westerners live in a milieu that is defined by the dialectical clash between faith and non-faith. Unless we live in a bomb shelter, the issues of life's meaning bubble on our stove every day. Such issues may not be explicit, but they certainly play implicitly through all our decisions and moods.

Solzhenitsyn stands by his analysis of contemporary Western culture because it best squares with his deep convictions about the human spirit. Going to the center of the human spirit, he finds it meant to embrace honesty and love. Then, looking about for the faith that best matches this conviction, he chooses the Christianity of his native Russian culture. By contrast, he rejects Marxism-Leninism and its basic atheism as a system of dishonesty and hatred. In the person of Lenin, he sees a sort of Anti-Christ—a father of lies and destruction.[8] Without scruple, Lenin would change his positions to suit his advantage. When one writes that principle large, one has a state like the Soviet Union.

The "faith" of Western materialism is almost a non-faith, in that it is confused on so many points. Still, it has a certain instinctive coherence, insofar as rejecting God, exalting science and technology, and acknowledging only a material reality go hand-in-hand. As in examining the Soviet system, the question is whether this Western materialism is in harmony with the human spirit. Can one be radically honest and radically loving on its terms? Or do radical honesty and radical love burst the bonds of materialism, insisting and demonstrating that reality is *more?*

That is the sort of question one must keep in mind when evaluating any faith, Christian, Marxist, Humanist, or Hindu. How well does it accommodate the inner postulates of the human spirit, the human drive to know and to love? How deeply does it illumine the human condition, how powerfully heal human ills? Keeping this question in mind, we explain Christian convictions, history, and curren movements so as to make them competitive in the dialectical search for truth. In the tradition of liberal education, we ask what light and healing Christianity offers. We hope the result is a study that could change a life. It has changed our lives, giving u what we hope is a sure footing in both the university and the church.

Summary

Mystery is at the core of religion. The best way to begin our study of the Christiar approach to mystery seemed to be to take up the Christian worldview. Challengin readers' assumptions that they already know what Christians think, we hoped to ge a good start on the Christian approach to life's most profound issues. We will dea with that topic in more depth in the next part. Following that, we promised, will come a sketch of Christian history and a survey of some of Christianity's contemporary appearances.

Aleksandr Solzhenitsyn's speech at Harvard served to articulate the challenge that traditional Christian faith puts to the modern West. In attacking Western materialism, Solzhenitsyn showed the quarrel to ripple out from the Christian conviction that God, not human self-satisfaction, is the center of a sane worldview. We then took this quarrel as an instance of a dialectic, the clash between different horizons, and suggested that dialectics serve liberal education well.

Study Questions

1. Why is mystery at the core of religion?
2. What is your impression of Solzhenitsyn's Harvard address?
3. Is the traditional way, rooted in the primacy of God, as logical as the materialistic way of the contemporary West? Why?
4. How does faith function as an interpretational horizon?

Notes

1. T. S. Eliot, "Burnt Norton," line 62, in *The Four Quartets* (Harcourt Brace and World, 1947).
2. George Steiner, "Books," *The New Yorker*, August 25, 1980, p. 94.
3. Aleksandr I. Solzhenitsyn, "A World Split Apart" [Harvard address, June 8, 1978], in his *East and West* (New York: Harper & Row, 1980), p. 44.
4. *Ibid.*, p. 48.
5. *Ibid.*, pp. 50–51.
6. Our colleague Michael Kalton, who was at the 1978 Harvard commencement, informed us that another multitude praised Solzhenitsyn's courage. Kalton's analysis of this praise is intriguing. He sensed that it was impossible for Solzhenitsyn or anyone else to offend many Harvard academicians. They have become people capable of absorbing any challenge and trapping it in the bland realm of the "interesting." Beneath this attitude, however, likely lies the pernicious faith that nothing finally matters very much. For Solzhenitsyn's own impressions of the reactions to his Harvard speech, see *The Mortal Danger* (New York: Harper & Row, 1980), pp. 64–67.
7. Margaret Atwood, *Life Before Man* (New York: Simon & Schuster, 1979).
8. See Aleksandr Solzhenitsyn, *Lenin in Zurich* (New York: Farrar, Straus and Giroux, 1976).

NICENE CREED

(THE NICAEO-CONSTANTINOPOLITAN PROFESSION OF FAITH, 381 C.E.)

I believe in one God, the Father almighty, maker of heaven and earth, and of all things visible and invisible. And in one Lord Jesus Christ, the only-begotten Son of God. Born of the Father before all ages. God from God, Light from Light, true God from true God. Begotten not made, consubstantial with the Father: through whom all things were made. Who for us men and for our salvation came down from heaven. And was incarnate by the Holy Ghost of the Virgin Mary: and was made man. He was crucified also for us under Pontius Pilate, suffered and was buried. He rose again the third day according to the Scriptures; and ascended into heaven: and is seated at the right hand of the Father. And he will come again with glory to judge the living and the dead. And of his kingdom there will be no end.

And in the Holy Ghost, the Lord and giver of life; who proceeds from the Father. Who together with the Father and the Son is adored and glorified: who spoke through the prophets.

And in one, holy, catholic, and apostolic Church. I acknowledge one baptism for the remission of sins. And I look for the resurrection of the dead. And the life of the world to come. Amen.

PART 1

The Christian Worldview

Part One deals with the Christian horizon. Assuming that liberal education should sponsor a dialectical clash among different points of view, we strive here to explain the Christian viewpoint. What does their tradition tell Christians they should think about physical nature, society, the human self, and God? How does Christian faith configure these four primal realities? (Eric Voegelin has said, "God and man, world and society form a primordial community of being.")[1] These are the questions we pursue in Part One.

The answers have only developed slowly, through centuries of Christian history, and they shape many Christian consciousnesses only partially. Nonetheless, there is a logic to the faith of a major religion like Christianity, and that logic affects all persons whom it touches. With biblical **revelation**, Greek philosophy, and Roman law, Christian theology long was the soul of Western culture. Even today, when many feel we are living in a post-Christian age, Christian theology is influential, if only as the prior worldview, the *ancien régime*, that contemporary secularism has rejected. The work that we do in Part One therefore will deepen our understanding of the Christian history that we study in Part Two. Being familiar with Christian logic, we shall be better able to appreciate Christian history's most significant developments.

The same holds for the contemporary trends that we study in Part Three. Catholic, Protestant, and Orthodox Christians largely share the worldview described in Part One, as do black Christians and Christian feminists. The worldview goes with the territory marked "Christian"; one cannot have a Christian personality or movement without it. Thus, the worldview sets the stage for the debate between leftist and rightist Christians in Latin America. As they argue about the best way to effect social justice, both sides draw on traditional convictions about **creation**, **sin**, **grace**, and **incarnation**. In fact, the argument comes down to determining which side better interprets the tradition in applying it to present circumstances and needs. The better we understand the traditional worldview, the better we are able to pass judgment on such arguments.

As we explain the central notions of the Christian viewpoint, we draw on theologies from throughout Christian history, from biblical, **patristic**, medieval,

reformation, and contemporary times. In this way, we see that Christian theology, history, and contemporary trends intertwine. The philosophical portions of Christian faith that receive primary attention in Part One relate intimately to the historical developments we focus on in Part Two and the contemporary trends described in Part Three. It is important to emphasize these connections, for they give coherence to the Christian faith as a whole. This text will have succeeded if you grasp Christianity as a whole—what it has meant in "ages past" to live by faith in Jesus Christ, and what it means today.

Before we end this brief introduction to Part One, we should note that North American culture arose from a matrix grounded in the Christian worldview. More than Native American influences and African influences that came with black slaves, Christian beliefs of English, French, and Spanish colonizers shaped the legal, social, and political institutions born in the New World. Therefore, in Part One you meet much of your cultural heritage.

You will find that the Christian worldview is a double-edged sword. While it finds good in the high aspirations that moved many North American colonizers to labor and build, and in the Christian motives that stirred the Pilgrims and some of the western frontiersmen to their great exploits, it also condemns what happened to the American Indians and the blacks. Similarly, the Christian view of creation that we draw from biblical, traditional, and contemporary theologies condemns as malicious and sinful the pollution of nature that we see our society perpetrating.

So take the Christian worldview to heart and you feel that it cuts to the North American joint and marrow. But you also feel it as a source of radical healing, for Christians believe that grace has abounded over sin. Indeed, they believe that recognizing sin, casting it out, and healing the wound are the essence of the spiritual life, the life of deepest humanity. Unless one is converted from living a life of superficial humanity, from living in service to **mammon** and self, there is no good life, no good news. The Christian worldview claims there is great good life and good news—much better than unchallenged human perception realizes. Let us now expose that claim and test it.

Note

1. Eric Voegelin, *Order and History, Volume 1: Israel and Revelation* (Baton Rouge, LA: Louisiana State University Press, 1956), p. 1.

CHAPTER 2

Creation

The Cosmological Myth

What we call "the cosmological myth" is the view of creation common to most nonbiblical peoples. The purpose of this section is to provide background from the history of non-Christian religions, so that the biblical notions may stand forth more clearly.

Ancient peoples generally did their cultural business through **myths**, according to historians of religion. Myths are essentially stories that try to explain primary realities or mysteries in the space-time terms of ordinary human experience, to impose on the world sufficient order so that a people can comprehend it and live harmoniously. Granted this objective, it stands to reason that a story of creation (a "cosmological myth") should be especially important to a people. A myth describing the way things were ordered at the beginning, when the world was formed, could serve as a guiding pattern for the people to live in harmony with nature. Living in harmony with nature was precisely ancient peoples' first concern. Why? Because to them nature *was* reality. It was the most solid, dependable, powerful, ultimate, holy thing that they experienced.

The particular myths that different peoples developed to describe how the world began are so many expressions of a spontaneous interest in nature's constitution. A piquant little myth of the Cupeno Indians of California expresses this interest in simple, almost childlike pondering. In the Cupeno beginning all was dark and void. A bag hung in space. After a while, the bag opened out into two halves. A coyote came from one half and a wildcat came from the other. They immediately began arguing about which of them was older. Human beings had already been created, but they could not see, for they were in mud and darkness. They heard the coyote call first, so they knew that he was older than the wildcat. The people arose from the mud and began to sing. Today **shamans** are able to understand the coyote, because the people heard him first.[1]

What a strange little story! There is a sense, first, that "in the beginning," at the start of the present order of things, all was dark and void. Like the night before the dawn, or the ignorance that precedes understanding, or the time in the womb before life in the world, the first movement of creation is muted, negative, a "that from which" rather than an impressive *something* in its own right. As we shall see, the biblical account of creation also conveys this sense of a negative first moment. So the intuitions expressed in cosmological myth and those expressed in the Bible are not ultimately so different. At the borders of consciousness, as at the borders of the universe, is darkness. There our light of understanding stops, there we have to shift and make progress by "unknowing." The origins of the world are obscured in an uncertainty that makes words like *God* and *mystery* inevitable in the human vocabulary, regardless of how one comes to understand creation.

The Cupeno imagination went to a bag hung in space, as though this people's contemplation of the heavens through mild California nights had fused with a practice of hanging their possessions in the branches under which they camped. Their imaginations also went quickly to the origin of the animals that were interesting to them. Like twins fighting in the womb, coyote and wildcat disputed for seniority. Their dispute was of interest to human beings because human beings interact with animals intimately in ancient society, and even more intimately in ancient mythic imagination of how things were when the world first began. Though the first human beings were in mud and darkness (hardly a self-exalting view), they were party to what went on between coyote and wildcat, those cats of intriguing grace. So, in the full speech called *song*, human beings affirmed their oneness—their feelings of camaraderie—with animals like coyote and wildcat. Today only the shaman, the privileged person of special religious powers, retains those bonds with the animals, but when human beings first came out of the mud, when they were fresh and original, they all understood animal creation. Implicit even in this poor little myth, then, is a sense of "fall." Compared to the time of creation, humans today have lost an intimacy with nature, a knowledge and harmony that they once had.

Had we the space, we could document these "premodern" thoughts in the myths of many other peoples, adding many nuances and intriguing details. But the point here is the sufficiency of nature, the immersion in the details and rhythms of the cosmos, that premodern peoples' creation accounts suggest. Despite intuitions of darkness and void, of mystery and reality of a **transcendent** order, premodern peoples generally accept the orbit of the heavens, the waters, and the earth as their reality. They are fascinated with the rise of the things of this earth, because harmony with them is the basis of a holy (a most realistic) life.

The Biblical Account of Creation

"In the beginning God created the heavens and the earth" (Gen. 1:1). This is the first line in the Christian Bible. Its implications are more remarkable than most of its readers realize. For the God written of in Genesis, and the creation that God worked, stand apart from the gods and creations of most other peoples. By the time that Jewish and Christian tradition developed the Genesis story, the biblical God made the world in full freedom from nothingness. That is not true of most other peoples' creation accounts, and the biblical difference produces a distinctive view of the world.

The Bible is interested in a holy life, but it conceives a holy life in terms of harmony with, and obedience to, a God who stands outside the world. By the time that biblical literature arose, putting Jewish and Christian ponderings about creation into written form, the God who stood behind the world as its first source had been experienced as a **redeemer**, an agent of release from human beings' historical dead ends. "In the Bible . . . the doctrine of creation does not stand by itself but depends upon and elaborates the redemptive activity of God in history."[2] In the Hebrew Bible (the Old Testament) creation is viewed in the light of the **covenant** that God made with Israel. In the New Testament, it is viewed in the light of Jesus Christ, who is the beginning of a new creation. Both portions of **scripture** agree that all things created depend completely on God.

The Genesis story of creation depends on the notion, common to the culture of the ancient Near East, that the divine agent worked with an original watery chaos. It is distinctive, however, in the degree of power and autonomy that it attributes to its God. Bracketing the question of where the original watery chaos came from, Genesis emphasizes that the things of heaven and earth came to be by God's simple fiat. The implication, of course, is that all things of heaven and earth owe their being completely to God. For any creature to claim independence or self-sufficiency would be error, amnesia, and ingratitude all in one.

It is this implication that gives the story of the first human beings' disobedience its bold relief. God made human beings in the divine image and likeness; they derived utterly from God's own fullness of being and life. The denial of this origin, which is implicit in the disobedience of the first couple, is the primordial lie that Genesis sees as the basis of human wreckage.

So, for all its reflection of Israel's understanding of God as a redeemer, Genesis begins with a description of the way things are for all creatures. Biblical scholar Brevard Childs makes this point exactly: "The canonical role of Gen. 1:11 testifies to the priority of creation. The divine relation to the world stems from God's initial creative purpose for the universe, not for Israel alone."[3] In the mythic mode, Genesis proposes a novel, ultimately transcendent understanding of reality. Because of God's utter priority, the world does not have the comprehensive status that the cosmological myth gave it. In Genesis, God and the world are not considered coextensive. The world—the panoply of inanimate, animate, and human—is seen to be derivative. The implication is that there was a time when the world was not, though time does not predominate in the mentality of Genesis. What predominates is a reverence for the beneficent power that made all things come to be, and a shrewd grasp of what happened to human beings when they lost that reverence.

In the Bible, when human beings lose reverence for God, their creator, they become foolish. For the Psalmist, it is the fool who says in his heart that there is no

God. To the author of Genesis, that fool waits at the edge of every human consciousness. Given the slightest invitation, it will dart to center stage, begin to leer and loll. Puffed up with self-importance, weary of the work it takes to be wise, the human personality loses sight of its creaturehood, the fact of its having been created, easily. When the classical Christian theologians contemplated this phenomenon, in the context of their reflections on the effects of **original sin**, they spoke of a weakening of the will and a darkening of the mind. Like victims of a severe winter virus, human beings feel too enervated to confront the reality of their creaturehood. As though they have been drugged, they can't quite remember the original dispensation. So they stagger over an earth grown steamy with miasma, with lethal clouds of forgetfulness.

Though it is not her precise intention, novelist Doris Lessing, author of *Canopus in Argos*, plays out the vast implications of this forgetfulness in her account of the degenerative disease visited on Shikasta, the planet Earth seen in the celestial order of things.[4] The inhabitants of Shikasta can't quite summon the concentration to follow Johor, emissary of the good system of Canopus. Their eyes cloud over, their minds wander off. So they stumble in a stupor, a sort of sleepwalking. Unlike physical sleep, however, their state is not broken by the hard knocks of reality. War, violence, disease, and destruction only deepen their mental aberration. With nightmarish energy, they increase their commitment to ways that destroy. So their bloodshed, lies, and hatreds grow almost exponentially. So their souls sicken, warp, and atrophy.

From the early Greek philosophers to the Baal Shem-Tov (the father of the religious movement called Hasidism), spiritual masters have deplored such signs of human degeneracy. The early Greek philosophers thought that most human beings had turned waking life into dreaming. The Baal Shem-Tov's counsel to "*Remember*" is written today on the walls of Yad Vashem, the memorial to the victims of the Nazi concentration camps. And the biblical view of creation? It labels most of us amnesiac. We have forgotten our main designation, the one thing necessary for our peace.

Radical Monotheism

"Hear, O Israel: The Lord our God is one Lord; and you shall love the Lord your God with all your heart, and with all your soul, and with all your might" (Deut. 6:4–5). The one thing necessary for our peace, according to biblical Israel, is following these verses from Deuteronomy. Known as the **Shema**, they encapsule the religious effect that the biblical doctrine of creation should produce. At the origin of the world, as at the center of Israel's religious history, stands one sovereign power. This God is not the divinity of the nations who believe in the cosmological myth. He is not a local god, a deity of a particular place. The true God, the God of Moses, the God of Abraham, Isaac, and Jacob, is one universal Lord. To love this God utterly, making him the treasure of one's time, is to find the center of good human living.

A line from modern Irish poet William Butler Yeats puts this conviction another way. Speaking of the European culture of the late nineteenth and early twentieth century, Yeats said, "The center does not hold." Like German poetic philosopher Friedrich Nietzsche, who spoke of "the death of God," Yeats was prophetic. Like a true artist, he felt in his bones disorders that the general populace only appreciated generations later. It was not until the late 1940s, after the Second World War, that the existential pessimism of Yeats and Nietzsche touched the bones of an entire generation. Even then, only the theologically astute realized that existentialism indirectly confirmed the deep monotheism lyrically postulated by the Shema.

The center of Yeats's European culture was not holding because many no longer found credible that a single source of power and love could secure human life in meaning. The failure of Christian culture to prevent two world wars, to offer a more effective social reform than Marxism, and to correlate its traditional theology with modern science had dealt its authority almost a death blow. In our judgment, Christianity had failed adequately to distinguish the passing, culturally variable aspects of its faith from its invariant center in a transcendent, mysterious God. As a result, the passing away of traditional European culture seemed to many the passing away of God. Deeper Christian minds knew better. Protestant theologian Karl Barth, for instance, knew that the God who had died in the collapse of "Christian" culture was an imposter. At the roots (*radices*) of human existence, the mystery of God vibrated as strongly as ever.

The radical question, as deeper-thinking existentialists like Martin Heidegger saw, is "Why is there something and not nothing?" This question returns radical monotheism (the belief that there is only one sovereign God) to center stage. For the question spotlights the mystery of be-ing, the aboriginal wonder that anything steps forth from the void. Parmenides, the early Greek philosopher of be-ing, grasped this mystery in an ecstatic vision. Driven to express it, to rip from his viscera a word that would give the mystery form, he could only exclaim, "Is!" The ultimate fact of the world is its "is-ness." The radical mystery is our inexplicable ex-istence—our standing forth in reality when nothingness could lap us away.

This is ontological talk, muttering about the deepest structures of reality. It bakes little bread in most kitchens. But the "ontological shock," as Protestant theologian Paul Tillich has called it, from which such talk flows has been capital in the history of Christian theology.

More than Jewish theology, Christian theology appropriated Greek philosophy, for which **ontology** was the bottom line. Like Indian philosophy, which greatly influenced Hindu and Buddhist theology, Greek philosophy tried to get at the ultimate causes of human being and knowing. When Christian theologians applied Greek philosophy, they filled out the Bible's appreciation of the One God. Roman Catholic theologian Karl Rahner has translated a full appreciation of the One God into a contemporary stress on divine mystery: "For a Christian, his Christian existence is ultimately the totality of his existence. This totality opens out into the dark abysses of the wilderness which we call God. When one undertakes something like this [Rahner's effort to write an introduction to the idea of Christianity], he stands before the great thinkers, the saints, and finally Jesus Christ. The abyss of existence opens up in front of him. He knows that he has not thought enough, has not loved enough, and has not suffered enough."[5]

"The abyss of existence" is the One God of the Bible given a contemporary ontological accent. That Rahner can use this phrase while standing before the saints and Jesus Christ shows how Christian he finds it to be. Not for him, then, the facile opposition between the God of the Bible and the God of the philosophers that some Christian thinkers have proposed. The God of biblical creation is the God we seek when we go to the depths of our own existence. At root, there is only One God, one Lord of meaning. As we shall see, when Christian meditation clarifies the abyss of existence, it finds the unbegotten Father of Jesus the divine Son.

God's Relation to the World

What causes the One God who is the fullness of existence to create? Only her* own goodness, her own outflowing love, Christian tradition has answered. God is the only being who is necessary, who exists in his own right. All other beings are contingent: they easily could not be. In the thinking of most Christian theologians, necessary being gives rise to contingent beings purely because necessary being is fruitful. In terms of human experience, the best analogy is probably love. Love between spouses tends toward fruitfulness in children and homemaking. Between friends it tends toward likemindedness and mutual support. At work, love moves us from drudgery to art, original science, or social services that repair. In the fields, love makes farming a matter of care and living with the land, resulting in a yield no agribusiness can match. Wherever we go, to hospitals or schools or laboratories, the message is the same. What is fresh, fruitful, and creative derives from personal investment, care, and gentleness—from love.

When the Christian regards the world faithfully, the world is a consummate expression of God's love. Does this view conflict with contemporary astronomical and evolutionary science? We doubt it. Both the Bible and the brunt of Christian theology deal in symbols that try to render something of the ultimately mysterious font of human life. Properly understood, neither the Bible nor the brunt of Christian theology purports to provide empirical facts. Their concern is rather the ultimate horizon, the faith-attitude, against which empirical facts or evolutionary science are finally set. Regarding the origin of the universe, for instance, we find no necessary conflict between a Christian view of creation arising from God's love and a scientific view that proto-hydrogen started things with a "Big Bang." Where did the proto-hydrogen come from, the believer asks the scientist. Why could not God

*Following the traditional Christian conviction that God is beyond gender, we use masculine and feminine pronouns interchangeably.

have used proto-hydrogen in the empirical working of creation (as opposed to the mythical account in Genesis), the theologian asks the untutored believer.

Discovery of proto-hydrogen does not answer the radical question of why there is something rather than nothing, and a retreat to the scientific assumption that proto-hydrogen has always existed is an act of faith at least as great as believing in a truly mysterious God. Likewise, we distort Genesis and the rest of the Bible when we read them literalistically, as just about all biblical scholarship today agrees. It is poor method, bad questioning, to ask Genesis for scientific data, because Genesis was not written for that purpose.

In our opinion, much the same holds true regarding human creation, the origin of *homo sapiens*. The biblical account of Adam and Eve is a religious analysis of our species' beginnings. Its interest is God's care for a kind of being that would know and love and so image the divine nature. Whether *homo sapiens* developed by the evolutionary mechanism postulated by Darwin falls outside the Bible's interest and competence. If the marvelous stories implied by current paleontology, genetics, and molecular biology hold true, the Creator's workings were more imaginative than Genesis ever conceived. However, nothing in these sciences needs to conflict with a faith interpretation of humankind's beginnings. Humankind's beginning is finally a question for philosophy and theology, a question inextricable from the mystery of be-ing. It is scient*ism*, an illegitimate effort to infiltrate a realm beyond science's competence, that causes conflicts between evolution and religion.

Having taken care of these methodological issues and tried to clear the waters, we can turn to the major point of this section: in the Christian view, God's creation is ongoing. The contingent beings who derive from the necessary divine being are dependent in their every moment and action. **Conservation** and **concursus** are the words we use to denote this relationship. God keeps providing the love on which all creatures depend (conserves them); God acts with all created beings (concurs with their actions). Speculatively, these theses of traditional Christian theology lead to difficult questions about the Creator-creature relationship: how to reconcile divine knowledge with human freedom, how to absolve God of responsibility when evil agents (for example, Hitler) act, and so forth. Theologians have done their best work when they have pointed out the difference between the divine and created orders (for instance, God does not act in time, with a before and after, although time exists in the world she created) and have respected the mystery of what Kierkegaard called "the infinite qualitative distinction" between divine and human.

For religion, the implication of conservation and concursus is the nearness of the Christian God. In Saint Augustine's phrase, he is more intimate to us than we are to ourselves. We have no reality, movement, or life that God does not grant. Accepted in faith, correlated with the grace that Christians find in Jesus, the notion of conservation and concursus is expressed in prayers like this: "You nourish and sustain the world from day to day and wherever we go you are present more fully than we dare presume. We thank you for this presence, this hidden, vulnerable, yet faithful presence here and now. We believe in it and live from you as we live from bread, as we hunger and thirst for peace."[6]

The Image of God

Prayers like this suggest a Christian version of the Israelite notion of covenant. The covenant between God and Israel was a sort of compact. The Israelites would be God's people and he would be their God. For their fidelity they could expect protection. For their faith they could hope to find life good. Throughout the Hebrew Bible, the covenant remained a form for the Israelites' religious experience. Bonded to God, they expected to share time with him, almost the way that a wife shares time with her husband. To the prophet Hosea, God was Israel's husband. However unfaithful Israel might be, he could not stop loving her. According to Exodus, the people would only come to know their God by sharing time with him. In the self-revelation that God made to Moses (Exod. 3:14), the divine name was almost a tease: "I am as I will be with you." These temporal and marital motifs made the covenant a most intimate bond. As Eve was known by Adam and conceived a child, so Israel hoped to be known by God and to bear fruit. The prayer we quoted recalls this hope, this reliance on a God present to nourish and fertilize.

There is a tantalizing dictum from Christian tradition that puts the covenantal relationship between creator and creature in the form of a practical maxim. "Act as though everything depended on God, and pray as though everything depended on yourself."[7] This maxim is so contrary to most Americans' expectations that frequently they invert it. Surely action, they reason, is our human affair, and prayer is where God comes in. But deeper Christian instinct confounds such a superficial view of the creator-creature relationship, as it confounds many other aspects of contemporary Western culture. To the Christian, the priority in all that we observe or do belongs to God the creator, the conserver, the concurer. She is the first cause and the final cause comprehensively.

When people really believe this, Christians assert, their action or work or doing straightens out. Like runners who have learned about stretching, they move more easily, with fewer tightnesses and cramps. Like people who have appropriated a trust walk, making it something adult, they let themselves go, expecting that God will catch them when they fall. The results are often impressive. In contrast to the "Type A" behavior of the stereotypic American executive, tight-jawed and hell-bent for a coronary, those who feel God's presence keep their work in perspective, taking cues from the subtle initiatives that a given situation offers. Because they are not pushing, they can receive such initiatives, take in the delicate signs that nature or other people give of how things are flowing. Because their egos are not blocking their horizon, they can move their bodies and minds dexterously. So they resemble a realized Zen master, who has no self and can follow Buddha-nature's flow. So they conjure up T. S. Eliot, who set the still point of union with God in the context of a reality that was a dance. "Dance with me," the Christian God says. "Follow my lead, my music of the spheres."

At prayer, deeper Christian instinct focuses on God's priority with the effect of making the self a petitioner. When we face ultimate reality honestly, we ourselves are very small and unenlightened. This truth prompts humble dispositions like that of John the Baptist: "He must increase, I must decrease." Then, locating the responsibility for history properly, it leads to prayer like that of Abraham and Job. Abraham haggled with God to save Sodom. Job brought a law suit against the One finally responsible for a world in which evil is strong. Bonded to God by covenant, married to divinity in time, John the Baptist, Abraham, and Job prayed as if everything depended on themselves, for they knew they were totally inadequate to the tasks of **salvation**.

We shall come to the tasks of salvation in due season. The upshot of the creator-creature relationship to be driven home here is the image of God that it clarifies. In addition to the biblical understanding of how human beings are God's image (through their spirituality, stewardship for the natural world, and male-female communion), later Christian theology added a covenantal human creativity. Working gracefully in love, human agents express the Creator's poetic molding of matter in time. Praying deeply, contemplatively, in both petition and rest (the abiding with God of the Gospel of John), human patients are purified in their wellsprings. Such action and passion slowly draw forth a warm knowledge, a bright love, that makes glowing icons of God's heavenly being. The coexistence of the creature with the Creator, and their co-action, brings a new humanity into relief. Christian faith attributes this bringing into relief to God the **Holy Spirit**, and it speaks of a *new* creation. The Spirit of Christ can restore the image of God intuited by Genesis. Despite all the marrings of sin, God's deepest work and presence, at the depths of the human personality, is a labor of love not lost. The saints exemplified the successes the Creator can have, when the creature makes itself docile, and all the faithful are called to be saints.

Nature

Good Harbor Beach in Gloucester, Massachusetts, is a place where a person can feel called to reinterpret the cosmological myth. It has North Shore waters so cold, so clear, that your vacation begins with aching ankles and wondering eyes. As you become acclimated and start riding the waves, the ache leaves and the wonder spreads to your whole body. Shocked alive by this return to evolution's life-site, you realize again how narrow city existence has made you. There is an immersion in living nature, an ecological connection, that your heady work and cement surroundings have short-circuited. At the curl of a gorgeous breaker, you come back to your body and your world like a prodigal coming home. And the day that the lowering clouds move out to sea, letting the sunbeams dance on that pure, pure cold water, is the day that nature's radiance completes your homecoming. It is an incredibly beautiful world that the Master Maritimer has fashioned, an abundance of light and power and life.

Through most of their millennia, human beings have had an instinctive intimacy with nature. The cosmological myth largely was a matter of putting that intimacy into stories and songs. Since the time of the Greek discovery of mind and the Israelite discovery of divine Spirit, nature has been more distant. The discovery of mind accentuated the way human beings stand out from the rest of physical creation. As the animals who could think, speak, and blush, we became somewhat alien to the boulders and the bees. As the species addressed by a divine Word from beyond the cosmos, we could no longer be wholly comfortable in nature, for nature now was delimited by a God ever greater, ever farther than the skies and the seas. Western technology increased this alienation, as Northern European peasants devised giant plows to rip the bosom of Mother Earth with little compunction. With similarly little compunction, their descendants developed modern science and technology.

Today the ambiguity in humanity's relationship to nature has come home to roost nightmarishly. The capabilities we have developed are a dazzling display of the virtuosity latent in the mind that the Greeks discovered, but our unblushing destruction of the ecosphere says we have little understood the creative God. Though not all scholars agree on the role that Christian religion played in the destructive process,[8] there is good agreement that the Christian fracture of the cosmological myth, the Christian exaltation of a world-transcendent God, and the Christian exaltation of an Adam placed by God at the head of creation inclined many Westerners to lay nature waste cavalierly. In face of the nuclear, chemical, and other pollutions this has brought, contemporary observers sometimes turn back to archaic religion. The way traditional American Indians, Africans, Eskimos, Australians, or even European peasants treated the land seems sane to the point o nostalgia.[9] How long will it be before the West again tastes such sanity?

Feminists thinking along this line have urged a return to good witchcrafts Novelists have tried to break the madness by displaying how it poisons the home "She stands as she has done for millennia, cutting bread, setting out sliced vegeta bles on a plate, with a bottle of wine, and thinks that nothing in this meal is safe that the poisons of their civilization are in every mouthful, and that they are abou to fill their mouths with deaths of all kinds. In an instinctive gesture of safety renewal, she hands a piece of bread to her child, but the gesture has lost its faith a she makes it, because of what she may be handing the child."[10]

". . . the gesture has lost its faith. . . ." High on the list of Christianity failures, in our view, is its failure to motivate its people to love nature more tha comfort, power, riches, and ease. The ecological crisis is the most profound cris we face today, because it threatens the very matrix of life. We shall deal with th sinful sides of this crisis, as we shall deal with the interrelated problems of econom injustice and war, in the next chapter. Let the final task here be to suggest ho Christian faith might resurrect gestures like giving bread to one's children.

Simply, it might resurrect them by replumbing the traditional doctrines incarnation, to which we come in Chapter 5, and of creation, which we have bee translating here, so that nature again becomes venerable, again is seen as a divi gift. Coming from a good God, all creation has intrinsic value and dignity. To Sai Augustine, all creatures were vestiges of God—footprints showing where he ha walked. The lawyer-ecologists who want to write statutes guaranteeing nature rights, protecting wilderness areas and deserts and prime fishing banks from developers' greed, have a solid warrant in Christian tradition. Alternative life-stylers like Ernest Callenbach,[11] who want an ecotopia, a new culture living with the land, are buttressed by Christian sacramental theology. In traditional Christian **liturgy** (worship), water, wax, bread, wine, incense, flowers, and oil all bear the Holy Spirit. They all are sacred signs reminding the faithful that God has shot creation through and through with grace. The new heaven entails a new earth, according to Revelation. According to the best ecological monitors, Christian faith had better re-entail such a new earth very soon.

The Freedoms of Creaturehood

Were the Christian view of creaturehood, the fact of our having been created, again to inform Western consciousness, several old freedoms might be re-revealed. We have already suggested an ecological freedom. It is the liberty to enjoy beautiful places—Good Harbor Beach, Yosemite Valley, Okefenokee Swamp—with a sense of homecoming. It is also the freedom to eat unpoisoned food, breathe unpoisoned air, drink unpoisoned water. The Christian theology of creation, renovated in the face of today's natural crises, pits God's no! against the forces that fill the land with cancer. It says that aberrant technology is a sacrilege. Many Westerners now know this tacitly. An articulate retrieval and updating of Christian biblical tradition might render their knowledge express and politically effective. It might free our grandchildren down to their genes.

A second freedom latent in a good theology of creation is an emancipation for radical contemplation. Responding to the God of radical monotheism, the One Mysterious Love who is creation's source, the knowing creature turns poetic, grateful, and communing. Gerard Manley Hopkins turned poetic through naturalist contemplation: "Glory be to God for dappled things. . . ."[12] The Christian **Eucharist** is an act of gratitude for the prime grace of salvation, but also for a beautiful creation. And the saints who have enjoyed deep communion with the divine Mystery often have delighted in physical creation. Saint John of the Cross loved the quiet solitude of the woods. Saint Francis of Assisi sang to Brother Sun and Sister Moon.

In these and other ways, contemplatives have enjoyed the Creator heart-to-heart. Below the plodding mind, below even the sprightly imagination, they have been with God, dwelt in God's artful patterns of making. Scientists tracking the heavens sometimes have felt Dante's God: the love that moves the stars. Philosophers probing the world sometimes have stepped back to marvel at Kant's starry heavens above and moral law within. In each instance, a soul has crossed a border to capacious freedom.

A third freedom that a solid grasp of creaturehood entails is political. From their earliest clashes with repressive political powers, Christians realized that they had to obey God rather than men (Acts 4:19–20). The immediate cause of this realization was their experience of Jesus's resurrection, but undergirding it lay the Creator of radical monotheism. For when a person realizes that her being comes from no state, no this-worldly organization, she necessarily limits her allegiance to any state, any this-worldly organization. That does not mean she cannot be patriotic or loyal. It does mean she cannot be a chauvinist, a jingoist, or any other species of political slave.

This forgotten political freedom is further evidence that the Christian worldview is largely unknown. The relationship between a mature Christian religious practice and secular politics is far more nuanced than most Americans realize. In our view, a mature Christian religious practice reads the doctrine of creation as a critique of all secular politics. No party, program, or cause merits full allegiance. All parties, programs, and causes are at best intermediate, penultimate. To place any at the center of life is to commit idolatry. Similarly, a mature Christian religious practice grants one great freedom of political choice. It never dictates that one identify with conservatives or liberals, capitalists or socialists, because it knows that they all can serve or frustrate the ends of creation and so must be judged case by case.

A complementary consequence of creaturehood is a maturing political responsibility. Not compelled by state or party, the individual has a vocation to influence society so that society enjoys the health of existence under the truly mysterious God. Paradoxically enough, the more intensely a creature relates to God, the freer, more individual, healthier, and more fulfilled that creature is. The result is citizens who love their land but cry out when the emperor has no clothes. Free of compulsive madnesses, they are the citizens who bring society to balance, justice, and sanity.

Summary

We have begun our study of the Christian worldview with the doctrine of creation because creation goes to the bedrock—the relation between God and human beings. The majority of human tribes expressed this relationship in terms of the cosmological myth. Divinity—sacred power—virtually overlapped with nature. Thus the biblical view that a divinity beyond the natural world created it in sovereign freedom differs from the generality of cosmogonies. Pursued into its depths, the biblical view yields radical monotheism: there is only one source from whom all creation issues, before whom all creation should bow. Through many centuries, Christian theologians meditated on these implications of the Israelite Shema. Using the somewhat cumbersome notions of conservation and concursus, they showed that creatures depend on God for their every moment and breath.

Because they can activate this truth, Christians believe, human beings are special images of God. Sharing time with him, they can let a covenant relationship draw out a warm love reminiscent of the Spirit moving over the waters. Then, as their images clarify, they can glimpse a relationship to nature as their home. Despite all the denaturing constraints, they can recognize that an intimate ecology is their birthright. That is just one instance of a marvelous freedom. In a proper understanding of the Christian doctrine of creation, allegiance from the heart, the center of one's being, is due only to the source of that being. For that reason an ancient Christian prayer began, "O God, to serve whom is to reign. . . ." The implications of this freedom for our ecological, military, economic, and political crises is dynamite usually kept well-defused.

Study Questions

1. How does the story told by the Cupeno Indians express the cosmological myth?
2. Does the biblical doctrine of creation make much modern culture seem like amnesia or sleepwalking? Why?
3. How does radical monotheism respond to the proposition that the center of existence now does not hold?
4. How does the prayer quoted in the section on conservation and concursus assume these notions?
5. What image of God does Eliot's notion that reality is a dance conjure up?
6. Can you reconcile a Good Harbor Beach and a nature on the verge of causing a gesture like giving bread to a child to lose its faith? How?
7. Describe a concrete situation in which awareness of the freedoms of creaturehood could change ordinary behavior.

Notes

1. See Barbara C. Sproul, *Primal Myths: Creating the World* (San Francisco: Harper & Row, 1979), p. 242.
2. B. W. Anderson, "Creation," *The Interpreter's Dictionary of the Bible, Vol. I* (Nashville: Abingdon, 1962), p. 725.
3. Brevard Childs, *Introduction to the Old Testament as Scripture* (Philadelphia: Fortress, 1979), p. 155.
4. Doris Lessing, *Canopus in Argos: Archives, Vol. I: Shikasta* (New York: Alfred A. Knopf, 1979).
5. Karl Rahner, *Foundations of Christian Faith* (New York: Seabury, 1978), p. 2.
6. Huub Oosterhuis, *Your Word is Near* (New York: Newman, 1968), p. 33.
7. There is a profound commentary on this dictum in Gaston Fessard, *La Dialectique des Exercices Spirituels de Saint Ignace de Loyola* (Paris: Aubier, 1956), pp. 305–363.
8. See David Spring and Eileen Spring, eds., *Ecology and Religion in History* (New York: Harper & Row, 1974).
9. See Denise Lardner Carmody, *The Oldest God: Archaic Religion Yesterday and Today* (Nashville: Abingdon, 1981).

10. Doris Lessing, *Shikasta*, p. 199.
11. See his *Ecotopia* (New York: Bantam, 1977).
12. Gerard Manley Hopkins, "Pied Beauty," in *Gerard Manley Hopkins: Poems and Prose*, W. H. Gardner, ed. (Baltimore: Penguin, 1963), p. 30.

CHAPTER 3

Sin

Human Evil

It is a common opinion in literary analysis that depicting evil characters, citizens whose warpings twist the social fabric, is far easier than depicting good characters. In fact, some appreciations of Dostoevski's *The Idiot* account it a more difficult achievement than *Crime and Punishment* or *The Brothers Karamazov* because its central figure is saintly rather than villainous. This illumines a puzzling aspect of human nature. War, disorder, evil, and social fracture get the headlines, because their effects are more gripping. Peace, order, goodness, and social harmony are something we expect, even when they seldom occur. We are "programmed" for health rather than disease, for truth rather than falsehood—so much so that we may only appreciate health when we are first laid low by sickness, or truth when we first suffer because of lies. In terms of our human constitution, evil is our greatest problem. As nothing else, it calls into question our whole makeup.

The varieties of human evil are legion, unfortunately. On the big screen flash scenes from Stalin's Gulag Archipelago and Hitler's Auschwitz. On the medium-sized screen flash scenes from the Uganda of Idi Amin, the Iran of the Shah, the Cambodia of Pol Pot. On the little eight-millimeter screen flash scenes from any American neighborhood, office, or factory. Racism, sexism, ageism, and religious bigotry fight for a prominent place in evil's showings. In the news, torture and crime, pollution and profiteering strut their stuff. Alongside accounts of My Lai, where Americans slaughtered Vietnamese villagers, stand accounts of Vietcong who drove chopsticks through Vietnamese children's ears. In the back pages, behind reports of Nicaraguan President Anastasio Somoza's murder, run reports on Rock Kansas, where the Air Force still denies responsibility for its Titan Missile accidents. The news, then, is not encouraging. The evil reported in a single week says that the human constitution, the human orientation toward order and truth, is under fierce attack.

At least this evil brings religious and ethical discussion down from the clouds. For those with eyes to see, it rivets attention to the concrete, the here and now struggle to limit destructive forces and advance good. Recently we saw this point clarified on the editorial pages of our local newspaper. The editors had picked up a story saying that Amnesty International thought the Begin regime in Israel might be guilty of torturing Arab prisoners whom it held as suspected terrorists. A friend of ours who had spent eight years living in Israel wrote a letter pointing out that the "torture" involved usually was roughing up the terrorists in order to gain information that would prevent their accomplices from killing more Jews.[1] The reaction to our friend's letter was outrage that anyone could defend torture. In the name of impeccable principles, liberal university types and others branded our friend a monster. It seems they could not condone dealing strongly with harsh evil.

The Biblical Notion of Sin

In our view, biblical religion is concrete, in good measure because it acknowledges human evil and still considers God the source of protection. The prime biblical word for human evil is *sin*. Studying the biblical notion of sin, one sees a strange knowing and unknowing, culpability and impotence, in the cluster of human evils.

The Hebrew word most commonly translated as *sin* is *het*, the verb form of which means "to miss the mark."[2] This connotes that sin is not so much intellectual error as failure to attain one's goal. Aimed at goodness, made for truth, sinners fail to fulfill their makeup.

In the ancient Akkadian language (related to Hebrew), the word commonly used for sin meant "rebellion." It was also used to designate a breach of agreement between nations and peoples. So to the image of an arrow missing the mark, we must add a sense of willfulness. The sinner turns away from her goal deliberately. She breaks a compact, disrupts an agreed-upon relationship. Along the same line, sin can take the form of disloyalty, as in the falling out between Saul and David (1 Sam.). It shows in an inferior's failure to fulfill his responsibilities to a superior, a host's failure to fulfill his duties of hospitality. In all these cases, something expected, at least implicitly agreed-upon, is neglected or refused willfully. Thus, sin is a breach of covenant, a failure in responsibility and community.

Another Hebrew word for sin is *awon*, which is usually translated "iniquity." It means a deviation, a failure (to fulfill one's obligations) that distorts the social order. As a result of *awon*, something that ought not to exist has come into being, and it produces guilt. In several passages, the guilt that the sinner bears is said to be crushing, too heavy for him to carry (Gen. 4:13, Ps. 38:5, Isa. 1:4). Other passages describe guilt equally vividly: it is etched in the heart like an inscription in stone (Jer. 17:1); it is like rust eating into a metal cup (Ezek. 24:6). Thus, sin is not merely the corruption of a social relationship, whether between human beings or between a person and God. It is also the sinner's ruin, the distortion or corruption of her very person.

A third Hebrew word for sin is *ra*: "evil." Evil is that which lacks its proper form. It is ugly, twisted, crippled. For that reason, Yahweh (the Hebrew God) finds it intolerable, cannot abide it. Related to this, sin is a lie (*seker*), for the sinner pretends to be something he is not, denies reality by his actions even more than his words. The result is folly: the sinner is a fool, a troublemaker, a cause of affliction. Genesis 3–11 is an extended commentary on this theme.

In these and other expressions, the biblical conception of sin shows its sense of a nuanced corrosion. At heart, beneath the many variants of sin is ignorance of God. Because they do not know God—willfully refuse to know God intimately—sinners feed an evil heart, a deliberate unrealism. According to Catholic scholar John L. McKenzie, the Bible is much harder on sinners than current analysts are: "There is never any question in the [Old Testament] whether sin is a deliberate and willful act for which man must bear full responsibility. There is no suspicion of any compulsion or neurosis, nor of any failure of society which excuses the individual. Sin is indeed a breakdown of society, and the prophets often speak of this; but society breaks down because of the failure of its members."[3]

If that is the psychology of sin, what about its history? Genesis 3–11 says that humans began sinning because they wanted things that didn't belong to them. Such sin destroyed the intimate relation to God we ought to have, and then our social order. Loosed on the world, sin grew like a cancer. The result was a curse and manifold disaster, death and a state of constant suffering. This complex of sin is a mystery that the Bible never pretends to fathom, except insofar as it absolves God of all blame. The upshot of the biblical view of sin's history is that death and disorder lie on humanity's own head.

The New Testament assumes this background and adds several new concepts. For instance, it sharpens both the notion that sin can be a single act and the notion that it is a state or a condition. The New Testament also interprets sin as a power. But the most novel element pervading the entire New Testament is the idea that Jesus conquers sin. Without diminishing the Old Testament vision of sin's malice, the New Testament sees Jesus's conquest as a sign of God's greater power and goodness. If it is a central Old Testament doctrine that only God can save human beings from sin, it is a central New Testament doctrine that in Jesus God *has* saved human beings from sin.

Thus, the first three books of the New Testament (Matthew, Mark, Luke) show Jesus consorting with sinners, to forgive them. The fourth book (John) probes the depths of sin, finding an opposition to God rooted in darkness and the devil. For Paul, the Old Testament Law spotlights the impotent sinfulness in which human beings suffer, subject to a terrible power of malice. The seat of sin is the flesh, weak humanity prone to evil, but Christ's greater power of grace has made it possible to conquer the flesh and live in the spirit.

War

Flesh and spirit are the great counterplayers that Saint Paul's theology sees dueling through history. Nowhere is their contest more horrifying than in the phenomenon of war. Throughout human history, war seems to have dominated most empires.[4] Estimates of those killed in World War II alone reach fifty-five million, while some say that a thermonuclear war could kill three hundred million people in a matter of hours.[5] With the curse of Cain (Gen. 4:15) on our foreheads, we human beings have moved from fratricide to the brink of genocide. Our will to power and bloodlust testify that flesh is far stronger than spirit.

In traditional Christian reflections on war, the mainstream has moved between the Machiavellian position that any war seeming to serve one's interests is legitimate, and the pacifist position that no war is legitimate. After laying down the principle that maintaining peace is a duty incumbent on all human beings, the mainstream of the tradition has admitted that unscrupulous people can force good Christians to resist crime by violent means. If there is no other way to remedy injustice, one may have recourse to war.

Thus there arose the Christian theory of the "just war," whose conditions were quite stringent. First, one side had to persist in committing an injustice, and so force the other side to legitimate self-defense. Second, all peaceful means of settling the dispute had to have been exhausted. Third, there had to be a due proportion between the gravity of the injustice and the damage that the war would cause. Fourth and last, one had to have a reasonable hope of winning the war. After enumerating these four traditional conditions, theologian René Coste expresses the sober mood that they ought to engender: "War can only be a desperate remedy in a desperate situation, used in order to spare humanity a still greater evil when all essentially reasonable and peaceful means have proven ineffective, for only in these circumstances can war acquire the necessary (though accidental) rationality. Unjust war is a monstrous crime."[6]

Even when the stringent conditions for a just war are met, the conduct of hostilities ought to restrain sinful flesh and honor Godward spirit. Thus good conscience binds combatants to continue respecting human life, so that they will not kill except in lawful self-defense. They must avoid inhumane treatment, preserve a distinction between combatants and noncombatants, and not let war cloak such evils as assassination, rape, torture, treason, or defamation.[7]

In the atomic age, it is especially difficult to fulfill the third condition, that there be a due proportion between the gravity of the injustice and the damage that war would inflict. Thus many Christians now find a greater imperative to pacifism than was true in ages when the weapons of destruction were less lethal. Following the model of Jesus, who suffered the evil of his enemies without striking back, or the Hindu Mahatma Gandhi, whose nonviolence was part of a total commitment to make politics truthful, many contemporary Christians lay a great burden of proof on any military venture. It must make clear that the injustice it would remove cannot be removed by peaceful means, that it would not do more harm than good, and that it is prompted by humane motives rather than by profit or pride.

Thus, many Christians judge conflicts case by case, according to criteria like those for a just war. Nations have to make their determinations in the concrete, and so do individual citizens. While it is legitimate for the individual citizen to assume the state's right to self-defense, and to grant the state's leaders the benefit of the doubt in determining when self-defense comes into play, it is not legitimate for the individual citizen to grant the state carte blanche. No individual can support a military establishment or an active war ethically without a personal judgment of their legitimacy here and now. This requirement leads many Christians to crises of conscience, especially concerning active military service.

According to Dietmas Mieth, author of an article on military service in *The Concise Dictionary of Christian Ethics*, the individual is free to choose "the absolute preference for symbolic nonresistance or the relative, realistic and objectively rational preference for military preparedness."[8] In other words, individuals may differ in their conscientious assessments of a given military service and so legitimately come to different conclusions. One may choose to object to a given service, and so symbolize the pacifist strain in the Christian view of conflict. Another may agree to serve, and so symbolize the "just war" strain. A humane state will recognize this possible diversity, provide alternate forms of service, and take all conscientious protest as a salutary pressure to keep its defense systems functioning as means to peace.

Thus, war reveals the tangled state to which sin has brought the human race. The very existence of today's military arsenals underscores the dividedness, the fallenness, that sin imports. Realistically, one has to reckon with many persons' sinful will to violence. Theoretically, the faithful Christian has to work to move human conflicts toward peaceful solutions. Concretely, the avoidance of war is very demanding.

Pollution

For Christianity, reality has four irreducible dimensions: nature, society, self, and divinity. None can be reduced to another, without losing the richness that wise consciousness intuits. Each must be given its due, if we are to have sanity and prosperity. War shows the interrelatedness of these four irreducible dimensions. Primarily a social evil, it also wastes the land, corrodes individual personalities, and cries to God for judgment. Still, it is most potently a symbol of social sin—the moral evil that people conspire to accomplish. In societies that are militarily developed, conspiratorial war-making can take on a life of its own, becoming a system almost independent of human control. The current arms race may be a good example. Though distinct individuals keep fueling it, the arms race has momentum of its own. Submitting the military budget, mining the required materials, manning the factories, assembling the parts, training the personnel, evaluating the enemy's arms production, submitting the next military budget—the suboperations mesh like spiraling gears, making their upward climb very difficult to stop.

Parallel to the social phenomenon of war is the natural phenomenon of pollution. If war is a prime symbol of social sin, pollution is a prime symbol of "natural" sin—the wanton abuse of nature. And as war implicates all the irreducible dimensions of reality, so does pollution. The chain of noxious chemical dump sites that now stretches across our country came into being because individuals deliberately chose not to control them, because society generally chose comfort over ecological sanity, and because worshipping God seemed to have nothing to do with protecting nature. Knowingly, human beings now pollute the air, the land, and the sea, sinning grievously. Our uncontrolled chemicals, radiation, and garbage show the disorder in our souls.

The mind grows inured to statistics on pollution, and suspicious of the arguments they serve. However, now and then a set of statistics is so striking that it makes the case for the sinfulness of pollution incontrovertibly. For instance, the statistics on pollutants found in Love Canal, near Niagara Falls, place the ethics of the Hooker Chemical Company, accused of dumping pollutants into the canal, in serious doubt. Nonetheless, we recently came across a set of figures that puts even Love Canal in the shade. It concerned Cubatao, Brazil, one of Latin America's leading petrochemical centers. As we recite some of the figures on Cubatao, keep in mind the Christian conviction that things like this need not be—that they are the free choice of warped wills.

Cubatao rests atop coastal lowlands intersected by four now lifeless rivers. Over it sits a venomous mist fed each day by a thousand tons of toxic gases that are trapped by a two-thousand-foot range of hills nearby. The city has eighty thousand inhabitants, but neither its mayor nor its state officials will live in it (because their request for gas masks was turned down). Of every thousand babies born in Cubatao, forty are dead at birth and another forty perish within a week (at least eight times the infant mortality rate of the USA). Most of the eighty victims are deformed. A pollution monitoring machine set up in 1975 broke down in 1977 because of the intensity of the contamination. Before breaking down, however, the machine found that residents of Cubatao were being showered continuously with twelve hundred particulates per cubic meter of air, more than twice the amount that the World Health Organization says produces "excess mortality" after twenty-four hours of exposure.

More precisely, the atmospheric tests said that Cubatao's 50-square-mile area was being bombarded daily with 473 tons of carbon monoxide, 182 tons of sulfur dioxide, 148 tons of particulate matter, 41 tons of nitrogen oxide, and 31 tons of hydrocarbons. The giant foundry of the Paulista Steel Company is the largest polluter, but other Brazilian firms, the American firms Dow Chemical, Du Pont, and Union Carbide, and French and German firms all contribute. The newspaper account from which we got this information may provide the motive for these companies' abuses of nature: "The industries of Cubatao have given the city the highest average per capita income of any city in Brazil, but the profits do not reach most of the city's inhabitants."[9]

Is Cubatao a preview of an industrialized third world? Do the deformed fetuses in its women's wombs, the deformed fish in its waters, prophesy the ecology of Latin America in the year 2000? Perhaps the answer to these questions is no, but it could conceivably be yes. For the profit in it, some people are willing to kill the air, the land, the sea, and with them many living inhabitants. In Christian faith, such sin cries to God for vengeance.

Injustice

When the human spirit rejects a Cubatao or a Love Canal as sinful, it activates an inbuilt mechanism expressed by the word *justice*. One image that many peoples apparently spontaneously have used for justice is a scale. From within, the human spirit weighs things as though placing them in a scale. When they do not balance, it suspects an injustice. Whether this image comes from a deeper sense that there should be harmony throughout the world (a sense almost always found in the cosmological myth) or depends on a slightly developed civilization doesn't greatly matter. By the time that Christian theology came on the scene, "pondering" (weighing) was an activity natural and proper to the Spirit-led spirit.

There are too many candidate examples of injustice to ponder, too many ways that, functioning as Christian theologians, we might concretize injustice. The scales of American justice do not balance racially, for black people obviously do not have the economic, educational, or health opportunities that white people do. Similarly, our scales do not balance sexually. Women get paid less than men even when they perform the same jobs. They are underrepresented in Congress, overrepresented on the welfare rolls. Many churches will not accept female leadership. Many professions drag their feet and hold back. Injustice therefore molds the lives of a majority of our population. In one of the nations most respectful of the human person, tens of millions are shortchanged.

The scales tip more when we place in them the different nations' standards of living. In 1976 the per capita GNP in Kuwait was $15,480. In Bhutan it was $70.[10] In the USA it was $7,890. Kuwait to Bhutan is a ratio of about 221 to 1. Out of its instinct for justice, traditional Christian teaching said that the goods of the earth are for all the earth's people, and no person has the right to superfluities while another person lacks necessities. If you want to stir up a heated argument, take these two theses to any circle where *The Wall Street Journal* is read reverently. Most likely you will be called a Communist. If the spirit moves you, you can reply that you are just speaking as a traditional Christian should.

Perhaps that "should" needs underscoring. Western culture largely derived from Christian sources, and those sources obviously did not raise a steady stream of generations who treated the goods of the earth as though they existed for all people, or who gave away their superfluities whenever they met people who lacked necessities. "Physician, heal thyself" has applied all too regularly. Nonetheless, the two theses do represent the social doctrine that theologians tended to derive when they pondered Christian faith deeply.

An instinct for human solidarity and practical charity caused the Christian tradition to account great disparities in wealth another sign of sin. At the least, the wealthy had an obligation to give alms to alleviate the sufferings of the poor. At its strongest, the tradition recalled the teaching of the Sermon on the Mount: God blesses the poor (and will redeem the injustice they suffer). Thus, only a bastardized Christianity supports unbridled capitalism. Through two thousand years, legitimate Christianity has said that one cannot serve God and mammon. To serve God, and love one's neighbor as oneself, great disparities in wealth have to go. It is easier for a camel to pass through the eye of a needle than for a rich person to enter the Kingdom of God (Matt. 19:24) because great wealth usually depends on injustice.

When British economist E. F. Schumacher converted to Christianity, he found an ultimate rationale for his progressive ecological and labor theories.[11] Schumacher had had considerable practical experience in industry (such as the British coal industry), and in later years he consulted extensively abroad. One of the specific experiments with which he was involved was the Scott Bader Commonwealth, a chemical firm that attempted to organize itself more equitably than most British firms had. At Scott Bader work units were kept rather small, so that workers could know one another well and develop a sense of collaboration. There also was an effort to distribute profits fairly. Schumacher lamented the fact that a seven-to-one ratio, top to bottom, was the best that Scott Bader could accomplish in its salary scale, but when one compares that with the salary scale of a large American firm, such as General Motors or ITT, Scott Bader looks quite good. At General Motors or ITT the salary ratio, top to bottom, is about seventy to one.

The point, of course, is not to argue about specific decimals or fractions. The point is that in a dozen directions, many of them economic, the scales have long gone tilt. Again and again we find that due proportion, fair distribution of resources and profits, does not obtain. Again and again there is massive injustice. We shall return to this theme in our last chapters, when we deal with Latin American, black, and feminist liberation theologies. Right now, in the midst of piecing together something of the Christian worldview, the import of such injustice is sin. The best in us knows that God hates injustice. The best in us senses, with the Hebrew prophet Amos, that God wants justice to roll down like a mighty stream (Amos 5:24).

Death

"The wages of sin is death" (Rom. 6:23). In this one sentence the apostle Paul distanced Christian faith from detached biological science. For while it is true that death has a metaphoric weight in Paul's theology, standing for the whole atrophy and self-ruin that sin creates, it is integral to Paul's vision that physical death is also linked to sin and the old order of Adam, the first man. Indeed, the crux of Pauline theology is Jesus's passover from death to resurrection. Christians believe that in that movement the reign of sin gave way to the reign of grace. Through dying to death, Jesus showed that God's life burned in him unconsumably. The Greek thought that underlay the earliest Christian philosophical theologies understood death as the prime difference between humanity and divinity. Humans were mortal, the gods were immortal. Dying, Jesus showed that he was fully human. Resurrected, he showed that he was deathless, and so divine.

Cued by Jesus's passover, Christian theologians have probed death from many angles. Early Greek Fathers reflected that their philosophy should be the practice of dying like Jesus. In this they resembled Plato, whose beliefs were crystallized by the death of Socrates. That Athens should put its most just man to death on the charge of impiety shocked Plato to his soul. Christian theologians reflecting on the death of Jesus felt a similar shock. That human beings put to death God's very Son was a profound revelation of human malice.

Through the Middle Ages, when long lives were few, *memento mori* ("remember dying") was a watchword. Influenced by the plagues, a late medieval classic, *The Imitation of Christ*, set Christian piety in a sober, almost macabre mood. The *danse macabre* of the same period was a combination of gallows humor and sober theology. Joined mortal hand to mortal hand, pope and pauper alike danced across time to the same graveyard.

Recent Christian piety has reacted against this almost morbid spirituality of the past. Impressed by the vital human intelligence and energy that has transformed the world technologically, much twentieth-century piety has tried to be optimistic, life-affirming. Somewhat ironically, secular thought has returned lately to the centrality of death. As courses on death and dying proliferate on college campuses, secular humanists have tried to come to grips with the widespread denial of death in American culture. The result has been a somewhat cross-purposed, unintended agreement between theologians and secular humanists that death and life knot together at the human core. As psychologist Erik Erikson has put it, the consummating strength that human beings need, in order to complete the lifecycle well, is the wisdom to love life in the face of death.

Sensing this, a cluster of Christian theologians have reflected on the way death summarizes human time. Prior to death, all our acts are partial. Slowly, bit by bit, we build a personality, but none of our acts in time can be exhaustive. We cannot fathom ourselves, so we do not *know* how we stand before God's mystery. We cannot commit ourselves completely, so none of our decisions is once-and-for-all. The most we can do in our lifetimes is to launch a **fundamental option** (a basic choice for or against honesty and love) and sail with it. Only when we come to term do we have the chance to write *finis*. Only at death can we finally say yes or no to the concrete destiny God has dealt us.

Psychologist C. G. Jung analyzed the crises that commonly occur in the second half of life and found them to be uniformly religious. Under the increasing pressure of its aging, the personality is forced to take stock. Pondering what it has become in its time past, it can panic before the tasks of its diminishing time future. Or, in happier cases, death can emerge from the hidden side of one's motivations and take a prominent place in the light.

For personalities not open to mystery in faith and hope, the approach of death easily prompts a snatching at carnal pleasures, or an accumulating of possessions, or a grasping to consolidate power. All these reactions suggest a sinful unreality and fear. People flee the light that death should cast because their deeds are evil (John 3:19). What should be the greatest reality factor, the greatest stimulus to raise their minds to mystery's sovereignty, causes many to run in circles.

Human death, then, is more than a biological inevitability. Concretely, its approach triggers either **conversion** or more animated sin. Christian faith says that we should not die in moral agony, and this "should not" is another sign of our divided human condition. Because of the guilt we bear, the wrongdoing on our accounts, we go into the night fearfully. Will we find harsh judgment, or will a good God wipe away every tear? In the eye of Christian faith, life and death are paradoxical. Jesus was so full of life that he made death die. Saints have been so dead to secular life that their spirits have grown fat. Deuteronomy says, "Behold, I set before you this day two ways, of death and life" (30:15). The human task is to choose life.

Utopian Conscience

In his efforts to choose life, the human person finally is dependent on his own moral sense. A peculiarity of human consciousness is its ability to be both subject and object, both judge and judged. As we suggested in discussing human evil, there is an ingrained bias for truth and goodness. Strangely enough, the species that wreaks so much havoc on the world does so only by aberration. We know that lying is a misuse of reason and speech, so we brand the habitual liar *pathological*. We see that even great evildoers—Hitler, Stalin, Lenin—presented their murders as a species of good. As the primal ontological question is why there is something rather than nothing, so the primal ethical question is why our humanity is essentially good. If we answer these primal questions realistically, our answers show the prior action of God. Before we judge or act, God has been at work inclining us to the positive, to being and goodness. This is the fundamental tenet of a Christian view of human origin.

Christian philosopher Blaise Pascal said that we would not seek God had we not already found God. By this he meant that God prompts even our seeking. What we call *utopian conscience* derives from such divine prompting. **Utopia** (literally "no place") is where what ought to be obtains; utopia is the direct product of God's lures. The Christian symbols of **heaven**, judgment, and **beatific vision** all exemplify utopian conscience guided by grace (God's self-gift). Extrapolating its sense that sin and death should not be, Christian utopian conscience fashions a place where sin will be judged, good rewarded, and death overcome. It calls this place *heaven*, joining the archaic human tendency to place conscience, light, and judgment in the sky, where an all-seeing wisdom dwells.

Through heaven, Christians believe, evil will get its comeuppance. Murderers, profiteers, liars, and cheats who prosper in time will be corrected by eternal truth. If grievous sinners, they will be sent to hell and deprived of eternal truth. Of course this thought can spring from petty minds and express little more than bloodthirsty vengeance. The core impulse behind imagining a heaven, however, seems quite laudable. Unless there is a judgment fairer than that of human history, our lives are but sound and fury. Even the deep truth that people suffer in their selves for their evil does not make history sane, for what about the victims of evildoing? It is not enough to see that Hitler's evil left him a spastic personality. The six million Jews and six million non-Jews who perished in the camps still remain on humankind's heads. Somehow, a God who is Lord of history must recompense those millions, as she must recompense all the innocents whom time has crushed. Otherwise, there is no deep sense to existence, and so no anchor for morality. If chaos is king, the goodness or evil of our actions does not matter.

But chaos is not king in most consciences. Even when people are weak and sin often, few of them give up on morality completely. The criminal still feels that he has some human rights. The bully continues to think that she should not be bullied. By and large, human beings are amazingly committed to having things make sense. Through some deep instinct, they flee absurdity like the plague. A few intellectuals can argue that this is a mass self-deception, an instinctive reaction like the release of adrenalin. In the Christian view, a better analysis, more responsive to such a massive phenomenon, is that the human person is coded for the path of life. However frequently he wanders the way of destruction, however monotonous his sin, the human person seldom gives up on life and goodness, because they are innate in him.

Hell, then, is for Christians but the privation of the truth and goodness that humanity naturally seeks. Laying aside the flames and the devils, serious Christian theologians have conceived of hell as humanity without God. By contrast, heaven is essentially the beatific vision of God: the knowing and loving without restriction that humanity at heart seeks. Augustine, the leading Father of the Latin Church, put it unforgettably: "You have made us for yourself, O Lord, and our hearts are restless til they rest in You." Hell is the restlessness of hearts made to know God and ever separated from God. Heaven is the fulfillment, the "abiding" spoken of by John, that makes light and life and love overflow outside time. Demythologized, translated, these utopian concepts disclose profound realities, for they are inseparable from a personhood set for God.

Evil therefore serves the Christian as a strong impetus to measure time well. If time were all that the human person had, the human person would be ill-made. We do have a reach that exceeds our grasp. The attainment of heaven is the exercise of that reach that time never allows. It is true that reaching for heaven can upset a fine balance. It is true that religion can be an opiate diverting people from social change, and that otherworldly energies have been perverted into terrible fanaticisms. For Christians, though, those energies, those refusals to consider evil intrinsically human, have powered the noblest human ventures. Indeed, otherworldly energies are what have kept human beings human, and what have kept Christian theology most aware of sin. Sin is the mystery of iniquity, of the evil and non-being that should not be. It is ungodliness's powerful intermediate say. But Christian faith says that God is ever greater than ungodliness, and so it always has good news to proclaim.

Summary

The Christian doctrine of creation spotlights human finitude, as well as the constant dependence of all who exist on God. The Christian doctrine of sin spotlights human evil. In the hurly-burly of concrete events, human beings show a dark inability to do what they should. Thus, many of our actions occur in situations tilted from the beginning. For the Bible this state of affairs rests on human beings' own heads. Sin is a missing of the mark, a lack of due proportion, both irrational and personally chosen.

Perhaps the greatest social blight caused by sin comes through war. When injustice forces people to pursue violent means of redress, the usual result is carnage. For that reason, Christian tradition limited the conditions for a just war severely. Impressed by the history of sinful violence, it put the great burden of proof on the warmakers. Today the situation is rapidly becoming the same with industrialists. As pollution comes within sight of destroying the very matrices of life, the great burden of proof is on any firm that would add more toxic chemicals, radiation or nonbiodegradable garbage to the ecosphere.

War and pollution are prime manifestations of sin's social abuses, but a dozen other evils warp human intercourse. Racism, sexism, and great economic disparities all exemplify the sinfulness of injustice. Metaphorically, injustice is traveling a way of death, a way destructive of the good life for which human beings have been made. In the apostle Paul's view, all species of death manifest the reign of sin Rooted in Christ's resurrection, utopian Christian conscience produces the symbol of heaven and hell to show the human spirit's power over injustice and death.

Study Questions

1. How does the contemporary Israeli dilemma concerning "torturing" terrorist epitomize concrete ethics?
2. Is the biblical view that sin rests on human beings' own heads outmoded? Why
3. What are the four conditions that a just war must fulfill?
4. Explain to a pregnant woman living in Cubatao what religion has to do with the air she breathes.
5. How does traditional Christian social teaching buttress the Scott Bader Commonwealth?
6. What ought the increasing realization of mortality mean for the second half of human life?
7. What do the symbols that utopian conscience has developed say about human nature and destiny?

Notes

1. *The Wichita Eagle*, September 26, 1980, p. 2c.
2. John L. McKenzie, *Dictionary of the Bible* (Milwaukee: Bruce, 1965), p. 817

3. Ibid., p. 818.
4. See Arnold Toynbee, *Mankind and Mother Earth* (New York: Oxford University Press, 1976); Geoffrey Barraclough, ed., *The Times Atlas of World History* (Maplewood, NJ: Hammond, 1979).
5. René Coste, "War," *Sacramentum Mundi*, ed. Karl Rahner et al. (New York: Herder and Herder, 1970), vol. 6, p. 353.
6. Ibid., p. 354.
7. Ibid., p. 355.
8. Bernard Stoeckle, ed., *The Concise Dictionary of Christian Ethics* (New York: Seabury, 1979), p. 181.
9. Warren Hoge, "Valley of Death," *The Wichita Eagle*, September 24, 1980, p. 13a (N.Y. Times News Service).
10. See Barbara Ward, *Progress for a Small Planet* (New York: W. W. Norton, 1979), pp. 283, 290.
11. For Schumacher's ultimate rationale, see A *Guide for the Perplexed* (New York: Harper & Row, 1977). His ecological and labor theories are to the fore in *Small is Beautiful* (New York: Harper & Row, 1973) and *Good Work* (New York: Harper & Row, 1979).

CHAPTER 4

Grace

Faith

We have gone to the nadir of human existence and found a malice, a deliberate refusal to love God and neighbor, that biblical religion calls sin. Destructive of the individual sinner, it is also the darkest aspect of war, pollution, economic injustice, and the other social evils that spoil the human span. In this chapter we turn toward the apex of human existence, the surplus wonders and fulfillments Christianity finds God to provide. If sin collects the worst about our species, grace collects the best.

The word *grace* ordinarily means poise, smoothness, easy flow. When we say that a man, or more frequently a woman, is graceful, we stir images of lovely dancing, skating, or social gestures. The graceful person moves easily, inhabits patterns or moments that do not jar. Theologians take these connotations of grace and apply them to the repair and elevation of human nature they believe God has worked through Christ.

Almost always, seeing such repair and elevation of human nature demands eyes especially focused. That is somewhat true regarding sin, too, but human evil is so dramatic that seeing sin, recognizing a mystery behind human malice, is not very difficult. Grace, however, tends to be subtler. It is like a clear October day when you feel unusually alive but are only half aware why. Sin is like the violent thunder-storm of July or the bone-chilling blizzard of February: you can hardly miss its major manifestations. Grace is the barometer rising a degree, a seven-mile-an-hour wind playing on your cheek. As Saint Ignatius of Loyola, the sixteenth-century founder of the Jesuits, put it in his rules for the **discernment of spirits**, when Satan (evil personified) works on the basically good personality the impact is violent and wrenching. When God works on the basically good personality the touch is light, dexterous, consoling.[1]

Faith is the Christian focus that enables one to see sin and grace. There is a general axiom in Catholic Christianity that grace perfects nature. In other words, God's action in our lives rounds out, complements, and fulfills the capacities we have simply by being human. In consequence, the eye of faith is not wholly different from the eye of any person alert and sensitive. The eye of the mature theologian is quite like the eye of the mature novelist. So the short stories of a writer like Grace Paley,[2] which describe nuances of human behavior the ordinary person probably would miss, are a good model for the mature theologian's longer story. Paley describes a family squabble or two mothers airing their kids in the park with such perception, such sympathy, such intelligence that they are no longer commonplace happenings. Indeed, she makes us realize that no one, no human event, is commonplace. Each is unique and revelatory, if we have eyes to see. And having eyes to see seems to be especially the province of the priest and the poet.[3]

A first sense of *faith*, then, is seeing that God's Spirit inspires—with new light, horizon, and sensitivity. As authors trying to translate Christian notions into lay terms, we have found this meaning of faith especially useful. However, theologians generally tend to explain faith in more analytic, less figurative terms, so let us move on to sharper analysis.

Theologian Van Harvey, representing a rather moderate Protestant view, analyzes faith as follows. The history of Christian thought shows two general tendencies regarding faith. The first regards faith as belief or mental assent to some truth, whether about God or about a historical event. The second tendency regards faith as a basic orientation of the whole person. This may include belief but it shows itself more as trust, confidence, or loyalty. The first tendency is more **intellectualist**, the second more **voluntarist**. Roman Catholics have tended to the first view, Protestants to the second.[4] (It is typical of American theologians, unfortunately, that Harvey ignores Eastern Orthodoxy completely.)

In general, theologians of the early Church tended to regard faith intellectualistically—as the acceptance of tradition or the apprehension of certain eternal and divine truths. Thus, early theologians did not identify faith with the whole of Christian life or salvation, and they often sought to supplement faith with mystical experience. For instance, Clement of Alexandria, a leading Father of the Greek church, spoke of a *gnosis* or higher knowledge. Augustine was more voluntaristic, but even he sometimes presented faith as but the preparation for the higher stages of Christian life, where the love of God would rule.

During the Middle Ages Saint Thomas Aquinas brought the intellectualist model of faith to its peak in his impressive *Summa Theologiae*. For Thomas faith was at core an assent to **dogma**, official truth backed by divine authority. Martin Luther, a leading Protestant **reformer**, had a more holistic notion, in which the core of faith was the total person's trusting response to God's graciousness. Thus Luther tended to include hope and love within faith. John Calvin, another leading Protestant reformer, spoke more about a knowledge component, but this knowledge was of God's benevolence rather than of his essence. Thus Calvin was closer to Luther than to Aquinas and made faith a matter of affection as well as of mind. Since the

Reformation, Protestants, **Pietists**, and **Evangelicals** have tended to opt for the second, more holistic view of faith in terms of the priority of the heart over the head.

As Harvey's brief sketch implies, faith can carry more or less freight. Overall, however, the emphasis that Jesus himself gave to faith, and the emphasis of the New Testament gospels and epistles, have made faith crucial. It is one of the **theological virtues** (powers given by God) because it pertains directly to the divine life of Christ and the Spirit. As the orientation of the Christian personality to Jesus's God, it is primordial in Christian religion. Like a new set of senses, faith finds a world that atheism cannot perceive. Believers say faith comes from God, is amazing grace, and fulfills both the head and the heart.

Hope

Hope is another of the theological virtues. It also is a gift of God, an amazing grace. A tangled sentence by Karl Rahner, a contemporary Roman Catholic theologian, from the *Theological Dictionary* suggests the richness that traditional Christianity has found in hope: "In the [New Testament] sense, hope is ultimately constituted by the intersection, on the one hand, of that divine predestining plan for man whereby the love of God—which, being incarnate in Christ, has become human history—has efficaciously and permanently affected man, and on the other hand of the responsive attitude towards this plan shown by the person (or the Church, in which the highly personal response of which each individual is capable is preserved and sustained) who confidently awaits the final consummation of the divine economy of salvation in the coming of Jesus Christ (Heb. 6:18 f.; Rom. 8:24 and *passim*), in reliance on the saving plan which has already and irrevocably been initiated by God, as he knows with the certainty of faith."[5]

Because of Germanic sentences like that, folklore has it, Karl Rahner's brother Hugo, who was also an eminent Roman Catholic theologian, used to wait until Karl's writings were translated into French before reading them. Nonetheless, such sentences have the merit of suggesting, by their very rush and complexity, the interconnections that basic Christian notions beg. Thus, Rahner shows us that hope conjoins God's plan of salvation, which centers in Christ, and human beings' faithful response. Hope is the expectation of a good future, based on a belief in Christ's past accomplishments.

God, then, is the primary agent of hope, as God is the primary agent of all the theological virtues. The relation between God's agency and our own is the mysterious cooperation we sketched when dealing with the creator-creature relationship. Rahner's further notion, that hope helps form an intermediate stage in the historical development of general dogmatic faith into the absolute personal intimacy of love amounts to a Roman Catholic acknowledgement that the emphasis on personal, holistic faith that the Protestant Reformation brought has much to commend it.[6] On the way to the Church's contemporary emphasis on the primacy of love, hope bridges the gap between the intellectualist emphasis of the Fathers and the volun tarist emphasis of the Pietists. Leaning into the future, the Christian trusts that God will provide. Such trust is almost the abandonment of concern, the complete confidence, that the saints' profoundly loving union with God produces.

When we specify this hopeful orientation, we find that it takes up other central themes. For instance, the Christian hopes for the forgiveness of his sins, and for a complete fulfillment in heaven. Because of Jesus, she expects that God's goodness will consummate her life with mercy and bounty. One day God's Kingdom will come, God's will will be done, on earth as it is in heaven. On that day evildoers will receive their just deserts and peacemakers will be called children of God. There will be a new heaven and a new earth, for the former things—the dispensation of sin, suffering, and death—will have passed away. Thus hope is innate in the Christian view of death. Hope is of the Christian essence. One cannot really believe in Jesus's God and not lean into the future trustingly, expectantly.

Largely in the context of a dialogue with Marxists, many Christian theologians recently have reexamined the importance of hope. One of the most interesting books that has come from this reexamination is José Miranda's *Marx and the Bible*.[7] Miranda's thesis is that Marx and the Bible largely agree in insisting that the prime human task is to do justice, and in taking a hopeful view of history. Marx thought that human beings *can* bring about a just society; Christians reading the Bible alertly find that God *has* given the grace to bring about justice and peace. Two major currents of deep reflection therefore might join in stressing a hopeful view of the future. They would have to iron out their differences about the divine element (grace), but humanistic Marxists like Milan Machovec suggest that they could.[8]

Of course Christians like Aleksandr Solzhenitsyn, who have suffered at the hands of a version of Marxism, think such an agreement is impossible. They may be right, but their own lives usually reflect a hopeful view of the future. Indeed, such Christians usually invite all persons to work for a just social order and expect that life's mystery will turn out to be gracious. Such Christians are not uncritical optimists. They never stray very far from the massive evidence of evil. But the mystery of Jesus's God is so real to them that they are confident all things will one day be well.

Love

Speaking of the (heavenly) time when all things will be well, the apostle Paul concluded his famous hymn to charity with the words: "So faith, hope, love abide, these three; but the greatest of these is love" (1 Cor. 13:13). Joining this with Jesus's emphasis on love (for example, in Matt. 22:37–39) and the **Johannine** "God is love" (1 John 4:16), Christians traditionally have made love their central treasure and prime command. That is not to say, of course, that Christians have been remarkable for their loving kindness. Empirically, one would be hard put to show that Christianity has treated humanity better than Hinduism or Buddhism. But theologically, in terms of the worldview that their faith has laid out, Christians have made love more central than Hindus have made *bhakti* (devotion) or Buddhists have made *mahakaruna* (great compassion). Love is the very stuff of the Christian God. So not your brains, not your money, not your pious works, but your love, is the matter of your Christian final examination, your Christian trial before the judgment of God.

There are different kinds of love, and Christian theology has made some distinctions among them. The love that the tradition finds saving, divine, exemplified by Jesus, is *agape*. *Agape* connotes light, warmth, creativity, and above all self-spending. It is not desire so much as benevolence, not self-enrichment so much as help for others. When God "so loved the world that he gave his only begotten Son" (John 3:16), he gave the greatest example of *agape*. That which the Father held dearest, most intimate and self-expressive, he gave over "for us men and our salvation," as the traditional creed says. In **Pauline** terms, Jesus's incarnation, death, and resurrection resulted from an amazing self-emptying (Phil. 2:5–11). In the New Testament, then, *agape* is the great sign of God. It is God's way of doing business, concretized in the way that Jesus did business—in Jesus's healing, instructing, forgiving, and laying down his life for his friends.

Two other kinds of love that Christianity has found worth considering are *eros* and *philia*.[9] *Eros* is the love of beauty, the love of romance, the love that fired Romeo and Juliet. The Greek cultural world in which the early Church found itself was sensitive to *eros*, if only because *eros* figured so prominently in Plato's thought. It was the god, the human energy, the creative fire with which the Platonic soul burned after the Idea of the Good. Christianity showed itself leery of *eros*. Not only did *eros* relate to Greek homosexuality, it was part of an aesthetic approach to life that stressed human feeling more than Christianity found comfortable. When the early Latin Father Tertullian asked rhetorically, "What has Athens to do with Jerusalem?", he was opposing a culture based on *eros* to a biblical culture based on salvational *agape*. The salvation that God had worked through Jesus was, in his view, incomparably more valuable than the Idea of the Good. Not all the early Fathers were so opposed to "Athens," but the Christian mainstream seriously qualified the rights of *eros*.

Nonetheless, through history *eros* and *agape* have kept a tension in Christian love. Insofar as *eros* represents a natural part of the human being, it cannot be intrinsically evil. It is liable to abuse, yes, but in itself it is part of the human image of God. Thus, traditional Christianity defended the intellectual *eros* manifest in study, the aesthetic *eros* manifest in art, and the bodily *eros* manifest in conjugal sex, whenever more rigorous movements called them evil. Patristic, medieval, and Reformation theology all were ambivalent about *eros* (especially bodily *eros*), but the refrain in the Genesis account of creation, "God saw that it was good" (Gen. 1:10), forced them to defend what God had seen fit to put into the human makeup.

Philia is the love of friendship. Classical Greek thought, which was much interested in friendship (in part because it did not see marriage as the union of two friends), rooted *philia* in *homonoia*: likemindedness. Two people were friends when they shared a common mind, when they agreed enough to forge a bond. A true friend became another self, the other half of one's soul. Christianity seems to have found friendship less interesting than *agape* or *eros*. It had scriptural stimuli to exploit friendship theologically, for instance the love of David and Jonathan (1 Sam. 18:1–4) and Jesus's saying that he had not called his disciples servants but friends (John 15:15), but these stimuli seldom started great movements, in either thought or politics. Some medieval monks wrote warm treatises on friendship, but most theology employed either *eros* or *agape* in its analogies.

In modern and contemporary times, love has come in for rather cynical treatment. Put off by human savagery, or by vapid emotionalism, serious persons have tended to put large parentheses around affairs of the heart. True, Pascal spoke of the reasons of the heart that the mind doesn't know, implying that love is finally more revelatory than knowledge, but Pascal was an exceptional man. Since the Enlightenment, most intellectuals have deemed reason and gravity more proper than great passion. But we are in a post-Enlightenment age, so artists like Patrick White, the Nobel-Prize-winning Australian novelist, are daring a return to old Christian verities: " 'Love' is an exhausted word, and God has been expelled by those who know better, but I offer you the one as the proof that the other still exists."[10] Without love there is no Christian God; without love human beings are but tinkling brass and clanging cymbal.

Salvation

Salvation overcomes the terrors and frustrations of a world without God, a world where human beings merely tinkle and clang. If you are shrewd, or a post-Enlightenment thinker, you may already have intuited that salvation is principally a matter of love. Patrick White won his Nobel Prize for a series of novels—*Riders in the Chariot*, *The Vivesector*, *The Eye of the Storm*—that shrewdly study the human hunger for love. Speaking of a confused, post-modern woman, another victim of our contemporary normlessness, he wrote: "Yet whatever form she took, or whatever the illusion temporarily possessing her, the reality of love, which is the core of reality itself, had eluded her, and perhaps always would."[11] If the reality of love is the core of reality itself, as we have shown Jesus, Paul, and John to insist, then salvation is mainly a passover from lovelessness to wholehearted *agape*. Let us meditate on this pillar of the Christian worldview.

The basic connotation of *salvation* is health. To save someone is to return her to health, wholeness, well-being. By implication, prior to salvation she is sick, fragmented, ill at ease. Protestant theologian Paul Tillich played variations on this analysis, especially in his *The Courage to Be*.[12] Some of his findings were historical. For instance, he thought that the breakup of classical civilization brought about a crisis in meaning, especially meaning strong enough to counterbalance human mortality. The Middle Ages were possessed by moral anxiety: fear of hell and God's wrath. The end of modernity brought many persons close to despair. They were tempted to prefer nonbeing, the cessation of their existence, to the spiritual sufferings their times imposed. For our purposes, these historical negatives are but different faces of the human need for salvation.

It is true, of course, that personalities differ in their sense of the human need for salvation. In *The Varieties of Religious Experience*, American psychologist and philosopher William James distinguished between "once-born" and "twice-born" personalities.[13] The once-born personality is relatively whole and content. He does not experience the world as sundered. By contrast, the twice-born personality must "die" and be "reborn" if he is to find any peace. Unhappy, lacerated, seeking peace desperately, he is a prime candidate for religious conversion. Christianity can grant this difference in temperament or intensity, but it says that all human beings need salvation, because all have "sinned and fallen short of the glory of God" (Rom. 3:23). More or less aware, all human beings sense that humanity is sick, people are alienated, nature is a terrible stranger. Every military camp, hospital, and sweat shop blares forth this message. Every sleepless night of guilt or worry adds a footnote.

In Western Christianity, salvation has been seen largely as a redemption from sin. By the cross of Christ, the God who was far and threatening has become near and welcoming. Perhaps the classical statement of this Western view was Saint Anselm's theory that Christ atoned for our sins by paying the debt of punishment we had contracted. That theory has struck most contemporary theologians as legalistic, but it puts a sharp point on the Western tendency to see sinful, divided creatures as separated from God, and to see Christ's work as the restoration of good relations with God—the **atonement** that overcomes alienation. In its train such atonement brought a renewal of human integrity, the chance for social peace and greater harmony with nature, but its core was rebuilding the bridge to God. For Anselm, God became human in order to save us from sin.

In addition to Anselm's view, two other species of the Western moral emphasis in salvation are the Augustinian-Calvinist (derived from Saint Augustine and John Calvin) notion of freeing an enslaved will, and the Thomist (derived from Saint Thomas Aquinas) notion that redemption proceeds by the law of the cross. In the Augustinian view of salvation, which owes a great deal to Paul's descriptions of human beings' inner division (Rom. 7), God must give us a new, liberated will. The great choice that human beings face is between a love of God unto contempt of self and a love of self unto contempt of God. Wretches that we are, many of us choose the second, enslaving love. Unless we are seized by God's grace, we spend our time pampering bodies that will soon feed worms, egos that become more and more ridiculous. For Augustine, true freedom is not being able to do whatever one wants; it is being able to do whatever one should. The grace of Christ that saves us is the power to do what we should: love God utterly and love our neighbors as ourselves.

Saint Thomas Aquinas's view of salvation focuses on how such grace works. In the dismal state of sin, our instinctive law comes from the jungle. Eye for eye and tooth for tooth, we exist in a whirl of false justice. Our wars, legal banditry, and closure to God's better life of love all spin off from this whirl. Thus, God's man had to break the jungle law, stop the whirling tit for tat. He did this by suffering evil in love, by taking sin into the greater divine goodness. The new law of the cross is the consummate statute of *agape*: as God has loved us, so should we love one another (1 John 4:11).

Divine Life

Eastern (Orthodox) Christianity has been less concerned with the acting out of grace than with its being. Without neglecting the deeds to which faith ought to conduce, the Orthodox Church has revered the divine being from which the deeds of faith proceed, and has seen the divine being as pertaining to humanity. By God's grace, human beings can become "partakers of the divine nature" (2 Pet. 1:4). Thus the Orthodox Church has spoken much of **deification**. God's salvation of humanity not only heals humanity, it also elevates us to divinity. As the Greek Father Athanasius put it, God became human so that humans might become God. The ultimate reach of grace is to the human core, where divine *agape* draws both body and spirit into God's own (trinitarian) life.

Eastern Christianity as well as Western Christianity has seen the dangers in this view, especially the danger of **pantheism** (identifying God with everything). In order to make it absolutely clear that God remains God and human beings remain human, Orthodox Christianity has stressed that the union between divinity and humanity that Jesus's birth made possible was with God's energies, not with God's essence. The divine essence remains beyond human knowledge, intrinsically mysterious. The energies are God in action revealing himself to the world.

Orthodox theologian Timothy Ware has clarified the Orthodox position on this point: "It is through these energies that God enters into a direct and immediate relationship with mankind. In relation to man, the divine energy is in fact nothing else than the *grace of God*; grace is not just a 'gift' of God, not just an object which God bestows on men, but a direct manifestation of the living God Himself, a personal confrontation between creature and Creator. 'Grace signifies all the abundance of the divine nature in so far as it is communicated to men.' When we say that the saints have been transformed or 'deified' by the grace of God, what we mean is that they have a direct experience of God Himself. They *know* God—that is to say, God in His energies, not in His essence."[14]

So, Eastern Christianity has considered grace to be deification. Its great Fathers took up the pagan Greek theme of immortalization (becoming deathless) and found in the incarnation, death, and resurrection of Christ a new human destiny. Beyond the grave, heaven would be an eternal sharing of God's own life. In time, grace and the sacramental life began such sharing. Four implications of this Orthodox view of grace merit comment. First, as grace grants humanity a share in the nature of the Christian God, it also implies the existence of the **Trinity**. We will take up this topic in the next chapter. Second, as exemplified by the life of Jesus, grace deifies not only the human spirit but also the human body. Indeed, the entry of the Son into the material order has exalted all of creation to the divine order, physical and biological nature included. Thus Lutheran theologian Joseph Sittler, a pioneer in recent Western theologizing about ecology, noted that the Orthodox doctrine of the *Pantokrator* (Logos as Lord of Creation) has much to offer the West, where grace historically has meant little in relation to physical nature.[15]

Third, this Eastern Christian understanding that grace extends to the body and physical creation undergirded what came to be the victorious position in the East's protracted controversy about **icons** (holy images used in devotional practice). Whereas Asiastic Christians, often influenced by Jewish and Muslim abhorrence of representations of God, tended to be **iconoclasts** (icon-smashers), Greeks argued that the Incarnation (enfleshment of God) sanctioned icons of Christ, Mary, and the saints. True, icons were not to be worshiped like God, but they were holy, grace-laden, and so presences of the power and love that came into the world with God's Logos and Spirit. Without icons Christian religion would be poorer, less expressive of God's goodness, of God's power to touch all our senses, all parts of our minds and hearts. Without icons, humble, illiterate people would lack a major mode of religious instruction. As John of Damascus, a leading Eastern Christian theologian said, "If a pagan asks you to show him your faith, take him into a church and place him before the icons."[16]

Fourth, the Eastern Christian notion of grace implies a powerful concept developed by Karl Rahner called the **supernatural existential**.[17] Simplified, it says that the gracious God manifest in Jesus Christ has made herself present everywhere. Through all history, no place has lacked a divine offer of shared life. In their very struggles after authenticity, their very battles to be honest and loving, human beings accept or reject God's offer of love-life. Deification, then, is nothing added on to the profound human labor to grow wise and good. Taken seriously, this thesis opens the whole world to the intimate energies of deification.

Thus, like all primary Christian notions, grace can swell to epitomize the whole. It can carry the entire order of salvation that Jesus's Kingdom represents, his entire dispensation of love. That God is good rather than wrathful, loving rather than harsh, is implied by grace. That divinity should number every hair of our heads finally derives from grace—from God's desire to give himself, to offer his life like a marriage-minded lover.

Community

The concept of the supernatural existential expresses the Christian God's desire to share the divine community. Father-Son-Spirit want to give themselves like lovers. As they themselves share a rich life of knowledge and love, so they want human beings to have more intimate associations, with other human beings as well as with the Trinity. Therefore, another mark of grace is that it is edifying. Grace builds up relationships, collaborations, communities. By contrast, sin tears down relationships and communities. Introverted, self-seeking, it whispers the tainted words, prompts the sour thoughts, that set people at enmity. Real sinners can never be real lovers. They are too closed and self-serving. Real lovers are always children of grace. Their tact, kindness, and self-spending reflect the best in human nature, its images of the Trinity.

The Christian community *par excellence* is the Church, which we discuss directly in the next chapter. Here it is appropriate to note that the Church derives from grace as well as from ordinary social dynamics. So much is this the case for Roman Catholicism that Pope Pius XII's **encyclical** on the Church, *Mystici Corporis* (1943), spoke of the Holy Spirit as the Church's soul. Across space and time, the Church forms a community in which believers are to Christ as his mystical body, as branches to his vine. These images, which derive respectively from Paul and John, stress the organic sharing, the common life, that flows between divinity and humanity. It flows as well among all Church members. Thus, as the Orthodox Church especially has stressed, the divine life of grace takes embodied, worldly form. The Church ought to be a city on a hilltop where all human beings can see the community possible when people are honest and loving.

We mentioned that the Church ought to embody the life of grace across space. In fact, it has been remarkably international. Despite the Eurocentrism that has plagued Christianity's missionary efforts, the Church has retained a sense that divine life cannot be captive to any particular culture. Similarly, divine life cannot be captive to any particular historical period. When Eastern Christians look back to the time of the first Church councils (assemblies of bishops) with nostalgia, or Roman Catholics gild the strong faith of the thirteenth century, or Protestants canonize the sixteenth century Geneva of John Calvin, they show themselves much smaller than God's gracious offer. On the other hand, all the major churches have retained a sense of tradition, and also a sense of the **communion of saints**.

The communion of saints is the society of all believers, whom faith makes holy. Thus, Christian liturgy commemorates outstanding martyrs, teachers, and **confessors** of the past. When it buries the dead it does so with a sense that the bonds of faith continue beyond the grave. Unlike some other religious traditions, however, Christianity has little encouraged direct efforts to commune with the dead. Seances, mediums, and divinations (efforts to spy out the future) have always been denigrated. There is a mystery about "the Church triumphant" in heaven, as there is a mystery about "the Church suffering" in **purgatory**. (Orthodoxy and Protestantism have shied away from the notion of purgatory—a place of purification before entry into heaven—because it seems to have little scriptural warrant.)

A remarkable artistic rendition of the Christian sense that the community of faith transcends time is El Greco's *The Burial of Count Orgaz*. Interestingly enough, El Greco was trained as an icon painter, so his mystical vision owes a great deal to the Eastern Christian sense of grace. *The Burial of Count Orgaz* adorns a tiny church in Toledo, Spain, the church of Santo Tomé. In the bottom half of the painting, the scene is earthly. The Count is being buried in the midst of his family and friends. However, even the earthly scene is miraculous, for the brilliantly robed clergy who are interring the Count are Saint Augustine and the martyr Saint

Stephen. The upper half of the picture shows the far reaches of the communion of saints. The heavens are open so that we can see angels, saints, apostles, the Virgin, and the triumphant Christ. Bathed in glory, they suggest both judgment and welcome. The body is being laid in the grave, but the Count's virtuous soul is proceeding to heaven. In the life of grace, temporal barriers fall away.

El Greco's sense of mystery and grace is so powerful that it communicates even in our secular age. Even as contemporary and mannered a writer as Louis Auchincloss has fallen captive: "Auntie became inscrutable. 'I don't know [whether I believe in God]. But I know this. I know that I like El Greco's feeling that what we see and hear is not all. That there's another world all around us and in us. You can divide the people in his pictures into those who sense this keenly and those who sense it only dimly. I can't think of any who don't sense it at all.' 'But why do you *like* that?' 'Because it makes life more exciting! Anyway, it makes painting more exciting.' "[18]

Resurrection

Toward the end of a weighty book that deals mainly with the New Testament experience of grace, Roman Catholic theologian Edward Schillebeeckx says: "Belief in the Resurrection gives Christians—assured in their conviction of victory over death—unshakable freedom, boldness in the face of the 'powers of this world.' "[19] The anchor for the religious excitement that Auchincloss's character found in El Greco's work is the Resurrection. In the dispensation of grace, the Resurrection is the dramatic pivot, the place where time yields to eternity. The Resurrection of Jesus was his passing over to God's sphere definitively. The Resurrection to which Christians look forward in hope is the materialization of the concepts of their utopian conscience.

Through most of Christian history, the Resurrection of Jesus from the dead has been taken quite literally. Reading the New Testament with uncritical eyes, believers have encountered accounts of the empty tomb, and Jesus's appearance to the disciple Mary Magdalene and to the apostles. There was doubting Thomas, invited to place his finger in the wound in Jesus's side; there were Peter and John breakfasting with the Lord by the shore. Finally, there was Paul's ringing judgment: "If Christ has not been raised, then our preaching is in vain and your faith is in vain" (1 Cor. 15:14).

Lately matters have become more complicated. Summarizing the consensus of New Testament scholars, Reginald Fuller has reported the opinion that the Resurrection cannot be considered a historical event.[20] What has interceded between the traditional literalism about the Resurrection and the contemporary scholarly reservations? Sophisticated historical and literary analyses. These analyses have shown discrepancies among the different New Testament accounts of the Resurrection, as philosophical analyses have shown difficulties with the very concept of a historical Resurrection. The discrepancies remind us that the New Testament authors were not historians in today's sense. They were believers writing to other believers about matters that both parties accepted in faith. The philosophical difficulties with the concept of a historical Resurrection are almost a matter of the definition of *history*. In most understandings of history there is no room for divine agency. This assumption may finally be untenable, and so prove that most understandings of history are faulty, but the burden of proof is on those who claim that the Resurrection is historical, since clearly it is not an ordinary, everyday event. To be historical the Resurrection would have to have the same type of empirical evidence, credible witnesses, and the like that are necessary to establish other events as historical. Because of the supernatural character of the Resurrection's claim—that God raised a dead man and endowed him with heavenly life—its proof is quite difficult.

Nonetheless, New Testament accounts likely had experiential sources, and the concept of a historical Resurrection is not contradictory if history is not by definition foreclosed to God's agency. In the total context of a commitment to Christian faith, which acknowledges all aspects of Jesus's personality and message, the Resurrection makes an intriguing kind of sense. Like many other species of grace, it is not necessary but it is fitting. Just as God need not have offered to share her divine life, so God need not have fulfilled human beings by taking the whole personality, body and soul, friends and world, into the divine deathlessness. Thus, with reasons of the heart, mature believers can find the New Testament picture of the Resurrection more plausible than seeing Jesus's life stop at the grave. The Song of Songs thought that love is strong as death. Reflecting on saying to another human being, "I love you," Christian philosopher Gabriel Marcel found the conviction, "You at least will never die." The Resurrection takes these profound human intuitions up and fulfills them at a level barely glimpsed.

Both monks and married folk have rooted their Christian faith in the Resurrection. Monks who gave up this-worldly life could look on the resurrected Christ as a warrant for their sacrifices. In time, they were trying to live a life opened to the eternal power that filled Christ the Lord. Married folk whose love went deep found great pathos in their mortality. Despite the saying that "in the resurrection they neither marry nor are given in marriage, but are like angels in heaven" (Matt. 22:30), married folk assuaged this pathos with the hope that their spouses, children, and relatives would return to them in the general resurrection, the time when all the faithful would receive a glorified flesh.

Sometimes Christian theologians have gotten sidetracked, troubling themselves with such questions as how God would restore the body of a person drowned at sea and eaten by several fish. However, despite all the sidetracks, false literalism, credulity, and naivete, a central tenet has held firm. God's salvation promises fulfillment for the real human personality, which is embodied. Though Christianity found merit in the Greek notion of the immortality of the soul, it never abandoned the biblical notion of the resurrection of the body. Begotten by late Israelite religion, this notion entered the Christian creed: ". . . I believe in the Holy Ghost, the Holy Catholic Church, the Communion of Saints, the forgiveness of sins, the resurrection of the body, and life everlasting. Amen." Without the promise of resurrection, grace would not have the full impact it does in Christianity.

Summary

Creation expresses the basic Christian understanding of the relation between God and the world, sin expresses the mystery of iniquity that mottles that relation, and grace expresses the repair and the elevation that God freely works in love. Taken as a set of powers, a repair and elevation of basic human nature, grace entails the theological virtues of faith, hope, and love. Faith has an intellectual component (assenting to truths that God has revealed), but its deeper import is trusting surrender to God. Hope is the Christian's faith-filled stance toward the future. By the warrant of Jesus—especially of Jesus's resurrection—the Christian expects that somehow all will be well. Love is both the best indication of God's nature and the substance of the healing that salvation connotes. Though *agape* has been the preferred name for the love one experiences in grace, *eros* and *philia* also have a valid place in Christian religion.

The Western Christian view of grace, focused on salvation, has stressed the healing and repair of sin. For the West, God sent his only begotten Son because of human beings' moral impotence. The Eastern Christian view of grace has not denied salvation, but it has stressed divine life. In addition to remedy for human impotence, divine generosity caused God to offer *agape* and communion. Such communion is the core of the Christian community called the Church. On the model of the sharing of the divine persons, Christians in all places and times are an extended family. Finally, the grace that makes religious community has most embodied itself in the Resurrection. Jesus's conquest of death tells believers that their bodies, those whom they love, and the world are part of the creation God has chosen graciously to save for eternity.

Study Questions

1. In what sense does Christian faith imply a priority of the heart over the head?
2. How does hope offer Christians a basis for dialogue with Marxists?
3. What are the assets and the liabilities of *eros*?
4. Give an example of how contemporary Americans experience a need for salvation.
5. How has the Eastern understanding of grace sponsored the art of religious icons?
6. Is it true that "real sinners can never be real lovers"? Why?
7. How has the Resurrection stabilized the Christian faith of both monks and married folk?

Notes

1. *Ejercicios*, in Ignacio Iparraguirre, ed., *Obras Completas de San Ignacio de Loyola*, Edicion Manual (Madrid: Bibliotheca de Autores Christianos, 1963), no. 335, p. 267.

2. See Grace Paley, *Enormous Changes at the Last Minute* (New York: Farrar, Straus, Giroux, 1974).
3. See Karl Rahner, "Priest and Poet," *Theological Investigations* (Baltimore: Helicon, 1967), vol. 3, pp. 294–317.
4. From Van Harvey, *A Handbook of Theological Terms* (New York: Macmillan, 1964), pp. 95–98.
5. Karl Rahner and Herbert Vorgrimler, eds., *Theological Dictionary* (New York: Herder and Herder, 1965), p. 216.
6. See ibid.
7. José Miranda, *Marx and the Bible* (Maryknoll, NY: Orbis, 1974). See also his *Being and the Messiah* (Maryknoll, NY: Orbis, 1977).
8. See Milan Machovec, *A Marxist Looks at Jesus* (Philadelphia: Fortress, 1976).
9. A clear treatment of the topic of the Christian conception of love is C.S. Lewis, *The Four Loves* (New York: Harcourt Brace, 1960).
10. Patrick White, *The Twyborn Affair* (New York: Viking, 1980), p. 426.
11. Ibid., p. 336.
12. Paul Tillich, *The Courage to Be* (New Haven: Yale University Press, 1952).
13. William James, *The Varieties of Religious Experience* (New York: New American Library, 1958), pp. 140, 280, 369.
14. Timothy Ware, *The Orthodox Church* (Pelican Books, Revised Edition, 1980), p. 78. Copyright © 1963, 1964 by Timothy Ware. Reprinted by permission of Penguin Books Ltd. Ware's quotation is from Maximus the Confessor, *Ambigua* (Migne, *Patrologia Graeca*, XCI, 1148 D).
15. Joseph Sittler, *Essays on Nature and Grace* (Philadelphia: Fortress, 1972).
16. See Ware, *The Orthodox Church*, p. 41.
17. See Karl Rahner, *Foundations of Christian Faith* (New York: Seabury, 1978), pp. 126–133.
18. Louis Auchincloss, *The House of the Prophet* (Boston: Houghton Mifflin, 1980), p. 97.
19. Edward Schillebeeckx, *Christ* (New York: Seabury, 1980), p. 800.
20. See Reginald Fuller, "The Resurrection Narratives in Recent Study," in Thomas J. Ryan, ed., *Critical History and Biblical Faith* (Villanova: The College Theology Society, 1979), pp. 99–107.

CHAPTER 5

Incarnation

Christology

Were a Christian theologian to engage in a dialogue with a historian of religions, the theologian probably would argue that Christianity's views of creation, sin, and grace are distinctive. The historian could point to parallels in other religions, especially Judaism and Islam, but the theologian probably would feel that Christianity has perceived the world, society, and the self at least a little differently than any other religion. If pushed for the reason for this feeling, the astute theologian would finally point to Jesus Christ. Because of Jesus of Nazareth, whom Christians believe God resurrected and showed to be the **Christ**, the **Messiah** foretold by Jewish prophecy, all of Christianity's perceptions of reality are distinctive. To be a Christian is ultimately to set one's gauges by Jesus Christ.

The **Incarnation** is the doctrine that the Word of God (the **Logos**) took flesh from Mary and abode in Jesus, who was fully human. We shall expand on this doctrine momentarily. It seems useful to point out here, however, that the theme of this chapter is broader than the doctrine of the Incarnation. From its faith in the God-man, Christianity has developed a view of matter that makes the world, the human body, and all the things that we sense revelatory, sacramental. In many periods it did not exploit this view very well, with the result that the world seemed alien or threatening. Nonetheless when the Christian worldview comes to high polish it is a beautiful, positive humanism. Our intent in this chapter is so to polish the staple notions radiating from the Incarnation that this positive humanism shines forth.

Christology is the portion of Christian theology that develops the implications of the Resurrection. Taking the Resurrection as Jesus's historical finale, as the consummating achievement from which one could best discern Jesus's significance,

Christians early spoke of messiahship. Messiahship is a notion derived from the Jewish milieu contemporary with Jesus. The Jews of Jesus's time awaited the Messiah, the "anointed One" who would free them for peace and prosperity. *Christ* is another word for *Messiah*. The first basic difference between Jews and Christians was their rejection or acceptance of Jesus's messiahship. Experiencing Jesus's goodness, wisdom, and power, early Christians thought he fulfilled the scriptures and was all the Messiah should be. Unable to accept Jesus's claims, or the interpretations of his life that his followers developed, Jews judged him *not* the Messiah. Indeed, many Jews await the Messiah to this day, still hoping to find him "next year in Jerusalem."

We shall deal with the historical aspects of Jesus and the New Testament in the next chapter. Doctrinally, Christology begins with the belief that Jesus was fully human. This belief is unquestioned in the New Testament, but some of the earliest **heresies** rejected it out of hand. Influenced by the later Greeks or Hellenists, and by a small group of deviants called Gnostics, a considerable number of deviant Christians found unfitting the idea of divinity joining itself with humanity. Consequently, they rejected the notion that the Divine Word really took human flesh. In their eyes Jesus only appeared to be human, only appeared to die on the cross. The heavy emphasis on Jesus's flesh that we find in the Gospel of John seems designed to combat such Gnostic tendencies. When the prologue of John's Gospel says, "The Word became flesh" (John 1:14), it means a literal incarnation.

The pivot of Christian faith, then, is the humanity of Jesus. As we shall make clear in the next section, his humanity is the prime source of Chrstian revelation. No doubt the first three Gospels of the New Testament (known as the **synoptic** Gospels) have been a staple of Christian piety because they have shown Jesus's humanity in action: preaching, healing, consorting with sinners, suffering rejection, dying, and encountering the disciples after the Resurrection. In fact, much Christian piety has been explicitly an imitation of Christ—an effort to follow Jesus's example. To be most human, in Christian interpretation, has been to use time as Jesus did, to love as Jesus did. Where other religions have sacred codes or precepts, Christianity has an exemplar who once lived. Where other traditions stress ethics or meditation, Christians want above all to walk in Jesus's footsteps, to follow Jesus's way.

Eastern Christianity has especially venerated Mary as the source of Jesus's flesh. To chisel the Incarnation into the structure of faith, it has pointed to the young Jewish girl who conceived Jesus by the Holy Spirit, and has given her the status of *Theotokos*, "God-bearer." In this phrase we see the extraordinary character of Jesus's humanity. As later theologians like Luther and Kierkegaard stressed, Christianity's pivot turns out to be a paradox. Jesus is so human that he stands apart from humanity. He is like us in being limited, historical, able to suffer, and mortal. He is unlike us in being sinless, resurrected, the literal Son of God. Because Christians have found Jesus's wisdom, love, and power unique, they have confessed Jesus to be God in human terms. His humanity is more than human; the deepest identity of his flesh is the Logos of God.

When theological language became precise, it called the union of Jesus's humanity and divinity **hypostatic**. This term appeared in the early bishops' teaching at the Council of Chalcedon (451): in Jesus Christ there is one person (*hypostasis*) and two natures. Jesus has one identity, but he is both human and divine. He has what we would call a human personality, because every true man and woman does, but his final integrity is not that of a creature but of the Creator. When, prior to this precise language, a group called the Arians drew a dividing line between creatures and the Creator and placed Jesus on the side of creatures, the bishops assembled at the Council of Nicaea (325) denounced this as blasphemy. In the bishops' interpretation of evangelical faith, there was no moment when Jesus's deepest identity, the Logos, did not exist. The Word that took flesh existed from the beginning (John 1:1).

Revelation

Throughout the New Testament, Jesus's flesh is the prime revelation of both divinity and humanity. The basic meaning of *revelation*, of course, is 'disclosure.' When a person opens herself, or an event shines with unexpected meaning, it is as though a veil has been removed.

Consider, for instance, the difference between Joe the toll-taker and Joe the good father talking with his troubled daughter. Joe the toll-taker seldom drops your quarter, nearly always is courteous, but offers you no great encounter. Indeed, many states have replaced Joe with a metal basket, and few people have complained of a great loss—because few people expect revelation at the toll booth.

On the other hand, most adolescents are desperate for revelation. Above all, they want to know who they are, what they will become. The best, if not the only, way for parents to help such adolescents is for parents to reveal their own struggles, especially those they had at the awful age of fourteen. So, removing the veil of his usual taciturnity, Joe takes a walk with sniffling Sarah and reminisces a bit about *his* freshman year. Lord, he was 5′ 3″ and still singing soprano! He laughs so hard his belly shakes, but Sarah catches enough rue to make some startling connections. Jeez, even solid old Dad agonized about his looks, about his future. Somehow he got through it. Maybe his daughter will get through it too.

If God is personal, as most Western instinct has suspected, then God, too, has the choice of being closed, of showing only his functional aspects, or of opening up and revealing his inner life. Much of the Christian distinction between nature and grace has been an elaboration of this personal divine choice. For God to exist and create a world does not necessarily entail a profound revelation. What we can infer from creation, our "natural" theology, is important, but it is largely negative. From the limitations of creatures we can suspect that God is unlimited. From the perfections of creatures we can argue that God somehow is good, loving, and wise. But little of this inference is positively engaging. Most of it keeps us at arm's length, and is somewhat abstract and antiseptic.

The God of gracious love does not want arm's-length relationships, any more than warm-hearted human beings do. The God of gracious love wants interpersonal knowing and sharing. Were we especially shrewd in our analyses of human relationships, we might be able to conjecture this aspect of God. Being impressed by the centrality of human love, we might extrapolate a self-revelatory God of grace. However, our extrapolation would be very fragile. History shows us too much divine silence, too much human evil, for the God of grace to be certain. The real warrant for the Christian God of grace, then, is not fragile human inference but the concrete historical life of Jesus.

As Titus 3:4 puts it, God showed her "goodness and loving kindness" through Jesus Christ. The Logos who is the eternal Word of God's heart became a word that human beings could hear, a self-disclosure that human beings could see and touch. Building on this "verbal" divine revelation, 2 Cor. 1:19–20 makes Christ the expression of God's yes. The life of Jesus is God's once-for-all affirmation, God's once-for-all acceptance of humanity and the world. Freely, outgoingly, with something of his veil torn asunder, God says a personal word, makes an embodied gesture. Amazingly enough, the Father of Jesus Christ puts himself on the line. In order to achieve a lover's intimacy, he risks a lover's rejection.

Thus, in this interpretation, revelation is of a piece with God's grace, God's personal love. Through Christian history, however, the word *revelation* has frequently connoted holy Scripture. Moving from the flesh of Jesus to the place where they could experience Jesus somewhat vicariously, Christians became habituated to thinking of Scripture as God's Word. Usually they did not separate Scripture from Jesus, nor from the Holy Spirit who inspired both scriptural authors and scriptural readers. Often Christians also remembered the **liturgical** context in which Scripture first flourished, and so remembered the living Lord who continued to be the gracious God's prime revelation. But churches that centered in reading Scripture afresh, especially churches begotten by the Protestant Reformation, tended to equate revelation with the Bible.

Thus, revelation became the picture of the world's creation that Genesis gave, the picture of sinful humanity sketched by Romans. In contrast to natural science, Genesis was a privileged account of creation. In contrast to social science, Romans was a privileged account of human nature. When Christians proferred these judgments without qualification, they made revelation the enemy of reason. Non-Christians might labor industriously, might display brilliant intelligence, but their labors were as straw. Real truth was what God zapped from heaven into the Bible.

Today most university theologians abjure such a simple, potentially self-serving view. They point out that Jesus solicited faith and that Scripture assumes a commitment to faith. Like the bond between lovers, faith (openness) is necessary for revelation, and revelation mainly pertains to salvation, healing humanity's depths. It is no substitute for empirical information, no pipeline that bypasses the brain.

Christian revelation, then, derived from Jesus, the Logos incarnate, and had written form in Scripture. The New Testament became finally the privileged set of Christian writings, but the first Christian Scripture was the Hebrew Bible. Later called the Old Testament, it testified that God had been revealing himself long before Jesus. In disclosures to Abraham, Noah, Adam, and above all Moses, God had given the mysterious divine name (Yahweh) and the **Torah**, guidance for a life of covenant. When early Christian apologists like Justin Martyr reflected on Jesus Christ, in the context of trying to demonstrate Christianity's superiority to Judaism and paganism, they admitted that both Jews and pagans had (lesser) forms of divine revelation. The Hebrew Bible displayed the marvelous disclosures that God had made to Israel. The lofty speculation and ethics of the best pagan philosophers suggested that God "did not leave himself without witness" (Acts 14:17) among the Gentiles. Thus Justin spoke of a *logos spermatikos*, a seminal reason, through which even pagans had participated in the divine Word.

Trinity

Apologetics is the effort to defend or promote faith to those outside the family of the Church. Doctrine is teaching mainly directed to those who have faith and are striving to grow in Christian life. Jaroslav Pelikan sets the stage for our discussion of the Trinity when he says: "The climax of the doctrinal development of the early church was the dogma of the Trinity. In this dogma the church vindicated the monotheism that had been at issue in its conflicts with Judaism, and it came to terms with the concept of the Logos, over which it had disputed with paganism."[1] We shall place the doctrine of the Trinity in its historical context in Chapter 7. Here we are concerned with its place in the Christian worldview, and we can start our reflection with a description of the doctrine and the two points that Pelikan mentions, monotheism and the Logos.

The traditional Christian doctrine of the Trinity asserts that there is one God in three divine persons. Christian theologians developed this doctrine in early conciliar debates, based on references to Father, Word, and Spirit that abounded in the New Testament, and on the Old Testament tendency to speak of God's Word and Spirit as substantial entities. Throughout, the early Christian anchor was Jesus's own usage. He had addressed God as *Abba* ("Father") and been moved by the Spirit. When it became clear that he was divine, the Logos incarnate, his relations with the Father and the Spirit begot the basic notion that he derived from the Father and communed with the Father and the Spirit. Thus, the basic Christian notion of God made God a Trinity. At the peak of love, God was variety without disunion.

Jews, Muslims, and others have advanced against the doctrine of the Trinity the objection that it denies and detracts from God's unity, but Christians have always maintained that it does not. Christianity thinks of itself as a monotheism; the doctrine of the Trinity does not imply that there are three Gods. As much as Judaism in its Shema or Islam in its profession of faith ("There is no God but God"), Christianity says that God is one. Father, Son, and Spirit, the three divine "persons," share one identical divine nature. Each is fully God, and the totality of the three is not more divinity than Father, Son, or Spirit has alone. Indeed, the three are distinguished only relationally—by the ways they relate to one another and express the divine fullness.

Various elaborations of this core sense developed in later Christian theology, and presented themselves as analogies. Basically, the Father was the unbegotten source, the fathomless ground zero. The Son was begotten by the Father, spoken forth like an exhaustive Word expressing an infinite mind. The Spirit was like a processive, encircling love. For Western Christianity, the Father and the Son both breathed forth the Spirit. For Eastern Christianity, the Spirit proceeded from the Father alone. Saint Augustine led Western Christians to what came to be called the **psychological analogy**. The Father was like an infinite memory, the Son was like an infinite knowledge, and the Spirit was like an infinite love. Saint Thomas Aquinas sharpened this analogy. For him the Father was like an infinite act of understanding, the Son was like the intellectual concept that such an infinite act of understanding would beget, and the Spirit was like the act of love that such expressive understanding would develop. This psychological analogy enhances the core intuition that God is an active community of the richest knowing and loving.

Scripture and Sacraments

In light of the doctrine of the Trinity, the mystery of human life, its brightest knowing, and its warmest loving all are seen as participants in a divine interiority. The mystery of human life participates in the Father's fathomless fullness. The brightest human knowing occurs in the stream of the Son's procession from the Father. The warmest human loving is carried by the Spirit, who is the divine love. At core, then, Christian life is holy because it is the life of the triune God. Thus, the Christian community was seen, especially by Protestants after the Reformation, as a society of saints. In their being, if not their every act, those baptized into Christ were holy with divine life. We see this especially in the Reformed notion of the Church as "the congregation of saints wherein the Gospel is rightly preached and the sacraments rightly administered."[2] This brings us to our next topic, the Scripture and sacraments. In contrast to the Catholic and Orthodox notions of the Church, which tend to picture the Church as *expressing* itself through the Scripture and sacraments, the Protestant notion stresses the Church's *formation* through the Scripture and sacraments. Throughout this book our effort is to vary the viewpoint, so that no one tradition predominates, and here we take the Protestant view.

Scripture, as we have seen, became a prime locus of revelation. In the Scripture one could find God's Word—the truth that moved both the prophets and Jesus. Without denying that Jesus was God's Word, Protestant theology after the Reformation was drawn to the way that the biblical Word came to life in preaching. When the Scripture was at the center of a worship lively with faith, God's Word could be as Hebrews described it: "The word of God is something alive and active: it cuts like any double-edged sword but more finely: it can slip through the place where the soul is divided from the spirit, or joints from the marrow: it can judge the secret emotions and thoughts" (4:12).

Like a nation's legal constitution, but more powerfully and personally, the Scripture gave form to the Christian assembly. It was the good news that kept Christians going, the book of judgment and consolation apt in all times. The New Testament picture of the Church was a template for later generations. Its record of the first believers' holiness, ardent expectancy of Jesus's return, and mutual love was meant to give their descendants in faith great encouragement. Even the problems and divisions of the early Church were consoling, for they showed that God had chosen weak vessels from the beginning: "Take yourselves, for instance, brothers, at the time when you were called: how many of you were wise in the ordinary sense of the word, how many were influential people, or came from noble families? No, it was to shame the wise that God chose what is foolish by human reckoning, and to shame what is strong that he chose what is weak by human reckoning; those whom the world thinks common and contemptible are the ones that God has chosen—those who are nothing at all to show up those who are everything" (1 Cor. 1:26–28). Along with the picture of Jesus that it offered for believers' emulation, the Scripture gave the Church a marvelous sense of its own election by God.

As we shall make even clearer in the next section, the Christian Church is the gathering, the assembly, of the people who believe in Jesus Christ. The Church is not primarily either the building in which Christians congregate or their hierarchical leadership. Rather, the Church is those who take the scriptural word for their meat and drink and celebrate Christ's sacraments. Christ's sacraments are the holy acts that embody faith and the action of the Spirit. They are the ways that people of flesh and blood can sense God's deification of their humanity. Baptism is one of the sacraments; the baptismal sign of pouring water, for instance, symbolizes the new beginning that comes when one enters the Body of Christ. As is clearest when baptism is by immersion, one goes down with Christ into death (to the old life of sin) and rises with him to the life of a new creation. Similarly, the Eucharist (partaking of bread and wine) is a sacrament commemorating the Lord's last Supper and giving concrete form to God's ongoing nurture of divine life in believers. Jesus's flesh and blood, for which the bread and wine stand, is food for immortality. Ignatius of Antioch, a much revered early bishop and martyr, showed how the young Church lived by such teaching: "I have no taste for corruptible food nor for the pleasures of this life. I desire the Bread of God, which is the Flesh of Jesus Christ, who was of the seed of David; and for drink I desire His Blood, which is love incorruptible."[3]

The Church has been especially manifest when it has gathered to attend to God's Word and celebrate the Lord's Supper. Thus, the Eucharist has been its most central sacrament. In the main, all three families of churches have agreed on the sacramentality of baptism and the Eucharist. By late medieval times, based on the assemblage of traditional texts that scholars such as Peter Lombard had provided, Western Christians spoke of seven sacraments. In addition to baptism and the

Eucharist, Western Christians listed confirmation (a consecration for coming of age), penance (a holy ritual for the forgiveness of sins), marriage, holy orders (ordination for ministerial service in the Church), and extreme unction or anointing (spiritual help for grave sickness or preparation for death). Eastern Christians accepted this list of seven sacraments in the seventeenth century, but they have never been so exact or dogmatic about it as Roman Catholics. Protestant Christians have tended to call only baptism and the Eucharist sacraments in the strict sense (because the scriptural warrant for the other five is unclear or lacking).

Ecclesiology

In its sacraments and rituals, the Church has shown itself to be "the People of God," "the Body of Christ." These are two biblical ways of describing the Christian *ecclesia* (gathering). Around the idea of the *ecclesia*, there has grown up a body of **ecclesiology**, theological doctrine relating to the Church and its purposes. The Church was not founded simply for itself. It was founded, according to the New Testament, for mission, witness, and service. While it was right and just to praise and thank God through public worship, it was also incumbent on Christians to carry on the work of their Master. *Mission* connotes being sent. As Jesus was sent by the Father on an errand of salvation, so Jesus sent his followers: "Go, therefore, and make disciples of all nations; baptize them in the name of the Father and of the Son and of the Holy Spirit, and teach them to observe all the commands I gave you. And know that I am with you always; yes, to the end of time" (Matt. 28:19–20). Traditionally, therefore, Christians have considered missions intrinsic to Church life. When Pilgrims took up residence in seventeenth-century New England, they did so in the context of what historian Perry Miller called "an errand in the wilderness." When European traders discovered East Asia and the New World, missionaries soon followed in the traders' train.

Traditionally, the Church also has thought of itself as called to witness. When one considers the Greek root of the word *witness*, *martyria*, it loses any overtones of blandness. The martyrs have been the prime Christian witnesses, for they have been willing to lay down their lives for their beliefs. And while current historians suggest that the number of Christians put to death in the Roman persecutions of the first three centuries was considerably smaller than the early chroniclers implied,[4] the number was great enough to make a profound impact on many observers, and to give the later Church a sense that the martyrs' blood had been its seed.

When the Roman persecutions ceased, a new movement arose to translate the martyrs' fervent faith to a more peaceful time. Thus, the red martyrdom of those tortured and thrown to the beasts gave way to the white martyrdom of ascetics and virgins. In both cases, an essential motivation was witnessing to the primacy of divine life. To this day many Christians continue such witnessing, through their sufferings for their faith. For example, when Solzhenitsyn accuses the West of grossly misunderstanding the evils of communism, one of the evidences to which he points is the suffering of Russians persecuted for their Orthodoxy.[5] One could also point to the suffering of East Asian Christians under communism.

Service is a third task for which the Church was founded. As Jesus came not to be served but to serve (Mark 10:45), so the Church was founded to work for the welfare of all human beings. At times this service was understood as mainly spiritual: preaching the good news and forgiving sins. Through most of Christian history, though, it has also been understood to include corporal works that intend social betterment. Thus the Church has sponsored schools, hospitals, soup kitchens, and other charitable organizations, from its sense that Christian life entails service. The judgment scene in Matthew 25 puts it most vividly: whatever is done for a brother or sister in need is done to Christ and merits a heavenly reward; whatever is not done merits a hellish punishment. Implicitly, then, the Christian concept of service envisions the solidarity of all human beings. One is to love one's neighbor as oneself because that neighbor really is potentially a part of one's self, a fellow in the body of Christ.[6]

The Church also has described itself with four "notes." It is one, holy, catholic, and apostolic. By their common commitment to Jesus, the members of the Christian assembly form a single body. By the divine life that inspires that body, they are holy. Since one basic faith is held everywhere, the Church is catholic or universal. Since that faith has derived from the apostles, the close disciples of Jesus who became his most authentic witnesses, its tradition dates back to the beginning. Obviously these terms describe the ideal Church, not always realized. Christians have been divided, sinful, partisan, and forgetful of their traditions. For that reason, the Reformers spoke of a Church always needing to be reformed. It is a happy sign that Roman Catholics and Orthodox Christians today largely accept this Reformed notion.

Ecumenism

There are other happy signs today that the Church is unifying, becoming **ecumenical**, but they are not so numerous, nor so official, as many Christians hoped in the mid-1960s. After the euphoria of Vatican Council II, when it looked as though Roman Catholicism finally was opening to Protestantism and Orthodoxy, many in all branches of the Church awaited dramatic progress toward reunion. It has yet to come. The World Council of Churches, which institutionalized a Protestant movement toward reunion that began early in the twentieth century, has come under attack for its support of revolutionaries trying to overthrow unjust third world regimes. Roman Catholicism has kept the more positive assessments of other world religions and recognition of the ecclesial status of the other churches of the Christian family developed at Vatican II, but it has balked at serious negotiations on the questions still dividing it from Protestantism and Orthodoxy. Orthodoxy has continued to participate in the World Council of Churches, and it has agreed to consultations with Roman Catholic theologians, but its own internal problems have held center stage.[7]

Insofar as it connects intimately with the traditional Church note of unity, ecumenism is more than an accidental matter. As judicious ecclesiologists have long sensed, the division of the Christian churches is a glaring sign of their collective sin. By the will of Jesus preserved in the Johannine "high priestly prayer" (see John 13–17, especially 17:11–24), Christians are to be one as Jesus and the Father are one, and their unity is to be the great sign to the world that the Father sent Jesus and loves Jesus's disciples as He loves Jesus himself. Consequently, Christians' disunity mars the continuance of the Incarnation. The Church has a basic commission to keep embodying God's love for the world; when its own house is a place of enmity rather than love, it fails this commission egregiously. Confusions in foreign missionary activity, domestic witness, and social service result almost inevitably.

The points that divide the Church today are more political than doctrinal. Most of the doctrinal disputes that historically have divided the East from the West have calmed to manageable proportions. For example, the Orthodox objection to the Western notions of purgatory and the **filioque** (the Western view that the Spirit proceeds from the Son as well as the Father), now seem largely matters of different emphasis or theological style. So too with the Protestant reformers' demurs from the Roman Catholic teachings on justification, scripture, tradition, and Eucharist, and the like. It is the question of Church organization, Church political power, that divides the Church nowadays. One does not have to be a cynic to observe that this is a case of the churches being all too human. Power corrupts, Lord Acton observed; power continues to corrupt the Body of Christ today.

According to the New Testament, Christian power or authority is for service. Those who hold office in the Church are to be the prime ministers, the first rank of servants. In this spirit the popes coined their motto, "*servus servorum Dei*": "the servant of the servants of God." But the popes and the curias, the Protestant church officers and their staffs, and the Orthodox episcopacy and its retinues have all fallen prey to the self-service seemingly inseparable from bureaucracy. Shielding themselves with lofty words like *tradition* and *biblical authority*, they have let the scandal of division continue. Though theologians have found creative solutions to most past doctrinal difficulties, Church administrators have failed to move. Concerning the significance of Peter, Mary, sacramental intercommunion, and a variety of orders (ways of deploying Church power), they have not effected active cooperation and consensus.[8] The New Testament says, "By their fruits you will know them" (Matt. 7:16). In our view, this criterion convicts most Church leaders, and most Church laity, of not really wanting the unity for which Jesus prayed and gave his life.

Nonetheless, considerable ecumenical unity now obtains *de facto*, despite official cautions. Robert McAfee Brown, a front-line Protestant ecumenist, has described a spontaneous ecumenical communion service that expresses this *de facto* crossing of denominational lines:

> We have come into the dining room after hearing four Roman Catholic women tell us about a meeting of two thousand Roman Catholic women in Baltimore discussing the role of women in the church. Their conclusion: there is nowhere to go but up. They are discouraged and hopeful.

> It suddenly seems important that the moment around the table be more than an ordinary moment. Canonically and liturgically we are separated from one another at the Lord's Table. At least we should not be separated from one another at this human table. I say something to that effect and we pray together.
>
> Without benefit of clergy, without an act of consecration that would be canonically acknowledged, the four women who have been at Baltimore distribute bread and wine to the rest of us, and it is indeed "the bread of life" and "the cup of wholeness." We are nourished, restored, healed. There is a real presence. For a few moments life is as it is meant to be—everyone included, no one excluded.[9]

On the day that a majority of the Church leadership and membership realize that the Church exists to provide moments when life is as it is meant to be, moments when no one is excluded, ecclesiology will have come of age in our view, and ecumenism will not be an accusation. That may not bring a new heaven and a new earth, but it will bring a mature expression of the Incarnation.

Sex

As the quotation from McAfee Brown suggests, a mature ecclesial expression of the Incarnation would incorporate women into the political structure of the Church far better than most Christian traditions have thus far. It would also interpret the Incarnation in such a way that Christ's maleness would not remove the feminine from Christian analogies for God. Both the politics and the theology of women in the Church are concerns that we take up in Chapter 15. We narrow our discussion here to what a free, liberated reading of the Incarnation might imply for love's sexual expression.

There is no doubt that the question of sex has been a bugbear in Christian history, as it has been in the history of almost all other religious traditions. Erotic energy is the most explosive in the human arsenal, and the sexual forms of erotic energy are dynamite in most human lives. Since Freud we have had the beginnings of a scientific psychoanalysis of sexual *eros*, but the Tantra (sexual yoga) of ancient India, to cite but one religious instance, acknowledged long before Freud that libido plays a formidable role in salvation.

Describing Alexandria, a significant city in the development of the classical Christian doctrine of salvation, contemporary novelist Lawrence Durrell has one of his characters muse: "I remember Nessim [another character] once saying—I think he was quoting—that Alexandria was the great wine-press of love; those who emerged from it were the sick men, the solitaries, the prophets—I mean all who have been deeply wounded in their sex."[10] It is not clear grammatically whether Durrell equates sick men, solitaries, and prophets; it is very clear to us theologically that the salvation offered in the incarnate Logos has to embrace human sexuality.

The free, liberated reading of the Incarnation mentioned above has some sanction from the apostle Paul: "For freedom Christ has set us free" (Gal. 5:1). Paul's main intent in saying this seems to have been to shore up Christians' freedom from the Jewish law, but the saying can also serve the Christian worldview as a counsel to approach the implications of the Incarnation largeheartedly. There are positive reasons for the vocations to solitude and prophecy; neither all flight from the world of noise nor all reception of God's Word depends on wounded sexuality. Traditional Christianity has tended to stand up for these theses whenever deviant movements attacked them frontally. For example, the orthodox refused to hold with the second-century dissident Marcion that sex and childbirth are unclean and can have nothing to do with salvation.[11] Similarly, the Manicheans and Albigensians (more Christian dissidents) who deprecated sex, the body, and marriage received a firm denunciation.

However, in times of relative doctrinal peace, monks, fathers, doctors, and reformers all showed not a little fear of sex, not a little suspicion of women. Augustine in the West and Chrysostom in the East were prime offenders, but almost everywhere there was a tendency to consider sex part of the "flesh" that is opposed to "spirit." Modern emancipation has not uprooted this tendency. As recently as the Roman Catholic bishops' synod at the end of 1980, there were authoritative voices saying that the primary end of marriage is procreation and that the mutual love of the spouses is secondary. The relation of this quite traditional view to the bishops' judgments on contraception, divorce, and abortion is rather knotted, but there is little doubt that they run together. On account of similar views held by the bishops, one survey of recent theological trends branded Roman Catholicism "especially objectionable" and "deeply neurotic."[12] A literary display of the same opinion is Mary Gordon's fine novel *Final Payments*.

But what has Christian instinct been in what we would consider its better moments? First, and minimally, that sex is as natural, created as good, as any other human endowment. Thus the main theological line has abjured such practices as the Russian Orthodox discouragment of menstruating women from communion. Second, in its better moments Christian instinct has been that God positively encourages sexual love, as Hosea and the Songs of Songs imply. Judaism has maintained this conviction better than Christianity, making marriage one of life's primary blessings. True, Judaism has had its own problems with sex, because of its strong patriarchalism and the prudery of many rabbis, but it has not had the institution of celibacy to compound its struggles for erotic balance.

Third, celibacy and marriage are complementary in a fully incarnational view. The Incarnation holds together a salvation that is both final and present here and now. To the celibate, sexual fulfillment is promised in final salvation. To the married couple, sexual fulfillment is a manifestation of salvation here and now. In faith, hope, love, and good cheer, spouses can fulfill one another, let their love overflow to children, and make their family circles little churches. Not fearing space and time, or one another, they can use their bodies as sacraments of both *eros* and *agape*. As archaic peoples sensed that maleness and femaleness are both necessary for wholeness, so can Christian marriage, Christian use of sex, produce wholeness. Plato's myth that originally some human beings were androgynes, combining both male and female qualities, gives an insight that Christian **exegesis** (interpretation) is free to affirm. As flesh of one another's flesh, a woman and a man united signify the great mystery of God's marriage to humanity (Eph. 5:29—32).

Time

The Incarnation in Christianity celebrates God's marriage to humanity. At the moment of the Incarnation, when the Logos took flesh, it became clear that humanity was to work out its salvation on the material plane. Thus the Incarnation became a central point in the Christian perception of time. Not only did the West reset the calendar to adapt to the God-man, Christian reflection configured history in terms of the privileged span when divinity sojourned in human flesh. Under the assaults of new knowledge that came in from traders and missionaries dealing with the Far East and the New World, later Christian historians had to broaden their conceptions. They did this reluctantly, so the first universal histories, not centered around the Incarnation, came from non-believers like Voltaire. That does not mean that universal history has furnished a more adequate explanation either of history's structures or the human experience of time and its limits.

Among the most impressive explanations of history in recent times is Eric Voegelin's *Order and History*,[13] whose debt to Christianity is only partial. Among the most impressive explanations of human temporality in recent times is Martin Heidegger's *Being and Time*[14] which, despite Heidegger's stay in a Catholic seminary, similarly owes Christianity only a partial debt. For all their erudition and depth, neither of these impressive works affirms that the human cry for salvation will be answered. In different ways, they both imply that the usual forms of that cry for salvation do not square with the realities of the human condition. For Voegelin the "leaps in being" that came with Israelite revelation and Greek philosophy did not penetrate or express divine mystery definitively, once and for all. For Heidegger human being is care-ful and anxiety-ridden to the core, because we are being-unto-death, destined to die. No resurrectional inrush of deathless divinity, no Incarnational inrush of deathless Logos, works the **sublation**, elevation by grace, that would take human time to a new realm of faith, hope, and love stronger than death. To the best and brightest of our secular moderns, then, the Incarnation and the Resurrection continue to be stumbling blocks they cannot o'erleap.

There are two responses to this discouraging view of time that Christians tend to make, and their conjunction gives us a good last word on the Christian worldview. First, wise Christians tend to respect the integrity and wisdom of humanists like Voegelin and Heidegger. Such humanists underscore the mystery of God's ways, the unlikelihood of grace, better than do most Christian theologians. Neither the historian's picture of the human temporal span nor the philosopher's picture of the human spirit shows a God that is obvious, comfortable, a secure human possession. Like the formidable realities of Auschwitz and Babi Yar, human use of time and human performance in general make a good case for absurdity. They provide many good reasons for nonbelief. That the Incarnation and the Resurrection redeem human time is by no means obvious.

Second, for Christian faith the Incarnation and the Resurrection are fitting. It may not be necessary that God should be gracious, but it is uncanny how exactly God's grace reveals our hearts' finest aspirations, history's best inner formations. Without removing the necessary mystery of God, Christianity gives it human form. Where there might well be abysmal nothingness, there is instead the life of Jesus, as evidence of a fathomless, unbegotten divine parenthood, evidence that there is mercy and forgiveness. Above all, where there might be spiritual death by distraction and triviality, Christianity in flesh and time finds all moments capable of becoming sacraments. Indeed, it finds each moment an intersection of time and eternity, since the Logos incarnate married these two orders once and for all time.

Summary

We began our study of the Incarnation, the fourth notion chosen to explain the Christian worldview, with Christology. The mysterious fusion of humanity and divinity in Jesus Christ is central to the Christian's reality. Jesus is the prime revelation both of what human beings should strive to become and what God can be in human terms. Substantially, there is little difference between incarnation and revelation, or between revelation and grace, because they all take their first denotations from Jesus Christ.

In the same way, the Christian view of God finds its first insights in Christology. Historically, both Jesus's own way of addressing God and early Christianity's understanding of Jesus as the Logos incarnate were crucial in the development of the Christian notion of the Trinity. The triune God is the ultimate picture in the Christian gallery because it is the limit to which Christian reflection on divine mystery has gone. Experiencing the triune God, baptizing and communing in his name, Christians have gathered to form the Church. The prime actions of the Church are its attendance to the Scripture and its celebration of sacraments. In addition, the Church has understood its purposes to be witnessing, mission, and service. One, holy, catholic, and apostolic, it has strived to continue the enfleshment of God's Word.

Largely in recognition of the Church's failure to be one, the ecumenical movement has charged all Christian traditions to update their ecclesiologies. By repenting of their abuses of power and their inhumane interpretation of such incarnational areas as sex, the traditions could repair the fractures in Christ's Body and make a great sign of God's having drawn time into eternity.

Study Questions

1. In what sense is Christology "the portion of Christian theology that develops the implications of the Resurrection"?
2. What is the meaning of Christ as God's yes?
3. How does the psychological analogy represent the persons of the Trinity?
4. Compose a contemporary prayer for Christian baptism.
5. What was the relationship between the early martyrs and the early ascetics and virgins?
6. What are the problems in ecumenical actions that express a *de facto* unity across denominational lines?
7. What light should a theology of incarnation shed on marriage and sex?
8. Is it traditional to say that the Incarnation makes human history occur in God? Why?

Notes

1. Jaroslav Pelikan, *The Christian Tradition, Vol. 1: The Emergence of the Catholic Tradition (100–600)* (Chicago: University of Chicago Press, 1971), p. 172. Reprinted by permission.
2. Richard P. McBrien, "Theological Brief," in R. Evans and T. Parker, eds., *Christian Theology: A Case Method Approach* (New York: Harper & Row, 1976), p. 204.
3. "Letter to the Romans," 7:3, in W. Jurgens, *The Faith of the Early Father* (Collegeville, MN: Liturgical Press, 1970), vol. 1, p. 22.
4. See, for instance, William A. Clebsch, *Christianity in European History* (New York: Oxford University Press, 1979), p. 285, where the number suggested is between 10,000 and 1,000.
5. See Solzhenitsyn's *The Mortal Danger* (New York: Harper & Row, 1980), pp. 34–35.
6. A fine study of Christian service is Bernard Cooke's *Ministry to Word an Sacrament* (Philadelphia: Fortress, 1976).
7. See Michael A. Fahey, "Orthodox Ecumenism and Theology: 1970–78," *Theological Studies* 39/3 (September 1978), 466–85.
8. For examples of ecumenical theological consensus see Raymond Brown et al *Peter in the New Testament* (New York/Minneapolis: Paulist/Augsburg, 197 and *Mary in the New Testament* (Philadelphia: Fortress, 1978).

9. Robert M. Brown, *Creative Dislocation—The Movement of Grace* (Nashville: Abingdon, 1980), p. 28. Reprinted by permission.
10. Lawrence Durrell, *Justine* (New York: Pocket Books, 1961), p. 4.
11. See Pelikan, *The Christian Tradition*, vol. 1, p. 73.
12. John Carmody, *Theology for the 1980s* (Philadelphia: Westminster, 1980), p. 101.
13. Eric Voegelin, *Order and History* (Baton Rouge, LA: LSU Press, 1956).
14. Martin Heidegger, *Being and Time* (New York: Harper & Row, 1962).

Christianity: Twenty-Five Key Dates

CA. 30 C.E.	Death of Jesus of Nazareth
CA. 65	Death of Apostle Paul
CA. 95	Last of New Testament Writings
CA. 100–165	Justin Martyr, Leading Apologist
CA. 185–254	Origen, Leading Theologian
313	Christians Freed of Legal Persecution
325	First Council of Nicaea
354–430	Augustine, Leading Theologian
451	Council of Chalcedon
CA. 480–550	Benedict, Founder of Western Monasticism
CA. 540–604	Pope Gregory I, Founder of Medieval Papacy
787	Second Council of Nicaea (last one that the Orthodox Church considers ecumenical)
869–870	Rome Declares Photius in Schism
1054	Mutual Anathemas between Rome and Constantinople
1096–1099	First Crusade
1225–1274	Thomas Aquinas, Leading Theologian
1369–1415	John Hus, Bohemian Reformer
1517	Luther's Ninety-Five Theses
1509–1564	John Calvin, Leading Theologian
1545–1563	Council of Trent
1620	Mayflower Compact of the Pilgrims
1703–1791	John Wesley
1869–1870	First Vatican Council
1910	Beginning of Protestant Ecumenical Movement
1962–1965	Second Vatican Council

PART 2

Christian History

When we introduced Part One, we suggested that the Christian worldview has a far sharper edge than most of us appreciate. You must finally judge the validity of that suggestion, but let us briefly recapitulate the evidence, now that you have seen some of Christianity's capital notions. First, there is the Christian concept that the world was created by God from nothingness. That entails the ideas that the world depends on God completely, and that God was moved to create for no motive other than her own goodness. For the believing Christian, consequently, the whole world is charged with God's grandeur, alive with ontological mystery. No mastery achieved by science or technology removes this mystery, for no such mastery is itself creative in the deep sense of giving being from nothingness.

Second, the Christian concept of sin hones the creator-creature relationship to a still sharper edge. In place of the gratitude that reflective creatures should show the Creator, sin is a rejection and closure that are deeply ungrateful. For biblical religion, human beings are finally responsible for the evils that mar their social life, and none of that evil draws God into the dock. The slaughter of innocent children, the brutality of numberless wars—these are free perversions of human reason and will, not doings of the divine Creator. God *is* finally responsible for natural evils, such as earthquakes and volcanoes, but he at least balances them with nature's bounties and beauties. The moral evils that bring most shipwrecks of faith are deeds done by those who should recognize that they are brothers and sisters. By its conception of sin, Christianity accuses such persons bitterly, promising that they shall receive fair punishment.

Third, the Christian concept of grace predominates over that of sin. If sin is the strong man who pillages most human houses, grace is the stronger Christ who has re-formed the human condition and tied the pillager up. From the predominance of being over non-being which gives us a world, to the surplus gifts that bear us through social life, grace invites people to believe in a carrying Spirit, to entertain the subtle strengths of love. As deep as it follows the corrosions of sin, Christianity finds a more profound prevenience of God. Thus Paul said that where sin abounded, grace abounded the more (Rom. 5:15). At the far reaches of grace is deification: sharing God's own immortal love-life. Dying to death and sin, Jesus the Christ promised fulfillment beyond humanity's clearest hopes.

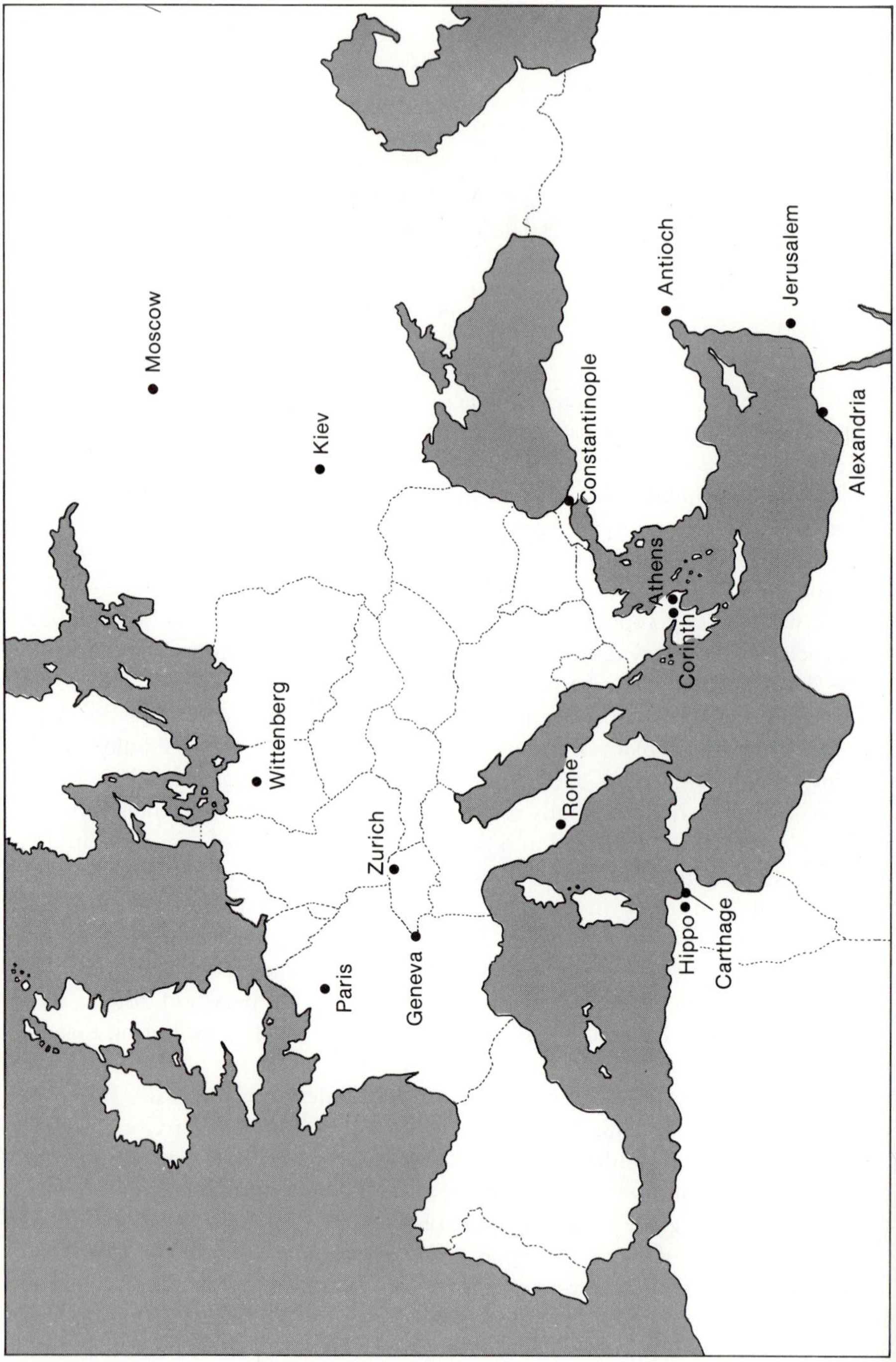
Moscow
Kiev
Wittenberg
Zurich
Paris
Geneva
Rome
Constantinople
Athens
Corinth
Antioch
Jerusalem
Alexandria
Hippo
Carthage

Fourth and last, encompassing creation, sin, and grace is the significance of the Incarnation, an event that has centered the Christian worldview around the enfleshment of divine Reason. For the knowing Christian believer, God is as near and revelatory as daily human flesh. If Christ and the Spirit are true, the community of divine persons abides in human hearts. If the New Testament is a book of wisdom, the Father labors for human beings' fulfillment. Through its gatherings, scriptures, and sacraments, the Body of Christ challenges the world with such utopian proclamations. Its faith is nothing so pedestrian as nationalism, Western superiority, or the self-service of a "moral majority." Rather it is a vision of God demanding radical justice and self-spending. As the Sermon on the Mount (Matt. 5–7) epitomizes it, an ethics based on the Incarnation makes Jesus God's mystery enfleshed.

Part Two traces the story of how this Christian faith developed over time from the seed of the New Testament. At times the beginning message seemed more a condemnation of Christians than a guarantee of their distinction. Insofar as Christians failed the twofold command of love, were not apostles of truth and service, their own Gospel wrote them judgments of shame. The Crusades, the Inquisition, witch-burnings, Church divisions, religious wars, bigotries, pruderies, sexisms, racisms—all the blots on the record gave large cause for nonbelief. On the other hand, the sublime parts of the message, and the ways Christians did imitate Christ, always kept hope alive. For all the human weakness displayed by Christians, they have had moments of glory that place their benefactions high on any fair list of the world's great achievements.

In Part Two we follow the development of Christian doctrine, the rise of major Christian institutions, and the story of Church divisions, to help us grasp what Christianity actually has been over space and time. Where the worldview that we have drawn is something of an abstraction, the history that we are about to sketch will take us a step closer to the concrete persons who have made up Christianity. Primarily, Christianity is the people who have been shaped by Jesus, the culture that Jesus has inspired, the saints who have given the Gospel its good name, and the victims who have cast the Gospel in doubt. Follow their stories as we discuss Jesus and the New Testament, the patristic era, medieval Christianity, the Reformation, and modernity.

CHAPTER 6

Jesus and the New Testament

Before Jesus

Like all human beings, Jesus was formed by the culture he inherited. However much the Christian doctrine of Jesus's divinity influenced either New Testament or early Christian theology, the equally Christian doctrine of Jesus's full humanity agrees with current social science that Jesus formed his outlook largely from his people's shared assumptions.[1] Since his people were Jews, Jesus inherited a Jewish religious outlook. Even the innovations he offered Judaism assumed its principal convictions.

For hundreds of years Jewish religion had been an ethically oriented monotheism. According to the Hebrew Bible (the Christian Old Testament), the transcendent God had called the Jewish patriarch Abraham to a special relationship (Gen. 14–15). Abraham and his descendants were to live in a covenant with God that would set them apart from the surrounding peoples, whose gods were essentially natural forces. The covenant came to dramatic focus with Moses, whom later Judaism regarded as the great lawgiver. In the account given in Exodus, God led the Israelites out of bondage in Egypt and solemnized the covenant relationship on Mount Sinai. The Law (Torah) that the Bible portrayed as originating with Moses on Mount Sinai was the basis of subsequent Judaism. Through the period of the Judges (charismatic leaders), as well as the brief period of the Monarchy of David and Solomon, the God (Yahweh) of the covenant was the great force in Israelite history. Through the period of the Prophets, when the kingdom was divided and both the northern and southern portions fell into foreign hands, Yahweh and the Covenant remained the central reference points.

For some commentators, the word *Judaism*, which was derived from the southern tribe of Judah, strictly refers to the religious and cultural phenomena datin from the Israelites' return from Babylon to Palestine in 538 B.C.E. (before the common era). The religion that followed the return from exile was characterized by a resistance to any influence from other civilizations which might have tended to absorb or change it. The people's religious heritage and original traditions were jealously preserved through scrupulous observances.[2] The returnees interpreted the law rigorously, and they rebuilt Solomon's Temple as the center of their cult. At first they were ruled by the Persians, then by Alexander the Great and his successors, the Seleucids. A good number of Jews remained outside Palestine, but both outside and inside Palestine the Hellenistic culture that Alexander had sponsored impinged on Jewish life. The rebel Maccabees and the Hasmoneans gave the Jews periods of political independence in the second and first centuries, but in 63 B.C.E. the Roman ruler Pompey annexed Syria to the Roman Empire and seized Jerusalem. Thus the culture of the generations immediately prior to Jesus was formed by the ancient Israelite biblical faith, Hellenistic influences, and a Roman military presence.

Though Rome ruled Palestine, Jews continued to think in ancient theocratic terms. Even in the Diaspora—the lands outside Palestine—Jews gathered in tightly knit communities to preserve their religious traditions. On the whole, the Romans allowed the Jews, who numbered about half a million in Palestine but seven to eight million in the Diaspora (about 10 percent of the Imperial population), to practice their traditions with little interference.

At the time of Jesus the various groups who shaped the Jewish religion placed different emphases on Torah and politics. The Samaritans, most of whom lived north of Jerusalem and the province of Judea, were accounted heretics because they limited Torah to the Pentateuch (five books of Moses) and did not acknowledge the Temple in Jerusalem to be the dwelling place of God. The Essenes were monks who lived in deserted parts of the country, especially along the Dead Sea, because they deemed both the worship in the Temple and the general religious observance impure. The Zealots were a militantly political group so opposed to Roman occupation that they performed terrorist acts not only against Romans but even against fellow Jews whom they deemed insufficiently patriotic.

The two main groups in official Judaism, however, were the Sadducees and the Pharisees. The Sadducees were an aristocratic, largely priestly group, who cooperated with Rome in order to conserve the religious traditions. They influenced the liturgy and worship in the Temple considerably but had little effect on the common people. The Sadducees accepted only the written law (the Pentateuch and, to a lesser extent, the Prophets) and tended to apply it formalistically. They did not fear Hellenism, for they thought that God had diffused the morality of the Bible beyond Judaism. In their desire to preserve the nation, the Sadducees downplayed many practices the Pharisees considered crucial.

The Pharisees were more influential than the Sadducees. Their roots went back to the pious who stood up for their religion in the period after the Maccabean war for independence (ca. 125 B.C.E.) and they upheld the Law staunchly, opposing Hellenization. The Pharisees urged close study of Torah, were spread throughout Palestine, and dominated the synagogues in which Jews outside Jerusalem gathered to pray and study. Although their background included a strong nationalism, by Jesus's time their interests were predominantly religious.

The Pharisaic instinct was to obey the Law with great attention to detail. Jesus ran counter to this instinct insofar as he thought the letter of the Law was detrimental to its spirit. Today scholars treat the Pharisees more kindly than past Christian generations did, removing "Pharisee" from being a term of contempt. The Pharisees were the only group to survive the destruction of the Temple and the exile that followed when the Romans crushed a Jewish revolt in 70 C.E. Without the ritual and sacrifice of the Temple, the Pharisees stressed even more intently the synagogue format of prayer and study. Before long they generated the collection of oral tradition that became Judaism's Mishnah and Talmud. Thus, the Pharisees were the progenitors of the Judaism that has dominated the common era (the history that Christians and Jews share).

Jesus's Life and Personality

Jesus was the heir of this history. His life seems not to have been important to nonbelieving historians who wrote soon after his time. Still, passing references by Roman historians Josephus, Pliny, Tacitus, and Suetonius, all of whom lived during or shortly after Jesus's life, and nonscriptural Christian documents like the Gospel of Thomas, remove any doubt that Jesus existed. He was born at Bethlehem in 6 or 7 B.C.E., lived in the northern province of Galilee, and died in Jerusalem between 30 and 33 C.E.[3] His public career probably began after his baptism by John in 27 or 28 C.E. Prior to this, Jesus likely lived in the city of Nazareth in Galilee, working as a carpenter. The Gospels suggest that after his baptism he withdrew to the solitude of the Judean desert, perhaps from a sense of vocational crisis,[4] and then emerged to preach the good news that the Kingdom of God was dawning.

In addition to preaching, Jesus performed healings and exorcisms. He kept company with poor people and social outcasts, and he showed special kindness toward women and children. Finally, he opposed the rigorism of some Pharisees and the revolutionary ardor of the Zealots. Leading a small band of itinerants, Jesus wandered the northern districts of Palestine and developed the implications of the dawning of God's reign. If the implications bewildered many of the common people, they largely alienated the religious establishment. The religious leaders apparently thought that Jesus's subordinating the Law to love of God and love of neighbor invited social chaos.

After King Herod Antipas had John the Baptist beheaded (Matt. 14:1–10), Jesus left Galilee and went to Jerusalem. According to the Gospels he entered the city in triumph and confronted the merchants doing business in the outer precincts of the Temple. This was the final straw in his conflict with the Jewish leaders, and after a passover meal with his disciples Jesus was arrested by the Roman authorities.

He was examined by members of the Sanhedrin, the Jewish political assembly, whose consensus was that he deserved death on the grounds of having blasphemed and claimed divine powers (such as the power to forgive sins). Roman prefect Pontius Pilate judged Jesus a danger to the civil peace and ordered him scourged and crucified. After Jesus's death his disciples claimed that he had returned to life and appeared to them. They began preaching his resurrection and messiahship, before long forming a new Jewish sect. When reunion with Judaism became impossible, this sect became the start of a new religion.

Even this brief biography is fraught with uncertainty, since its main sources, the Gospels, were written a generation after Jesus's death and are filled with faith assumptions. It is even more difficult to reconstruct Jesus's personality and teachings, but few scholars dispute the claim that Jesus's personality was extraordinary. For example, the modern Jewish scholar Geza Vermes describes Jesus as a holy miracle worker and approves an earlier scholar's view that in Jesus's ethical code there was "a sublimity, distinctiveness and originality in form unparalleled in any other Hebrew ethical code; neither is there any parallel to the remarkable art of his parables."[5]

Beneath Jesus's ethical code and parables, Christian scholars such as Lucas Grollenberg have found a singular trust in the Jewish God and covenant.[6] Jesus apparently spoke of God intimately, referring to him as "Father." Confident that this Father would always support him, Jesus moved with great freedom, reaching out to all the people who came to him. This seems to have made him a cause of crisis. People who could handle his freedom, his trust that God was utterly good and would always provide for him, could open themselves and come to what Scripture calls *faith*: wholehearted commitment. Such faith is the best psychological explanation for the cures and exorcisms Jesus worked. People who could not handle this freedom withdrew from Jesus. He seemed to undermine their traditions, to demand too much change. Thus his contemporaries divided. Jesus's personality was so strong that members of the same family sometimes took different stands toward him.

On the other hand, if we believe the Gospels, Jesus was not a "powerful personality" in the ordinary sense of the term. Often he was gentle and poetic. He did not fight for control of the religious establishment; he did not frighten women or children. Indeed, even the religiously outcast, the "sinners," found him approachable. He was so convinced that God was a good Father and a new era of intimacy with God was dawning that he offered sinners forgiveness. His good news meant new beginnings, for love could heal old wounds. It could reconcile enemies, even reconcile a disheartened person to himself. Possessed of this vision, Jesus seems to have found the world vibrant and beautiful. He loved the birds of the air, the lilies of the field that God clothed in splendor. He saw the small dramas of the widows who gave one of their few coins to support the Temple and the shepherds who went out of their way to save a single sheep. Musing, Jesus realized that if ordinary people often were like ungrateful children, God was like a father so full of love he immediately forgot their offenses. Above all Jesus prized being the child of such a Father.

Jesus's Teaching

Jesus saw in the Kingdom of God the potential extension of divine childhood to all persons. In his time the Jews had ardent hopes that God would finally come to free them from foreign rule. Their utopian imagination drew pictures of the justice and freedom God's rule would produce. Jesus interiorized these pictures. Because of his own sense of intimacy with God, he taught that anyone who believed in his Father could come to a similar intimacy. The works that Jesus did in testimony to his mission to proclaim the Kingdom—his cures and **miracles**—overflowed from his relation to the Father. They pointed away from Jesus himself to his divine source. For Jesus the cornerstone of human prosperity, individual and social alike, was right relation to God. This was a traditional Jewish conviction, but Jesus sharpened its personal accent. Because the Reign of God was dawning, as his own experience and works showed, the cornerstone of human prosperity now was loving intimacy with God. Like a guileless child, the follower of Jesus was to throw herself into God's keeping utterly. Indeed, the "Abba" that Jesus used was the speech of a toddler, equivalent to "Daddy," or "Pappa." That was how familiar with God the believer should be.

The second pillar of Jesus's teaching was love of neighbor. The Shema had urged Jews to a wholehearted love of God, and rabbinic teaching contemporary with Jesus was emphasizing love of neighbor. On neither of these capital points, then, was Jesus's teaching wholly novel. But just as his teaching about loving God was more intimate than that of the Shema, so his teaching about loving one's neighbor was more dramatic. To the man who asked him, "And who is my neighbor?", Jesus gave the parable of the Good Samaritan (Luke 10:30–37). Its implication was that neighborliness cuts across the divisions between Jews and Samaritans, orthodox and heretics, compatriots and foreigners. As the apostle Paul later saw, it cuts across the divisions between men and women, free and enslaved (Gal. 3:28). The Kingdom of God, and the Church of Christ, demanded new definitions of neighborliness. Any fellow human being in need deserved one's love. Every other creature made in God's image deserved to be treated like oneself.

These two tenets were the inmost structure of Jesus's teaching and, as Karl Rahner has shown,[7] they flow together. Perhaps the most striking revelation of their unity occurs in Matthew 25:40. There the King, who stands for God, says to those whose lives he is judging, "Truly I say to you, as you did it [a good deed like feeding the hungry or clothing the naked] to one of the least of these my brethren, you did it to me." 1 John 3:17 expresses the same notion: "But if any one has the world's goods and sees his brother in need, yet closes his heart against him, how does God's love abide in him?" The love Jesus had for his Father, and the love Jesus received from his Father in what he called *the Spirit*, had to overflow into practical charity toward his fellow human beings. Conversely, the love that anyone showed toward his fellow human beings, however instinctive or unthinking it might seem, went back to God, the source of all creation. So the core of Jesus's teaching was the simple experience and power of love. His interpretations of the Law, as his acts of healing and casting out demons, derived from his love.

Contemporary scholars advise us that matter and form go together in religious teaching, and we do well to apply their advice to Jesus. The form in which Jesus tended to cast his teaching about the Kingdom and the twofold command of love was the parable. Through concrete, pithy stories, such as the story of the Good Samaritan, Jesus tried to shake his listeners free of their preconceptions and show them the gratuity, the overwhelming goodness, of God's Reign. There are parallels to such parabolic teaching in other religious traditions—for example, Zen Buddhist koans—and they share Jesus's intent.[8] The God or Buddha-nature of ultimate religious experience is a mystery ordinary speech and conception cannot handle. For Jesus the mystery is the far side, or the summoning fullness, of divine love. God is so much better than we can imagine, so much better than we are, that we have to be stripped of our petty assumptions if divine reality is to crash through to us.

Jesus finally proved unacceptable to the Jewish establishment, most likely because he shifted the foundation of religious life from the Law to the love that filled him personally. He may have sensed that he would have to pay for this shift with his life, for John 15:13 puts in Jesus's mouth the conviction that there is no greater love than laying down one's life for one's friends. Consistently enough, Christians and Jews have also differed in their interpretations of the way that Jesus laid down his life. For Christians the crucifixion showed the farthest reaches of divine love, God's willingness to suffer death on behalf of human beings. For Jews it represented a degradation (death as a common criminal) and a cruelty incompatible with divine love. Thus we do more than pun when we say that the cross is the crux of the interpretation of Jesus.

Pauline Christianity

The cross surely was the crux of Paul's interpretation of Jesus: "For Jews demand signs and Greeks seek wisdom, but we preach Christ crucified, a stumbling block to Jews and folly to Gentiles, but to those who are called, both Jews and Greeks, Christ the power of God and the wisdom of God" (1 Cor. 1:22–24). On the cross God had displayed the depth of human sin and the depth of divine love. By raising Jesus from the dead, the Father had inaugurated a new creation. The old order of Adam had passed away, being done to death. The new order of Christ, the Second Adam, had restructured the human race. Where Adam's disobedience had led to death, Christ's obedience had led to life, immortality, and grace before God. Thus, the death and resurrection of Jesus was the pivot of Pauline theology. Like the *goel*—the "redeemer" of Jewish family law—Jesus had bought back those whom sin had sold into slavery. As a result, human beings could now enjoy the liberty of the children of God (Rom. 8:21).

Originally a Jewish persecutor of Christians, Paul was converted by a vision and soon thereafter began applying his Pharisaic training and immense energy to Christian missionary activity. He journeyed all over the eastern Mediterranean founding new churches, and he developed the major accommodation that cut the new Christian Church's umbilical cord to Judaism. Opening Christianity to non-Jews, Paul declared the Law nonbinding for them. He said they need not be circumcised nor obey Jewish dietary restrictions, for in Christ God had done a new thing, an act of grace for which the Law was but a preparation. Good in its own way, the Law had been superseded. In its place God had set the inner guidance of the Holy Spirit and the outer guidance of Church discipline.

Paul's letters show that the young churches he founded did not immediately grasp the full implications of Christian faith. While baptism meant such an immersion in the death and resurrection of Christ that thenceforth immorality was unthinkable, early Christians such as the Corinthians, Thessalonians, and Galatians to whom Paul wrote all continued to suffer burdens of the flesh. Paul provided them a judicious blend of firmness and compassion. As he applied his penetrating mind to Church affairs, Christ's import expanded. Whereas the early epistles, such as those to the Thessalonians, were written in the expectation of Christ's imminent return, the middle epistles (Philippians, Galatians, Corinthians, and Romans) stressed that the Spirit of Christ that remained was the assurance of his return. The last epistles (Colossians and Ephesians) meditated on Christ's cosmic exaltation and God's great plan of salvation. Ephesians 1:3–10 offers a good sample of the mature Pauline vision:

> Blessed be the God and Father of our Lord Jesus Christ, who has blessed us in Christ with every spiritual blessing in the heavenly places, even as he chose us in him before the foundation of the world, that we should be holy and blameless before him. He destined us in love to be his sons through Jesus Christ, according to the purpose of his will, to the praise of his glorious grace which he freely bestowed on us in the Beloved. In him we have redemption through his blood, the forgiveness of our trespasses, according to the riches of his grace which he lavished upon us. For he has made known to us in all wisdom and insight the mystery of his will, according to his purpose which he set forth in Christ as a plan for the fulness of time, to unite all things in him, things in heaven and things on earth.

Although scholars debate whether Ephesians came from Paul's own hand, it represents a cosmic Christology faithful to his theological style.

"The unity of the Christian community in the Church is Paul's great contribution to Christian theology—a unity that he derives from the single purpose of the divine plan of salvation," according to theologian Joseph Fitzmyer.[9] The great image in this ecclesiology is "the Body of Christ." Parallel to the way Jesus interiorized the Law, making it a matter of love of God and love of neighbor, Pauline Christianity continued the trend of some Pharisees to interiorize the covenant. Through Jesus's death and resurrection, God had created a new people and struck a new bond. This new people of God existed "in Christ"—a quasi-spatial location Paul favored. By baptism and participation in the Church's sacramental life, believers shared one life with Christ. Their divine childhood was based on the model of Christ's connection to the Father. The Father had sent Christ to accomplish thi organic bonding. To extend the divine family, Father, Son, and Spirit nurtured the Body of Christ. For example, the Spirit moved in believers' depths, making their prayer with sighs too deep for words (Rom. 8:26).

Thus, a basic thesis of Pauline Christianity was the holiness of the Church. Its members were married to Christ (Eph. 5:21–33) and shared his divine luster. With the help of the Spirit their daily lives could reflect this luster. Above all, they were to prize charity, the greatest of the Spirit's gifts. Loving one another as brothers and sisters in the Lord, they could endure earthly tribulations and merit a heavenly fulfillment. Indeed, the Resurrection of Jesus was a warrant for believing they too would be raised. Pauline Christianity therefore discounted both worldly trials and worldly advantages. The Body of Christ focused on higher things.

The Synoptic Communities

Today's New Testament scholars borrow some of their most fertile techniques from sociology. More aware of the importance of a group's sociological background than their predecessors were, today's analysts are probing the cultural movements contemporary with the different New Testament communities and theologies. For example, they are investigating the cults outside Christianity that might have influenced New Testament documents like Ephesians. Howard Clark Kee offers a glimpse of such influence: "References to enlightenment are found in the magical papyri and in inscriptions related to mystery cults. Its penetration into post-apostolic Christian usage is seen in the explicit reference to mystical illumination in Eph. 3:9 ('to illuminate the operation of the mystery which has been hidden in God for ages'). . . ."[10]

Such Hellenistic culture was influential in Pauline Christianity. Jewish culture appears to have been more influential as the background of the first three Gospels of the New Testament, Matthew, Mark, and Luke—the so-called synoptic (meaning "presenting a common view") Gospels. The synoptic Gospels are collections of Jesus's sayings, shaped to the needs and insights of early Christians in Palestine and Syria. Since the authors of Matthew and Luke likely had access to both Mark and another source (called "Q," from the German *Quelle* [source]) as well as their own distinctive sources, Kee finds he must characterize at least four synoptic theologies. The Q theology is **eschatological**—concerned with how to live in the time of final judgment. It presents Jesus as a charismatic leader and prophet dominated by eschatological concerns. The interests of the Q community, or communities, included the privileges and trials of Christian discipleship, the prophet's role as God's messenger, the process of repentance, and Jesus's function as the revealer and agent of God's rule. Q's Jesus moves from his baptism and successful contest with Satan to announce the time of decision, of spiritual combat. Its theology has an esoteric character, as though it stemmed from a group that felt marginalized and privileged because of its adherence to the eschatological prophet. Q also shows a strong sense that faith means persevering in the face of trials, as Jesus did. Thus Q gives us beatitudes such as "Blessed are you poor, for yours is the kingdom of God. Blessed are you that hunger now, for you shall be satisfied. Blessed are you that weep now, for you shall laugh" (Luke 6:20–21).

In Mark are found many of the same eschatological features, but the community that produced this Gospel seems to have been more reconciled to living in the interim between the present and the eschatological finale. Thus Mark manifests an interest in Jesus's words about divorce, marriage, the state, and wealth. It has the psychic leisure for speculation about the Resurrection, the First Commandment, the forgiveness of sins, and how to observe the Sabbath. The interest shown in Mark in Jesus's differences from Jewish interpreters of the Law follows the style of some of the Dead Sea Scrolls. Combining such features with other peculiarities of Mark, Kee offers the following opinion about its sociological context: "What we have in Mark is the foundation document of an apocalyptic Christian sect. Although there are only bits of evidence by which to hypothesize the provenance of Mark, there is a convergence of factors that point to rural and small-town southern Syria" about 65 C.E.[11] Focused on the revelation of the end-time, the community that produced the Gospel of Mark thought in terms of secret knowledge (4:11), private visions (9:2–9), and an early fulfillment of its hopes (13:30). Its members were ready to sacrifice their houses, families, and lands (10:30), which indicates that their contentment with the interim period was not total. These Christians subordinated community organization to the freedom necessary to wander about proclaiming God's reign, and they probably were the source of the literary genre we now call *gospel* which weaves traditions of Jesus's sayings and doings into a rough narrative.

Matthew took over materials from Mark and made explicit their submotif of Jesus's having fulfilled the Hebrew Scriptures. For example, Matthew's opening genealogies trace Jesus back to Abraham and David, setting his story within the history of Israel. Its narrations of Jesus's infancy, his baptism by John, and his temptations by Satan are all interlaced with scriptural references. In terms of literary structure, Matthew organizes its materials into five books, set off by the phrase "when Jesus had finished" (7:28, 11:1, 13:53, 19:1, 26:1), that likely are a conscious imitation of the five books of Moses. Connected with this scriptural orientation is Matthew's pointed contrast between the Pharisaic interpretation of the Law and Jesus's interpretation. The vindictive tone is striking, and it strongly suggests that the community that produced Matthew was in bitter competition with Pharisaic Judaism. A further mark of this community's Jewishness is its position on the question of what the status of the Law ought to be for Christians. In contrast to the Pauline position that Jesus had abrogated the Law, the Matthean position was that Christians were to outstrip the Scribes (religious lawyers) and Pharisees by the stringency of their religious observance (5:19–20). The only relaxation concerned food and ritual cleanliness, where Matthew bowed to Jesus's dictum that evil proceeds from the heart, not from what one touches or eats.

Generally, the Matthean community regarded the Church as the true Israel. Its main mission was to Jews, and the "lost sheep" whom it expected to respond to the

Gospel linked Jesus to the shepherd-king mentioned in the Old Testament book of Zechariah (21:5). On the other hand, Matthew also shows a universalist strain, for it expects the members of the covenant community eventually to come from all nations (28:19). Jesus dwells in the midst of the Church (28:20), and Matthew details juridical procedures for settling disputes (18:15–20), both of which suggest an established, almost institutionalized church rather than an apocalyptic sect.

With Luke and its sister book, Acts, one moves to a sociology more immersed in the Greco-Roman world. For example, while the story of Jesus begins in Jerusalem, the center of the Jewish world, the story of the Church moves toward Rome, the center of the Gentile world. Language, rhetoric, and literary models in Luke reflect Hellenistic influences, and Acts 17 commends the search of the Hellenistic poets and philosophers for God. Lukan theology solves the problem of Christ's failing to return by portraying God as present in the Church now through the Spirit (Luke 24 and Acts 1). Further, the outpouring of the Spirit at Pentecost, fifty days after Easter (Acts 2:5), prefigures a worldwide mission that comes to a first climax when the Gospel arrives in Rome (Acts 28). Throughout, the author stresses divine providence, the unfolding of a secure heavenly purpose. Thus Luke's stories of the journey of the holy family to Bethlehem, the martyrdom of Stephen, and the vacillation of Roman authorities in Paul's legal case all are made to serve salvation-history.

In addition to Gospel materials from Mark and Q, Luke employs Hellenistic and Roman biographic writing and shows a strong sense of the entire Hellenistic world. These are signs that the Lukan community was Gentile and cosmopolitan in character. Other signs are its attitudes toward the state, the significant role it accords women, and its stress on reconciling different theological viewpoints. Where Markan and Pauline Christianity showed Jesus acquiescent to Roman rule, Lukan Christianity went out of its way to emphasize that both Jesus and the early Christians were always found innocent when they were brought before civil authorities. As Christians grew in numbers, their position in the empire became a pressing matter. Throughout the first two centuries they had public relations problems, but Lukan Christianity sensed early on how to handle them: if the Church seemed an oasis of peace and charitable works, it would give the lie to all charges of sedition.

The Lukan Church stressed the variety of Jesus's followers in the Christian community: women, the poor, Roman officers, Samaritans, even the demon-possessed. The Church ought to be a **catholic** group, open even to persons that Judaism or polite society scorned. Still, Lukan theology also opined that the Christian community has room for the wealthy, the law-observing Jew, and the nonobservant Gentile convert. Indeed, as Acts (Chapters 6, 10, 15, and 21) shows, the Church ought to pacify different theological outlooks, considering itself an inclusive rather than an exclusive institution. With a propagandist's keen eye, the author of these writings painted the Church as apolitical, peace promoting, and catholic across ethnic and social lines. He wrote urbanely, so as to persuade educated Gentiles that Christianity was intellectually respectable, and sensitively, so as to extend God's care to underdogs and little people.

Johannine Christianity

The religious experiences and sociological forces in the background of the Johannine literature (the Gospel of John, Epistles of John, and Revelation) add still another dimension to New Testament Christianity. Raymond E. Brown, a distinguished Roman Catholic scholar who has specialized in Johannine studies, has recently sketched the history of the Johannine community in four stages.[12] In Brown's view Johannine Christianity likely originated with Palestinian Jews of fairly standard Messianic expectations. They may have included followers of John the Baptist, and they quickly accepted Jesus as the Messiah. For them Jesus came in the line of David, fulfilled the scriptural prophecies, and was confirmed in his messianic role by miracles. Their leader was a man who had known Jesus during his ministry and had become designated as "The Beloved Disciple."

Joining this originating community was a second group made up largely of Jews opposed to the religion of those who worshiped in the spirit of the Jerusalem Temple. They believed in Jesus and made converts among the Samaritans. For them, however, Jesus was less the successor of David than the successor of Moses. Like Moses, Jesus had been with God, had seen God, and had brought God's words back to the people.

When these two groups joined, they produced a "high" Christology that stressed Jesus's preexistence as the Logos. This doctrine outraged the Jews with whom these Palestinian Jewish Christians still had ties, because they thought it made a second God out of Jesus and destroyed Jewish monotheism. When the Jews had the proponents of the high Christology expelled from the synagogues, the latter saw the Jews as children of the devil. To compensate for what they had lost in Judaism, the Christians stressed that Jesus was the fulfillment of God's eschatological promises. The Beloved Disciple was the leader in this development, which left the Church with both a realized eschatology (the view that the end-time had come in Jesus) and a polemical stance toward Judaism.

Brown emphasizes that his reconstruction of the history of Johannine Christianity is hypothetical, and he suggests that this first stage covered the years from the mid-50s C.E. to the late 80s C.E. The second stage probably occurred around 90 C.E. Its main phenomenon was the conversion of numerous Gentiles, whom the Johannine Christians welcomed because "the Jews" (an almost technically pejorative term in the Johannine literature) had shown themselves blind to Jesus's messiahship and preexistent dignity. It is likely that the Johannine community moved from Palestine to the Diaspora and concentrated on teaching the Greeks, which further developed its universalist tendencies. There was enough rejection by Gentiles, however, and enough continuing opposition from Jews, to convince the Johannine community that the world was under Satan's sway and almost intrinsically opposed to Jesus. Although they kept communications open with the apostolic Church—the Church directly connected to the eyewitnesses of Jesus—the Johannine Christians were less institutionalized and more sectarian in their consciousness.

The third stage, which occurred around 100 C.E. and is expressed in the Johannine epistles, brought a decisive split among the Johannine Christians. The adherents of the author of the epistles held that to be a child of God one had to confess that Jesus had come in the flesh, and to keep the commandments. Persons who withdrew from this teaching were considered children of the devil and Antichrists. Since Jesus had given his followers the Spirit of truth, the adherents had no need for human teachers. Testing the charity of all who claimed to have the Spirit, they could discern the wise and righteous. Opposed to the adherents of the author of the epistles was a band of secessionists whose main tenet was that the One who had come down from heaven was so divine that he was not fully human. He did not belong to the world, so neither his life on earth nor that of the believer had any significance for salvation. The only important thing was knowledge that God's Son had come into the world. Those who believed this already were saved, said the secessionists.

The fourth and last stage in Johannine Christianity occurred early in the second century C.E. The community represented by the epistles found that it could not combat the secessionists successfully simply by appealing to tradition. It therefore decided to accept authoritative official teachers (presbyters or bishops), and so moved closer to the "Great," or Catholic, Church, linked to the apostles, which by then had a firm hierarchical authority. The Great Church's acceptance of the Johannine high Christology facilitated the enactment of this merger and slowly the Johannine group melded into the Great Church.

On the other hand, the secessionists, who may well have been the numerical majority, took the road to heresy. Developing the notion that the One who came from above was not fully human, it fell into **Docetism** and **Gnosticism**. That is, it agreed with those who said that Jesus merely seemed to be human and with those who talked of believers' preexistence in heaven. In addition, the secessionists fell in with the heretical **Montanists**, who held that the Holy Spirit gave them new revelations additional to the Scriptures. The secessionist group took the gospel of John with them and helped to make it popular with the Gnostics.

Whatever the merits of the details of Brown's reconstruction, it does justice to the distinctive themes of the Johannine literature. Clearly this Church especially revered Jesus's heavenly status, found themselves fiercely opposed by Jews guarding monotheism, and stressed the interior guidance of the Spirit. To distinguish themselves from heretics, the more moderate Johannine Christians stressed Jesus's having come in the flesh—his full humanity—and the Church's sacramental authority. The Johannine literature now stands in the New Testament as the most profound meditation on Jesus's relations with the Father and the Spirit, as well as the most artful presentation of the signs the incarnate Logos worked in the world. It may be ironic that this contentious group laid special stress on brotherly and sisterly love, but this stress has been an important counterweight to hierarchical authority. If the Johannine Christians' own experience revealed the need for a decisive external authority, it also made a persuasive case that only the Spirit of faith and love led one into the mysteries of the Trinity and the Incarnation.

Christianity ca. 100 C.E.

Our sketch of Johannine Christianity touched on many of the main features that Christianity had developed at the turn of the first century C.E. By that time the literature of the New Testament was essentially complete and the main structures of the Church were essentially settled. In this section we round out the picture, giving an overview of the situation in which the apostolic Church found itself around 100 C.E.

At the turn of the first century the Church was multi-ethnic. Whereas Judaism had allowed a mild proselytizing, the Christian Church reached out to non-Jews aggressively. This policy brought Christians into close contact with Hellenistic culture and with the many religions that had come into the Roman Empire from the East. Hellenistic culture included not only Greek art, architecture, drama, and the gymnasium (center of physical development) but also philosophy and the mystery religions.

The philosophy most influential in the first century was not the classical thought of Socrates, Plato, and Aristotle, but the natural law theories of philosophers called Stoics and Epicureans. They probably made subtle contributions to Christian theology, like Paul's doctrine that since the creation of the world God's invisible nature—his eternal power and deity—have been clearly perceivable from the things that he made (Rom. 1:20). The Hellenistic mystery religions also influenced Christianity more obliquely than directly. They stressed a new knowledge that would give the initiate a happy afterlife, and they entailed secret ceremonies that bonded members to one another. By stressing their own saving knowledge and sacraments, the early Christians made themselves competitive.

The religions that had come into the empire from the East stressed fertility themes, such as the rhythms of the vegetative cycle. Thus the originally Egyptian gods Isis and Osiris offered followers an initiation into dying and rising that would secure them blissful immortality. Similarly, those who participated in the cult of Mithra, originally an Iranian god who helped the chief deity Ahura Mazda, but later a solar deity especially dear to Roman soldiers, sacrificed bulls and spiritually ascended to different astral (star) levels on the way to winning the release of their souls. As excavations under the present-day church of St. Clement in Rome have revealed, the Mithraic assembly had altars and schoolrooms quite like those of a local Christian church.

The Gnostic sects, who became early Christianity's most formidable competition, were like the mystery and fertility religions in that they offered saving esoteric knowledge. They tended to wander intellectually among different levels and ages that had preceded the present creation, and to teach that current human nature had fallen from a holy spiritual level into the sad mire of the flesh. In competition with the Gnostics the early Christians had both to defend the full humanity of Jesus, the perfect human being, and to argue persuasively that the knowledge imparted by Jesus's Spirit gave a more secure salvation.[13]

When it competed for members, then, the early Church fought on several fronts. To Jews it offered Jesus as the Christ, the fulfillment of their messianic expectation. To Gentiles it offered Jesus as the source of truly saving knowledge. Reluctant Jews found Jesus's sufferings scandalous and feared that venerating him would fracture their monotheism. Reluctant Gentiles found Jesus's resurrection incredible and balked at his full humanity. Apologetically the Church tried to walk a middle road, developing its doctrines in terms of an incipient Christology that held Jesus's divinity and humanity together.

By trial and error, as well as the influence of this moderate instinct, the Church's internal affairs shaped themselves to an implicit principle of "both/and." Both Jewish traditions and Gentile insights could enrich a core commitment to Christ. Both official leaders and free-wheeling charismatics could serve the upbuilding of faith. Lukan theology could complement Matthean theology. Poor people and women could complement wealthy people and men. Christianity was a religion with strong social implications, since its members constituted a single body and shared a single command of love, but it was also a religion of individuals who had to pray privately—indeed, in Paul's injunction, to pray always (1 Thess. 5:17). The liturgical life pivoted on both the Scriptures and the sacraments, especially the sacraments of baptism and the Eucharist. The water and bread of life entailed an exalted morality, but from early times there were penitential rites that ministered to sinners and the weak. Marriage was a holy vocation, and most of the early Church leaders were married, but so too was virginity a holy vocation. The final consummation of faith would only come when the Lord returned, but present times offered many occasions for fulfillment and good work.

Thus when commentators speak of the early Church as "catholic," they should mean more than that a religious group spread thoughout the Mediterranean. Implicitly, the median instinct of the early Church, which it derived from its central doctrine of the Incarnation, was that the full range of reality, from the heights of divinity to the dregs of humanity, lay in its province. The Roman poet Terence had given the imperial world the ideal that it should think nothing human foreign to itself. The early Christian poets who sang the good news of Jesus Christ accepted most of that ideal. As Paul put it in Philippians 4:8, "Finally, brethren, whatever is true, whatever is honorable, whatever is just, whatever is pure, whatever is lovely, whatever is gracious, if there is any excellence, if there is anything worthy of praise, think about these things."

Summary

The Judaism prior to Jesus centered on Torah, but different Jewish groups offered varying interpretations of what Torah meant, especially for compliance with Roman rule or opposition. The Pharisees were the most influential party. They stressed a religious exactitude in obeying the prescriptions of Torah and left political issues alone. Jesus agreed with them in making politics peripheral, but he disagreed with their punctilious attitude toward Torah. Like the Sabbath, the Law was made for man, not man for the Law. Jesus gave his public ministry over to proclaiming the dawning of a new era, the Reign of God, in which love superseded the Law. He finally died because of the opposition that this message, as well as his cures and miracles, raised among the Jewish and Roman leaders.

Pauline Christianity took as its axis the redemptive significance of Jesus's death and resurrection. Opening the Church to the Gentiles, Paul taught them that the Law was now secondary to the leading of Jesus's Spirit. "The Body of Christ," as Paul designated the Church, was the new Israel, just as Christ was the new Adam. Synoptic Christianity focused more on the traditions about the historical Jesus. Against different sociological backgrounds, Mark, Matthew, and Luke shaped Jesus's sayings for the theological needs of apocalyptic, Jewish, and Gentile churches. Johannine Christianity, born of bitter conflicts with Jews and Gnostics, stressed a high Christology and a sacramental interpretation of Jesus's flesh. It finally had to confess the need for external authorities and firm disciplinary structures, but it bequeathed the Great Church a strong reliance on the inner guidance of the Spirit. By 100 C.E. these different theologies had prepared the Church to compete effectively with the Hellenistic religions and Gnosticism.

Study Questions

1. What were the principal merits of Pharisaic Judaism?
2. What was the center of Jesus's powerful personality?
3. How could the judgment scene in Matthew 25 anchor a humanistic Christian theology?
4. How did Pauline Christianity enlarge the significance of Christ's death and resurrection?
5. What are some of the main contrasts between the sociological background of Matthew and that of Luke?
6. Why did Johannine Christianity come to define the Jews and the world as its enemies?
7. Would the Church have found itself stronger in 100 C.E. if it had chosen a mentality of "either/or"? Why?

Notes

1. For theoretical background see Alfred Schutz, *The Phenomenology of the Social World* (Evanston, IL: Northwestern University Press, 1967).
2. Xavier Leon-Dufour, *Dictionary of the New Testament* (San Francisco: Harper & Row, 1980), p. 27.
3. Ibid., p. 246.
4. See Joachim Jeremias, *New Testament Theology: The Proclamation of Jesus* (New York: Charles Scribner's Sons, 1971), pp. 68–75.
5. Geza Vermes, *Jesus the Jew* (London: Fontana/Collins, 1976), p. 224.
6. See Lucas Grollenberg, *Jesus* (Philadelphia: Westminster, 1978), especially pp. 100–116.

7. Karl Rahner, "Reflections on the Unity of the Love of Neighbour and the Love of God," *Theological Investigations* (Baltimore: Helicon, 1969), vol. 6, pp. 23–249.
8. See William A. Beardslee, "Parable, Proverb, and Koan," in *The Poetics of Faith* (Missoula, MT: Scholars Press, 1978), pp. 151–177. For further background on the parables see Norman Perrin, *Jesus and the Language of the Kingdom* (Philadelphia: Fortress Press, 1976), and John Dominic Crossan, *Cliffs of Fall* (New York: Crossroad, 1980).
9. Joseph A. Fitzmyer, "Pauline Theology," in *The Jerome Biblical Commentary*, ed. R. Brown, J. Fitzmyer, and R. Murphy (Englewood Cliffs, NJ: Prentice-Hall, 1968), vol 2, p. 826.
10. Howard Clark Kee, *Christian Origins in Sociological Perspective* (Philadelphia: Westminster, 1980), p. 113.
11. Ibid., p. 138. Our characterization of all the synoptic communities draws heavily on Kee, pp. 135–151.
12. See Raymond E. Brown, *The Community of the Beloved Disciple* (New York: Paulist, 1979), especially pp. 166–167.
13. On the Hellenistic religions and Gnosticism see M. J. Vermaseren, "Hellenistic Religions," in *Historia Religionum*, C. J. Bleeker and G. Widengren, eds. (Leiden: E. J. Brill, 1969), vol. 1, pp. 495–532, and J. Doresse, "Gnosticism," ibid., pp. 533–579.

CHAPTER 7

The Patristic Era (100–600)

Apologetics

The concluding section of the last chapter gave us a glimpse of Christianity around the year 100 C.E. This chapter takes us from 100 to 600 C.E., the period called the *patristic era* because the influential Christian thinkers of the time are considered to have been the "Fathers" of the Church. The main accomplishment of this five-hundred-year period was a marriage of doctrinal and organizational developments that begot the catholic or universal tradition. Whereas by the end of the New Testament period the Christian community was merely diverse and energetic, by the end of the patristic era it was the most influential religious body of the Roman world. On the way to such influence the Church had to pass through fires of persecution, but the Fathers who guided it did their work so well that Eastern Christianity still considers them its foremost teachers. These Fathers were bishops, theologians, and often martyrs. They combined piety, learning, and pastoral care as perhaps no Church leaders of later ages did. From their conciliar controversies emerged the classical dogmas that became the infrastructure of Christian faith. From their sense of tradition they forged an apostolic chain back to Jesus himself.

The Fathers are an imprecise collection of authors sometimes divided into ante-Nicene and post-Nicene groups, relative to the assembly of bishops at Nicea in 325, which historians consider to have been a watershed. Preeminent among the ante-Nicene fathers were the *apologists*. Their main work was to interpret (give an apologia for) Christianity as a religion superior to both Judaism and classical Greco-Roman thought. After 135 C.E., when the Romans closed Jerusalem to the Jews and sent them into the Diaspora, Hellenistic Jews and Hellenistic Jewish-Christians fought constantly over the question of the continuity of Christianity from Judaism. The New Testament (for instance, Acts 15) gives evidence of the early Christians' indecisions, but as more Gentiles came into the Church the tenor of the controversy shifted:

> What was offensive about Christianity in the eyes of Gentiles was, to a considerable extent, what it had inherited from Judaism. Celsus and other pagan critics ridiculed the claim that God had put in an appearance at, of all places, "some corner of Judea somewhere"; and the emperor Julian scored the Jewish and Christian conception of God as "essentially the deity of a primitive and uncivilized folk," even while he chided the "Galileans" for forsaking Judaism. Not only the Gentile critics of Christianity, but also the Gentile converts to Christianity demanded a decision about just how much of the Jewish tradition they were obliged to retain.[1]

This bad repute of things Jewish in cultured circles played a part not only in early Christian heresies such as **Marcionism**, which rejected the Old Testament, but also in moderate early Christian writings, such as *The Epistle to Barnabas*, which downplayed Israel's covenant with God.

The basic line that the early Christian apologists took regarding Judaism had been laid down in New Testament writings like Matthew. By interpreting Jesus as the correction and fulfillment of previous Judaism, the apologists could claim for the Church all the saints and believers back to Abraham, or even to Adam. Something in the temper of Hellenistic culture made antiquity a valuable quality, so the Christian Fathers were anxious to connect the faith of the present Church with that of the most pristine times, when God had called heroes like Abraham and spoken with men like Moses face-to-face.

The most famous specimen of this early Christian interpretation of Judaism as a prefiguring of the Church is the *Dialogue with Trypho* of Justin Martyr. In apologetic writings like the *Dialogue*, Christians tried to assemble proof from the Old Testament to show how Christ had fulfilled Jewish prophecy. The authors varied in their estimates of the Mosaic Law, but the more artful among them resorted to **allegorical** interpretations of Old Testament customs. For example, Christians said that the Mosaic commands against eating animals thought unclean were meant to be taken spiritually, while the circumcision of Abraham referred not to the flesh but to purifying the heart. There was Pauline precedent for the latter interpretation (Rom. 2:29), and Jesus's own words seemed to carry the former interpretation (Matt. 15:11), but the apologists' main motivation was their conviction that Jesus Christ had changed Judaism into something new. Identifying themselves with the Hebrew prophets, the apologists railed against the Law. Taking the missionary momentum away from Judaism, and being increasingly unable to read the Hebrew Bible in its own tongue, the early Christians swept Judaism to the sidelines. Since history was running with the Christians, the dubious scholarly grounds for many of their scriptural interpretations finally mattered little.

On a second front, the apologists contested classical Greco-Roman thought. A few repudiated pagan culture entirely, taking as their model the bitter diatribes of the New Testament Apocalypse of John, but the more intellectually inclined, such as Clement of Alexandria, tried to show that Christianity took good pagan insights to a higher level of fulfillment. Before reaching this plane, however, the apologists usually had to rebut two charges that pagans leveled against Christians. The first charge was civil disobedience. In correspondence between the governor Pliny and the emperor Trajan, for example, the two leaders worried that the Christians would turn out to be seditious. Insofar as civil and religious fealty to the emperor was the glue holding the Roman Empire together, sects that had different centers of loyalty were ready sources of unrest. The apologists therefore tried to show that Christians could be good citizens.

The second charge was immorality. Usually this charge was rather vague, tied perhaps to an accusation that Christians ate human flesh or devoured loaves steeped in blood. Informers would get wind of the Christian Eucharist and garble the teaching about eating Christ's body. Here again the apologists argued merely for Christians' ordinary morality. More refined classical opponents such as pagan philosopher Celsus, who felt that Greek philosophy had only won a purified view of divinity after hard struggles with classical mythology, charged that Christianity was a regression to fables about gods in human dress. Celsus also attacked the Christian doctrine (teaching) of the forgiveness of sins, arguing that it encouraged immorality. In response the apologists tried to clarify Christian teaching and ethics, interpret scripture allegorically, and show how the Logos purified the best of Greek philosophical thought. Fathers such as Clement praised the inspiration of Greek thinkers, while the Latin Father Tertullian advanced beyond Platonic cosmology, in which divinity stayed within the world, to a doctrine of creation from nothingness.

Ante-Nicene Doctrine

Through its apologetics, second-century Christianity clarified its differences with Judaism and classical Greco-Roman thought. Increasingly, its own faith, whose pivot was the decisive revelation of Christ, determined its interpretation of both Scripture and philosophy. The contrast between Gospel and Law led Christians to think that their religion had begun a new phase of human history, but internal problems forced the Church to sharpen its own law. Against Marcionists, as we mentioned, the Church had to defend its Old Testament heritage. Against Montanists (second century) it had also to control a Christian prophecy and subordinate it to ecclesiastical leadership, for Montanists claimed direct inspiration from the Holy Spirit. To combat such claims, Church leaders began the process that we now call **canonization**. As deviants picked over Scripture, tossing out what did not fit their predilections, Church bishops reached a rough consensus as to which writings made up the "rule" (*canon*) of faith. For example, Marcion relied only on certain Pauline and Lukan writings. In rebutting him, Church leaders raised the status of the other synoptic Gospels and John.

During the second century, salvation was a central theme. While churches that expected the end of history were on the wane, as it became clearer that the Second Coming was delayed, Gnostic groups offered elaborate systems of redemption based on secret knowledge.[2] The Church's response to these Gnostic groups was to stress not only the historical life of Jesus but also its own sacramental means of grace. Irenaeus was the early Father who did most extensive battle with the Gnostics, and his language suggests that it was often hard to clarify the differences between true believers and heretics. For example, Irenaeus said that "to follow the Savior is to participate in salvation, and to follow the light is to perceive the light."[3] Gnostics could have used much the same terminology. It was crucial, therefore, to define the salvation Jesus brought as the removal of Adam's sin and the imparting of divine life. Similarly, it was crucial to show that the light of Christian illumination (baptism), given by Christ's Spirit, reinforced the chain of apostolic teaching.

The Gnostics' basic error, in the eyes of the orthodox, was their aversion from the given world of matter, sex, and history. By placing salvation in an elitist insight into the human spirit's supposed destiny (to return to the good God who had made it and escape the evil powers that detained it in matter), the Gnostics denied both the biblical understanding of creation and the Christian understanding that Jesus was the privileged revelation of divinity. A group called the **Monarchists** also earned the ire of the orthodox by failing to give Jesus, the Incarnate Son, his due. The Monarchists, who flourished in the second and third centuries, so stressed the unity (monarchy) of the divine substance that they seemed to deny the independent reality of the Son. They said that Jesus was God only in the sense that a divine power rested on him from the Father. The subgroup of Monarchists called Sabellians denied the differences within the Trinity in such a way that they made the Father suffer in Jesus's passion. This was abhorrent to the orthodox. The orthodox held that divinity could not suffer, and that Jesus's suffering (in his humanity) was the very anchor of salvation that fixed it in the real world of space and time.

By the fourth century, Christians had organized salvation in terms of Christ's life and teachings, sufferings and death, and resurrection and exaltation. They held that by his life and teachings Christ had revealed the truth that saves human beings from sin and death; by his sufferings and death he had brought forgiveness of sins and justification; by his resurrection and exaltation he had given human beings immortality and deification. These themes grew more and more interrelated. Though they all had a basis in the New Testament, and most of them also were foreshadowed in the Hebrew Bible, the (largely Greek) rumination to which they were subjected in the second and third centuries sharpened them considerably. For example, Christ's victory over all the powers hostile to humanity gained great prominence. Indeed, historian Jaroslav Pelikan suggests that modern Western Christians have to work hard to appreciate what power Christ's victory used to carry:

> Yet when a modern Western Christian turns to the Christian writers of the second and third centuries for their understanding of salvation in Christ, it is neither their attention to the teachings and example of Christ, (which he may, rather superficially, identify with that of Protestant liberalism) nor their preoccupation with the passion and death of Christ (which he may, with some justification, see as an ancestor of the orthodox doctrine of vicarious atonement), but their emphasis on the saving significance of the resurrection of Christ that he will find most unusual. So great was that emphasis in the soteriology [theory of salvation] of many church fathers that the definition of salvation through Christ's victory over man's enemies has been called "the classic" theory of the atonement.[4]

Using our imaginations, we can see that such a stress on Christ's victory would have underscored Christian freedom. Celebrating together, Christians would have rehearsed the liberation—from sin, for divine life—that made Jesus a glad tiding. Against the manifest forces of evil, they would have raised the banner of the One who had defeated the Prince of Devils. Against human mortality, they would have sung songs to the One who was "the first and the last, and the living one; I died, and behold I am alive forever more, and I have the keys of Death and Hades" (Rev. 1:17–18). The victory Christ had won was all-pervasive. For the philosophically-minded, it went to the core of the human condition, overturning what had been a nearly unavoidable frustration.

Insofar as the Church was the great ark of salvation, Church unity bulked large among the early Fathers. Ignatius and Cyprian, for example, both laid great stress on keeping communion with the local bishop, and sound doctrine was critically important, for wrong faith closed the doors of grace. Thus Tertullian, arguing against Marcion, claimed that his heretical followers would receive none of the gifts of baptism: neither remission of sins, nor deliverance from death, nor regeneration (in divine life), nor the bestowal of the Holy Spirit.[5]

It is important to remember that the theme of salvation dominated the first Christian centuries; otherwise neither the fierce battles with heretics nor the great dogmatic councils make much sense. The Fathers thought that only correct faith (*ortho-doxy*) kept one joined to the Body of Christ, which was the sole font of salvation. As we turn to the cardinal dogmas of the Trinity, the Incarnation, and grace, salvation does not lose this urgency. What one confessed about the Father, or the Logos, or the work of the Spirit remained the pith of human success or failure.[6]

Post-Nicene Doctrine

Between 325 and 451 there were four major Church councils (assemblies of bishops) that to this day retain a special dignity: Nicaea (325), Constantinople (381), Ephesus (431), and Chalcedon (451). The Council of Nicaea was convened to deal with the teachings of the dissident priest Arius about the relation of the Logos to the Father. The creed that Nicaea produced became the touchstone of orthodoxy. The Council of Constantinople clarified the status of the Holy Spirit; the Council of Ephesus developed the Nicene Creed to answer new Christological questions that had arisen; and the Council of Chalcedon promulgated the dogma that Christ is one person in two natures. None of these councils settled the controversy with which it dealt, but each was a further articulation of patristic faith.

The councils of Nicaea and Constantinople focused on the Trinity. The starting point of their discussions was the traditional view that Christ was divine. For example, the oldest surviving Christian sermon originating after the New Testament began with the words: "Brethren, we ought so to think of Jesus Christ as of God, as of the judge of the living and the dead. And we ought not to belittle our salvation; for when we belittle him, we expect also to receive little."[7] The question, however, was whether such liturgical identification of Jesus with God could stand up to hard analysis. Wanting to be monotheists, yet also wanting to respect the scriptural differences between Father, Son, and Spirit, the early Christians cast about for a trinitarian theory. Against the force of Arius's teaching that the Logos was not of the same substance as the Father, a majority of the Nicene Fathers rallied behind the bishop Athanasius and confessed it as traditional faith that the Logos was indeed of the same substance as the Father.

The matter was a good deal more complicated than that, of course, since neither Scripture nor earlier tradition had spoken with a single voice. Jesus manifestly was a human being (despite the claims of some heretics that he only appeared to be human), so the question of how his divinity and humanity related remained on the conciliar agenda. Before the councils at Ephesus and Chalcedon took it up, the Council of Constantinople had the task of filling out the Nicene trinitarian doctrine by confessing the Holy Spirit to be consubstantial with the Father, as the Son was. Mysteriously, the One God was a Trinity of "Persons." Father, Son, and Spirit were not three different deities, nor just three different names for the same single divine nature. Son and Father, for example, were not identical, because Jesus clearly had distinguished himself from the Father. On the other hand, Son and Father were thoroughly united, for one who saw the Son saw the Father (John 14:9). So too with the Spirit, whom the Gospel of John showed to be thoroughly united with both the Son and the Father. Further, the traditional formula for baptism used the name of all three persons, showing that Christian faith confessed salvation to come from union with the precisely triune God.

Searching Scripture, liturgical practice, and their deepest instincts of faith (and responding to the political pressures of the emperors), the Fathers of Nicaea and Constantinople concluded that any positions detracting from the co-divinity of the three Persons were unorthodox. The ultimate power that made things be, the power of salvation and holiness, was the community of interpersonal relations revealed by Jesus's speech and religious experience. When further controversies developed over how to understand Jesus Christ himself, the Nicene conviction about Jesus being of the same substance as the Father served orthodoxy as a firm foundation. If Jesus had been defined to be of the same substance with God in order to save his divinity, then defining him to be of the same substance with us human beings ought to save his humanity.

Beyond that, the problem was how to conceive the union of Jesus's divinity and humanity. With different terminological accents, a group called the **Nestorians**, and followers of Cyril, bishop of Alexandria, tried to make the divine Logos the locus and source of union. All sides presupposed that divinity could not change, but orthodoxy came to accept that one could predicate things like birth and death of the Logos because of his intimate union with humanity from Mary. The doctrine that called Mary the God-bearer therefore was a crucial issue, but the major resolution of the Chalcedonian controversy came when Pope Leo I gave the formula "one person in two natures." The ultimate person of Jesus Christ was the Logos, but this did not detract from Jesus's full humanity. When later councils clarified how Jesus had a rational soul and a human will, they carried Leo's balanced formula to its logical conclusion.

In addition to such trinitarian and christological discussion, which mainly took place in the Greek-speaking East, the fourth century also witnessed discussions about freedom and grace, especially in the Latin-speaking West. Augustine was the outstanding figure in these discussions, so we shall postpone our treatment of them until we come to our sketch of Augustine. Suffice it to say that they, too, were not academic controversies but robust arguments about the very heart of salvation, for whether grace was gratuitous, and how it was channeled through the Church, struck to the heart of Christian life.

Establishment

For the first three centuries Christianity led a shaky existence, always subject to Roman persecution. The emperors Nero, Decius, and Diocletian attacked Christianity as a danger to Roman culture, which they thought centered around Roman religion. Thus Decius revived the office of the Roman censor and ordered all inhabitants of the empire to sacrifice to one of the Roman gods in the emperor's behalf. Christians felt that their consciences forbade such sacrifice, but they were divided over how to respond. Many Christians purchased certificates falsely testifying that they had offered sacrifices, but this outraged staunch resisters. After Decius died in 251 the Church had stormy battles over how to deal with those who had compromised.

Emperor Constantine gave the Christians civil peace. In the process of becoming ruler of the Western empire in 312, he had had a vision that led him to put the cross on his standards. In 313 he proclaimed toleration for Christians and began patronizing the Church. The sole emperor after 323, Constantine was convinced that Christianity offered the best basis for unifying his empire. Consequently he took a lively interest in the Council of Nicaea, approving the condemnation of Arianism in the East and **Donatism** in the West. (Donatism held a rigorist position against the readmission of Christians who had lapsed during the persecution of Diocletian.) He recentered Byzantium in Constantinople, rededicated the emperor's churches at Jerusalem, and was seen by church leaders such as Eusebius as a thirteenth apostle. Upon Constantine's death in 337, his sons Constans and Constantius began to support the Catholic and Arian parties respectively. Constantius outlasted Constans, but he in turn was outlasted by Julian, who produced a short-term revival of paganism.

Valentinian I, Western emperor from 364–375, was himself a Christian and restored a policy of toleration. Pope Damasus used such toleration to fuse the old Roman civic and imperial pride with Christianity.

> The rich adornment which Damasus lavished on martyrs' shrines and the stress on the founding apostles asserted a claim that the real glory of Rome was not pagan but Christian. In one epigram which reflects East-West tension during

> the Arian controversy, Damasus remarked that "although the East sent the apostles, yet because of the merit of their martyrdom Rome has acquired a superior right to claim them as citizens." Under the potent patronage of the apostles who were intimate with Christ, the city could be assured of security and of a more lasting grandeur than the old gods had conferred. It is characteristic that Damasus is the first known Pope to speak of Rome as 'the apostolic see' [center of power].[8]

The relation of imperial and ecclesiastical powers troubled Christianity almost from the time of Constantine. In addition, ecclesiastical power itself was distributed among Rome and the four patriarchal (fatherly) sees of the East: Alexandria, Antioch, Constantinople, and Jerusalem.

Based on its understanding of the role of the apostles in the New Testament Church, the Church of the early centuries lay great stress on the succession of the bishops from the apostles. A special dignity attached to the bishop of Rome, who was thought to have succeeded to the office that Peter, Jesus's prime apostle, had held. As the Church came to base its institutional structure on the organization of the Roman Empire, the bishop of Rome (called the pope) became its most powerful figure. Although Pope Leo the Great (440–461) asserted the universal episcopate of the Roman bishop successfully, he admitted that the Greek emperor was invested with not only secular but also priestly rule, in which latter capacity the Holy Spirit preserved the emperor from doctrinal error.

Later popes such as Gelasius and Gregory the Great clearly recognized the authority of the emperor in temporal matters, but a dramatic conflict between the two powers occurred in 390 when Ambrose, bishop of Milan, successfully required the emperor Theodosius to do penance for massacring thousands of citizens at a circus in Thessalonica. After this capitulation, Theodosius supported imperial policies opposed to heretical Christianity.

Between 300 and 500 C.E., therefore, Christianity established itself as the predominant religious force in the Roman Empire. Although rent by division, especially between the Orthodox and the Arians, Christianity grew from being the adherence of a significant minority to being the faith of the empire's power-bearers. Even the Germanic tribes that overthrew Rome in the fifth century were Arian Christians, and from Britain to Palestine the cross marched at the head of Christian troops.

Probably the Church never recovered from this hurly-burly plunge into power. Something of the cosmological myth (the placing of divinity within the cosmos) revived in the veneration accorded the first Christian emperors, and something all too human showed in the zeal with which prelates like Ambrose fought for the Church's privileges. For example, in 388 Ambrose used his episcopal powers to prevent the emperor from forcing Christians in Callincum on the Euphrates to make restitution for having burned a synagogue. The temporal power to which the Church gained access in the fourth century was a heady brew. Throughout the Middle Ages the monarchical model of this power greatly influenced the papacy, taking it far from the New Testament model of service. On the other hand, the establishment of Christianity as the dominant religion of the Roman Empire, east and west, laid a foundation for Christian culture. Thinking itself part of the imperial order, Christianity had to take new responsibility for political, educational, and artistic institutions. This responsibility deepened Christian incarnationalism.

Monasticism

Polar to the Church's increasing influence in the Roman Empire was an **ascetic** movement designed to offset Christians' worldliness. During the second century some individuals in local communities had renounced marriage, embraced poverty, and devoted themselves to prayer and works of mercy. As Christianity grew, this ascetic ideal threatened to make a split-level Church. Impatient with worldly life, numerous ascetics withdrew to concentrate on spiritual perfection fulltime. Although many bishops viewed such a withdrawal with suspicion, the ascetics gained the support of some influential theologians, who began to adapt the theology of martyrdom to justify a life of contemplative witnessing. Early in the fourth century Antony and Pachomius, Egyptian ascetics, furnished the monastic movement two striking role models. Pachomius started a community along the Nile at Tabennisi that was devoted to manual labor and strict obedience to a superior. Antony became a celebrity due to Athanasius's biography of him, which pictured him as a Christian warrior in combat with the demons. As a prudent bishop, Athanasius took pains to show Antony's devotion to orthodoxy. Relatedly, a synod of bishops who convened at Gangra in Asia Minor in about 340 expressed disapproval of monks who separated themselves from church attendance and the sacraments.

In the middle of the fourth century, Basil, bishop of Caesarea, wrote a rule that stressed monks' union with the bishop. According to Church historian Henry Chadwick,

> [Basil's] principle of episcopal control worked admirably as long as the bishop was good. But within thirty years of Basil's death the bishop of Caesarea was using his monks to terrorize the city militia when it was protecting the exiled John Chrysostom [an eminent Greek bishop]. In Egypt the successors of Athanasius did not take long to discover that a force of peasant monks was an ideal instrument for destroying pagan temples and for conflicts with heresy. To the second and third generation of the monastic movement it was clear that the ascetic life had special problems of its own. It might easily provide a home for people wanting to contract out of responsibilities in civil society, for those bankrupted by oppressive taxation, sometimes for criminals on the run, sometimes for homosexuals, rather more often for people with compulsions to make some striking gesture and urges to be self-assertive in their mortifications. It was always likely, even at its best, to be a movement dependent upon striking leaders and personalities.[9]

Through Basil's rule in the East, and Saint Benedict's rule in the West, monasticism gained more control over the personalities it attracted. From the fifth century many communities of monks and nuns supported themselves by manual labor, leading prayerful lives centered on the liturgy. Through their vows of poverty, chastity, and obedience, these ascetics developed what later came to be known as *religious life*. With adaptations in later times, especially the thirteenth and sixteenth centuries, religious life furnished the Church many of its most understanding saints, teachers, and ministers.

Thomas Merton, a twentieth-century Trappist monk, has edited a collection of sayings that convey something of the piety of the early ascetics. Many of these sayings amount to a dialogue or interview between a novice and his teacher. Like similar conversations between a Buddhist disciple and his guru, these dialogues strain with implications. Since the desert monastery was steeped in silence, each word from the spiritual father flew like an arrow to the heart. Consider this brief exchange between Abbot Pambo and Abbot Antony, reported by Merton: "Abbot Pambo questioned Abbot Antony saying: What ought I to do? And the elder replied: Have no confidence in your own virtuousness. Do not worry about a thing once it has been done. Control your tongue and your belly."[10]

How ordinary the message appears. The great ascetic hero Antony merely says to be humble, not to have scruples, and to live in silence and fasting. His regime is bare as the Egyptian desert, stark as the fight between good and evil, ruthlessly simple. There is nothing specifically Christian in this saying. One sees why bishops might worry about a depreciation of Christ and the sacraments. On the other hand, one sees how strong an antidote the ascetics offered a Church tempted to worldly accommodation. So long as Christian heroes lived in silence and fasting, Jesus's words about John the Baptist would echo well: "What did you go out into the wilderness to behold? A reed shaken by the wind? Why then did you go out? To see a man clothed in soft raiment? Behold, those who wear soft raiment are in kings' houses. Why then did you go out? To see a prophet? Yes, I tell you, and more than a prophet" (Matt. 11:7–9).

A saying of Abbot Pastor's shows the freedom or mystery in the wisdom of the desert fathers: "If there are three monks living together, of whom one remains silent in prayer at all times, and another is ailing and gives thanks for it, and the third waits on them both with sincere good will, these three are equal, as if they were performing the same work."[11] In the psychic space of the desert, any work could become a way to perfection. Perfection was loving God utterly, loving one's neighbor as oneself. Perfection was humility and deep faith. Layer after layer, monks peeled their pride like an onion. Level after level, they pursued a deeper gratitude and peace. From their ardent religious lives the early Church gained a great storehouse of experiential wisdom.

Athanasius

Perhaps the quintessential Eastern Father, in whom the doctrinal, political, and spiritual themes of the first four centuries find a natural convergence, was Athanasius, bishop of Alexandria. Born about 296 C.E. in Alexandria, he became the great champion of Nicene orthodoxy, fighting the Arians steadfastly until his death in Alexandria in 373. From his *Life of St. Antony* it appears that Athanasius had contacts with monks of the upper Nile valley, the cradle of Christian monasticism, during his youth. He was educated in the catechetical school of Alexandria, which numbered the theologians Clement and Origen among its assembly of past great teachers.

Athanasius was ordained a deacon in 319, and he served Alexander, bishop of Alexandria, as his deacon and secretary during the Council of Nicaea in 325. It was Alexander who had excommunicated Arius in 321, so Athanasius knew the Arian controversy intimately from its outset. He gained considerable renown during the debates of Nicaea, and in 328 he succeeded Alexander as bishop of Alexandria. Athanasius served in this capacity for the next forty-five years, five times being exiled on account of his Nicene orthodoxy. His life therefore renders almost too concrete the historian's commonplace observation that conciliar theology mingled inextricably with imperial politics.

Specifically, Athanasius was first exiled by the emperor Constantine, after the Synod of Tyre (335) had deposed him from his episcopal seat because of his refusal to restore Arius to communion with the Church. When Constantine died in 337 Athanasius returned to Alexandria, but he was deposed again by a Synod in Antioch (339) and had to flee to Rome. Although the Council of Sardica (ca. 343) sought his restoration, the emperor Constantius would not grant it until the death of the Arian bishop Gregory, who had been installed in Athanasius's place. At Constantius's behest the Synod of Milan deposed Athanasius again, and this time he fled to the Egyptian desert and took refuge with the monks. At the accession of the emperor Julian in 361 Athanasius returned to Alexandria, but Julian forced him into exile again until 363. His last exile was but a brief four-month span in 365, apart from which he served as bishop of Alexandria, and leader of the Nicene party, until his death in 373. Largely because of Athanasius's theological and organizational abilities, the Nicene party won a resounding victory at the Council of Constantinople in 381, making his name practically synonymous with trinitarian orthodoxy.

Despite his many flights into exile, and his deep immersion in ecclesiastico-imperial politics, Athanasius found time for a goodly quantity of writing. By 318 he had written two short works, *Contra Gentes* and *De Incarnatione*. *Contra Gentes* is an apologetic piece concerned with showing the folly of pagan worship and the truth of monotheism. *De Incarnatione* focuses on the redemption, emphasizing that when the Logos took flesh he restored the image of God lost in Adam's fall. In later polemical writings against the Arians, Athanasius defended the Nicene doctrine of the divinity of the Father and the Son. In letters to other bishops or his flock, he defended the divinity of the Holy Spirit and gave orthodox interpretations of controversial scriptural passages. His thirty-ninth Festal Letter, written for Easter of 367, is important because it is the earliest listing of the twenty-seven canonical books of the New Testament in the order that since has become standard.

Theologically, Athanasius's greatest contribution was to bring Hellenistic reason to Christianity's efforts to understand its faith in the God-Man. Opposing both

Arian **rationalism** and biblical **fundamentalism**, Athanasius paved the way for the catholic position that faith and reason can dovetail. Reason cannot plumb the mysteries of faith, such as the Trinity and the Incarnation, but it can defend them from the charge of irrationality. Religiously, Athanasius probably made his greatest impact through his *Life of St. Antony*, which championed Egyptian monasticism. The *Life* was composed in 357, the year after Antony's death (supposedly at the age of 106). It was designed more to present Antony as a model Christian than to furnish the historical details of his life. Athanasius wrote from firsthand acquaintance with Antony, setting the saint's renowned holiness in the service of Nicene orthodoxy. A high point in the *Life* is the moment when Antony comes out of solitude, at the appeal of the orthodox bishops, to preach against Arianism: "He said that their heresy was the worst of all and a forerunner of the Antichrist. He taught the people that the Son of God is not a creature nor has He come into being 'from nonexistence' but He is the eternal Word and Wisdom of the substance of the Father."[12]

Athanasius goes on to picture Antony's warfare with the demons, stressing how his sound doctrine and humble reliance on God won the day. Perhaps Athanasius's own warfare with emperors and heretics made Antony's spiritual combat especially intriguing. In any case, here as elsewhere Athanasius is "the compleat Greek father," vigilant for the defense of traditional faith and morals. Conceiving all his labors as being in the service of Christian salvation, he distinguished little between theological and pastoral works.

Augustine

To introduce its short article on Augustine, *The Westminster Dictionary of Church History* simply says: "The most influential of the Fathers of the Western Church."[13] He was born in 354 and died in 430, spending most of his life in northern Africa. Although his mother Monnica was a devout Christian and he received instruction as a catechumen (one approaching faith), the young Augustine never was baptized. Indeed, for thirty years he struggled with problems of faith, as his famous *Confessions* relates. Trained as a rhetorician, Augustine was attracted to **Manicheanism**, whose principal teaching was the duality of good and evil. He took a mistress, fathered a son, and journeyed to Rome. By turns he was weaned away from Manicheanism and attracted to **Neoplatonism**, which stressed the mind's participation in divine light, beauty, and goodness. Coming to Milan as a professor in 384, Augustine was inspired by the preaching of Ambrose and in 386 experienced a full, mystical conversion to Christianity. He was baptized in 387 and returned to Africa in 388 to form a semi-monastic community. In 391 the people of Hippo, on the African coast, prevailed upon him to be ordained a presbyter, and in 395 he was consecrated a bishop. For the remaining thirty-five years of his life he was the bishop of Hippo—pastor, preacher, administrator, theologian, and the dominant figure at the councils of the African church.

Augustine's early writings were philosophical and apologetic in tone, stemming as they did from his personal involvement with Manicheanism and Neoplatonism. After his ordination he was preoccupied with the Donatist controversy, which absorbed the whole African church. Whereas the Donatists conceived of the Church as purely a communion of saints, Augustine conceived of the Church as a worldwide catholic communion. He also recognized the validity of the sacraments of separatist Christians, further qualifying the sanctity required for Church ministry. From early in his own ministry Augustine concerned himself with scriptural exegesis, not only for his controversial work but also for regular preaching.

The three mature works for which Augustine is most famous are the *Confessions*, the *City of God*, and *On the Trinity*. As Jaroslav Pelikan has said, "Any theologian who would have written either the *Confessions* or the *City of God* or *On the Trinity* would have to be counted a major figure in intellectual history. Augustine wrote them all, and vastly more. He was a universal genius."[14] The *Confessions*, written shortly before 400 C.E., were an amazing leap into "modern" subjectivity. Largely from his own creativity, Augustine probed the center of his self and religious journey, drawing an incomparable portrait of the soul struggling for faith. The famous incident of the pears renders both Augustine's rhetorical style and his near-fixation with the enslavement of the faithless will:

> A pear tree there was near our vineyard, laden with fruit, tempting neither for colour nor taste. To shake and rob this, some lewd young fellows of us went, late one night . . . and took huge loads, not for our eating, but to fling to the very hogs, having only tasted them. And this, but to do what we liked only, because it was misliked. Behold my heart, O God, behold my heart, which Thou hadst pity upon in the bottom of the bottomless pit. Now, behold let my heart tell Thee what it sought there, that I should be gratuitously evil, having no temptation to ill, but the ill itself. It was foul, and I loved it; I loved to perish, I loved mine own fault, not that for which I was faulty, but my fault itself.[15]

The *City of God* is an immense work written to defend Christianity against the charge that it was responsible for the decay of the Roman Empire. What began as an apologetics became a full theology of history centered on the conflict between the true love of God and the false love of self. The Church and the empire were visible expressions of these two disparate loves, but they would be mixed inseparably until the Final Judgment. Until the seventeenth century the *City of God* gave Western historiography its basic pattern.

On the Trinity made an enormous contribution to Western trinitarian theory through its close analyses of human knowing and loving, which came to be the prime analogies for the processions of the Son and the Spirit. Although written to contest Arian trinitarian theory that had come to Africa with Germanic soldiers, it became a formative influence on medieval theology.

The topic that dominated Augustine's final years was grace, the gratuity of salvation. In part he was drawn to grace by his own sense of having been freed from an enslaved will gratis. In part he was forced to deal with it because of **Pelagianism**.

Pelagius was a British monk who stressed human freedom and responsibility. To Augustine's mind he compromised God's freedom to save whom He willed. Of course there was a great mystery in predestination, but certainly the priority in salvation always remained with God, whose love alone could save human beings. The rest of the Church tended to reject Augustine's doctrine of "double predestination," according to which God actively assigned saints their heavenly destinies and sinners their hellish ones, but it stood with him in insisting on the gratuity of Christ's work. Thus the Council of Orange (529), drawing largely on Augustine's writings, expressed what became the normative Western view: God's help must begin the work of salvation and carry it through, but all persons have sufficient grace for salvation and none are lost except through their own fault.

Summary

At the turn of the first century, the Christian Church had most of the present New Testament writings, with the mosaic of theologies and organizational structures they suggest. Church intellectuals next addressed themselves to apologetics: trying to show that Jesus fulfilled Jewish prophecy and bested pagan wisdom. In their doctrinal battles with Christian heretics, the Fathers were driven by the conviction that salvation depended on both right faith and communion with the Church. Either heresy or schism could endanger salvation. The four great councils held between 325 and 451 focused this concern for salvation on the dogmas of the Trinity and Christology. By the close of the Council of Chalcedon, the orthodox had the foundations of their theology firmly laid down.

Politically, the fourth century brought an end to persecution by Roman authorities and the beginnings of imperial patronage. Although Arians and Catholics still fought fiercely, martyrdom became quite rare. The rise of monasticism at the end of the third century supplied fervent Christians an alternative to martyrdom. Insofar as the monastic movement has shaped seventeen centuries of subsequent spirituality, its rise has proved to be momentous. Indeed, the bishop Athanasius, who epitomized Eastern orthodox faith in the fourth century, was prophetic in fusing monastic fervor and Nicene faith. The late fourth- and early fifth-century bishop Augustine, who tutored Western Christianity in grace, cast Nicene faith and monastic spirituality into a grand intellectual vision that molded medievals and reformers equally. Further councils in the fifth and sixth centuries dotted the i's and crossed the t's of these bishops' faith, so that by 600 the Church was quite well defined.

Study Questions

1. Why were the early apologists forced to allegorical or spiritual interpretations of Scripture?
2. What tenor did the notion of Christ's victory give patristic faith?

3. In what sense does the Nicene doctrine of the Trinity assume that God is too full for us to understand?
4. Did the Christian emperors of the fourth century reinsert Christianity into the cosmological myth? How?
5. What psychodynamics could Christian monasticism hold in common with Buddhism?
6. How does our brief sketch of Athanasius's career present the office of the bishop in the patristic era?
7. Why would Augustine have fought so vehemently for the gratuity of grace?

Notes

1. Jaroslav Pelikan, *The Christian Tradition, Vol. 1: The Emergence of the Catholic Tradition (100–600)* (Chicago: University of Chicago Press, 1971), p. 14. Reprinted by permission.
2. See Elaine Pagels, *The Gnostic Gospels* (New York: Random House, 1979), and Pheme Perkins, *The Gnostic Dialogue* (Ramsey, NJ: Paulist, 1980).
3. Irenaeus, *Against Heresies* 4.14.1.
4. Pelikan, op. cit., p. 149. Reprinted by permission.
5. Tertullian, *Against Marcion* 1.28.2.
6. See Robert C. Gregg and Dennis E. Groh, "The Centrality of Soteriology in Early Arianism," *Anglican Theological Review*, LIX/3 (July 1977), 260–278. We owe this reference to our colleague Gregory Robbins.
7. *II Clement* 1:1–2.
8. Henry Chadwick, *The Early Church* (Pelican Books, 1967), p. 163. Copyright © 1967 by Henry Chadwick. Reprinted by permission of Penguin Books Ltd.
9. Ibid., pp. 179–180. Reprinted by permission.
10. Thomas Merton, *The Wisdom of the Desert* (New York: New Directions, 1960), p. 25.
11. Ibid., pp. 42–43.
12. Quoted in Johannes Quasten, *Patrology, Vol. III: The Golden Age of Greek Patristic Literature* (Westminster, MD: The Newman Press, 1960), p. 41.
13. Ed. Jerald C. Brauer (Philadelphia: Westminster, 1971), p. 72.
14. Ibid., p. 292.
15. Augustine, *The Confessions of Saint Augustine*, trans. E. B. Pusey (London: Collier-Macmillan, 1961), Book 2, pp. 30–31.

CHAPTER 8

Medieval Christianity (600–1300)

The Eastern Tradition

We begin our overview of medieval Christianity by taking stock of the deposit of faith that had accrued in the East by the beginning of the seventh century. In his famous history of dogma, German Protestant scholar Adolf von Harnack put forth the opinion that dogma in the Greek Church stopped evolving in the seventh century.[1] Perhaps the first thing we should note is that Greek patristic theology, which had been the matrix of the majority of conciliar developments, would have quarreled bitterly with Harnack's view and with its underlying assumption that stability was a token of lifelessness. To the leading proponents of classical Greek theology, orthodox doctrine had been changeless from the beginning. Rooted in the changeless God, it at most had unfolded new implications, as new situations turned it to new angles of God's saving light. In the words of the Latin Vincent of Lerins (fifth century), orthodox faith was what had been believed "everywhere, always, and by all."[2]

Nonetheless, the apparent changelessness of Greek doctrine cloaks considerable historical movement. Although the patriarchs and monks of the Byzantine part of the Eastern empire generally were a bulwark of conservatism, Byzantine theology (unlike Western theology until the Renaissance) included an educated laity who perforce were in touch with many socio-political changes. The impact of Islam, which arose in Arabia in the seventh century, forced Greek theologians to sharpen their apologetic arguments in favor of Christian revelation, while the persistence of christological controversies after the Council of Chalcedon meant further reflection on the union of the Logos with a humanity fully conscious and voluntary. To speak of the "ahistorical character" of Greek theology therefore requires some distinctions.

Inasmuch as the Greek Fathers thought orthodox doctrine came from God, it was one and the same from the beginning. The truths of Scripture, the Nicene creed, or the consensus of the Fathers remained valid in all times and places. Thus Greek theologians could join authorities across several centuries and feel little need to note their differing historical contexts. On the other hand, whether they were fully aware of it or not, Greek theologians were constantly reinterpreting traditional teachings in the light of current circumstances. Whether those teachings were scriptural, creedal, conciliar, or patristic, the necessity to interpret imposed itself on even the most conservative traditionalists. Simply to keep pace with old notions in new circumstances, Greek theologians had to keep moving.

The central idea in the Eastern Christian tradition that had accrued at the beginning of the seventh century was deification. When the Greek fathers spoke of the Christian **economy**, they emphasized that the Logos had taken flesh so as to draw humanity into divinity. Thus the knowledge that came with Christian initiation was not an end in itself. However interior, however much the product of the illuminating Spirit, it was but an intermediate stage on the way to union with God. As the ultimate reality, God was beyond intellectual grasp. The communion of love gave light sufficient for holy living, but the divine light itself was so bright that for finite beings it was a great darkness. Thus the idea of deification was an almost ready-made foundation for a **mystical** theology like that of Dionysius the Areopagite, which exerted an enormous influence in the East after 500. To Dionysius, theological **mystagogy** (emphasis on mystery) transcended the dogmas formulated by the Church councils, and statements about what God is not were considered truer than statements about what God is. This was not to deprecate conciliar dogmas, but rather to keep them in proper perspective. To Dionysius, the God whose own life was the substance of salvation dwelt in inaccessible light, and Christians properly appreciative of salvation should be content to cling to the traditions that mediated it safely.

Thus Eastern Christianity came to a sense of the relation between faith and reason quite like that of Western Christianity. Faith, correlated with revelation, opened the human personality to truths beyond its natural capacity. An unknowing bounded all human knowing that was aware of its proper character. Still, it was right for human intelligence to try to grasp the divine mystery accessible to it. Maximus the Confessor (580–662), John of Damascus (675–749), and similar Greek luminaries agreed with Anselm of Canterbury (1033–1109) and the Western **Scholastics** that theology should be "faith seeking understanding." So long as understanding did not overreach itself, forgetting such scriptural warnings as "Seek not what is too difficult for you, nor investigate what is beyond your power" (Ecclus 3:21–22), it could serve faith well.

Another safeguard limiting theological speculation was what Eastern Christians called the Divine Liturgy. The worship of God was bound to be fuller than the study, since the worship included the obeisance and delight of all the senses. Nonetheless, the worship of God included the adoration of the mind. At the Divine Liturgy the mind turned to God's light, rehearsed the scriptural record of salvation

Byzantine book cover, Syria, sixth–seventh century C.E. Nelson Gallery–Atkins Museum, Kansas City, Missouri (Nelson Fund).

and confessed the creedal faith. It was true that the scriptural record of salvation adapted divine truth to the needs of limited human beings. It was true that revelation used figures and stories that in a sense were unworthy of God. But Scripture itself taught the believer to recognize this divine accommodation and so not to confuse what was said about salvation with God's inner being. The immanent life of the Trinity remained mysterious, but the economic life of salvation that the Trinity communicated through the incarnate Logos and the Church was available to all who faithfully attended on Scripture and the Liturgy.

Through the centuries of conciliar controversy, east and west, an important rule had been *lex orandi, lex credendi*: The law of liturgical prayer was the law of creedal faith. For example, in the controversies over Original Sin an important argument had been the ancient practice of baptizing infants for forgiveness. In the controversies over the divinity of the Holy Spirit an important argument had been the ancient practice of baptizing in the name of the Spirit, as well as the Father and the Son. Thus a keen sense of its faith as it had been lived kept early Church theology close to Scripture and liturgical tradition. Along with its sense of God's changelessness, the Eastern Church used Scripture, liturgical tradition, its notion of deification, mystical theology, and the prestige of the Fathers to generate a massive sense of continuing in the divine truth.

Iconography and Liturgy

Reverence for holy images (iconography) became deeply rooted in Greek piety in the fifth century, but in the eighth and ninth centuries theological controversy challenged Greek iconography. The theologians who emerged as the great defenders of icons, furnishing the traditional reverence a solid rationale, were John of Damascus, Theodore of Studios, and the patriarch Nicephorus. At the Second Council of Nicaea (787), they argued that images "of our God and Savior Jesus Christ, as well as that of our immaculate Lady, the Holy Mother of God, and those of the revered angels and of all the saints and holy men"[3] were appropriate to the dullness of the human body and pointed beyond themselves to their heavenly archetypes. Indeed, John of Damascus described an icon as "a triumph, a manifestation, and a monument" in commemoration of the victory of Christ and his followers over the demons.[4] Contrary to the iconoclasts, who destroyed images as idolatrous, these orthodox defenders denied that iconography encouraged the faithful to consider image and reality one. Image and reality were distinct, but so related that in the image one could venerate the imprint of the venerable archetype.

What was the motivation of the iconoclasts? They were influenced first by the **monophysites**, who had organized in the fifth century in opposition to the Christology defined at Chalcedon, and who tended to minimize the human side of the Incarnation, and so to cast a pall on the use of material elements in worship. Second, a group called the **Paulicians** that arose in the seventh century influenced the iconoclasts by their attraction to the Manichean notion that matter is evil. Third, some historians also see an influence from Islam, whose stark monotheism led to a prohibition on representational art.

The iconoclastic energies came together in the person of Emperor Leo III the Isaurian (ruled 717–740), who had been brought up under Paulician influence. He thought that the use of icons, which even sympathetic historians admit had become excessive, was the chief obstacle to the conversion of the Jews and Muslims. In 726 Leo published an edict declaring all images idols and ordering their destruction.

The reaction was uproarious. When the church patriarch Germanus appealed to the pope, Leo deposed Germanus and began a systematic persecution of the **iconodules** (reverers of icons), especially the steadfast monks. In 731 Pope Gregory III held two synods in Rome that condemned Leo and his supporters.

Leo's son Constantine V continued his father's iconoclastic policies. Under his patronage the Synod of Hieria (753) alleged that since an icon only represented the humanity of Christ, worshipping it either divided Christ's unity or confounded his two natures. Worse, worshipping icons of Mary or the saints was pure idolatry. Persecution grew even more intense, and a great many monks became martyrs in the cause of the icons. The Second Council of Nicaea (787) reversed the Synod of Hieria, defined the degree of veneration to be paid icons, and decreed their restoration. However, iconoclastic tendencies remained strong within the imperial army, and in 814 a second controversy broke out under Emperor Leo V the Armenian. The patriarch Nicephorus was deposed in 815 and the monk Theodore of Studios sent into exile. Persecution continued until 843, when the regent Irene had the monk Methodius elected patriarch and a great feast was celebrated in honor of the icons. Since that time the Eastern Church has kept "the Feast of Orthodoxy" on the first Sunday in Lent to commemorate this and other instances of the triumph of right faith.

The iconoclastic controversy had relatively little impact on the West, but the Liturgy was no less influential there. Attendance at mass, the sacraments, and other forms of public devotion was the way the common people took in their Christian doctrine and theology. The Mass looked back to the Last Supper of Jesus, which itself had the form of a Jewish passover meal. In fact, such stylized prayers as "the Lord be with you," "let us pray," and the people's affirmative response "amen" reflected the usage of the synagogue. The special emphasis of the medieval Mass in the West was the sacrifice that Jesus had made on Calvary. While the opening prayers, scriptural readings, and sermon provided for a full rehearsal of the New Testament message, the high point was the moment of consecration, when the priest pronounced the words "this is my body" and "this is my blood" to change the bread and wine into Jesus's own substance. Medieval sacramental theology read this change (**transubstantiation**) in view of Jesus's giving himself on the cross to redeem human sins.

Thus all the color and sound of medieval liturgy, its gorgeous vestments and lovely Gregorian chant, embellished a central fixation on Jesus's death. Western medieval Christians knew that Jesus had risen from the dead, but their great symbol of God's love was Jesus's death on the cross. This outlook influenced the other sacraments, making the whole system quite sober. Thus baptism was taking the child from the domain of Satan to a life of Christ that would only be joyous after death, penance was trying to cleanse the soul so that it could avoid consignment to hell at death, and the other sacraments were mainly helps through a lifetime conceived as a vale of tears.

Since the second century the Church had celebrated Easter each year, and since the fourth century, when peace had come under Constantine, the Latin liturgy had assumed a public character and formal garments, in many cases simply adopting secular customs. For example, since public officials were preceded by candles and incense on solemn occasions, candles and incense became customary during liturgical solemnities. Several geographically distinct liturgical rites of the catholic Church arose in the fourth and fifth centuries. Greek rites prevailed in the East, Latin rites in the West, and the vernacular in the cluster of areas dominated by Antioch (in Syria).

It was in the sixth and seventh centuries that the Latin or Roman rite came to full development. From the eighth century, often under monastic influence, the Roman rite became quite elaborate. Since many of the laity did not understand Latin, liturgists developed an allegorical interpretation of the actions of the Mass. The formal liturgy also expressed the many different ranks in the Church (bishops, canons, monks, priests, and more), contributing greatly to the Church's increasingly hierarchical self-image. From the thirteenth century the elevation of the host and chalice at the consecration became the climax of the Mass, for by then sacramental communion was rarely permitted, due to an excessive sense of God's distance from human beings.[5]

The East-West Schism

The liturgical differences between East and West, illustrated by the East's iconoclast controversy, were but one expression of an increasing cultural separation, or **schism**. Although this separation became explicitly schismatic with the mutual excommunications of 1054, and irreparable with the Crusaders' vengeful destruction of the Byzantine Empire, which covered most of present-day Greece and Turkey, in 1204, division had been growing for many centuries. Certainly the language gap between the Greeks and the Latins was an important factor, for even in such central doctrinal matters as the Trinity and Christology it caused misunderstandings. Equally important, however, was the political rivalry between Rome and Constantinople, the two poles of the Christian empire. During the Acacian Schism of 484–518 the Roman see had pressed claims to primacy on the basis of its having been founded by the apostle Peter. Significantly, however, it went on to add the further claim that its ecclesiastical power was superior to the secular power of the emperor. The Byzantine branch of Christendom directly opposed these claims, resulting in Rome fighting the rule of the emperor Justinian and Pope Hormisdas refusing to attend the Second Council of Constantinople in 553.

The Sixth Ecumenical Council (680) reestablished peace between the Byzantine Empire and Rome, but continued papal claims to ecclesiastical supremacy made the peace uneasy. In 691 the emperor Justinian II summoned a council that met in the imperial banquet hall in Constantinople and passed canons (for example, prohibiting Saturday fast and permitting priests to marry) that flew in the face of

Roman practices. Pope Sergius rejected these canons, as well as a more offensive one giving the patriarch of Constantinople status equal to the pope. Justinian attempted to enforce the canons by having Sergius arrested and brought to Constantinople, but he was thwarted by the Roman populace.

Other acts of antagonism followed on both sides. The West dealt with the iconoclast controversy clumsily, and Pope Leo III offended Byzantium's imperial sensibilities when he crowned Charlemagne emperor in 800. In the mid-ninth century the Photian Schism further aggravated the hard feelings. In 858 the emperor Michael deposed the patriarch Ignatius and appointed Photius, a learned layman. Ignatius was a bitter opponent of the iconoclasts, Photius was more moderate. Pope Nicolas (858–867) annulled the consecration of Photius and reinstated Ignatius. His major motive, however, was pique over a previous failure to secure jurisdiction over Bulgaria, which had been more Eastern than Western. In the midst of further maneuverings over Bulgaria, Photius convoked a council in Constantinople in 867, condemned the Latin mission to Bulgaria, and also condemned the *filioque* clause as a heretical addition to the Nicene Creed. When the eleventh-century German popes formally introduced the *filioque* into the creed, and Pope Sergius included it in a letter written to Constantinople on his assumption of the papacy, Constantinople responded by dropping the pope's name from the diptychs, the lists of living and dead Christians for whom it made special prayer at the Liturgy. In effect this act called the pope's orthodoxy into question.

The Synod of Siponto, assembled by Pope Leo IX in 1050, ratified a number of reforms, stemming from the monastic renewal centered at Cluny, that overturned long-standing Greek usages. The Eastern patriarch Michael Cerularius took the Synod's decrees as a threat to Greek-rite churches of southern Italy and ordered all Latin churches in Constantinople to adopt the Greek rite. When the papacy lost influence in southern Italy through the victory of the Normans, it sent an embassy to Constantinople headed by an avid anti-Greek, Cardinal Humbert. Humbert was intransigent on points of doctrinal difference, and was so choleric that he placed on the altar of the cathedral of Santa Sophia a bull (letter) excommunicating patriarch Michael and the Greeks. Michael responded by anathematizing the Latins. Nonetheless, East and West did not reach definitive animosity until the late eleventh century, when the West forced a Latin patriarch on Antioch. In 1182 the citizens of Constantinople rose in bloody revolt against the Latin Crusaders, and in 1204 the Crusaders sacked Constantinople brutally.

In the fifteenth century, when the Byzantine Empire was approaching its end, leaders of the Eastern Orthodox realm approached the West for help against the impending onslaught by the Turks. At the Council of Florence (1439) representatives of East and West met to deliberate on their religious differences. Dropping many disputed points of Church discipline, such as whether bishops should wear rings or the clergy should shave their beards, the Council focused on the four issues thought to be central: the prerogatives of the papal see, the *filioque*, the doctrine of purgatory, and whether leavened or unleavened bread was to be used at the Eucharist.[6] Political pressures forced the Greeks to agree to largely Latin views on these matters, but Eastern Orthodox synods later refused to ratify the agreements.

At a distance from both the Council of Florence and the entire East-West division, theologians tend to emphasize the disagreements over the prerogatives of the papal see and the *filioque*. We shall study the rise of the papacy and the claims of Rome in the next section. Some theologians see the *filioque* as having important implications for the structure of Christian faith, but most see it as a matter of different traditions that could have accommodated one another.

The Papacy

"Dominating the jurisdictional and theological conflict between East and West was the massive fact of Rome's spotless (or nearly spotless) record for doctrinal orthodoxy."[7] The supreme example of Roman doctrinal influence in the conciliar period was the role of Pope Leo I in resolving the main controversy during the Council of Chalcedon in 451, when he called Jesus "one person in two natures." By 862, when Pope Nicholas I was feuding with the patriarch Photius, Rome claimed that all the councils came under papal jurisdiction. Although Photius opposed this claim, one of his predecessors at Constantinople, the sixth-century patriarch Ephiphanius, had prayed to unite himself to the pope "and to embrace the divine dogmas that had been handed down by tradition from the blessed and holy disciples and apostles of God, especially from Peter the chief of the apostles, to your holy see."[8]

By the fact that it had been on the winning side so many times, the Roman position came almost to predetermine the settlement of controversies. Although the Council of Constantinople (681) had denounced Pope Honorius for teaching that Christ had only one will, to the mid-ninth century the record of the Roman pontiffs for orthodoxy was remarkable overall. Thus while Photius could cite Honorius as evidence that popes were fallible in matters of doctrine, he could not crush the Roman claims. Indeed, the Easterners who had opposed the doctrine of one will in Christ had themselves appealed to Rome as "the apostolic and chief see." Similarly, the iconodules had appealed to Rome, and by the time the conflict between Rome and Constantinople heated up, the pattern of Eastern deference had been set. Constantinople had an unfortunate association with heresies, including those of Arius and Nestorius, so that Cardinal Humbert could embellish his excommunication of 1054 with an unflattering string of historical references.

On the Western front, papal supremacy drew support from documents forged in the eighth and ninth centuries. These documents (the *Donation of Constantine* and the *False Decretals*) joined with the more intrinsic authority generated by Church reforms stemming from the influential abbey of Cluny in France to keep the popes strong in face of the increasing alienation of the East. Pope Leo I had frankly asserted the Petrine foundations of papal supremacy in the fifth century, and Pope Gregory the Great had provided strong organizational and doctrinal leadership at the end of the sixth century. The spread of Western monasticism had raised up a corps of clergy loyal to the pope as the universal bishop, while the conflicts among the many Western tribes had allowed the Church to increase its strength relative to the secular powers. The revival of the Holy Roman Empire in the eleventh century under Otto the Great brought a new challenge to papal primacy, but the failure of the empire to overcome the emergent spirit of political nationalism left the pope as Europe's first source of unity.

A high point of the medieval conflict between pope and emperor was the encounter of Emperor Henry IV and Pope Gregory VII at Canossa, Italy, in 1077. Henry is said to have stood in the snow three days doing penance so that the pope would lift his excommunication. However, this was merely one salvo in a protracted controversy (called *the Investiture Controversy*) that raged between 1075 and 1122. The controversy turned on the question of who had the power to invest a cleric as the custodian of the rights, spiritual and material, embodied in a bishopric, monastic abbey, or local parish. Both ecclesiastical and secular rulers claimed this power. Henry and Gregory locked horns, and eventually Henry defeated the papacy in military combat. Bitter antagonisms followed in England and Germany, for investiture came to symbolize the entire issue of Church-State relations. Finally the Concordat of Worms (1122) struck a compromise. The elections of bishops and abbots in the German kingdom would take place in the presence of the king, but the bishops and abbots would be invested with their ring and staff by a representative of the pope.

The peak of medieval papal power came in the pontificate of Innocent III (1198–1216), whose authority reached into every corner of Latin Christendom. Innocent's ambition was to bring all Europe together under one ruler and one Christian morality. He reformed the Roman curia (then the judicial body of final appeal for all Europe), reorganized the papal chancery courts, and modernized the canon law. On the occasion of Philip Augustus's refusal to fulfill his betrothal of marriage to Ingeborg of Denmark, Innocent used his power to force the capitulation of both Philip and the French bishops who supported him. In 1197 Innocent became the guardian of Frederick II of Sicily, securing as the price for this service the papacy's temporal power over much of Italy. When Emperor Otto IV violated this agreement, Innocent declared him deposed in favor of Philip of Swabia. He also imposed his will on England, forcing King John to accept the papal candidate for the see of Canterbury.

The Fourth Crusade (1204) that Innocent raised reestablished the emperor in Constantinople and enabled the pope to nominate a Latin patriarch. In doing so he claimed that "the Lord left to Peter governance not of the church only but of the whole world."[9] Innocent's other accomplishments included establishing the Inquisition that tore out the **Albigensian** heresy (a sort of revival of Manicheanism) and presiding over the Fourth Lateran Council that proclaimed the transubstantiation of bread and wine into Christ's body and blood, legislated annual confession and communion, suspended clergy living in concubinage, and required Muslims and Jews to wear distinctive garb.

Medieval Mysticism

Balancing their political activism, medieval Christians developed an impressive mysticism. In a broad sense, mysticism is the experiential side of religion, the interior feel or taste that makes religious realities come alive. Medieval Christianity, both Eastern and Western, was especially rich in mystical currents. In the East monastic piety was particularly strong during the last several centuries of Byzantine culture. Beginning in the eleventh century and climaxing in the fourteenth, a movement called **Hesychasm** rooted theology in silence, prayer, and intense spirituality. The monks of Mount Athos in Greece were a major force in the Hesychast movement, and it drew much of its rationale from St. Simeon the New Theologian (949–1022), who explained how deification was the crown of spiritual endeavor. Byzantine mystical theology linked this doctrine of grace to ecclesiology by stressing the reality of the Church as the Body of Christ. Thus monastic piety, indeed all Orthodox spirituality, immersed itself in the Church's sacraments and liturgy. Thereby it became richly trinitarian and christological—grounded in the most central Christian mysteries. In fact many accounts of spiritual ecstasy stressed that the mystic had felt the touch of God during the chanting of the *trisagion* ("Holy, Holy, Holy") or the *kyrie* ("Lord have mercy")—dramatic liturgical moments referring to the three divine persons or the risen Christ.

Hesychasm gave this ecclesial, liturgical context an ascetic complement. Its chief tenet was that a person could, through an elaborate system of ascetic practices that included pursuing perfect quiet of both body and mind, arrive at a vision of the uncreated God. As they gave more attention to such methods, the Hesychasts introduced other practices such as rhythmic breathing and repetition of the prayer, "Lord Jesus Christ, Son of God, have mercy on me." Many who used their methods claimed to feel an ineffable joy and to see a surpassing light, which they identified not with the divine essence but with the divine energy. Although this identification drew opposition from theologians steeped in Western thought, which was not comfortable with such a distinction between divine essence and divine energy, it infused Eastern Christianity with much religious fervor. After numerous trials and tribulations, both Hesychasm and its main defender, Gregory Palamas, were vindicated. Indeed, for a while they were even acclaimed in the liturgy for the Feast of Orthodoxy. When opposition to things Western intensified, Hesychasm became identified with distinctively Eastern Christian spirituality, but in the sixteenth and seventeenth centuries, when there was a swing back to Western theology in the Russian church, Palamas was removed from the liturgy of the Feast of Orthodoxy. Nonetheless, such Hesychast practices as rhythmic breathing and the Jesus prayer remained very influential in Russian Orthodoxy.[10]

Monasticism also was a font of mystical thought and practice in the West. The revival of the spirit of Benedict, the West's great monastic Father, that began with the founding of an abbey at Cluny in 910, was a source of spiritual renewal for much of Europe, while the Cistercian branch of Benedictinism exemplified by Bernard of Clairvaux sponsored a life of ardent asceticism and prayer. Bernard was himself a mystic of high order. His numerous writings on the *Song of Songs* reveal a soul passionately espoused to God. He argued that God should be loved sheerly for His perfect goodness and he made such charity practical by denouncing wrong-doing such as the persecution of Jews. On the other hand, he supported the Crusades.

In the twelfth century a group of French canons at the Abbey of St. Victor in Paris contributed a sound blend of spirituality and theology that helped give Western mysticism a solid founding. In keeping with the Platonic and Augustinian traditions, they linked prayer to intellectual analysis, balancing faith and reason in contemplation. In the thirteenth and fourteenth centuries a group of Dominicans (followers of Saint Dominic, 1170-1221) known as the Rhineland mystics formed another influential school. Although their founding father, Meister Eckhart, was accused of pantheistic tendencies, Henry Suso and Johann Tauler were accounted solid spiritual masters. The Rhineland mystics stressed communion with God in grace, the soul's being carried by the divine Spirit.

Many medieval nuns won a reputation for sanctity and mystical prowess, among them Saint Mechtilde and Saint Catherine of Siena. The Church seldom allowed women to hold formal teaching positions or give spiritual direction, but Saint Catherine illumined the fourteenth century by her labors to overcome the schism that afflicted the papacy.

Perhaps the most beloved of the Western medieval mystics, however, was Saint Francis of Assisi (1181–1226). He gave up considerable wealth to embrace a life of poverty, prayer, and service of the poor. The order that Francis founded took the name "Little Brothers" (Friars Minor), and his own seraphic joy, preaching to the birds, and canticles to brother sun and sister moon soon became legendary. Toward the end of his life he received the stigmata—wounds like those of Christ on the Cross—in token of his identification with his Incarnate Redeemer.

Gregory the Great

Parallel to the role that Athanasius played in the patristic era is the role that Pope Gregory I played in the medieval era. If Athanasius was the compleat bishop, Gregory was the compleat pope: administrator, pastor, practical theologian, and spiritual leader. He gave historical reality to Augustine's vision of the Church as the renovated Rome and fitted the papacy for government by perfecting the Roman curia. Much of his spirit comes through in his influential *Pastoral Rule*, a work that some historians consider the key to the medieval bishop's life and so to medieval civilization.[11] It reveals the great influence of Benedictine monasticism, which not only formed Gregory's personal spirituality but also poured into the medieval Church through his liturgical and administrative reforms.

Gregory was born about 540 and died in 604. Thus he stands at the very beginning of the period we are calling medieval. He was the son of a Roman senator and himself became prefect of Rome in 573. Although these positions brought him considerable wealth, he sold his property, gave the proceeds to the poor, and founded several monasteries, entering one himself about 574. After a few years of monastic life Gregory was compelled by the pope to become one of the seven deacons of Rome. In 578 he was given a diplomatic post in Constantinople, where his experience convinced him that the West could expect little from the decaying Eastern empire. About 585 he returned to Rome and became abbot of his former monastery. He was elected pope in 590, accepting only after a severe internal struggle.

The Italy of 590 was in a terrible state. Floods, famines, and pestilences had laid waste the land; the Lombard tribes had invaded; and Western Christianity was severely challenged by the claims of the emperor in Constantinople. Had the Church not gained a leader of Gregory's stature, it probably would not have survived to dominate the following centuries. In the years 592–593 Gregory negotiated a peace with the Lombards, in effect setting aside the authority of the exarch of Ravenna, the representative of the emperor. Such independent action, bold and decisive, became the mark of Gregory's administration. From the outset he refused to subject the Church to the weakness and treachery of the Byzantine authorities. He appointed governors to the Italian cities, provided materials for war, and generally established the papacy as the foremost Italian temporal power. It soon became clear that Gregory was the most talented administrator the Church had seen, and that the Church's vast estates were going not only to prosper but to serve the needs of the poor.

Furthermore, Gregory's administrative talent went hand in hand with an ecclesiology that exalted the bishop of Rome. His relations with the East were constantly strained, in large part because he refused to recognize the title "Ecumenical Patriarch" adopted by the patriarch of Constantinople. Even though Constantinople was the political center of the Empire, Rome would remain the center of the Church. From this center Gregory sent missionaries throughout the West. Among the greatest of their successes was the conversion of England. He also strengthened the Church in Spain, Gaul, and northern Italy. By concentrating on the lifestyle and administrative responsibilities of the bishop, he provided the Church a much stronger government than it had previously had. The bishop was above all to be a shepherd of souls—a pastor concerned for the religious welfare of his flock.

"Gregory's was a true innovation in the legitimation, indeed the sanctification, of the authority of certain persons to rule others. On the assumption that all Europeans would become Catholic Christians he was legitimating the authority and power of one person over all others. This breakthrough symbolized the emergence of a new form of human existence."[12] Whereas the secular rulers had stressed their personal virtue as the basis of their authority, Gregory stressed service to Christ and conformity to Christ's standards. Because of the influence of Gregory's pastoral theology, both medieval bishops and medieval kings sought Christian sanction for their rule. Actually, popes and bishops were the winners in the power struggle, for their succession from the apostles became more prestigious than the emperors' succession from prior emperors. Thus more than a century after Gregory's death his successor Pope Gregory II told the emperor Leo the Isaurian, who had threatened him with arrest for refusing to pay taxes, that a pope, as the successor of the prince of the apostles, could pass judgment on an emperor. Leo replied that he himself was both a king and a priest, but the Western Church maintained that the papacy mediated the sacrality of both those offices.

Gregory's prelacy served well the transition from the citified empire of antiquity to the agrarian and incipiently feudal society of the Middle Ages. This agrarian society placed the ownership of vast lands in the hands of a relative few. The Church was perhaps the greatest land owner, so its administrative style was doubly important. Gregory offered both the diocese and the feudal estate an adaptation of Benedictine stewardship. With persons of virtue serving the common good, the hierarchical Church could sponsor a paternalistic society in the best sense.

Thomas Aquinas

If Gregory the Great stands at the beginning of our medieval period, Thomas Aquinas (1225–1274) stands at its end. Both men were Italians, brought up close to the center of Western Christendom. Gregory initiated reforms that made the papacy the effective leader of Western Christendom. Thomas achieved a systematic expression of Western Christian faith perhaps second only to Augustinian theology in its influence.

Thomas Aquinas was educated at the famous Benedictine school of Monte Cassino, but he found his vocation in the intellectual apostolate of the newly founded Dominican order. His family initially opposed his desires, but he eventually entered the Dominicans in 1244, studied in Paris under the great teacher Albertus Magnus, and accompanied Albert to Cologne in 1248. He returned to Paris in 1252 and became a Master of Theology in 1256. From 1259 to 1269 he taught in various parts of Italy, and from 1269 to his death in 1274 he taught in Paris and Naples. In 1278 the Dominican order imposed his teaching on its students, and he was canonized in 1323 by Pope John XXII. Pope Pius V declared him a Doctor of the Church in 1567, but both before and after this declaration his teachings were attacked as rationalistic. Pope Leo XIII inaugurated a new era for Thomism in 1879 by enjoining the study of Thomas on all Roman Catholic theology students, and through slow percolation this renewed Thomism joined with a greater openness to historical studies to produce the Roman Catholic scholars most responsible for the *aggiornamento*, the bringing-up-to-date, of the Second Vatican Council (1962–1965).

Corpus Christi, Spanish, about 1250 C.E. Nelson Gallery—Atkins Museum, Kansas City, Missouri (Nelson Fund).

Thomas wrote on both theological and philosophical topics with a self-conscious borrowing from Aristotle, whom he called "the philosopher." He accepted the medieval sense of a great chain of being running from heaven to earth, and he was considerably influenced by the mystical theology of Dionysius the Areopagite, which enriched his theology not only with Neoplatonism but also with the sense that we speak of God more truthfully by negations than by positive declarations. Thomas had the whole of Scripture at his fingertips, knew the Fathers well, and counted Augustine a great mentor. To the philosophy of Aristotle, which stressed the essence of things, he added a new, restructuring focus on existence. This gave him an ontology of considerable depth, in which God's own being was best described as an infinite act of existence. Such a description dovetailed well with the Christian doctrine of creation from nothingness and it also led to the Thomist hypothesis that the hypostatic union between Christ's divinity and humanity occurs in the act of existence of the Logos.

It was characteristic of Thomas's mature work to distinguish between reason and faith but to keep them coordinated one with the other, and to do the same with nature and grace. The revealed truths that faith confesses lie beyond our natural capacities, but they more fulfill reason than confute it. Similarly grace perfects nature and the beatific vision of God that our minds naturally desire turns out to be an unmediated sharing in the mysterious life of the divine Trinity. Thomas defended the *filioque* and specified the biblical and patristic doctrine that human beings are images of God to mean images of the Trinity, extending the psychological analogy initiated by Augustine.

As Roman Catholic theologian Bernard Lonergan has argued with great textual specificity, Thomas's central inspiration in trinitarian theory and philosophical anthropology alike came from his grasp of insight, the human act of understanding.[13] Insofar as this experiential center expressed the high medievals' respect for disinterested intellectual inquiry, it provides a theologian's framework for the late medieval science that prepared the way for modern physics and mathematics. Overall, Aquinas achieved a system remarkable for its balance and serenity. Dry when taken too rapidly or divorced from its presuppositions of faith, it comes alive with considerable power when one starts to penetrate the magisterial mind behind it.

Summary

By 600 C.E. Christianity had a solid doctrinal tradition. Defined principally in the great councils of the East, it stressed the balance of reason and faith. For Greek theologians the central notion was deification. It named not only a rich view of grace as a transformation but also a mystical ascent to God. The East formed its common people in these doctrines through the Liturgy. As the controversies over icons suggest, the Liturgy became a battleground of passionate convictions. The West did not experience such heated polemics in its liturgical development; its various rites often expressed Christian hopes in beautiful sight and sound.

The schism between East and West that occurred in 1054 had been building for centuries. Through increasing cultural estrangement and political strife, the two poles of the Christian empire had grown farther and farther apart. Doctrinally, the worst causes of friction were the *filioque* and the claims of the Roman pontiffs to supreme jurisdiction over the entire Church. The papacy had won genuine esteem during the conciliar period for its solid orthodoxy, with Pope Leo I emerging from the Council of Chalcedon as a hero. Although they battled emperors and kings throughout the medieval period, the solid achievements of Roman bishops like Gregory the Great made the papacy the foremost Church leader. Gregory developed an efficient administration and a style of pastoral service that brought the medieval papacy much distinction. Balancing such external influences were the currents of mysticism that invigorated both Greek and Latin piety, as well as the theological vision of great thinkers like Aquinas. With Aquinas's writings, medieval Western Christianity produced its comprehensive *summa*, though before long voices of protest called for reform.

Study Questions

1. What was the theological basis for the Eastern tendency to think of Christian doctrine as changeless?
2. To what extent did the controversy over icons stem from different understandings of the Incarnation?
3. What was the relation between ecclesiology and politics in the East-West schism?
4. What were the major advantages of a strong papacy?
5. How did Hesychasm make rhythmic breathing and the Jesus prayer vehicles of mystical union?
6. What were the major disadvantages in the monastic assumptions behind the pastoral style of Gregory the Great?
7. Explain Thomas Aquinas's notion that God's own being is an infinite act of existence.

Notes

1. Adolf von Harnack, *Dogmengeschichte* (Tubingen: J. C. Mohr, 1931), vol. 2, p. 511.
2. Vincent of Lerins, *Commonitory* 2.3.
3. Acts of the Council, 7 (Mansi 13:378).
4. John of Damascus, *Orations on the Images* 2.11, 3.10.
5. Joseph A. Jungmann, "Liturgy," in *Sacramentum Mundi*, ed. Karl Rahner et al. (New York: Herder and Herder, 1969), vol. 3, pp. 322–328.
6. Nicholas Zernov, "The Eastern Schism and the Eastern Orthodox Church," in *The Concise Encyclopedia of Living Faiths*, ed. R. C. Zaehner (Boston: Beacon Press, 1967), p. 95.
7. Jaroslav Pelikan, *The Christian Tradition, Vol. 2: The Spirit of Eastern Christendom 600–1700* (Chicago: University of Chicago Press, 1974), p. 148. Reprinted by permission.
8. Ibid., p. 150. Reprinted by permission.
9. *The Westminster Dictionary of Church History*, ed. Jerald C. Brauer (Philadelphia: Westminster, 1971), p. 433.
10. See *The Way of a Pilgrim*, trans. R. M. French (New York: Seabury, 1965).

11. See William A. Clebsch, *Christianity in European History* (New York: Oxford University Press, 1979), p. 110.
12. Ibid., p. 112.
13. See Bernard Lonergan, *Verbum: Word and Idea in Aquinas* (Notre Dame, IN: University of Notre Dame Press, 1967).

CHAPTER 9

Reformation (1300–1700)

Ecclesia Semper Reformanda

Medieval Christianity reached the peak of its development in the thirteenth century, after which the need for its reform became increasingly manifest. When the floodgates of reform burst in the sixteenth century, Christians on both sides of what became the Protestant-Roman Catholic dividing line had long realized that reform had to mean more than a cosmetic freshening. For Protestant theologians, reform began to be seen as a constant ingredient in a life of genuine faith. Their subsequent slogan "*ecclesia semper reformanda*" (a Church always having to be reformed) expresses a keen intuition that the Church always stands before its God as an imperfect servant. Catholic theologians were reluctant to commit themselves to such a slogan for political reasons, but the program they developed at the Council of Trent, which we discuss in this chapter, was an implicit endorsement of it.[1]

The biblical basis for considering reform an ongoing ingredient of Christian faith is solid. The Bible's first commandment proscribes idolatry—setting anything finite in place of the infinite God. All too clearly in human history, both outside the Church and inside, men and women have tended to idolize wealth, pleasure, and power. Everywhere, therefore, men and women need to reform their consciences, so that only the holy mystery of God sits in the sanctuary. An alternate way of expressing this is the biblical notion that we possess the treasures of religion, which give us right relationship to God and our neighbors, in fragile containers: "We have this treasure in earthen vessels to show that the transcendent power belongs to God and not to us" (2 Cor. 4:7). In the dialectic between sin and grace, it is God's doing that grace abounds over sin. According to the apostle Paul, whose perception of this dialectic sparked Luther and the other Protestant reformers, all of us have sinned and fallen short of the glory of God (Rom. 3:23). Thus, looking to itself, the Church always finds solid grounds for echoing the apostle Peter: "The time has come for judgment to begin with the household of God" (1 Pet. 4:17).

Patristic and medieval Christianity had both offered many occasions for applying this Petrine dictum. East and West, they had both given many examples of falling short of God's glory and requiring reform. However, the fourteenth and fifteenth centuries were especially disgraceful for the Church. The intellectual style called **Scholasticism** sometimes became a matter of word games and so began its long career as a term of reproach. The Christian populace was under great strain because of widespread plague. "The most widespread epidemic began in Constantinople in 1334, spread throughout Europe (returning Crusaders were a factor in this respect), and in less than twenty years is estimated to have killed as much as three-quarters of the population of Europe and Asia."[2] The savagery of the Crusades of the twelfth and thirteenth centuries had brutalized the very notion of Christendom, the Hundred Years' War (1337–1453) between England and France gave the lie to "Christian Europe," and the highest spirituality of the early fifteenth century, which spread out from the Brethren of the Common Life in Holland, acquired an almost lugubrious tinge. *The Imitation of Christ*, an enormously influential work written by Dutch ecclesiastic Thomas à Kempis and stemming from that spirituality, had a meditation on death that suggests the depression of the times: "Very soon the end of your life will be at hand: consider, therefore, the state of your soul. Today man is here; tomorrow he is gone. And when he is out of sight, he is soon out of mind. Oh, how dull and hard is the heart of man, which thinks only of the present, and does not provide against the future! You should order your every deed and thought, as though today were the day of your death."[3]

Obviously, there is nothing wrong with a sober remembrance of death. Equally obviously, however, the fifteenth century had lost the early Christians' hopefulness, which had flowed from their preoccupation with the Resurrection. In the face of the mortality revealed by the Black Death, late medieval Europe had little hope for humanity's physical prospects. In the face of the breakdown of civility and morality presented recently in Barbara Tuchman's *A Distant Mirror*,[4] the fourteenth century became cynical about humanity's ethical prospects. Above all, the disarray of the Church itself led to a smoldering cry for reform. When those who should have been teachers and exemplars of faith failed dramatically, better spirits became convinced that a thorough housecleaning was in order.

The most egregious example of Church disorder began with the exile of the popes from Rome to Avignon during the years 1309–1377. Satiric writers such as Francesco Petrach referred to this as the Church's "Babylonian Captivity." During these years, a series of French popes lived in southern France for a variety of reasons. The first exiled pope, Clement V, was involved in delicate negotiations with Philip the Fair, king of France. His successors feared the disorder in Italy, were involved in trying to end the Hundred Years' War, and had numerous ties with the French court. War in Italy, international projects such as the Crusades, and the great papal bureaucracy that had grown up all contributed to an increasing need for money. This led the popes to centralize ecclesiastical appointments in their own hands and develop a sophisticated market in ecclesiastical futures. The many office-seekers who flocked to Avignon soon made the papal court a den of influence-peddling and bribery.

Madonna and Child in a Gothic Room with Saint Joseph In the Distance, by Petrus Christus, Flemish, about 1410–1472. Nelson Gallery–Atkins Museum, Kansas City, Missouri (Nelson Fund).

The nadir of Church disarray came with the Great Western Schism of 1378–1417. During this period, two and sometimes three rival popes claimed power. After the death of Gregory XI, who had returned the papacy to Rome in 1378, the conclave that was to elect his successor could not agree on a single candidate. Urban VI finally was elected, but he soon alienated the French cardinals. They proclaimed a new pope, Robert of Geneva (Clement VII), a cousin of the French king, and pronounced Urban's election invalid. Europe divided its loyalty between these two pontiffs, largely for political reasons. Eventually most of Europe considered Urban the legitimate ruler, but for forty years the Church was in schism, military force and legal machinations both failing to bring about unity. A general council at Pisa in 1409 deposed the successors of both Urban and Clement and put forth a new pontiff, with the result that there were then three claimants. By the time that the Council of Constance reunited the Church in 1417, such mockery of faith, and the greedy exactions of three papal courts, had fired a widespread desire for reform.

Finally, we should note that the Reformation started building at the same time as the influential movement known as the Renaissance. Europe in the fourteenth, fifteenth, and sixteenth centuries witnessed a rebirth of intellectual and artistic spirit, much of it based on the humanism of the classical Greek and Latin cultures. Thus in poetry, art, and politics currents were flowing which, although they seldom challenged the prevailing Christian culture head-on, implied profound questions about the otherworldly orientation of late medieval religion. Many of the Christian participants in the Renaissance stepped back enough to see the need for deep Church reform, and the Renaissance contributed to the growing desire for a more learned understanding of faith, in contrast to the rather unlettered version many of the clergy were preaching.

Martin Luther

German theologian Martin Luther (1483–1546) exerted the eloquent leadership that made reform a European conflagration, but he had several significant predecessors. For example, religious reformer John Wycliffe presaged many of Luther's notions in fourteenth century England. Scandalized by the Great Schism, Wycliffe taught that the pope's claims were ill-founded in Scripture, that the pope's salvation was no more certain than anyone else's, and that the sole criterion of papal actions ought to be their conformity with the Gospel. He also questioned the doctrine of transubstantiation and fought for the private interpretation of Scripture. In Bohemia, John Hus (1369–1415) translated some of Wycliffe's writings into Czech and denounced the low morals of the clergy. Hus was especially attracted to Wycliffe's rejection of property rights and the nonegalitarian hierarchical organization of society. Burned at the stake in 1415, he almost immediately became a national hero. Indeed, the University of Prague declared him a martyr and made the day of his execution a public feast day.

Against this background, Luther's reform began tamely enough. He was born in Saxony and entered the monastery of the Augustinian Hermits at Erfurt in 1505. Ordained in 1507, he journeyed to Rome in 1510 and was scandalized by the laxity he observed. From 1511 he taught Scripture at the University of Wittenberg and assumed administrative duties in his Order. For the first part of his career, then, Luther was but a conscientious Catholic.

There were numerous intellectual influences that pushed Luther away from a Catholicism like that of Aquinas, his Order's traditional **nominalism** (distrust of ontology) and pessimism prominent among them, but his own personality was the major determinant of his fresh interpretations. So anxious had he become about his personal salvation that he had developed many scruples and had therefore given up such religious duties as celebrating Mass daily and reciting the Divine Office (the prayer incumbent on priests). Out of his deep turmoil came a revelation that the essence of the Gospel is that man is justified by God by faith alone, rather than by the works the Church had increasingly emphasized. The New Testament basis for this interpretation was Paul's polemic against the Israelite Law and the works it required, but Luther found further support for it in passages Augustine had written against the Pelagians, and in what the Rhineland mystics had written about the nothingness of the human soul before God.

From 1516 Luther began to flesh out his central conviction about justification by faith with the denial that salvation required the mediatorship of the Church and the priesthood. The Church had appropriated the power to grant **indulgences** (to excuse sinners from purgatorial penalty) and had begun exacting a price for these indulgences, an abuse that Luther deplored. In 1517 he encountered a preaching of indulgences by German Dominican monk Johann Tetzel that he found a stunning example of the interpretation that justification is earned by works. Luther published 95 theses against indulgences and soon had all Germany abuzz with his challenge to Rome. The Church authorities first hoped to settle the dispute as a disciplinary matter, but Luther's ideas gained wide support and by 1519 he felt secure enough to deny both the primacy of the pope and the infallibility of the General Councils (assemblies of all the bishops). He enjoyed the support not only of his local prince, but also of many other political authorities who had reasons for opposing Rome.

In 1520 Luther invited the German princes to take over the reform of the German church by abolishing tribute to Rome, the celibacy of the clergy, masses for the dead, pilgrimages, and religious Orders. In each instance his charge was that the practice was unscriptural and at odds with justification by faith. In his writing *On the Babylonian Captivity of the Church*, Luther castigated the denial of communion to the laity under both species (bread and wine), the doctrine of transubstantiation, and the notion that the Mass was a **sacrifice**. The papal bull (writing) *Exsurge Domine* of 15 June 1520 censured forty-one such theses of Luther's as heretical and ordered his writings destroyed. Luther responded by burning the bull and a number of Catholic books, and so was excommunicated in 1521.

While Luther was secluded at Wartburg in Germany for his safety, his ideas continued to gain adherents. (At Wartburg he also produced a fine vernacular translation of the Bible which influenced the modern German tongue.) Following his ideas, many priests married, many monks and nuns left their monasteries, and Luther eventually had to return to Wittenberg to help the authorities restore order. He resumed his lectures at the university and brought about the abolition of such practices as private masses, confession, and fasts. In 1525 he married Catherine von Bora, formerly a Cistercian nun, and advised the German princes to wage war on the unruly German peasants, an action that cost him much popular support. His spirited hymns kept spreading his teachings effectively, and the decisions of the Diet (assembly) of Speyer in 1529 to allow princes to organize national churches was a big boost to his cause, because many supported him against Rome.

The German reformation had spread to other countries quite quickly, but before long differences developed among the reformers themselves. Thus the Colloquy of Marburg that gathered leading reformers in 1529 revealed a deep difference between Luther and Ulrich Zwingli, the leader of the powerful German Swiss reformation, concerning the nature of the Eucharist. For Luther, Zwingli's denial of the real presence of Christ in the Eucharist was far too radical. On another front, Luther approved the Augsburg Confession of 1530, a declaration of faith made to Rome by Luther's followers in an attempt to soften differences.

In maturity, Luther's character was quite complex, expressing itself both in moving religious verse and in crude obscenities. With deep pessimism he spoke of the depravity of humankind and the uselessness of human reason, but from his personal experience of justification he drew lyric descriptions of Christ's power and grace. Luther's negative attitude toward human action gradually led him to dichotomize interior religious affections and external behavior, so that he finally left the latter, including even the outward manifestations of religion, to the regulation of the secular authorities.

The Protestant Reformation 1

The traditional date for the beginning of the Protestant Reformation is 1517, when Luther published his theses against indulgences. By 1522 the transformation of Zürich from Catholicism to Protestantism was under way, and by 1525 it was complete. The pattern of this transformation was repeated in many other receptive free cities. Leading citizens embraced the doctrines of reform; they repudiated the authority of the local Catholic bishop; the city council legislated the reform of local parishes; the leading pastors then supervised a thorough reform of faith and morals. Specifically, Protestant reformation meant such changes as allowing clerical marriage, removing images deemed superstitious, suppressing monasteries or transforming them into educational institutions, and substituting a simpler vernacular liturgy for the Latin mass.

As mentioned in the previous section, the leader of the reform movement in Zürich was Ulrich Zwingli (1484–1531). Like Luther, he had been influenced by the church criticisms of Erasmus of Rotterdam (1466–1536), a fine biblical and patristic scholar. Zwingli was of cooler temper than Luther, and he felt less affection for the past. Thus his reform of the liturgy and the churches was more thoroughgoing. Where Luther kept many features of the medieval mass, Zwingli stripped the service to a sermon on a biblical text and a simple consumption of unleavened bread and wine. Further, he removed relics and organs from the churches, had pictures and images sold or smashed, put the ministers in lay clothes, and replaced the altar with a simple table. Where Luther had used Scripture as a negative norm, removing anything from the worship service that conflicted with Scripture; Zwingli used the Bible as a positive norm, insisting that anything done in the worship service ought to have explicit sanction from Scripture. For example, Zwingli thought that hymns were unscriptural so he substituted metrical versions of the Psalms.

The leader of the French Swiss reformation was John Calvin (1509–1564), who both dominated Geneva and produced the most influential systematization of Protestant theology. Calvin had trained as a lawyer at Orleans and Bourges, and then had fled France when his Protestant sympathies made France unsafe for him. In 1536, while in Basel, he produced the first version of *The Institutes of the Christian Religion*, a lucid handbook of the Protestant position. When he came to influence in Geneva, first as a teacher and then as the architect of its religio-political changeover to Protestantism, Calvin began to put into practice the belief, common to all the early reformers, that church order and virtue would flourish if the shape of the primitive New Testament community were restored. For Calvin this especially meant replacing the authority of the pope with that of church ministers and elders.

In Geneva both ministers and elders were strenuously concerned with the morals of their congregations. Such concern was not new—bishops' courts and city councils long had shown it—but Calvin made it more exact than it had been in most medieval cities. Thus elders would summon heretics, parishioners who failed to attend church, and parishioners who treated the minister with contempt. Such persons would be admonished, and if they did not repent they would be excommunicated. Minutes of a meeting held in 1542 show the other sorts of disciplinary concerns that flourished in Geneva:

> A woman knelt upon the grave of her husband and cried *Requiescat in pace*; others saw her and started to copy her. A goldsmith made a chalice. Someone said that the arrival of the French refugees had put up the cost of living. A woman tried to cure her husband by tying round his neck a walnut containing a spider. Another danced. Another possessed a copy of the lives of the saints, the *Golden Legend*. A woman of sixty-two married a man of twenty-five. A barber gave a tonsure to a priest. Another blamed Geneva for executing people for their religious opinions.[5]

In this mishmash of items one finds the elders alert to preventing any backsliding into Catholic superstitions or unbiblical practices, a concern for unseemly behavior, and a sensitivity to any criticisms of the new regime.

Calvin's great virture as an expositor of faith was his clarity. The notion of **predestination**, which he placed front and center, illustrates this point. All Christian theologians—Paul, Augustine, Aquinas, Luther—had taught some version of predestination. Theoretically, the differences among their positions were rather slight. Practically, however, Calvin made the Christian's assurance of election to eternal life the deepest source of his confidence and freedom. In so doing, he did not shrink from the complementary notion that God has consigned some people to eternal destruction. Since *all* human beings are unjust and deserve hell, such consignment did not violate God's justice. Whether it violated God's goodness was another matter, much debated in Calvin's wake. In Calvin's presence it was little debated: when French refugee Jerome Bolsec said that this doctrine made God a tyrant, Calvin had him placed in prison.

The Protestant Reformation 2

Zwingli and Calvin made Switzerland the powerhouse of a reform more austere, both intellectually and morally, than that initiated by Luther. In England, King Henry VIII presided over a reformation of quite different proportions. If Germany and Switzerland mainly gave up Church power to the state, England (and the Scandinavian countries) consolidated temporal and Church power. Henry initiated this change because he wanted to divorce his wife Catherine of Aragon, who had failed to provide him a male heir. When the pope, Clement VII, would not grant him permission (because Clement would have had to declare invalid the previous concessions Henry had obtained from Rome in order to marry Catherine), the king put reform into action. He dismissed Cardinal Wolsey, the leading English prelate, and had himself recognized as the head of the English church. Thomas Cranmer, Wolsey's successor, declared Henry's marriage to Catherine null and void, and in 1533 Henry married Ann Boleyn, who was then crowned queen. Shortly thereafter Clement VII excommunicated Henry and invalidated both his divorce and his remarriage. While some of Henry's subjects remained loyal to Rome, John Fisher and Thomas More at the cost of being beheaded, most of the upper clergy went over to the king.

A major change that spearheaded Henry's reform was suppression of the monasteries. The announced grounds for this suppression was the monasteries' laxity, but the actual grounds were the Protestant view that monasticism was a mistaken form of Christian life and a pragmatic desire to gain the monasteries' sizeable land revenues. While some of the monastic revenues were used to relocate monks and nuns in lay life, and others were used for educational purposes, the English nobles and Crown profited handsomely.[6] Another major change concerned the liturgy. Cranmer's careful scholarship and delicate prose in his *The Book of Common Prayer* offered the English a judicious blend of Catholic tradition and Protestant renovation. Henry VIII's own faith remained Catholic in substance, apart from his rejection of papal primacy, but Protestantism steadily gained adherents and by the reign of Queen Mary (1553–1558), a fierce Roman Catholic, there were martyrs for the sake of Protestant convictions.

In the years after their founders' deaths, the Lutheran, Calvinist, and Anglican reformations all suffered discord, both doctrinal and political. In Germany states followed the faith of their prince. Elsewhere in Europe, a nation was officially either Catholic or Protestant. With his Edict of Nantes (1598), Henry IV tried to stop France's religious warfare and provide religious freedom for its Protestants (Huguenots). The boon that the Edict offered Catholics was the recognition of

Catholicism as the established religion of France and the right to have mass in Protestant towns. Although the Edict was much infringed by Cardinal Richelieu in the seventeenth century, and finally was revoked by Louis XIV in 1685, it was a herald of religious toleration. Conflicts in Holland and Scotland had few such heralds. In both countries politics and faith made bloody conjunction, with the Calvinists the main beneficiaries. In seventeenth-century England the extreme Calvinists known as Puritans came to political power under Oliver Cromwell, who had King Charles I beheaded, crushed ruthlessly the Roman Catholic Irish, and defeated the insurgent Scots.

While the Lutheran, Anglican, and Calvinist movements had a strong political dimension, the so-called Radical Reformation which took those movements a step further was remarkably unconcerned about national or sectional loyalties. Its almost sole interest was a return to the roots (*radices*) of Christian faith in the primitive Church. The radical reformers also made special provision for religious experience, both individual and social, and often they produced a sort of revivalism.

Some scholars locate the beginnings of the Radical Reformation in the unhappiness of a number of early Lutherans with Luther's rejection of liturgical changes that had occurred at Wittenberg during his stay at Wartburg. These disaffected Lutherans wanted a more thorough reform of the worship service, just as certain disaffected Zwinglians wanted a more thorough reform of the baptismal doctrine, to prohibit infant baptism (on the grounds that infants could not make faith commitments). The "believer's Lord's Supper" and "believer's baptism" (stripped versions of these sacraments) that groups like these developed quickly won a considerable following in Switzerland and southern Germany. Those who opposed infant baptism sometimes were called *anabaptists* (re-baptizers), because some of the adults to whom they administered baptism had been previously baptized as infants. The radicals frequently are also considered to include eschatological groups that taught utopian social arrangements, pacifists, and groups that rejected "high" (literal) interpretations of the Nicene doctrines of the Trinity and the divinity of Jesus. Hutterites, Mennonites, and New England Puritans are sometimes grouped with the radical reformers, as are Quakers, because of their concern for a stripped, severe faith.

The Council of Trent

The Catholic response to the Protestant Reformation sometimes is called the Counter-Reformation. It had various levels and expressions, but a central feature was a rallying around the pope and Rome. In the main, Roman Catholics admitted a need for reform in both faith and morals but felt the Protestants were going too far. A strong arm of the Roman Catholic reform was the Society of Jesus (Jesuits), founded by Ignatius Loyola (1491–1556). Born a Basque, Ignatius lived a worldly soldier's life until he had a conversion experience while convalescing from a battle wound. Transposing his military ardor into spiritual terms, he formed a company of Christian soldiers to battle for Christ "under the standard of the Cross."

Ignatius's mystical experiences gave rise to an influential manual, *The Spiritual Exercises*, which became the most important literary tool of the Counter-Reformation. By attracting men of learning and devotion, and freeing them to serve the papacy wherever it wished, Ignatius gave the Catholic cause a cadre of shock troops to missionize new lands, engage Protestant theologians in dispute, give spiritual direction to influential laity, and staff some of the best secondary schools in Europe. The *Constitutions* that he drafted for his new Order became the model for most modern Catholic religious groups, and his ideal of finding God in all things significantly changed (or developed) the original monastic notion of finding God by withdrawing from the world. (An ecumenically minded observer might call this Ignatian ideal a cousin to Protestant "holy worldliness," which finds God in secular work.)

The most formal Roman Catholic response to the Protestant Reformation occurred at the Council of Trent (1545–1563). Both doctrinal and disciplinary reforms were on the agenda. The Council, which met intermittently, reasserted papal power and strengthened the power of Catholic bishops. It removed many of the exemptions from canon law that had weakened the fiber of the Church in the late Middle Ages, and it required those who received benefits from a diocese or church to be in residence there. Trying to alert its people to what it perceived as a profound crisis, the Council refocused Church life on intense prayer and participation in the sacraments. Since the low estate of the parish clergy was a prime reason for many of the abuses to which the Protestants could point, the Council made a strong effort to upgrade the intellectual and religious preparation of the parish clergy. It also called for better education of the laity. It condemned many superstitious practices and directed the Inquisition, whose cruel punishment of heretics and witches was a low point of late medieval Christianity, toward the suppression of Protestant doctrines.

Like almost all reforms of the sixteenth century, the Council of Trent was shaped by political considerations as well as religious. The popes played ecclesiastical politics with the Council, being unwilling to commit themselves in advance to its findings without an assurance of absolute control. The Spanish bishops and Emperor Charles V wanted the Council to reunite Christendom, while the popes considered it a way of arming the Church against Protestantism. The French king Francis I was hostile to Charles V and so supported the papal procrastinations. The result was that the Council made no progress until the king and the emperor were reconciled. By that time the Catholic-Protestant schism had hardened to the point where reconciliation was virtually impossible.

The doctrinal positions developed at Trent shaped Roman Catholic faith until the mid-twentieth century, when the Second Vatican Council made a full opening to modernity. Much of the doctrinal agenda was set by the positions of the Protestant reformers. Historian Benjamin Drewery has summarized the main doctrinal themes under the headings of Scripture/tradition, justification, and the sacraments.[7] Where the Protestants took their stand on Scripture, Luther's *sola scriptura* ("by Scripture alone") being a central slogan, the Roman Catholics spoke of two sources of Christian revelation. In addition to the written words of the Old and New Testament books they relied on a *traditio*, a handing on, guided by the Holy Spirit. Relatedly, they thought the interpretation of Scripture fell to the duly anointed leadership of the Church, whom the Holy Spirit empowered to judge faith and morals in fidelity to Christ. Thus they considered the popes and bishops to have been a constant conduit of God's Word. This effort to safeguard the interpretation of Scripture from individualist aberrations impressed itself on many Catholics and gave them a tendency to distrust Scripture. To read the Bible privately or try to commune there with God was a Protestant practice and so something they held suspect. As a result, Catholic scholarship largely remained aloof from the modern application of critical historical methods to the Bible, only changing its outlook in the mid-twentieth century.

On the second topic, justification, the Council of Trent again strove to distinguish the Roman Catholic position from that of the Protestant reformers. In this case, it argued that the teaching of the Catholic Church opposed justification by faith alone. While Trent admitted the Pauline basis for depreciating works, and also admitted the Augustinian teaching about the gratuity of grace, it pointed to both the Epistle of James and the long-standing penitential practices of the Church to argue that faith had to show itself in deeds. How much actual difference there was between this position and that of learned reformers is unclear, but in the gross terms that instructed the popular mind the two positions were antagonistic. Rome seemed to be depreciating the sovereignty of God's grace and the Protestants seemed to be denying the need for human moral effort. Relatedly, the Protestants seemed to be teaching a doctrine of human depravity, such that one could expect little good from the human will, while the Catholics seemed to be slighting the ravages of sin or the depths of an Augustinian vision of human evil. To this day Protestants and Catholics have different instincts in this matter, Catholics tending to think that grace perfects human nature and Protestants tending to think that grace opposes human nature.

The sacraments were a third bone of contention that worried the Council of Trent, because the Protestants denied the traditional seven sacraments and opposed the Roman view of the Eucharist. Where the teaching had grown up that baptism, confirmation, marriage, penance, the Eucharist, ordination, and extreme unction (anointing before death) were all sacraments, the Protestants taught that only baptism and the Eucharist were sanctioned by Scripture. And where Rome taught that the Eucharist was a sacrifice as well as a sacrament, reactualizing Christ's death on the Cross, the Reformers taught that eucharistic sacrifice violated the biblical notion that Christ died once for all. The two sides haggled over the interpretation of the *Epistle to the Hebrews*, which used sacrificial language, and many Romans admitted that popularly the mass had become rife with superstition. Eventually Catholics attended more to the Eucharist as a sacramental meal, but the first effect of Trent was to harden the Catholic defense of the mass as a sacrifice and to try to show that this teaching did not diminish the singularity of Christ's death on the Cross.

Virgin with the Carnation, by Joos Van Cleve, Flemish, 1485–1540. Nelson Gallery–Atkins Museum, Kansas City, Missouri (Nelson Fund).

Eastern Developments

Thus far we have been dealing with Western history. However, history went on in the East as well. In the ninth century Eastern Christianity reached out to the Slavs through the missionary brothers Cyril and Methodius. They set out for Moravia (modern Czechoslovakia) in 863, having translated the Bible and liturgy into Slavonic. When their missionary effort conflicted with one being carried out by Germans, Cyril appealed for protection from the pope, an action showing he did not take the quarrel between the pope and the patriarch of Constantinople very seriously. Emperor Hadrian II received the brothers in Rome in 868, approved their mission, and approved the use of Slavonic as the liturgical language of Moravia. However, the Germans ignored the papal directives and obstructed the brothers' mission. Still, their mission yielded fruit in Bulgaria, where Slavonic was more useful than Greek or Latin, and by 927 there was a Bulgarian patriarchate. Following the same principle, the brothers' disciples missionized Serbia and influenced the Christianity of Romania, which became a Latin-Slavonic amalgam.

Christianity started to establish itself in Russia in the tenth century. Princess Olga became a Christian in 955, and when her grandson Vladimir converted and married the sister of the Byzantine emperor, Christianity became the official religion. Vladimir imported priests, relics, vessels, and icons. He provided for mass baptisms in the rivers and for ecclesiastical courts. From a toehold in Kiev the new faith steadily won ground against the old paganism, tumbling the great idol of the old god Perun. Vladimir stressed the social ideals of the new religion, distributing food to the poor and the sick. Before long Russian monasteries flourished, providing a source of deep spirituality. Many of the Kievan abbots were especially solicitous for the poor.

Kiev was the power center of Russian Christianity until 1237, when the Mongol Tartars assumed power. Until that time Russia was under the ecclesiastical jurisdiction of Constantinople and most of its **metropolitans** (bishops in charge of large areas) were Greek. The Mongols dominated Russia until the mid-fifteenth century. During this period the Church kept Russian national consciousness alive, just as the Church preserved the national consciousness of the Greeks who later became subject to Turkish rule. In the fourteenth century Moscow came to the fore, Kiev never having recovered from the Mongol sack of 1237. A major reason for the rise of Moscow was the decision of the metropolitan Peter to settle there early in the fourteenth century. Saints such as Alexander Nevsky (a warrior who fought the Swedes and Teutonic Knights), Stephen (a missionary to pagan tribes), and Sergius (an explorer, monk, and mystic) provided Moscow with religious vigor. Russian religious art such as icon-painting flourished from 1350 to 1550, and when the Byzantine Empire fell to the Turks in 1453 Russia was ready to take the lead in Orthodoxy.

The transition from Greek to Turkish rule in Byzantium was not easy, "but it was made less hard by the Turks themselves, who treated their Christian subjects with remarkable generosity. The Mohammedans [Muslims] in the fifteenth century were far more tolerant towards Christianity than Western Christians were towards one another during the Reformation and the seventeenth century."[8] Nonetheless, Christianity under Islam was a second-class religion and Christians were second-class citizens. They paid heavy taxes, wore distinctive garb, could not serve in the army, and could not marry Muslims. The Church could not proselytize, for converting a Muslim was a crime. Since Islam saw little distinction between religion and politics, it organized the Christians into a civil unit, a sort of empire within the empire, under the leadership of the patriarch of Constantinople. The Christian bishops became political leaders, and before long Greek nationalism became synonymous with Greek Orthodoxy. All too often Church politics were corrupt, because the sultans sold church offices to the highest bidder. The sultans looked on the patriarch of Constantinople as the head of all Christians under Turkish rule, so the patriarchates of Alexandria, Antioch, and Jerusalem became subordinate to Constantinople, as did the peoples of Romania, Bulgaria, and Serbia.

The Ottoman Empire made Orthodoxy both more conservative and more western, forcing it to close ranks in order to survive and to turn to Latin sources for vigorous scholarship. The Protestant Reformation had some influence, but Orthodox sympathies lay with the Catholics, since they seemed more traditional. The Catholic monarch of Poland formed a "uniate" church that recognized the pope while keeping Orthodox traditions such as a married clergy and a Slavonic liturgy, but the Council of Brest (1596), where this church arose, embittered most of the Orthodox. Indeed, many Slavs came to prefer Muslim leaders to Roman Catholic. The patriarch Cyril Lukaris (1572–1638) so hated things Roman that he turned to Protestant sources, but his fellow Orthodox sharply repudiated his Calvinism. Mount Athos remained a potent spiritual center during the Turkish years, Hesychast practices continuing to flourish there.

From the middle of the fifteenth century, Moscow dominated eastern Russia. Many Russians looked on the Council of Florence (1438–1445), which attempted a Latin-Greek church union, and the fall of Constantinople as apocalyptic signs. Throwing off Constantinople's rule, Moscow started to think of itself as the Third Rome, called to be the center of a new Christian realm. However, in the theocracy that Moscow attempted the Church became subordinate to the Russian state. Orthodoxy slowly lost creativity, finally becoming hopelessly conservative.[9]

The Church as Missionary

From New Testament times Christianity had conceived of itself as a missionary religion, sent to spread the good news of salvation. The apostle Paul had spent himself missionizing the Gentiles of the Roman Empire, and after Constantine had given Christianity imperial status the Church had proselytized so successfully that by the beginning of the sixth century the only non-Christians in the empire were the Jews.[10] In the second century, Christians had established themselves in southwest India, and in the fourth century they had converted the German Visigoths. Saint Patrick converted the Irish in the fifth century. Christianity came to Britain in the third century, and Saint Augustine of Canterbury converted the English king in 597. Saint Boniface completed the conversion of the Germans in the eighth century, Cyril and Methodius inaugurated the Slavic mission in the ninth century, and Russia became Christian in the tenth century. However, during the seventh and eighth centuries Asian and North African territories fell to Islam. Islamic culture flourished to 1250, but Christian counterattacks were effective from the eleventh century. Scandinavia was converted from paganism during the years 1000–1200, quieting the depravations of the Vikings. By 1600 Scandinavia was largely Lutheran.

Most of these missions were led by monks or bishops. The missionary expansion that occurred in the sixteenth century was carried on by a combination of soldiers, merchants, and priests. Since Spanish and Portugese sailors initially predominated, the first missions to the Americas and the Orient were Roman Catholic. The Franciscans, Dominicans, and Jesuits were all effective missionaries, the Jesuits coming to the verge of great influence in China and Japan.[11] Orthodoxy only spread from eastern Russia to Alaska and Japan in the eighteenth and nineteenth centuries.

Protestant foreign missions came slowly after the Reformation. Among the first was the one that evangelized Indians in New England in the 1640s. About the same time chaplains of the Dutch East India Company began their work in the Orient. In the early eighteenth century Protestants trained by a group called the Danish-Halle mission went to southern India, while the Moravian Church sent pietists to St. Thomas in 1731. The Methodist and Baptist movements, which constituted a sort of second Protestant Reformation, led to the founding of British and American missionary societies at the end of the eighteenth century. In the nineteenth and early twentieth centuries, India and China received numerous Protestant missionaries. "The only countries in which there were no organized Protestant churches in the 1960s were Sikkim, Bhutan, Tibet, and Saudi Arabia."[12]

The American missions that proceeded in the wake of Columbus, Cortes, and Pizzaro began with the work of Franciscans and Dominicans, who later were joined by Jesuits. Since the Aztec rulers had been hated for their cruelty and the Inca rulers had robbed their subjects of initiative, the early Spanish and Portugese conquerers had a fairly easy time of it. However, these conquerers' own cruelty soon sowed enmity among the natives. While some missionaries championed the Indians' cause, Spanish historian Gonzalo de Oviedo y Valdes spoke for many Europeans when he described the natives as ". . . naturally lazy and vicious, melancholic, cowardly, and in general a lying, shiftless people. Their marriages are not a sacrament but a sacrilege. They are idolatrous, libidinous, and commit sodomy. Their chief desire is to eat, drink, worship heathen idols, and commit bestial obscenities."[13]

The Jesuit missions to India and China in the seventeenth century reflected a distinctly different view of the native peoples. Jesuits Roberto de Nobili in India and Matteo Ricci in China both adopted the cultures of their new lands and won reputations as savants. Francis Xavier, one of Ignatius Loyola's earliest companions thought the sixteenth-century Japanese the most refined people he had ever met.

French, Spanish, and English colonists wrote the early chapters of Christian history in North America, the English soon becoming the most important. A settlement on the James River in 1607 began the Virginia colony, and settlement in New England followed shortly thereafter. Puritans, whose fortunes were on the wane in England, came in significant numbers to Massachusetts Bay in 1630, and by 1641 at least twenty thousand had immigrated.[14] In 1636 Roger Williams left

Massachusetts for Rhode Island, before long making it a sanctuary for Baptists, Quakers, and other independent spirits who had split off from the main Protestant line. Dutch Reformed flourished in New York and New Jersey, Catholics gravitated to Maryland, and Pennsylvania was led by Quakers. The Carolinas initially were dominated more by merchants than preachers, while Anglicanism established itself in Virginia.

From this potpourri of largely Protestant sectarian groups bubbled up what Sidney Mead, the dean of American religious historians, has labeled "the lively experiment."[15] As the states strove to become united, they had to find a way of cooperating despite their religious differences. In Mead's opinion, the pluralistic federation that emerged was as momentous for Christianity as the Church's establishment under Constantine. Influenced by the seventeenth century's disgust with religious wars, and by the eighteenth century's Enlightenment, which we will discuss in the next chapter, the framers of the United States Constitution undercut the colonies' assumption of an established religion. Their toleration of religious differences had some historical precedents, but it flew in the face of most states' conviction that civic life needed a common religion. As recent studies of American national piety have shown, the lively experiment by no means disestablished a Protestant consensus. Being an American and being a Protestant long seemed to overlap. But in the narrow horizons of early eighteenth-century Christians, the American experiment seemed quite radical. Its relation to the secularizing tendencies that have challenged the Church as missionary in modern times takes us into our next chapter.

Summary

The rightness of the Protestant slogan, "*ecclesia semper reformanda*," is borne out by church history prior and subsequent to the Reformation. Again and again, Christians have fallen short of their self-assigned standards of justice, morality, and love. The centuries prior to the sixteenth-century Protestant Reformation were especially laden with such failures, so when Martin Luther seized on the issue of indulgences and proposed a wholesale return to biblical faith he found many sympathetic ears.

Indeed, before long other Reformers were proposing changes more radical than Luther's. The Calvinist wing of the Reformation developed the most lucid exposition of the new interpretations of justification, with special emphasis on predestination, and the most sober morality. Where Lutherans sought a halfway house in worship, and Anglicans struggled for a Catholic-Protestant middle way, Calvinists moved with a sure sense of election. Within thirty years of Luther's ninety-five theses the old Catholic order was broken irreparably.

The Council of Trent therefore became a Catholic rearming rather than a means to Protestant-Catholic reunion. Like the Protestant Reformation, the Catholic Counter-Reformation was political almost as much as religious, so the rearmaments of Trent became another step on the path to the religious wars of the seventeenth century. Doctrinally, Trent set the Protestant-Catholic differences c the interpretation of Scripture, justification, and the sacraments in bolder relief.

In Orthodox lands the continued spread of Slavic Christianity was a maj phenomenon, and by the mid-fifteenth century Moscow was considering itself th Third Rome. With the Greeks under Turkish rule and the Mongols overthrow Russian Christianity became the Eastern luminary. The European explorers of th sixteenth century paved the way for Christian missionaries to the Americas and th Orient, and by the seventeenth century the Western Church's divisions extended most of the globe. Only in the ecumenical movement of the early twentieth centu did Christians start to confront the gigantic reformation for which this global div sion called.

Study Questions

1. Does the Great Western Schism suggest that the Church always needs refor because it is capable of sin in both head and members? How so?
2. How does Luther's notion of justification by faith relate to Augustine's stress o the gratuity of grace?
3. In what way does Zwingli's reform of the liturgy and churches relate to th Protestant rejection of justification by works?
4. Why could Anglicans approve the suppression of the monasteries as a prop part of Church reform?
5. What are the strengths in the Catholic position that Christian faith consists tradition as well as Scripture?
6. Does the role of the Orthodox Church during the Mongol occupation of Russ and the Turkish rule of Byzantium parallel the role of the Catholic Church i contemporary Poland? Why?
7. Was the lively American experiment in pluralism an extension of the Church missionary impulses or a contraction of them? Why?

Notes

1. For patristic background see Gerhart Ladner, *The Idea of Reform* (Cambridg MA: Harvard University Press, 1959). On "*ecclesia semper reformanda*" se Robert McAfee Brown, *The Spirit of Protestantism* (New York: Oxford Unive sity Press, 1965), pp. 40–50.
2. *The New Columbia Encyclopedia* (New York: Columbia University Pres 1975), p. 2161, *s. v.* "plague."
3. Thomas à Kempis, *The Imitation of Christ*, Book I, Chapter 23, trans. Le Shirley-Price (Baltimore: Penguin, 1968), p. 57.
4. Barbara Tuchman, *A Distant Mirror* (New York: Ballantine Books, 1980).
5. Owen Chadwick, *The Reformation* (Baltimore: Penguin, 1964), p. 85.
6. Ibid., p. 108.

7. Benjamin Drewery, "The Council of Trent," in *A History of Christian Doctrine*, ed. H. Cunliffe-Jones (Philadelphia: Fortress, 1980), pp. 404–409.
8. Timothy Ware, *The Orthodox Church* (Pelican Books, Revised Edition, 1980), p. 96. Copyright © 1963, 1964 by Timothy Ware. Reprinted by permission of Penguin Books Ltd.
9. See Alexander Schmemann, *The Historical Road of Eastern Orthodoxy* (Crestwood, NY: St. Vladimir's Seminary Press, 1977), pp. 308–311.
10. *The Westminister Dictionary of Church History* (Philadelphia: Westminster, 1971), p. 558, *s. v.* "missions."
11. See *Silence*, a dramatic novel of the Jesuits' martyrdom in Japan, by Shusaku Endo (Rutland, VT: Tuttle, 1969).
12. *The Westminster Dictionary of Church History*, p. 559.
13. Quoted by Stephen Neill, *A History of Christian Missions* (Baltimore: Penguin, 1964), p. 171.
14. Sydney Ahlstrom, *A Religious History of the American People* (New Haven: Yale University Press, 1972), p. 106.
15. See Sidney Mead, *The Lively Experiment* (New York: Harper & Row, 1963).

CHAPTER 10

Modernity (1700–1965)

The Enlightenment

"The Enlightenment denotes the most revolutionary of all movements which the Occident has undergone in the course of its history."[1] This rather startling judgment is defensible if one understands the Enlightenment, a European philosophic movement of the eighteenth century, as the core phenomenon in the process known as **secularization**. Through that process, the modern view of the natural world and human society became divorced from transcendence. No longer did we see ourselves as creatures derived from a divine Creator; no longer did we acknowledge glimmers of an ultimate mystery. Insofar as such a mentality came to dominate the modern West, it distanced us from all previous historical periods, Eastern and Western alike. For throughout all previous historical periods mankind was religious—convinced that the natural world and human society were dependent, less than ultimate. Although secularization may never have dominated the Western masses, it made modernity a new era.

Many observers claim that since the mid-twentieth century we have entered a post-modern era, one in which we have started to challenge or even reject the assumptions of secularization. Nonetheless, those assumptions linger on, influencing a great many Western institutions. They dominated the ideas of leading thinkers of the eighteenth and nineteenth centuries.

The Enlightenment was the movement that most powerfully gave voice to the modern confidence in human reason. "It was assumed that through a critical exercise of reason man could arrive at a reasonable and thereby natural understanding of himself, of law, of religion, and of philosophy."[2] Along with this assumption went a rejection of outside authorities and a denigration of past forms of thought, which were considered "uncritical."

The foremost Enlightenment thinker was Immanuel Kant (1724–1804), who made critical reason modernity's most prized possession. Kant taught philosophy at Königsberg in East Prussia, and for much of his life the guardians of Lutheran orthodoxy found his views acceptable. Greatly influenced by the physics of Isaac Newton and the **empiricism** of David Hume, he led philosophers to focus on the problems of epistemology (theory of knowledge). Especially, he sought to uncover the grounds of Newtonian science. By insisting that human knowledge can only be based on empirical data, verifiable by the senses, Kant was led to conclude that we can know nothing certain about God, freedom, or the immortality of the human spirit. Thus, the only certitude we can gain about these entities comes from conscience and faith. Yet what speculative reason (concerned with being) cannot know, practical reason (concerned with doing) must know, for without God, freedom, and immortality our sense of duty and our ability to act would vanish. Kant therefore tended to base religion on ethics—the performance of the duties that conscience sets us—and by his last years he was denying the accustomed Christian understandings of sin, grace, prayer, God's action, and the like.

In Kantian terms, the watchword of the enlightened was *autonomy*. Whereas past, benighted ages had been heteronomous (directed by laws imposed from without), modernity ought to move by laws imposed by human reason itself. No God, church, or tradition standing over the human person ought to arbitrate his judgments or decisions. Fully human, fully authentic judgments and decisions were those produced by critical reason and dutiful will autonomously, in keeping only with evidence and logic. The progress in physical science that critical reason had produced made it plausible that autonomy would bring equal progress in the social realm. By the eighteenth century, Europeans realized that their culture was but one among many, just as their planet was but one among many. The confusion that the maritime explorations and new astronomy had produced pressured the intelligentsia to find a new rock on which to lean. Philosophers such as Descartes, Hume, and Kant nominated human reason to be their rock, even though they limited human reason's scope.

The Enlightenment therefore was a movement with many causes and many consequences. So far as Christian faith was concerned, a summary cause was the inability of the old doctrines adequately to explain the new science and worldview. A summary consequence was a shift from theocentrism to anthropocentrism—from centering on God to centering on humanity. To be sure, this shift never was complete or uncontested. Still, it showed itself on such frontiers as the American experiment in pluralism. Not only was John Locke, an English Enlightenment philosopher, a major influence on the framers of the Constitution, but Thomas Jefferson and Benjamin Franklin both hewed to the Enlightenment line that morality was more important than doctrinal faith. In this way they greatly contributed to an American tendency to deprecate speculative theology, contemplative prayer, and any ecclesiology beyond good fellowship.

In the Middle Ages, Aquinas had fit reason and revelation together carefully. While revelation went beyond reason, it extended capacities of reason and fulfilled them. Similarly, for many medievals, analytic, contemplative, and practical reason fit together quite nicely. Study could proceed with the confidence that natural and human data were intelligible, but it finally yielded to contemplative prayer, where one could experience the Creator directly, and to practical love of one's neighbor.

The Reformation occurred in good part because this medieval balance had come undone. In 1517 analysis was not vigorous, prayer was not deep, and charity was at ebb tide. The Protestant Reformation's stress on the primacy of individual conscience opened the gates to the Enlightenment's stress on autonomy, while its stress on faith helped the Enlightenment to divorce faith from reason. The irrationality of the religious wars between Protestants and Catholics blackened the name of faith still more, and many Enlightenment rationalists became leaders in the movement for tolerance. On the Catholic side, the efforts of the Counter-Reformation to strengthen Christian dogma often produced **dogmatism**, while its efforts to centralize authority in Rome easily seemed a prime instance of heteronomy.

The result of the Enlightenment, then, was the mortal wounding of traditional Christian culture. The supernatural, authoritative, clerical world to which biblical faith had given rise lay fractured and tattered. Like Humpty Dumpty, traditional Christian faith seemed broken beyond reconstruction. For the last two hundred years Christians have either blasted the Enlightenment as a terrible deviation or used it as a stimulus to rethink their faith.

Political Changes

If the Enlightenment was the prime intellectual expression of modern civilization's discontent with Christian religion, the political changes, especially those in the United States and France, were the prime social expressions. Eric Voegelin has described something of the connection between these two forms of expression:

> The eighteenth century has been variously characterized as the century of Enlightenment and Revolution or alternatively as the Age of Reason. Whatever the merit of these designations, they embody a denial of Christian transcendental experiences and seek to enthrone the Newtonian method of science as the only valid method of arriving at truth. The apostatic revolt, for such it was, released a movement of ideas which would shape decisively the political structure of the West. With the formal abolition of Christianity as the authoritatively unifying spiritual substance of mankind, the particular community substances could move into the vacuum. The mystical bodies of the nations which had been growing ever since the high Middle Ages had achieved by the eighteenth century a considerable coherence and articulation and now they could begin to substitute with increasing effectiveness for the mystical body of Christ.[3]

When Voegelin says that the eighteenth century denied cognitive value to spiritual experiences (saying they were not rational), he underscores the limits of the Enlightenment conception of reason. Characteristically, the savants of the eighteenth century were not persons attuned to the contemplative depths of the human spirit, where traditional religion has found wisdom to be nourished by loving communion with the divine. A major cause of this nonattunement, this narrowing of reason's span, was the Church's own divorce of theology from profound religious experience. Since the dogmas of Christianity and salvation no longer seemed to symbolize living, experiential truths, the Enlightenment rationalists easily could reject them. In so doing, however, they paved the way for the aridity, one-dimensionality, and even irrationality of much subsequent Western culture. For reason unanchored in contemplative love has nothing to stop it from such irrationalities as "destroying villages in order to save them" (a famous phrase of an American commander in Vietnam), just as at earlier times faith unanchored in contemplative reason had nothing to stop it from burning witches, beheading heretics, or branding foreigners *devils* (also a famous pastime of recent Iran).

Further, as Voegelin indicates, the modern revolt from Christianity led to nationalism with a vengeance. Disaffected by Christianity's many failings, the emerging nation states neglected the universal humanity that Christian revelation had advanced.[4] Thus America expanded the Pilgrims' errand in the wilderness to what eventually became the chauvinistic idea of "manifest destiny" to lead the world. That red people and black people suffered horribly in this expansion stayed at the edge of national consciousness. In the center grew a new mystical body, the holy community of the United States. This community has lost considerable luster in the late twentieth century, as other peoples have impressed their wills, but even now we Americans feel it fitting that we, about six percent of the world's population, should consume about forty percent of the world's natural resources.

The European results of the apostasy were equally momentous. While France had the most dramatic political revolution, as well as the most ambitious goal (liberty, fraternity, equality), many other European nations elected themselves to colonize non-Western peoples. Mixing manifest destiny and greed, they came to dominate Africa, India, and many other foreign territories. Obviously the colonial process had many stimuli, but a legacy from the political revolutions was the sense of being a nation noble enough, elect enough, to subjugate others for their own good.

To be sure, peoples had subjugated other peoples since time immemorial. Biblical Israel had subjugated surrounding peoples, Christians had gone on crusades, and the conquistadors of the sixteenth century had imposed "Christian" rule on the Americas. But the political revolutions of the eighteenth century, and the nationalism of the nineteenth century, begot new rationalizations through **civil religion**.

Prior to the discovery of universal humanity in the ecumenic age (after the reign of Alexander the Great ended in 326 B.C.), the civil and the religious had been almost indistinguishable. Thus, religious civilizations such as Egypt and Rome had thought that Pharaoh and Caesar mediated divine substance to their people. In the ecumenic age the effects of Israelite revelation and Greek philosophy somewhat broke such civil religion, for they showed that divinity transcended any national or

American Religious History: Twenty-Five Key Dates

1492	About 10 million American Indians living north of Rio Grande
1565	Roman Catholic colony at St. Augustine
1619	Beginning of black slavery
1620	Mayflower Compact
1654	First Jewish settlement in New Amsterdam
1683	William Penn founds Philadelphia
1734	Great Awakening in New England
1776	Declaration of Independence expresses nonconformist, Enlightenment-influenced religious outlook
1784	Death of Shaker leader Anne Lee
1799	Creation of Russian Orthodox Diocese in Alaska
1801	Beginnings of Western Revivalism
1836	Founding of Transcendentalist Club in Concord, Mass.
1847	Bushnell's *Christian Nurture*
1848	Mormons found Salt Lake City
1850	Oberlin College grants first theological degree to a woman
1863	Emancipation Proclamation
1866	Second Roman Catholic Plenary Council in Baltimore
1876	Mary Baker Eddy founds Christian Science Association
1885	Columbia Platform of Reformed Rabbis
1890	Massacre at Wounded Knee
1901–1902	William James's Gifford lectures, *The Varieties of Religious Experience*
1917	Rauschenbush's *A Theology for the Social Gospel*
1920–1933	Prohibition
1935	Peak of Neo-Orthodoxy
1964	Civil Rights Act; Martin Luther King, Jr., receives Nobel Peace Prize

civil regime. As well, humanity transcended any national or civil regime, for revelation and philosophy realized that divinity and humanity were relational terms (each playing a role in the definition of the other). Prior to the political revolutions the semi-sacral kings clouded divine transcendence, as did the semi-sacral popes, but enough theological vigor remained to keep the core of Christianity anti-idolatrous.

The emergent nationalisms led Westerners back to a civil religion that tended to eclipse divine transcendence. This becomes clear in sociologist Robert Bellah's statement that the American Revolution and American civil religion were one and the same thing.[5] The substance of American civil religion became the faith that a rather remote God had endowed human beings with certain inalienable rights. Noble enough in itself, this faith has proved all too liable to identify God with the

American way of life. Admittedly, American antitraditionalism was not so murderous as French, but many American intellectuals labored mightily to make the new nation profane.[6]

Modern Science and the Industrial Revolution

A signal feature of the modern era was the development of the physical sciences. Discoveries in physics, chemistry, and biology radically changed the West's conception of the world. Popularly, these discoveries seemed to challenge, or even destroy, the Christian worldview. But in fact, there are grounds for arguing that modern science could have developed only in the West because of the West's biblical faith that a Creator made the world rationally.[7] Nonetheless, the popular impression had merit, because the intellectuals who advanced the modern notions of enlightenment, autonomy, and progress often claimed natural science as their ally. Relatedly, they often described their cause as a fight against ecclesiastical obscurantism (deliberately withholding or obscuring the facts).

During the seventeenth century, Galileo had run afoul of the Inquisition because he had defended the heliocentric model of the universe developed by Copernicus against the geocentric model assumed by the Church. To most fair minds of the eighteenth century, Galileo was the party of integrity and the Church that launched the Inquisition was the party of dogmatism or even of bad conscience. The discoveries of Isaac Newton (1642–1727) proved even more disturbing to the Church. If his laws of motion and gravitation explained the operations of the universe, making it an efficient machine, where did divine causality enter in? Indeed, did not the notion of divine, providential care for events of the human sphere also come into question?

Although Newton himself remained religious, his faith was not orthodox Christianity. For example, he rejected the doctrine of the Trinity, because it was inaccessible to reason. Newton's belief in the **millennium** and his interest in alchemy (the science that attempted to turn base metals into gold) suggest that his hold on reason was less than firm, but still he became a patron saint to many Enlightenment leaders because his work demonstrated the power of rational inquiry. Thus the atheistically inclined judged God irrelevant to physical science, while the group called the **Deists** allowed only a clockmaker who set things ticking in the beginning but no longer intervened. Both agreed that miracles and doctrines undemonstrable by reason were but superstitions.

As science and technology made increasing progress, religion lost further ground. To persons educated in the new disciplines, the Genesis account of creation seemed absurd. When anatomists dissected corpses, they found no entity called a soul. When astronomers probed the galaxies, they found no angels and no God. Darwinian science struck the popular mind as a massive repudiation of the traditional notion that human beings had been made in God's image, for the popular mind interpreted evolution as swapping great-grandfather for an ape. Freudian analysis shocked the genteel as well as the religious, for it spoke of incestuous longings as natural and omnipresent. Both Adam Smith and Karl Marx produced economic analyses that many considered inimical to traditional Christianity, while the sociology of Auguste Comte made religion a stage of human development long passé.

From numerous voices, therefore, the educated person of the late nineteenth and early twentieth century heard counsels to consider Christianity something backward. Anyone up-to-date and progressive would reject faith and take up empirical science. The inventions that sparked the Industrial Revolution mainly led to more voices offering this counsel. However, as the results of the Industrial Revolution unfolded, the misery of the workers and their families provided humane persons food for thought.[8] Despite the warrant for Marx's view that religion was the opium of such workers, some church people spent themselves in programs of social welfare. Nineteenth-century Methodists, for example, served Great Britain, the foremost industrial nation, a powerful blend of evangelism and social concern. Considering that the typical workday in Britain around 1800 was fourteen or fifteen hours long, and that the average worker's life expectancy in the United States around 1900 was less than forty-seven years, the need for such concern is obvious. From 1891 on, the social encyclicals of the popes expressed the Roman Catholic Church's increasing interest in social welfare, while the Protestant Social Gospel movement that flourished from 1870 to 1918 convinced many that Christian faith entailed hard work for social betterment.

Overall, the churches' intellectual and social efforts did not make them impressive to modernity. In some Western nations church attendance remained high, but the trend was for Christian faith to seem irrational and unprogressive. Just as philosophy and natural science had been slow to differentiate historically, so modern science and theology were slow to appreciate their possible complementarity. Indeed, even today few Westerners have a firm hold on the different patterns of consciousness that would enable them to distinguish religious and scientific realms but relate them intelligibly.[9] Equally, the churches were slow to diagnose the causes of modernity's discontents in ways that would galvanize Christians to spend themselves for mental health or an equitable economy. Too often clerics and elders seemed part of the class that profited from ongoing insanity and maldistribution. Thus neither the Industrial Revolution nor modern science found the support or correction Christianity might have offered them.

Karl Marx

Instead, the Industrial Revolution was offered a correction in the form of the political philosophy of Karl Marx (1818–1883), a philosophy that would galvanize workers to fight for an equitable economy. Of Jewish family, Marx grew up in a German Lutheran atmosphere, studying law, philosophy, and history. As a student he was a militant atheist "whose creed was (and remained) 'Criticism of religion is the foundation of all criticism.' "[10] From his intellectual predecessor Georg Hegel,

Marx took a dialectical understanding of history according to which change comes about in the working out of contradictions inherent in situations. From philosopher Ludwig Feuerbach he took a materialism that rejected Hegel's **idealism** and viewed religion as a form of **alienation**. To this German philosophy, Marx added English economics and French socialism, making a heady brew that intoxicated many European intellectuals.

In 1848 Marx collaborated with Friedrich Engels on the *Communist Manifesto*, a pamphlet meant to be a statement of principles for the workers' movement. The *Manifesto* criticized capitalism as the source of the workers' woes, heralded true socialism, and issued a call to revolution. Expelled from Germany in 1849, Marx lived the rest of his life in England supported by Engels, who had a prosperous textile business. Marx did some journalistic work, and dominated the International Workingmen's Association from 1864 to 1872, but his major accomplishment was *Das Kapital*, a historical and analytic critique of capitalism's evils constructed from materials in the British Museum. Insofar as capitalism was the modern West's dominant economic structure, Marx's critique went to the heart of modern Western culture. Those who found the status quo beneficial reacted harshly, while those who wanted change found *Das Kapital* an arsenal.

Robert Heilbroner has offered a balanced study of Marxism that fixes Marx's major contribution in his "socioanalysis." By revealing the social relationships necessitated by the central triad of land, labor, and capital, Marx greatly sharpened an understanding of the human implications of Western economy. Specifically, he spotlighted "the fetishism of commodities." Heilbroner's explanation of this phrase and his appreciation of its significance are both worth quoting.

> . . . a commodity is not just a thing, but also a container of invisible social relationships. It is this twofold nature of the commodity that mystifies our perception of capitalist realities. Marx calls this mystification *the fetishism of commodities*. By this he means that the exchangeability of commodities appears to result from their physical properties, not from the hidden social relationships that, by filling them with abstract labor, endow them with their attributes of exchange value. . . . the perception that commodities possess the property of exchange value because they are the repositories of an abstract form of labor; that this abstract labor testifies to the social and technical relationships of a specific mode of production; and *that a commodity is therefore the carrier and the encapsulation of the social history of capitalism*—all this comes as a stunning realization.[11]

By signifying the social relationship embodied in commodities, Marx was able to illumine the way that capitalism depends on the surplus value of labor (getting more from laborers' work than they are paid) and encapsulates a class conflict between owners and workers. This in turn fit his dialectical understanding of history (the worker-owner conflict was a prime contradiction), and connected with his views of ideology and religion. *Ideology* (a term usually carrying negative overtones) was a mental scaffolding that a society threw up to frame its social relationships, while religion largely served to distract workers from the inequalities of a capitalist society. Some of Marx's further findings (that capitalism was intrinsically "anarchic," that it would give rise to large-scale industry, that it would spread out internationally, that it would produce a continuous squeeze of technology on employment, and that it would increasingly mechanize itself) seem confirmed by subsequent history.[12] His prediction that the proletariat (the working class) would become so "immiserated" that they would revolt and form a classless society has not been confirmed to date.

We have spent this space on Marx because his ideas spurred the series of movements that made communism modernity's new world religion. In the lineage of the Hebrew prophets, Marx's cry for justice has lit revolutionary fires in dozens of countries. Despite its many failings in theory and practice alike, the movement he fathered has given Christ's second commandment a razor's edge. How can a person claim to be loving her neighbor as herself if her income is $100,000 and the neighbor's is $10,000, or even $1,000? Moreover, if society is built on such gross differences in wealth, how can one prevent class conflict? When twentieth-century Christian ethicists laid down the thesis that no one has the right to superfluities so long as anyone lacks necessities,[13] they were in large part trying to accommodate Marx's challenges in their traditions.

Atheistic, trying to be scientific, concerned with the dynamics of historical change, materialistic, and sensitive to ideological self-serving, Marx epitomizes late modernity in opposition to Christianity.[14] Like Freud and Einstein, he combined a Jewish background with German culture and made a leap of genius that opened vast new vistas. Now Latin American theologians, blacks, and feminists all give credence to his work, and Part Three of this book echoes his analysis in every chapter. Now the Soviet Union and the Republic of China control hundreds of millions by his theses. Clearly any post-modern Christianity worth its salt will have to come to terms with his ideas.

Eastern Orthodoxy

Eastern Christians living under communist regimes have perhaps felt the most direct impact of Marxism. To get to modern Eastern Christianity, one has to focus on Russia. After the Turks captured Constantinople in 1453, the leadership of Eastern Orthodoxy passed to Russia. Using the notion that Moscow was the Third Rome, the tsars fused Christianity to their own rule. But the faith of their people was still new and unassimilated. "There was no vigorous technological tradition. The clergy were painfully ill-prepared; indeed, they were often wholly illiterate. Christianity was identified with a certain system of established forms of prayer; and since these were regarded as possessing an almost magical power, the slightest change might rob them of their efficacy."[15]

Thus in 1653 when Patriarch Nikon proposed changes in church customs and the liturgy, a group called the "Old Believers" resisted staunchly. Many of the proposed changes were as small as altering the number of prostrations during prayer or the number of fingers to use in making the sign of the cross, but the resistance of many Old Believers led them to be slaughtered. The resisters gained large numbers of recruits when Tsar Peter the Great (ruling 1682–1725) tried to Europeanize Russia, and they suffered persecution again under Tsar Nicholas I (ruling 1825–1855). Nonetheless, they constituted about 20 percent of the population before the Revolution of 1917 and symbolize a wound that Russian Orthodoxy has yet fully to heal.

Peter's reforms subjugated the Church to the government. He suppressed the Moscow patriarchate and established a Holy Synod ruled by a procurator he himself closely controlled. The Russian Church was kept in this indentured form of polity until 1917. Under the ultraconservative procuratorship of Pobedonostev (1880–1905), the church functioned as a department of the state. It had a monopoly on religious propaganda, power of censorship over religious literature, and was hated by liberal elements in Russian society for its red tape and its corruption. Despite all this, the mass of the uneducated peasantry filled their lives with Orthodox devotions. Indeed, the religious life of the Russian Church gained stimulus from a variety of spiritualist movements, some of them derived from European Protestant influences. Priests were better trained, and there was a shift from Western Scholastic sources back to the patristic tradition.

With the Revolution of 1917, Marxism and Christianity came into violent conflict. The Russian Church did not seem to fit the classical Marxist paradigm:

> The Bolsheviks were not well qualified to understand the Russian Church. They were dogmatic Marxists, for whom religion was 'the opium of the people', to be eliminated by hook or by crook. Engels had said that Christianity had become the perquisite of the ruling classes which they used to bridle the lower classes. Whatever justification for this view there may have been in Western Europe, it was far from being realistic in Russia where the Orthodox Church was essentially a Church of the people and the ruling classes were for the most part alienated from it. Whatever measures the communists adopted to extirpate religion would not hit the ruling classes but the peasants.[16]

Thus the Communist war against Eastern Orthodoxy often has gone hand-in-hand with an oppression of the peasants. For that reason Russian patriotism like Solzhenitsyn's combines a defense of peasant culture and Christianity with an assault on Marxism-Leninism.

With the mention of Lenin (1870–1924), we come to the figure most responsible for Christian Russia's transformation into the atheistic Soviet Union. Lenin began his revolutionary career while taking a law degree at St. Petersburg in 1891. He was imprisoned for revolutionary activity in 1895 and exiled to Siberia in 1897. From 1900 to 1917 he mainly lived abroad. He headed the Soviet Union from the Bolshevik victory in 1917 until his death in 1924.

Lenin's main work was developing the principles of Marxist social reconstruction into a political program, and his great genius was for partisan propaganda. He stressed the need to combine dialectical theory with revolutionary practice and forged a disciplined, ruthless central authority to control the proletariat. Seeing struggle at the heart of all change, he argued that capitalism was ripe for a struggle that would deal it a final deathblow. No longer would the Western state be an instrument of the bourgeoisie; the struggle against capitalist imperialism would establish the dictatorship of the proletariat. Some Western Marxists have been impressed by Lenin's ability to make Marxist ideas politically effective, but others have been put off by his ruthlessness, lack of moral scruple, and hatred of religion. Stalin was merely continuing Lenin's line when he wrote, "The Party cannot be neutral towards religion . . . it conducts an anti-religious struggle against all and any religious prejudices."[17] Those "prejudices" boiled down to any practice of theism, while that "struggle" regularly meant imprisonment.

Of the sixty to ninety million Eastern Orthodox Christians living today, about 85 percent suffer under communist regimes that only deviate from Lenin's line grudgingly. Christianity survives in part because many find it more reasonable and fulfilling than the ideological cant of regimes both ill-managed and repressive. However, state authorities watch churches and priests carefully. The rise and fall of Dmitrii Dudko, a Russian priest who recently dared to preach Orthodox faith openly, and whom we shall study in Chapter 13, summarizes the current situation.[18]

Colonialism

Marx postulated that capitalism would be inherently expansive, seeking ever more raw materials and markets. The colonialist expansion of the nineteenth century, bringing Western dominance and Christian values to vast new areas, seemed to verify his postulate. Whatever the precise analysis, the description of colonial expansion usually runs somewhat as follows:

> Between 1815 and 1914 Europe thrust out into the world, impelled by the force of its own industrialization. Millions of Europeans poured overseas and into Asiatic Russia, seeking and finding new opportunities in the wider world. Between 1880 and 1900 Africa, a continent four times the size of Europe, was parcelled out among the European powers. And when in 1899 the United States of America, following the European lead, annexed Puerto Rico, the Philippines, and other islands of the Pacific, and asserted a controlling voice in Latin American affairs, it seemed as though European expansion was turning into the domination of the white race over the colored majority. But expansion carried within it the seeds of its own destruction.[19]

Along with this expansion went an amazing growth in population. In the nineteenth century, world population grew from about 900 million to 1600 million. In the United Kingdom, Germany, and the United States (the leading industrial countries), the population increased fivefold. Vast waves of European emigrants settled in North and South America, South Africa, Australia, New Zealand, and Siberia. From China emigrants swept into Siam, Java, the Malay Peninsula, California, British Columbia, and New South Wales. From India emigrants crossed to Natal and East Africa, eventually surpassing the number of white settlers.

In the United States the former colonies became a vast country. During the nineteenth century they arranged the Louisiana Purchase, annexed Florida, secured the Oregon territory, annexed Texas, and obtained the present southwest from Mexico, virtually filling out today's borders. Napoleon's subjugation of Spain and Portugal precipitated the emancipation of Latin America between 1806 and 1826, but Latin America's economic emancipation from Europe and North America has remained a much slower process. In the East the Ottoman Empire was disintegrating, the Chinese Empire was collapsing, Russia was expanding, India came under British rule, Africa was partitioned among the European powers, and Japan was modernizing after 1868. Thus, during the years 1815 to 1914 European powers were dominating foreign territories all over the globe. Inevitably the primary European religion was involved.

Today it is customary to decry colonialism, and to point out that the colonizers imposed on their subjects a faith as much European as Christian. Soundings from the time show that what happened was a little more complicated than that, although not completely different in the final analysis. For example, in the proclamation by which she accepted responsibility for the rule and administration of India, Queen Victoria declared: "Firmly relying ourselves on the truth of Christianity, and acknowledging with gratitude the solace of religion, We disclaim alike the right and the desire to impose Our convictions on any of Our subjects. We declare it to be Our royal will and pleasure that none be in anywise favoured, none molested, or disquieted by reason of their religious faith or observance, but that all alike shall enjoy the equal and impartial protection of the law. . . ."[20] Nonetheless, this declaration provided legal protection for Christians as well as Hindus and Muslims. Missionaries and converts obviously benefitted from European administration, at least on the surface of things.

However, since the presence of Western powers seldom fully pleased native Indians or Africans, the Western powers' religion seldom got an impartial hearing. Those who converted to it might have thought they were securing temporal advantages, or they might have felt they were risking conflict with their fellow natives. Hard indeed was it for them to separate Christianity from its political entanglements and judge it solely on its religious merits. This proved true even when Western missionaries fought hard to de-imperialize the Gospel. Some of the missionaries realized quite well that Western culture carried as much greed as charity. Others knew from the outset that a native clergy could be their only legitimate goal. Those who spent themselves cheerfully in this spirit, often living in poverty, broke many interracial and intercultural barriers. Protestant and Catholic alike, they remembered that "in Christ" there was to be neither Jew nor Greek, slave nor free.

Such missionaries also realized the old Johannine ecclesiology with new pathos. In foreign lands such as Africa and India, the divisiveness of Christians was an especially massive scandal. Jesus had prayed for his followers' unity, so that the world would know he had sent them (John 17:23). The proliferation of Christian sects in the colonies told the world it was quite unlikely that Jesus had sent the West to dominate it. With such missionary experience in mind, the Protestant churches began a powerful movement towards reunification early in the twentieth century.

The Ecumenical movement, which we touched on briefly in Chapter 5, led to both the World Council of Churches and the Second Vatican Council.

The Second Vatican Council (1962–65)

Insofar as it brought the Roman Catholics—the largest single body of Christians—into the modern age, the Second Vatican Council perhaps will prove to have been the prime religious event of the twentieth century. On the other hand, there were Protestant events without which Vatican II probably never would have occurred. At Amsterdam in 1948 Protestants had formed the World Council of Churches from two earlier ecumenical movements, "Life and Work" and "Faith and Order." The Eastern Orthodox Church had joined the World Council (with mixed feelings), as had most of the mainline Protestant churches. The Roman Catholic Church had withheld membership, feeling that to join would compromise its claim to be the one true Church, but it had worked out numerous cooperative arrangements with World Council agencies.

The presence of a worldwide body of churches working together and perhaps moving toward reunion stimulated many Roman Catholics to reconsider their own place in divided Christianity. On the Continent, Protestant and Catholic theologians increasingly came into contact, for many Protestant and Catholic churches had established good relations during the Second World War. Indeed, a group called the German Confessing Church had given the entire ecclesiastical world a brave model of resistance to Hitler, drawing on strands of thought from theologians Barth, Bultmann, and Tillich. These three became the major Protestant theologians of the mid-century, and all of them tried to redirect the Gospel to a world shaken by modern war.

In 1959 Pope John XXIII announced his plan to convoke the Second Vatican Council. It was to be the twenty-second worldwide convocation of bishops by Roman Catholic reckoning, but the first in over ninety years. And while reunion with other Christians was on the pope's mind, the primary reason for convoking Vatican II was to bring the Church up to date. This meant facing the current state of Christianity in all its aspects, disunity quite included. A number of commissions set to work preparing for the Council; the Council itself met for three and a half years (with recesses); and it brought Roman Catholicism to grips with modernity as nothing previous had.

Following the Second World War, a number of European Catholic scholars had begun to press for theological and pastoral changes, based on several prior decades of hard work. In scriptural, liturgical, and ecclesiastical matters, they had opened to Protestant and secular sources. In philosophical theology they had opened to contemporary philosophy and science. Loyal to the Church beyond question, they began to win a hearing for their claim that the revival of Aquinas promulgated by Pope Leo XIII in 1879 was not by itself a viable twentieth-century theology. For an understanding of Scripture, sacraments, current ethics, and the like cogent to twentieth-century men and women, the Church would have to freshen its tradition at the biblical and patristic sources. Even more, it would have to open a sincere dialogue with the current, secularized world.

Considering Roman Catholicism's prior conservatism, Vatican II did well. In major documents on the Church, revelation, the Church in the modern world, non-Christians, and religious freedom, the bishops showed their contemporaries the most magnanimous face visible in many decades. Lesser documents dealt with the liturgy, communications, ecumenism, Eastern churches, bishops, priestly formation, the laity, religious life, priests, education, and missions. Much of the magnanimity came from Pope John XXIII himself. Other Roman Catholic leaders had been appalled at the plan to call a Council, fearing a capitulation to modernity, or had thought that the First Vatican Council (1869–1870), by placing so much power in the hands of the pope, had obviated the need for any future councils. But John XXIII had seen the obvious fact that his church was less effective than his God might have wanted it to be, and was less helpful to a confused world than it might have been.

From the Second Vatican Council, Roman Catholics received a more benign interpretation of their Protestant brethren and sisters, most of whose communities now were considered true churches in Roman eyes. They also received a loftier appreciation of Jews, Muslims, and persons of other faiths. The bishops underscored the competence of the laity in secular matters, and also the laity's full membership in the Church. They declared that every human being had the right to religious freedom, thereby opening the way to a society religiously pluralistic. In such a society persons of different faiths might cooperate more than compete. Finally, by emphasizing the importance of Scripture and the bishops' collegiality with the pope, the Council made giant strides toward harmony with the positions of other Christians, west and east, who had found past Roman Catholic practice an insurmountable stumbling block.[21]

Summary

Modernity has been shaped by the Enlightenment at its outset and secularization near its core. The Enlightenment said human beings ought to rely upon their own reason. Impressed by Newtonian science, and put off by religious irrationalities, many European intellectuals considered the eighteenth century the period of Christian faith's demise. The political changes in America and France at the end of the eighteenth century differed in the degree to which they rejected traditional Christian faith, but both countries expressed the new mood of freedom in active, social form.

From the seventeenth century on, many thought physical science was ousting the need for religion. In the nineteenth century, the Industrial Revolution offered complex evidence of the new humanity that irreligion would produce. Marx elucidated the energies at work in Western economics, but humanistic voices like his were not the only protests. Some evangelical churches ministered to the workers tirelessly. Marx did make plain the social relationships that commodities embody. Since his time, it has been impossible to overlook the class conflicts rooted in human labor.

Eastern Orthodoxy, which had become most vibrant in Russia, met Marxist tenets in the person of Lenin. Russian Orthodoxy had suffered a sizeable crisis in the seventeenth century with the Old Believers, but prior to the Revolution of 1917 there had been significant theological renewal. While much of the intelligentsia and upper classes were disaffected, the peasants clung to Orthodoxy steadfastly.

The colonial movements of the Western powers in the nineteenth century spread capitalism around the globe, especially the British movements in India and South Africa. By Vatican II even the largest church had been forced to deal dramatically with the many facets of modernity.

Study Questions

1. Why did developments in physical science cause Enlightenment thinkers to lose respect for religion?
2. Was the God of the American Revolution but a pale remnant of the Christian Trinity? How so?
3. How did biological science such as Darwin's further throw religion on the defensive?
4. What was the link between Marx's theory of labor and his theory of religion?
5. What does the resistance of the Russian Old Believers suggest about traditional religion?
6. Discuss the ambiguity in the missionary ventures that accompanied nineteenth-century European colonialism.
7. What was John XXIII's main reason for convoking Vatican II?

Notes

1. Heribert Raab, "Enlightenment," in *Sacramentum Mundi*, ed. Karl Rahner et al. (New York: Herder & Herder, 1968), vol. 2, p. 230.
2. *The Westminster Dictionary of Church History*, Jerald C. Brauer, ed. (Philadelphia: Westminster, 1971), p. 299.
3. Eric Voegelin, *From Enlightenment to Revolution* (Durham, NC: Duke University Press, 1975), p. 3.
4. See Voegelin, *Order and History, Vol. 4: The Ecumenic Age* (Baton Rouge, LA: Louisiana State University Press, 1974).
5. Robert Bellah, "The Revolution and the Civil Religion," in *Religion and the American Revolution*, ed. Jerald C. Brauer (Philadelphia: Fortress, 1977), p. 55.
6. William A. Clebsch, *From Sacred to Profane America* (New York: Harper & Row, 1968).

7. See Stanley L. Jaki, *The Road of Science and the Ways to God* (Chicago: University of Chicago Press, 1978).
8. See, for instance, E. P. Thompson, *The Making of the English Working Class* (New York: Vintage Books, 1963).
9. See Bernard Lonergan, *Method in Theology* (New York: Herder & Herder, 1972), especially Chapters 3 and 4; also Gary Zukav, *The Dancing Wu Li Masters* (New York: William Morrow, 1979).
10. Neil McInnes, "Karl Marx," *The Encyclopedia of Philosophy*, ed. Paul Edwards (New York: Macmillan/Free Press, 1967), vol. 5, p. 172.
11. Robert Heilbroner, *Marxism: For and Against* (New York: W. W. Norton, 1980), pp. 102–03.
12. For example, by 1970 the one-hundred largest enterprises in the United States owned almost 50 percent of all manufacturing assets (Heilbroner, p. 129).
13. See John A. Coleman, "Vision and Praxis in American Theology," *Theological Studies*, 37/1 (March 1976), p. 30.
14. He may also epitomize modern Gnosticism. See Eric Voegelin, *Science, Politics, and Gnosticism* (Chicago: Henry Regnery, 1968), especially pp. 23 ff., where Voegelin charges that Marx was an intellectual swindler.
15. Gerald R. Cragg, *The Church and the Age of Reason 1648–1789* (Grand Rapids, MI: Eerdmans, 1960), p. 109.
16. Alec R. Vidler, *The Church in an Age of Revolution* (Baltimore: Penguin, 1961), p. 232.
17. Quoted by Timothy Ware, *The Orthodox Church* (Baltimore: Penguin, 1964), p. 152.
18. See the collection of Dudko's discussions, *Our Hope* (Crestwood, NY: St. Vladimir's Seminary Press, 1977).
19. *The Times Atlas of World History*, Geoffrey Barraclough, ed. (Maplewood, NJ: Hammond, 1979), p. 207.
20. Quoted by Stephen Neill, *A History of Christian Missions* (Baltimore: Penguin, 1964), p. 323.
21. For a deeper interpretation see Karl Rahner, "A Basic Interpretation of Vatican II," *Theological Studies*, 40/4 (December 1979), 716–727.

Crucifixion, by El Greco, Spanish, 1545–1614. Nelson Gallery–Atkins Museum, Kansas City, Missouri (Nelson Fund).

PART 3

Contemporary Christianity

We have examined some of the principal notions of the Christian worldview and surveyed some of the major developments in Christian history. In Part Three our task is to render something of what Christianity is today—something of its current vitality, interests, and problems. Long before they became grand concepts fitted into theologians' schemes, creation, sin, grace, and incarnation were part of the experience of particular people in specific places. The Synoptics, the Fathers, the Scholastics, the Reformers, and the Modernists all thought about such concepts, but not in a vacuum. Rather they thought about such concepts in the context of their own lives and times, with the hope that understanding would improve their lives. The same is true of their successors today. We can approach the contemporary rethinking of Christianity as though we have a stake in it ourselves.

Modernity put a spotlight on individual rights and raised enormous hopes for material progress. The individual rights that liberals such as philosopher John Stuart Mill (1806–1873) espoused in the past century hardly have been secured around the globe, though they have entered the patrimony of the West, advancing it another step toward free speech and tolerance. Indeed, commentators such as Robert Heilbroner come to gloomy projections of the future in part because they judge Western liberties incompatible with global survival.[1] Despite material progress, the nuclear armaments, ecological poisons, economic disparities, and political instabilities that have surfaced since the Second World War force a sober view of humankind's prospects.

It is precisely the spread of this sobriety that justifies calling World War II the death-knell of modernity. While prophets like Friedrich Nietzsche had announced the death of God and the ungluing of Western culture at the end of the nineteenth century, the generations after Hiroshima were the first to take the announcement seriously. The many other things going on crowded the announcement off center stage, but behind the exploding communications, multinational corporations, space explorations, genetics, and the like grew a discernible spiritual malaise. It came closer in the civil rights and peace movements in the United States. Like a warning musk, it advanced at the edge of feminism. For the shifts in consciousness that dominated the 1960s and 1970s placed geiger counters at the foundations of Western society and found much to fear.

The same was at least equally true in other parts of the globe. If its Vietnam excursion clouded America's image in the world, the Soviet Union's Gulag Archipelago symbolized decades of violence against its own citizenry. One would not even know what violence occurred in the People's Republic of China, while throughout Africa and South America despots butchered citizens by the tens of thousands. Of course flood, famine, and earthquake continued, giving the lie to the nineteenth-century dream of progress, but their horrors paled before so many peoples' inhumanity. Uganda, Cambodia, Vietnam, Iran, Brazil—the question became, if God had not died, where was She?

Perhaps for that reason, the war between atheists and believers seemed to abate. At the elemental level of questions raised by the Nazi Holocaust or Hiroshima, the name one used for sanity, goodness, or hope mattered little. If invoking either "God" or "the people" led to concern and kindness, it was a blessed name. If invoking either led to injustice or destruction, it was a vile name.

Our last chapters take us to five outposts where the three major Christian traditions (Catholic, Protestant, and Orthodox) and two new schools of theology (black theology and feminism) pursue wisdom and love before Armageddon. From the taproots of tradition to the newest leaves of need, the contemporary Christianity we portray offers both a reprise of the faith we have seen and several new extensions. The Latin American liberation theologians, for instance, take their stand on the Bible *and* Marx. To do so they interpret Marx as a son of the biblical prophets and argue that Christianity should be a passionate call for justice. If Nicaraguan poet Ernesto Cardenal's community of *campesinos* in Solentiname is representative, the argument is eloquent indeed.

So too with the other snapshots of current Christianity we examine. To see the World Council of Churches puzzling over the implications of faith and science in an unjust world is to appreciate both the revolutions science implies and the irreplaceability of faith. To visit Orthodox prayer is to buttress such faith, while to hear black and feminist theologians is to yoke Marx, Freud, and Christ for the new defense of human hope. Centuries ago the Greek Father Irenaeus wrote that God's glory is human beings fully alive. Part Three sets out after God's glory, as some scattered—but we hope revealing—specimens of today's Christianity evoke it.

Note

1. See Heilbroner, *An Inquiry into the Human Prospect, Updated and Reconsidered for the 1980s* (New York: W. W. Norton, 1980).

CHAPTER 11

Latin American Catholicism

The Theology of Liberation

The classical definition of Christian theology is "faith seeking understanding." The theologian has been one who grows up in the Christian tradition, lives a sacramental life, and works to elucidate the mysteries that the tradition and sacramental life communicate. Thus the motto of the Dominican Order, the source of some of the greatest Roman Catholic theologians such as Thomas Aquinas: "To hand on the fruits of contemplation." Classical theologians and preachers were dealing with a reality they thought they could not change. Rooted in a changeless God, theology itself easily came to be regarded as immutable.

We came upon this mentality earlier, in our discussion of Eastern Orthodoxy after the great Fathers, and we could document it in other religious traditions. From the conservative instincts of community elders, who generally have wished to maximize social stability, has come the view that the world is stable, consistent. "The more things change, the more they stay the same."

Modernity contested this proposition. As scientific and historical information accumulated, modern people found things changed a great deal. Indeed, political changes in Europe encouraged left-wing thinkers like Marx to try to revolutionize philosophy itself. Whereas in the past philosophers had sought to understand the world, in the present their task was to change the world.

Liberation theology, a theology focused on freeing people from oppression, mainly accepts such a changed conception of the studies concerned with wisdom. Influenced by Marxism or American **pragmatism** (orientation toward action), it argues that truth is not best grasped from the sidelines. Many crucial political and social truths only emerge when one participates in their processes. The best philosophy or theology often will be that which links itself most intimately with *praxis* (action, practice). In contrast to merely academic or ecclesiastical schools of thought, liberation theology seeks to elucidate truths that matter practically.

Robert McAfee Brown has described more fully the new key in which the liberationists would have theology sing.[1] Whereas classical theology often started with nature, attempting to show God's presence in the physical world, or made tradition its point of departure, liberation theology begins with the experience of the poor. In the view of Latin American theologians who have promulgated liberation themes most successfully, the authority from which the next generation of Christian self-understanding should derive is society's most marginalized peoples. Dom Helder Camara, the Brazilian archbishop world-renowned for his defense of the poor, defines what Latin Americans mean by *marginal*: "Anyone who has stood by the road trying to hitch a lift in a hurry and watched the motor cars flash by him can understand what is meant by 'marginal.' A marginal person is someone who is left by the wayside in the economic, social, political, and cultural life of his country."[2] Marginalized peoples are expert in a country's most pressing failures. They are the people to consult if you want an agenda of truly basic needs.

Liberation theology would concentrate the light of the Gospel on the marginal, the people most in need of salvation. By preference it would dialogue with those accounted nonpersons, whom it believes God loves in a special way. Using the tools of social science, liberation theology would come closer to understanding and responding to society as it really operates, that old phrases about sin and grace might gain new life; that *barrios* empty of hope might hear how things could change. Conflict is high on liberation theology's list of watchwords. Refusing to sweep bankers and beggars together under one rug, it remembers Jesus's demand that we be reconciled with our enemies before making an offering to God (Matt. 5:23–24). Insisting that theologians share the realities about which they discourse, it makes experience in the practical side of salvation, engagement with liberation, requisite for all teachers. For the first Christian act is to engage one's faith. Theology is the second, reflective act that asks the Spirit to illumine as she will.

We shall see the lineage of these ideas, but already their potency should be clear. Take a continent where the contrasts between rich and poor are dramatic. Let the rich scramble to retain power any way they can. Derive the basic ethos of the continent from Spanish Christianity, and add a dedicated corps of well-educated clergy. Allow these clergy to convince their bishops that the Gospel opposes the going socio-economic structures, and your pot has reached the boiling point.

"For freedom Christ has set us free," Galatians 5:1 proclaims. In the course of history Christian understanding of such freedom has assumed many forms. By modern times in Latin America, blessing wretchedness as a short-cut to heaven seemed to be the only way Christianity could console the poor for the unfreedom of oppression. Not so should the Gospel of Christ sound, liberation theologists began to say. Not thus should the Word of God be polluted. The Word of God should be a two-edged sword, cutting to the joint and marrow. It should reveal the thoughts, the very makeup, of a person's soul. When those thoughts do not nourish love of God and love of neighbor, the Word of God turns to woe. Thus Jesus did not hesitate to proclaim: "Woe to you that are rich; woe to you that are full now; woe to you that laugh now; woe to you when all speak well of you" (Luke 6:24–26). For the liberation theologians, Jesus cast woe on these people because they were oppressing their countrymen, through greed or pride. By contrast, Jesus had come to set people free.

Biblical Themes

Reflecting on the many-sided captivity of their people, the Latin Americans have developed a many-sided analysis of the freedom Christianity ought to bring. Two theologians quite prominent in this work have been the Peruvian Gustavo Gutierrez and the Mexican José Miranda. In fact Gutierrez's *Theology of Liberation*,[3] published in Spanish in 1971, became the movement's primary text. It joined an analysis of the Church's situation with a reinterpretation of the biblical story in what became a typical liberation pattern. Front and center in the reinterpreted biblical story were freedom and sin: " 'For freedom Christ has set us free' (Gal. 5:1), St. Paul tells us. He refers here to liberation from sin insofar as it represents a selfish turning in upon oneself. To sin is to refuse to love one's neighbors and, therefore, the Lord himself. Sin—a breach of friendship with God and others—is according to the Bible the ultimate cause of poverty, injustice, and the oppression in which men live."[4] The root of the problem, then, is sin. Where human beings do not live openly, in love with God and one another, they develop poverty, injustice, and oppression.

Gutierrez's analysis depends on a full range of biblical notions for its depth and context. For example, his God is a Creator who has provided adequately for all people. Poverty, therefore, seldom is a matter of inadequate resources. The usual cause of poverty is human selfishness or noncooperation. However, the biblical God is more than a Creator. To combat human waywardness, God has encouraged the counter-energies of grace: faith, hope, and love. They offer the strength and perspective to cut through human selfishness. As well, they keep alive an incarnational religion, where divine mystery anoints all human flesh.

Genesis is the major biblical pointer toward a provident Creator; the prophetic writings underscore the social effects of sin; and Exodus is the great text on unexpected liberation. Getting their teeth into such paradigms, liberation theologians such as Gutierrez have treated the Bible and their people's situation dialectically. Their people, poor and suffering, are not receiving the benefits God intended from the Creation. Local leaders and foreign industrialists have siphoned away what should be common wealth. Like the avaricious Israelites against whom the prophets inveighed, these oppressors show themselves ignorant of God. But God is not ignorant of God. The divine nature, classically expressed in leading Israel from bondage in Egypt, remains intent on justice today. So God hears the cries of Latin America's afflicted and labors for their deliverance. For Gutierrez, he continues to side with the enslaved, to oppose the unjust pharaohs and generals.

José Miranda has condensed this Old Testament logic into the proposition that one only knows the biblical God by doing justice.[5] Why? Because the knowledge the Bible treasures is concrete and interpersonal. It is holistic, like the knowledge of friend and friend or spouse and spouse. Consequently, biblical knowledge is incompatible with dishonesty and self-closure. It rules venality, injustice, or oppression as out of bounds. Indeed, in the Bible God coincides with honesty and love. Human honesty and love do not exhaust God, but they are conditions absolutely essential for knowing God. This is the background for Jesus's linking love of God and love of neighbor. This is whence John derives the impossibility of loving God and hating one's brother.

Miranda's powerful book *Being and the Messiah*[6] develops such New Testament foundations of liberation theology. In his view, the Johannine community believed Jesus was a new beginning, a radical victory over sin. Thus Johannine faith meant access to a salvation that could heal human beings here and now. Far from postponing liberation to heaven, the Johannine theologians were incarnational through and through. They thought the Word's taking flesh had made grace closer than sin. If people really believed—really cast their lives into the Spirit's keeping—they could make heaven on earth. If they wanted justice badly enough, they could create the city of God.

A third Latin American, Jon Sobrino, has developed a Christology of liberation.[7] Drawing close to the synoptic Jesus, he has shown the centrality of justice to Jesus's message and the primacy of *praxis*. Really to believe in Jesus is to follow Jesus's way. It is a doing, an imitating, not just a verbal professing. Committed to the Kingdom of God, Jesus lived the Kingdom's creative, suffering life of love. His only treasure was his Father's desire for justice and love; his only program was to form a community of service. Translate these Christological theses for Latin America, or any other continent, and you fashion a socio-theology quite revolutionary.

Marxist Themes

The dialectic between biblical faith and their people's situation makes the liberationists socio-theologians. Not accidentally, this dialectic bears many similarities to Marxist thought. Disputing the total rejection of Marx that many Christians have been taught, the liberationists often distinguish Marx's social analysis from his atheism. The social analysis—of class conflict, ideology, and the effects of capitalism—seems to them largely accurate. How atheistic Marxism must be is debatable.[8]

Dispelling a number of myths, Marx showed the alienation at the heart of Western economics. The disparities in wealth following on industrialization were but part of a systematic abuse of one population segment by another. Recently some Brazilian bishops have applied this perspective to Latin America forcefully:

> Capitalism must be overcome. It is the great wrong, the cumulative sin, the rotten root, the tree that bears the fruit we know: poverty, hunger, sickness, and death to the great majority. For this reason the system of ownership of the means of production (of factories, of land, of commerce, of banks, of credit

> sources) must be overcome . . . we want a world in which the fruits of labor are shared by everyone. We want a world in which one works not to get rich but to provide everyone with the necessities of life: food, health, a house, education, clothing, shoes, water, and light. We want a world in which money will be at the service of men, and not man at the service of money.[9]

One can see why Jimmy Carter ordered the CIA to engage in surveillance of activist priests and nuns in Latin America, why Nelson Rockefeller warned that the agitation for change from the Church in Latin America could be detrimental to U.S. business interests.[10] Like Marxists, many Latin American church leaders look on North American capitalism as an enemy. More concerned for the welfare of their people than for the profits of North American businesses, they have decried their continent's poverty as an evil that should not be, a sin persons of good will should struggle to overcome.

In this sense, the liberationists have not backed away from class conflict. Where they have seen profiteering, the abuse of one sector by another, they have named it and called for its cessation. But most of the liberationists have striven to distinguish their species of class conflict from that of militant Marxists by setting it in the context of a love that reaches out even to one's enemies. Jesus obviously preached this love. He went to his death in good part because of it. The leading Latin American Christians are too close to Jesus, too intent on contemplating his way, not to recoil from a class conflict that would spawn hatred. They have their own version of the classless society in mind, their own beckoning utopia. A world "in which the fruits of labor are shared by everyone" would be a world where the Church fully flowered, for the Church is a gathering that should dissolve differences between Jew and Greek, slave and free, male and female. Human beings are so equal in God's sight that the hunger of one castigates the surfeit of another.

Insofar as Marxism has unveiled the ideologies that screen societies from their unjust socio-economic structures, Latin Americans have also developed a Marxist sensitivity to ideology. Each society tends to develop a mixture of religious, patriotic, and common sense notions that props its social arrangements. Obviously enough, this mixture is liable to be self-serving. For example, it is hard for North Americans to confront dispassionately the disproportionate fraction of the world's resources they consume, because consuming that fraction is essential to their affluence. In the same way, it has been hard for whites to confront racism, whether in South Africa or the United States, because racism has served whites' manifold advantage. Thus, one finds tortured defenses of apartheid in South Africa, of "gradualism" in the United States. Adopting Marxist insights, the liberationists call such defenses ideological—irrational, self-serving, and un-Christian. Without denying the complexity of many social problems, they insist that until justice, radical equality, is its bottom line, a program or analysis is tainted.[11]

Last, the liberationists have even appropriated much in the Marxist critique of religion. To Marx, religion was inseparable from a condition of oppression. So long as people existed in unjust, alienated socio-economic situations, they would take refuge in religious hopes and imaginings. Sometimes Marx criticized these hopes and imaginings bitterly, sometimes he was kindly toward them.[12] Always, however, he wanted practical changes that would remove the injustices causing religious escapes. This is what the liberation theologians want. Casting a critical eye on their own bailiwick, they have seen religion supporting many an unjust status quo. So they tend to read the New Testament as a critique of the "culture Christianity" that has grown up on their continent, denying that an authentic Christianity ever could have supported Latin American oppression.

Traditional Roman Catholic Social Teaching

Although the Latin American liberationists' mixture of biblical and Marxist themes is a fresh brew, it has a family resemblance to the social doctrine of the recent popes. By 1891 the popes had recognized the depth of Europe's social crisis and begun to update Catholic moral theology. Leo XIII's encyclical *Rerum Novarum* of that year was the first in what became a distinguished series of social pronouncements. As David Hollenbach's study, *Claims in Conflict*,[13] shows in detail, the issue central to the series has been the dignity of the human person.

Leo XIII was by temperament a conservative. His first reaction to late nineteenth-century social thought was to feel a need to defend the human person against the encroachments of the modern state. "Man precedes the state," Leo sloganized. In other words, political, legal, and economic structures are only as good as what they do for human beings. The state exists for its citizens, not vice versa. Still, social morality is not purely the product of human choice. For Leo it entailed the **natural law**, an objective order written into creation that balanced freedom with constraint. Politically this translated into a middle ground between either tyrannies of the left or tyrannies of the right.

Rerum Novarum also criticized the economic abuses of its time. Systems that stripped workers of their dignity, refusing to pay them decent wages, were but offspring of greed. By the time of Pius XI's *Quadragesimo Anno*, which commemorated the fortieth anniversary of *Rerum Novarum*, the economic and political situation had shifted dramatically. Pius wrote in the midst of the Great Depression, the consolidation of a Communist regime in Russia, and the rise of fascism in Italy and Germany. Decrying the vast disparities in wealth he saw in the modern world, the pope championed the proletariat. For example, although he rejected Marxist-Leninist philosophy, he condemned capitalism's tendency to reduce human beings to their economic functions as workers.

In opposition to nazism and the forces underlying the Second World War, Pius XII developed the Catholic defense of the human person still further. Insisting that all forms of social life depend on morally sound relationships, he detailed many of the specific rights all persons have: to develop their bodily, intellectual, moral, and religious dimensions; to choose their state in life; to work; to develop their national culture; and so forth. The influential encyclicals of John XXIII set these and other human rights in the more international context of the late 1950s and early 1960s. In fact, John's *Pacem in Terris* (1963) impressed many world leaders for its comprehensive view of the world community in terms of an updated, more flexible and historical theory of natural law.

When the bishops of Vatican II applied themselves to social questions, above all in *Gaudium et Spes*, the conciliar document on the Church in the modern world, they added a sense of history that natural law theory tended to lack. The international community was witnessing so much change that it required a more dynamic view of natural rights. This became clearer in Paul VI's post-conciliar *Populorum Progressio* (1967), which spoke of *development* as the new name for peace. Correlatively, it urged rich nations to curb economic expansion that would injure poor nations or wound their development.

The Synod of Bishops that met in 1971 affirmed the social teaching of Paul VI's encyclicals and gave the old criterion of personal dignity a new edge. When a society marginalizes a significant number of its people, shunting them to the economic, political, or cultural sidelines, it fails its major test. For the institutions of any society—its government bureaus, businesses, schools, and the like—are healthy in the measure they promote all citizens' share in its benefits. Thus a good index for any reform is the degree to which it increases the participation of the marginalized. Programs not drawing in the poor, racial minorities, women, children, the aged, the handicapped—all those who have tended to be marginal—cannot be considered progressive or Christian.

Let us summarize the recent Roman Catholic tradition.[14] It has criticized both communism and capitalism, because both have tended to brutalize the individual person. Nonetheless, its mainsteam has been quite positive. For example, it has preached the biblical perception that the goods of the earth are for all the earth's people. Also, it has kept the incarnational view that human beings should so enjoy material things that they more vigorously pursue spiritual things. Thus the tradition has thought teaching, curing, creating, worshipping, and cooperating more important than doing business or chasing pleasure. Thus it has accorded each human being an inviolable sanctity and condemned all torture, terrorism, and manipulation for profit.

John Paul II in Latin America

In January of 1979, John Paul II, the first non-Italian pope in modern times, went to Puebla, Mexico to preside at the opening of CELAM III, the third Conference of Latin American Bishops, convened to discuss evangelization. The scene was dramatic, because the pope was known (from his days as a Polish cardinal) to be a staunch opponent of communism, while many influential theologians of the Latin American Church had been urging Marxist analyses on the bishops. At CELAM II at Medellin, Colombia, in 1968, the bishops had adopted a prophetic stance, making a firm commitment to their continent's poor. They had spoken then of a "situation of sin." Those most responsible for this situation were Latin America's upper classes and the foreign monopolies, who represented "an international imperialism of money" leading to "institutionalized violence" against the people, who yearned for "liberation from all servitudes."[15]

However, in the decade between Medellin and the preparations for CELAM III, conservatives had gained power in the Latin American hierarchy and, with some encouragement from Paul VI and the Roman curia, had cast liberation theology into ill repute. Nonetheless, leaders such as Helder Camara of Brazil had warned that fascism was as much a threat as communism, and after the 1973 ouster of the freely elected Marxist Allende regime in Chile their warnings had gained weight: "Thanks to the work of such pioneers as Brazil's bishop Padim and theologian Comblin, who studied the new militarism in a systematic way, church leaders began to perceive the connection between U.S. counterinsurgency training and aid, the Rockefeller Report's advocacy of militarism, the sudden growth in multinational subsidiaries in Latin America, and the simultaneous rise of dictatorships. There was ample evidence to document this connection, in Brazil, Uruguay, Chile, Bolivia, and Central America."[16]

At Puebla John Paul II walked a middle line, praising the bishops' commitment to the poor but trying to qualify the participation of the clergy in politics. Using the conference's stated theme of evangelization, he began with a reminder that the bishops should be sure they taught Christ's full truth, pure doctrine radiating from solid Christology. Specifically, he rebuked those who kept silent about Christ's divinity or interpreted redemption merely as social improvement. Christ's redemption was a freeing from sin, a bestowal of divine life, that went beyond social improvement and did not resort to violence. Further, sound evangelization entailed traditional ecclesiology and anthropology (theory of human nature). The Church stood not by human means but by the Word of God, mediated through the sacred teaching office of the pope and bishops. And the truth the Church had to preach about human nature stressed the disorders that result when human beings do not center in God. John Paul II pointed to the immorality and violence of contemporary life as prime examples.

These were rather cautionary remarks, intended to keep Latin America's theologians away from innovations in Christology, ecclesiology, or theological anthropology. The pope balanced them with delicate but clear support for the bishops' defense of their continent's poor. For example, he referred to the constant tradition of the Church that private property does not constitute an absolute or unconditional right. Indeed, no one is justified in keeping what he does not need for his exclusive use when other people lack necessities. Rather, property owners have an obligation to serve the good of all. Christ did not neglect such issues of social morality, and neither can Church leaders. In a continent plagued with wealthy absentee landowners, these were firm challenges to the status quo.

The pope went on to decry Latin America's various forms of collective violence, including physical and psychological torture. Some of this violence was so long-standing it had entered the very fabric of Latin American culture, inducing a mass blindness to the oppression of many marginalized groups. The evangelization of Latin America had to include a proper liberation from such violence, one that helped men and women participate freely and without coercion in the structures that governed their lives.

In other speeches during his stay in Santo Domingo and Mexico, John Paul II dotted different i's and crossed different t's.[17] Associating himself with Paul VI's desire to be in solidarity with the poor, John Paul II told Indians and peasants that he, too, wished to be their voice and champion. Referring to the judgment scene in Matthew 25, the pope impressed the seriousness of social morality on his listeners. So long as the advocates of social change did not neglect the gospel's **supernatural** dimension, he blessed their efforts to promote their people's progress toward a better life and fuller dignity. The pope did caution that the distinction between lay and clerical roles should be maintained, so that priests would not appear to be working for particular political parties, but he reaffirmed priests' duty to preach social responsibility.

Overall, then, the pope gave each side in the Latin American debate over liberation theology some ammunition. He was explicit enough in reiterating the teachings of his predecessors' social encyclicals to be claimed by those advocating the church's involvement in building a new politico-economic structure, and he was cautious enough in reiterating traditional Christology and ecclesiology to please conservatives.

Comunidades de Base

The themes of John Paul II's visit to Mexico recurred in his first encyclical, *Redemptor Hominis*, which appeared in March 1979. Speaking in the broader context of the whole world's social and cultural needs, he repeated his predecessors' concerns about the great disparities in wealth and power that blind modern peoples to the unity of the human race. Equally, he repeated his predecessors' concern for justice, pointing out that the work of justice is peace and that human rights are justice's sign. These themes have remained prominent in the pope's subsequent allocutions, and they were deepened in his second encyclical, *Dives in Misericordia*, which appeared in November 1980. According to *Dives in Misericordia*, God's full plan for human beings requires that we go beyond a legalistic sense of justice to heartfelt mercy. This is the way God deals with human beings, as Christ's dramatic parable of the prodigal son (Luke 15) shows, and it is the way human beings can reverse the antagonisms that cripple social life on all levels.[18]

As though to demonstrate what liberation theology can mean at the grass roots, and to give John Paul II's rather solemn ecclesiology concrete form, the Latin Americans have been developing what they call *comunidades de base*: communities that are local, small-scale, at the grass roots, rooted in the actualities of the people's daily lives. A winsome expression of this development is Ernesto Cardenal's three volumes entitled *The Gospel in Solentiname.*[19] They represent the discussions of a little grass roots community in a remote archipelago of Lake Nicaragua. Its *campesinos* (farm laborers) would gather each Sunday for Mass, and after hearing the Gospel text of the day they would discuss its implications. Cardenal, a poet, priest, and political activist, usually led the Liturgy, and he was so impressed by the interpretations of the text the peasants produced that before long he began to record them.

This went on for several years during the mid-1970s, until October 1977, when the soldiers of President Anastasio Somoza burned the houses of the islanders, vandalized their library, and destroyed the other facilities of their little community. Cardenal and the *campesinos* were not surprised: the surveillance and threats of the government had been a running theme in their Gospel discussions. However, they were disappointed by the government's action, for Solentiname had become a beacon of hope. Cardenal had organized a lay monastery, a fish and farm produce cooperative, a clinic, and an artists' center. For miles around people had drawn strength from the Solentiname community, and from all over the world it had drawn visitors. When Solentiname was destroyed, because it was a supposed threat to "national security," the code word for repression in Latin America, Cardenal fled to Costa Rica, where he joined the Sandanista guerrillas. He participated in the revolution that ousted Somoza and served the new government as the minister of culture.

The design of Solentiname expresses the liberationists' notion of how the Church ought to function. First, it ought to be *with* and truly *of* the people. In most modern ecclesiology since the Reformation, the Church has been seen to consist of all the faithful. However, Roman Catholicism only fully affirmed this theology at Vatican II, where it first made "the people of God" predominate over older metaphors that stressed the clerical hierarchy. Solentiname was a gathering of locals opened to anyone else who wanted to come. Its axis ran from the Gospel and the Liturgy, taken as the prime expressions of universal Christian faith, to the local community, the band of neighbors who knew one another intimately and shared a common fortune.

Second, Solentiname was a model for a Church balanced between practical necessities and spiritual aspirations. Its cooperatives and clinic served the people's need to make a living and obtain decent medical care. Its monastery, regular liturgy, and artists' center served the spiritual aspirations of both the local people and outsiders. (The artists' center produced paintings, woodwork, handicrafts and poetry that became known around the world.) The major effort was to draw from the people themselves the initiative, creativity, and sense of self-worth that produces a rich, simple, profound communal life.

Third, the community did not sever itself from the political life of its nation but interpreted its faith as a call to promote justice all around. Cardenal is perhaps the most famous of its political activists, but many others, both local peasants and visitors, actively opposed Somoza and suffered persecution. In fact, their political reading of the Gospel was the most striking aspect of the Solentiname community's discussions. Again and again they interpreted Jesus and the New Testament in terms of liberation from suffering, inequality, injustice, or anything else that mottles human life. For example, in commenting on John the Baptist's saying (Luke 3:10–12) that a person who has two shirts should give one to a person who has none, a community member named Felipe said, "John is telling us that this is the society that we have to create. That nobody ought to have one shirt more than his comrade. . . . We're going to be all equal. That's what we have to seek: socialism, because that way we'd all be living a just life, like God wants."[20]

The aim of these last chapters is to show places where Christianity is alive and revelatory today. In our opinion, the Solentiname community, and much in Latin American Catholicism generally, recently has been alive, revelatory, and a sign of hope to the rest of Christianity. When *campesinos* like Felipe find the economics, art, and politics of their daily life illumined by the Gospel, freed by Christ's love, Christianity is alive and well. This does not mean that Christianity entails **socialism**, nor that all the vitality of Latin American Christianity comes from Roman Catholics. Socialism is too imprecise a term for the Christian theologian to approve it without close study of what it means in the concrete, and some of Latin America's most eloquent liberation theologians come from the Reformed traditions.[21] It does mean that some Catholic liturgies and Catholic priests have been offering Latin America an evangel so challenging and consoling that the rest of the Christian world would do well to take notice.

Summary

The theology of liberation assumes that the task of the wisdom disciplines is not merely to understand reality but to change it for the better. Specifically, it believes that "faith seeking understanding" must stand with the poor, engage in the *praxis* of following Christ, employ the resources of the social sciences, and concentrate on freeing whole persons, body and soul. The Latin American Catholics who have been foremost in this movement have employed both biblical and Marxist themes. From the Bible they have retrieved the themes that one only knows God by doing justice and imitating Jesus's self-sacrificing love. From Marxism they have adapted themes of class conflict, the self-protective function of ideologies, and the dangers of a religion that props the status quo.

Traditional Roman Catholic social teaching, as enunciated by the popes since Leo XIII at the end of the nineteenth century, supports many of the liberationists' emphases. Centered on the dignity of the human person, this traditional teaching has articulated the rights each person naturally has and criticized both Communist and capitalist systems for the ways in which they fail to honor these rights. Since Vatican II the authoritative teaching has sharpened its central criterion: where a system marginalizes significant fractions of its citizenry, it is in need of serious reform.

John Paul II walked a middle line between progressives and conservatives when he visited the Latin American bishops in 1979. He affirmed the bishops' call for reforms that would enfranchise Latin America's marginalized but cautioned about innovations in doctrine or clerical intrusions into partisan politics. Grass roots communities such as Solentiname exemplify the broader swell of the liberationists' vision, however, showing it to be a highly compelling fusion of justice, faith, and love.

Study Questions

1. How does *praxis* epitomize the changes the liberationists would bring to Christian theology?
2. Explain the logic of the biblical proposition that one must do justice to know God.
3. Is Christianity at core an ideology more supportive of change for social justice than opposed to such change? Why?
4. What are the pros and cons of the traditional Roman Catholic teaching that the well-being of the human person is the central criterion of social institutions?
5. Was John Paul II realistic in supporting the Latin American bishops' advocacy on behalf of the poor while discouraging the clergy from direct participation in politics?
6. How adequate a model for local churches was the grass roots community in Solentiname?
7. According to the liberation theologians, how should justice, faith, and love combine to empower liberation?

Notes

1. Robert McAfee Brown, *Theology in a New Key* (Philadelphia: Westminster, 1978).
2. Quoted by Brown, ibid., p. 60.
3. See Gutierrez's A *Theology of Liberation*, trans. and ed. by Sister Caridad Inda and John Eagleson (Maryknoll, NY: Orbis, 1973).
4. Ibid., p. 35.
5. See José Miranda, *Marx and the Bible* (Maryknoll, NY: Orbis, 1974), especially pp. 44–53.
6. José Miranda, *Being and the Messiah* (Maryknoll, NY: Orbis, 1977).
7. See Jon Sobrino, *Christology at the Crossroads* (Maryknoll, NY: Orbis, 1978).
8. See José Miranda, *Marx Against the Marxists* (Maryknoll, NY: Orbis, 1980).
9. Phillip E. Berryman, "Latin American Liberation Theology," in *Theology in the Americas*, Sergio Torres and John Eagleson, eds. (Maryknoll, NY: Orbis, 1976), p. 61.
10. Robert McAfee Brown, "The Significance of Puebla for the Protestant Churches in North America," in *Puebla and Beyond*, John Eagleson and

Philip Scharper, eds. (Maryknoll, NY: Orbis, 1979), p. 330. For broader background see Penny Lernoux, *Cry of the People: United States Involvement in the Rise of Fascism, Torture, and Murder and the Persecution of the Catholic Church in Latin America* (Garden City, NY: Doubleday, 1980).

11. On the importance of ideological sensitivity in theology, see Juan Luis Segundo, *The Liberation of Theology* (Maryknoll, NY: Orbis, 1976).
12. See Owen Chadwick, *The Secularization of the European Mind in the Nineteenth Century* (New York: Cambridge University Press, 1975), pp. 48–87.
13. David Hollenbach, *Claims in Conflict* (New York: Paulist, 1979).
14. See Joseph Gremillion, ed., *The Gospel of Peace and Justice* (Maryknoll, NY: Orbis, 1976).
15. See Penny Lernoux, "The Long Path to Puebla," in *Puebla and Beyond*, p. 11.
16. *Ibid*.
17. See *John Paul II in Mexico: His Collected Speeches* (New York: Collins, 1979).
18. These encyclicals may be found in *The National Catholic Reporter*, March 23, 1979 and December 19, 1980.
19. Ernesto Cardenal, *The Gospel in Solentiname* (Maryknoll, NY: Orbis, 1976, 1978, 1979).
20. Ibid., vol. 1, p. 107.
21. See, for instance, José Miguez-Bonino, *Christians and Marxists* (Grand Rapids, MI: Eerdmans, 1976).

CHAPTER 12

Protestant Focus on Science and Technology

The Conference at MIT

The international character of Roman Catholicism shows in its councils and synods, where representatives of such local views as Latin American liberation theology meet their counterparts from Europe, Africa, Asia, and North America. The international character of Protestant Christianity shows most forcefully in the assemblies of its World Council of Churches (WCC). Centered in Geneva, the World Council holds a variety of meetings on topics of pan-Christian interest that gather clergy, laity, and (Christian and non-Christian) technical experts from all corners of the earth. Its conference on "Faith, Science, and the Future," held at the Massachusetts Institute of Technology in July 1979, was a fine example of such meetings. It was also a good indication of where Protestantism is taking a cluster of important ethical issues. As we had to narrow our focus in treating Roman Catholicism, emphasizing its recent liberation theology, here we will focus on Protestant reflection on science and technology.

The title of the two volumes of papers published from the MIT conference summarizes its main thrust: *Faith and Science in an Unjust World.*[1] The delegates had gathered to consider science and technology, two of the main engines of contemporary culture. But they had gathered with a definite perspective, and in a definite context. The overriding perspective was that of faith, major genus Christian and dominant species Protestant. The context was nothing less than the global village created by twentieth-century transportation and communications, with an acute realization that the denizens of the village do not share its goods equally.

The MIT conference was the culmination of a long-developing concern first touched upon at the Universal Conference on Life and Work in Stockholm in

1925. More recently, the World Council had sponsored a conference on Church and Society at Geneva in 1966 with the theme "Christians in the Technical and Social Revolutions of Our Time." Its Fourth Assembly at Uppsala in 1968 had encouraged further work along this line, leading to a committee on "The Future of Man and Society in a World of Science-Based Technology." This committee had sponsored several meetings in the early 1970s and reported to the Fifth Assembly at Nairobi in 1975. That assembly's favorable reaction led the WCC's Central Committee to make "The Struggle for the Just, Participatory and Sustainable Society" one of its four programmatic emphases. Thus the MIT conference was the culmination of a long-developing concern.

Immediately prior to the conference at MIT, the Church and Society section of the WCC had published preliminary studies in its occasional bulletin *Anticipation*. To organize the work these studies outlined, the MIT conference was structured around four themes: 1) the relation between science and faith; 2) the ethical problems stemming from current science and technology; 3) the economic and political problems stemming from current science and technology; and 4) the new Christian social thought and action that has arisen to meet these challenges.[2]

The themes obviously overlapped, and the conference schedule provided for several approaches. In addition to plenary sessions, in which experts addressed the entire conference on a subissue of a main theme, there were working sections to tackle particular topics such as nuclear disarmament, energy, bioethics, and education. The two volumes of papers and reports conjure the image of a honeycomb or web. Across their pages the problems of today's industrialized world weave, reticulate, and interconnect. The result is an "ecology" for contemporary Christian faith. We shall come to this ecology momentarily, showing why it makes this leadership of the WCC a frontier of crucial importance. To complete the stage-setting, let us add brief descriptions of the international and liturgical dimensions of the conference, and then a digest of the keynote address by Philip Potter, WCC General Secretary.

Conference delegates came from all continents except Antarctica. They worked in five official languages (English, French, German, Spanish, and Russian) through simultaneous translation during the plenary sessions, and in many unofficial languages everywhere else. Among the 405 official participants, 91 college students from 55 countries comprised the largest bloc. The opening worship suggested the ecumenical outreach of the group. There were African drums and conch shells, Bach organ music, and choral music of Vaughan Williams. The conference moderator offered a meditation based on Col. 1:15–20; the chancellor of MIT brought greetings; and the cardinal archbishop of Boston represented the local Christian churches.

General Secretary Potter's keynote address stressed that today *scientists* are posing many of the most pressing ethical questions. The churches have been aware of science's impact, but one can hardly say they have responded adequately. Moreover, with the rest of society they have realized too slowly that those who control technology control development—that science leads to *power* as much as to knowledge. If 50 percent of today's scientists and technologists continue to be engaged in arms research and development, there will be no sustainable society at all. And until the poorer countries, which have only 10 percent of these scientists and technologists, begin fully to participate in global economics and politics, there will be no justice. For Potter, therefore, *participation* is a key component of the conversion that Christian faith entails.

Process Theology and Ecology

One of the first plenary presentations at MIT was an address by Charles Birch, the conference vice-moderator. A biologist from Australia, Birch spoke on "Nature, Humanity, and God in Ecological Perspective." Both the title of his address and its content placed it in the stream of **process theology**, a largely Protestant school of thought derived from the philosophy of Alfred North Whitehead. In accommodating relativity theory and the rest of early twentieth-century science, Whitehead had stressed the interrelatedness of all creatures.[3] As they have struggled to appropriate the new information pouring in about the natural and social environments, many Protestant theologians have found Whitehead's stress on interrelatedness and dynamism, or process, helpful. Birch's address exemplifies the insights and convictions they have developed.

For example, Birch claimed that both theologians and scientists are more aware today than they were in the past that science is a social construct. That is, the worldview derived from science reflects the society in which science is practiced. Thus, the dominant scientific-technological worldview of today reflects a society bent on mastering nature. For it the universe, including living organisms, is a contrivance, a matter of happenstance. As Richard Dawkins's book *The Selfish Gene*[4] put it, many biologists perceive the purpose of our lives to be only to perpetuate our DNA. Deeper scientific thinkers may reject this view, since contemporary quantum theory and some frontline thought in biology do not fit within it, but "most scientists think about the world about as much as bank clerks do," according to Birch.[5]

Many Christians think about the world just as little. Indeed, the general drift of Christian theology, especially in the West, has been to accommodate unthinkingly the **mechanistic** cosmology of science that says life is a machine with no soul. As a result, Christian theology has kept nature, humanity, and God dissociated. However, the developments and strains of the past half-century have revealed the inadequacy of the dominant mechanistic worldview. A major reason we have come to the brink of ecological crisis has been our loss of relation to nature. By treating nature as a factory, a production center existing only for our service, we have spent nonrenewable resources prodigally and seriously damaged systems of renewable resources. The pollution of our air, water, and soil is mechanism's telltale bequest, said Birch.

Still, Birch maintained, correctives to such an abusive view lie as near as personal encounters with the universe. One need only contemplate outer space, begin to appreciate sub-atomic particles, or sense the history of DNA, for wonder and mystery to arise. Far from being a dusty factory, nature is a treasury of living splendors. Whether they are Christians or not, scientists or not, many contemporary people have come to sense an inexhaustible fullness in nature. Paraphrasing God's answer to Job's complaints (Job 38), Birch has asked science to become more humble and less closed to humanistic and religious appreciations of nature.[6]

He implies that nature's color, vitality, beauty, and profusion are important, and links them with his growing conviction that science and religion can be conjoined. There are many approaches to the world, many approaches even within science, and each may bear a measure of truth. A mentality that is inclusive, cooperative, and relational acknowledges more of these measures of truth than does a disjunctive, mechanistic mentality. It also better helps us to see the continuities in the universe—the connections between nonliving things and living, between nonhuman life and human.

A good word for this inclusive approach is *ecology*. Ecology is the study of environments and systemic interconnections. It puts a premium on relationship, holism, and process. According to Birch, it points up the intelligibility and vitality *within* natural things that most make them valuable. Treating other creatures subjectively, refusing to regard them only objectively, the ecologist can move toward granting them independent rights. Then nature is valuable not merely for what it provides human beings, but also in its own right, as the marvelous collection of beings God sees to be good. This opens the possibility of a new ethics, in which pebbles, mosquitos, and pandas gain status and rights. It offers the possibility of a new model of the universe, in which a myriad of valuable entities play together in concert. Like a lecture hall full of students, who must cooperate for a class to proceed, the universe is a cooperative enterprise, not a machine run by a mechanic. It is a series of systems God guides gently, by persuasion more than force. Viewing the world ecologically, says process theology, might decrease the exploitation of the poor by the rich and more fully integrate the nonparticipants.

Process Theology and the Finite God

Numbering both scientists and church people on its roster,[7] process theology has sketched a truly ecological faith. While there certainly are other Protestant schools of thought, process theology has probed the implications of science and technology most deeply, so let us dwell on it a bit longer here.

The critical notion in the process theologians' repertoire is that God is finite, a real participant in the world's dynamics. Their belief is an adaptation of Whitehead's notion of a "dipolar" deity. According to Whitehead, divinity has a side that is eternal, unchanging, and antecedent to creation, but also a side that is temporal, changing, and consequent to creation.[8] Protestant theologian Langdon Gilkey's recent *Message and Existence*[9] is typical of process theology in utilizing this notion of a finite God to considerable effect. For Gilkey creation expresses "the unconditioned reality and power of God," who is the source of all beings. On the other hand, creation's relative autonomy, self-direction, and self-constitution suggest that God has chosen freely to limit his control over creation for the sake of better relationships with free, self-developing creatures. In her consequent nature God lets herself be affected by the world, plays in the dramas of the world's history, even suffers from the world. She grows, develops, becomes.

Thus process theology opens a channel through which faith may better affirm the divinity of the universe and its evolutionary processes, including the cultural evolution occurring through technology. For Gilkey and other process theologians, God is not the clockmaker of the Deists, who merely wound things up and left them to tick along as they would. He is not even the Pure Act of the Thomists, the inmost reality of everything that exists. Rather He is the head of a community of interacting beings, who lets them be and guides them forward toward fulfillment.

The crux of this conception emerges in its explanation of the **problem of evil**. There are things out of God's hands, limits to God's dominion. Consequently, there are limits to God's responsibility. Process theologians are convinced that God's purpose in evolution is to maximize beauty and enjoyment. They believe God acts on all wreckage or dysfunction, trying to bring from it whatever good is possible. But they reject any guarantee that God's will is always done, or any guarantee that evil, including the evil of the destruction of the human race, necessarily will be overcome. If the future truly is open, God's will may be defeated. To those burdened by a sense of **determinism**, a conception of God or the world that makes history and free will a charade and evolution impossible, this line of thought may be an emancipation proclamation. To those already deeply anxious about the way mankind has been exercising its free will, it may be but more cause for anxiety.

Some process theologians argue passionately that their conception of a changeable, limited, suffering God better represents the scriptural data than traditional Protestant theology has. Lewis Ford's *The Lure of God*,[10] for example, argues this way, exploring the Old Testament doctrines of God's persuasion and sovereignty and the New Testament doctrines of resurrection and reconciliation, in an effort to show that they make clearest sense when interpreted through process categories.

We had the privilege of knowing personally a member of the inner circle of process theologians, Harold K. Schilling. A physicist by training, a specialist in acoustics, his ethical sensitivity had led him in early adulthood to confront seriously the biblical question, "What think you of the Christ?" (Matt. 22:42). When he thought a great deal, and it brought him to Christian faith, he began a long study of the relations between science and faith. In maturity that study produced a marvelous book, *The New Consciousness in Science and Religion*,[11] that simply sings with wonder at the divinity creation carries. Undercutting sterile disjunctions between disciplines, Schilling used the holism of process thought as a challenge to investigate all reality. His investigation filled him with the conviction that all the pain of evolution is indeed worth it.

Economic Growth and Consumption

The MIT conference and process theology both spotlight the connections among technology, ecology, participation, and faith. The conference also focused on the ethical implications of contemporary science and technology. Perhaps the most fundamental ethical issue that emerged was whether economic growth should be limited. It came into sharp focus during a debate about "The Economics of the Just and Sustainable Society," so we shall report the gist of that debate, hoping it will illustrate the deep decisions that reflection on technology has laid before Christians.

To launch its discussion of the economics of the just and sustainable society, the conference asked Herman E. Daly, professor of economics at Louisiana State University, to speak on "The Ecological and Moral Necessity for Limiting Economic Growth." Daly is well known as an advocate of a nongrowth, **steady-state economy**,[12] and he did not disappoint those who expected him to apply steady-state philosophy to the MIT themes.

First, he informed the assembly about some ground-level economic facts. For a sustainable economy, two things are necessary: a renewable resource base and a population supportable within the sustainable yield of that resource base. There are four renewable resource systems, and indications are that each of them has peaked, in terms of global per capita productivity, and now is declining. Forest productivity peaked in 1967; fisheries productivity peaked in 1970; grasslands productivity peaked for wool in 1960, mutton in 1972, and beef in 1976; croplands productivity peaked in 1976.[13] It is possible these trends will be reversed, but not likely, reported Daly, because the peaks were attained in the first place only by directing large amounts of fossil fuels and minerals to mechanization, irrigation, fertilizers, insecticides, and transport. As population continues to grow, the four renewable resource systems likely will become less and less productive, in global per capita terms.

Some of the moral implications of this sober report begin to dawn if one looks at the current standard of living in the United States. In terms of the consumption of mineral resources, less than 18 percent of the current world population could live if the United States' rate were extrapolated globally. The first obvious implication is that the entire world can never share the U.S. standard of living. Another implication for those who believe in a basic equality among human beings is that the United States should drastically reduce its consumption of natural resources, and all nations should limit their populations. Daly may have extracted the ethical core of the economic issue when he extended the fifth commandment, "Thou shalt not kill," to an ecological "Thou shalt not destroy the capacity of creation to support life." Further, he suggested that the best way to confine the global economy within the world's permanent carrying capacity would be to impose maximal and minimal limits on individual income.

C. T. Kurien, director of the Madras [India] Institute of Development Studies, responded to Daly's paper with an address entitled "A Third World Perspective." The bitterness in Kurien's tone spoke volumes about the political problems involved in working toward a steady-state economy. For him proposals such as Daly's must be badly motivated: "May I submit that the 'limits-to-growth' slogan and its antidote, the 'sustainable society,' are both reflections of the anxiety of a pampered minority that its way of life is being threatened."[14] By the end of his speech Kurien had made it plain that he recognized many of the limits to growth that Daly and other steady-staters describe, but his first reaction was outrage that a member of an affluent society should call nonaffluent peoples to participate in a plan of constraint.

The outrage became more understandable when one learned the consumption levels at which many of Kurien's fellow Indians live. According to the figures available to him at the time, the per capita monthly expenditure of people in rural areas of India (80 percent of its 650 million) was about 53 rupees, 40 of which were spent on food. In U.S. dollars that was \$6.63 and \$5.00. Moreover, those were only the average figures, below which perhaps 75 percent of the Indian population fell. (Worldwide, similar figures would obtain for about two-thirds of humanity.) From 1951 to 1980 population in India increased from about 350 million to about 700 million. (Worldwide the progression has been from about 1.2 billion in 1850 to about 3.9 billion in 1975, with 6.2 billion projected for 2000.) Nonetheless, per capita income *increased* in India from 1951 to 1980, as it did in some other countries. Thus it seems from Kurien's figures that while Daly's call for reductions in the consumption levels of the affluent is long overdue, a steady-state global economy might deprive the poorest of any future improvement.

In terms of consumption, Kurien's rural Indians are to Daly's American consumers as apples to oranges. Not only do the Indians have minuscule incomes, they use virtually none of the world's scarce resources.[15] The matter is complicated, however, because the affluent are not likely to let the poor retain title to their land. Demographers Jorgen Randers and Donella Meadows have analyzed the status of arable land and concluded that presently there are only about 3.2 billion hectares. At current productivity rates we need about 0.4 hectares to support each person, which means that if current rates of productivity were doubled and population growth held steady (two very optimistic assumptions), we would run out of land about the year 2050.[16] Imagine the scramble that would ensue, and picture who most likely would lose out.

The ethicians of land use cannot concentrate only on the future, however. As MIT emphasized, plenty of moral choices are pressing right now, and they are all grist for the Christian theologian's mill. Although world hunger puts a premium on research and production to increase food supplies, a bigger problem is food distribution. Presently experts estimate that 450 million people suffer serious malnutrition, about 60 percent of them living in East Asia. "Raising the food intake of the over 450 million severely undernourished to the level of their nutritional requirements would involve the equivalent of 40–60 million tons of wheat per year. This is no more than 3–5 percent of present world cereal consumption, or 10–15 percent of the cereals now being fed to livestock in the developed countries."[17] A simple move on the part of affluent nations from feeding beef cattle grain to feeding them grass would provide most of what the starving need. Experience has shown that *getting* food to the starving is problematic, for their fellow countrymen are not above profiteering on their graves, but the MIT conference seemed to feel that the first step would be to mobilize a sense of global responsibility and shift the food production systems to the goal of feeding all the world's people.

Nuclear Weapons and Biological Manipulation

Human irrationality and greed seem to frustrate every such move toward a world order that is just, sustainable, and participatory. Thereby, they give theologians steady employment, for theologians most directly ponder the mysteries of sin and grace. At MIT theologians provided many of the strings that tied the numerous technological observations together. This proved true regarding ethical questions about nuclear weapons and biological manipulation, two further illustrations of recent Protestant Christian concern with technological pressures.

The topic of nuclear disarmament originally was not scheduled to come before the conference. The WCC has a major program on militarism, so it seemed a duplication of effort to put military issues on the MIT agenda. But many delegates sensed that any talk about future options would be quixotic unless they faced the paramount threat hanging over the future itself. Thus, biologist Jonathan King concluded his address on new genetic technologies with a plea that the conference speak out against the nuclear arms race.[18]

Therefore, on an impromptu basis, the conference arranged for sessions on nuclear disarmament. Drawing on local expertise, it invited Philip Morrison, professor of physics at MIT, to speak on "The Nature of Strategic Nuclear Weapons." Morrison explained how nuclear explosions occur, likening the blast pressure to high hurricane winds, the radiant heat to a volcanic eruption that ignites forest fires and burns exposed flesh, the ground shock to an earthquake, and the effects of water shocks to tidal waves. In addition, nuclear explosions produce deadly radiation. Most mind-boggling, though, was his set of statistics on the destructive power of current nuclear weapons.

A suitcase full of 10–25 kilograms of thermonuclear H-bomb explosive can release about a megaton of energy. A megaton is the equivalent of exploding a million tons of TNT. A million tons of TNT would fill a string of box cars 300 miles long. The train those box cars would form would take 6 hours to pass by, traveling at full speed. All the energy in the weapons exploded by the United States during the eight years of the Vietnam War equaled only about 6 megatons. The energy in the weapons held by United States strategic forces today is about 7,000 megatons[19]—7,000 of those trains, 42,000 hours of watching them pass by, 210,000 miles of those box cars. The Soviet Union has a comparable arsenal, and a number of other countries have a nuclear capability.

Compared to the unimaginable holocaust latent in such figures, other ethical problems tend to pale. Nonetheless, life and conferences go on, so the MIT participants bravely took up other moral dilemmas. A cluster of them grouped under "Ethical Dilemmas in the Biological Manipulation of Human Life." Increasingly this has been an area of interest to Christian ethicians, and the list of subtopics will show why: recombinant DNA technology, human genetic engineering, artificial insemination, abortion, behavior control, and just distribution of scarce medical resources.[20]

Recombinant DNA technology has great potential for good, as illustrated by the Eli Lilly Corporation's plan to produce human insulin by growing strains of *E. coli* bacteria containing the human insulin gene. On the other hand, such technology is sure to be muddled by the profit motive, and it has such potential for disrupting the ecosphere that Gabriel Nahas of the National Institute of Health in Paris attacked it at the MIT conference as "warfare against nature."[21]

Human genetic engineering raises fears of all the horrors possible in the name of eugenics (the effort to breed a better human stock), including Nazi-type racism. Artificial insemination and abortion both raise deep questions about marriage, procreation, and the human personality, while behavior control through drugs or advertising can assault the very image of God. Finally, the issue of just distribution hangs over all technological development, for one of the first questions on the road to a participatory society is why progress so frequently serves not the most needy but the least. Unless Christian theology can impress upon the scientific community a conviction that the human person is too valuable to be subjected to biological manipulation or the unjust distribution of resources, it will fail to achieve the goals MIT set before it.

Evangelicals and Science

A significant number of Protestant Christians do not belong to the WCC, but were present at MIT in ghostly fashion, as unseen counterplayers. Actually, they were not completely unseen, because a group of conservatives picketed the conference, protesting against what they considered the WCC's radical politics. Moreover, there were delegates inside the conference who would have been proud to identify themselves as Evangelicals, and who were present to represent what they firmly believed to be the heart of evangelical Christianity. Since much of the popular image of evangelical Christianity derives from an impression that it pits the Bible against science, and much Christian criticism of the Evangelicals derives from the impression that they slight social justice, this may be a good juncture at which to consider evangelicalism.

Evangelicalism is a complex, many-sided phenomenon. In the United States, "by the middle third of the nineteenth century, evangelical Protestantism, led principally by theological conservatives, dominated American religion."[22] The Civil War exacerbated divisions within the evangelical movement, and the critical methods of historical study that Protestantism developed in Germany at the end of the nineteenth century threw more confusion into the ranks. Some Evangelicals capitulated to the new biblical interpretation, or the new evolutionary science, while others withdrew into smaller assemblies, trying to preserve the pure faith. The nation perceived the Scopes Trial of 1925 over the issue of teaching evolution in the schools as a great contest between science and the Bible, and the apparent victory of science greatly depressed the Evangelicals. Until the 1960s evangelicalism seemed on the wane, left behind by contemporary progress. However, in the turmoil of the '60s, and perhaps even more in its aftermath, revivals of the evangelical spirit begun in the '40s and '50s began bearing fruit. With the nation in a mood of self-criticism, many Americans found the old biblical verities an answer to fill the void. Thus in the early '80s the Evangelicals were the growing edge of American Protestantism, adding to their numbers each year while the nonevangelical churches declined.

The doctrinal heart of evangelicalism is the Gospel, the good news enshrined in Scripture, but different churches unpack the Gospel differently. For the Evangelical Alliance formed in 1846 in London, Gospel faith led to nine verities: (1) the inspiration of the Bible, (2) the Trinity, (3) the depravity of man, (4) the mediation of the divine Christ, (5) justification by faith, (6) conversion and sanctification by the Holy Spirit, (7) the return of Christ and judgment, (8) the ministry of the Word, and (9) the sacraments of baptism and the Lord's Supper.[23] These verities could satisfy many Christians not usually considered Evangelicals. As in other instances, the name can mislead more than illumine. What has tended to distinguish the Evangelicals has been their heavy emphasis on the first affirmation. Deeply impressed by the Gospel message, they have tended to make the Bible the repository of all significant truth. One can imagine how this could lead to difficulties in several realms, such as biblical interpretation and the scientific study of creation.

From the intense work of historians and literary critics, who try to handle evidence and argument rigorously, biblical scholarship has borrowed a number of technical tools. Both the use of these tools and the findings to which they have led have upset many Evangelicals who sometimes are well called "fundamentalists," because they consider the Bible the foundation with which one cannot tamper. According to them, contemporary biblical scholarship is thoroughly wrong-headed, if not a work of Satan. For other Evangelicals, as disciplined in their use of historical and literary techniques as any other scholars, biblical revelation need fear no honest tool of inquiry. The Bible's **inspiration** concerns the truth necessary for salvation, not matters of historical or scientific detail.

As we see it from outside, these latter Evangelicals can avoid most of the pitfalls that have bedeviled their fundamentalist brethren and sisters in controversies about evolution and creation. Acknowledging the pluralistic nature of current American society (it was characteristic of many nineteenth-century Evangelicals to collapse Christianity and Americanism into one another), they have concentrated on tempering scientific dogmatism, and tempering as well the excessive claims of fundamentalist theology. Thus during the controversies that have raged in California since the early '70s about the presentation of cosmic and human origins in public school textbooks, the moderate Evangelicals have pressed for a distinction between science and scientism. Actual science, careful in its claims, explicit about its assumptions, and sensitive in its evaluation of evidence, is a splendid affair. Scientism, dogmatic in asserting that the world originated apart from God, or that human beings arose apart from God, is vicious, because it oversteps its competency and passes into ideology. Considerable work remains if Evangelicals are to correlate their theology with other disciplines, but there are many signs of progress.

Evangelicals and Social Justice

The widespread impression that they slight social justice is the second stigma that Evangelicals bear among outsiders. Along with being accused of anti-intellectualism, they are accused of badly privatizing Christian ethics, or even of throwing in their lot with big business, the military, and other pillars of an unjust status quo. There is considerable justice in this charge against twentieth-century Evangelicals, but considerable irony, or even tragedy, in it as well. Donald W. Dayton's *Discovering An Evangelical Heritage*[24] acknowledges all three aspects in a moving inquiry into the background of the tensions in the Evangelical community today.

Dayton attended an Evangelical college during the '60s. It was one of a chain that crossed the Midwest, providing fortresses against the modern, pagan world. At his college the traditional Evangelical prohibitions against drinking, smoking, dancing, card-playing, and theater-going were in force, and the weight of these prohibitions, when added to that of a formidable list of college regulations, became overwhelming. Trying to read the signs of his times, he felt he was drowning in trivia: "While other students responded to calls for civil rights workers or took to the streets in protest about Vietnam, we fought our administration over whether the yearbook could picture male swimmers without T-shirts, struggled for the right to watch TV in the lounge on Sundays, and wondered if the Christian should attend the theater (legitimate or cinema) or read twentieth-century literature."[25]

In many ways representative of many Evangelicals, Dayton and his fellow students tended to be passive politically, but to sympathize with conservative politicians. Their great fear was communism, the great foe of *Christianity Today*, the foremost evangelical journal. *Christianity Today* also was more than leery of civil rights. Its editors editorialized that voluntary segregation was consonant with "the biblical point of view," found communism implicit in Martin Luther King, Jr.'s views, and supported the American presence in Vietnam as necessary for the security of Christian missionaries. The whole experience became too much for Dayton. He left the school, worked in Mississippi and Harlem during 1964, and pursued further education at Columbia University and Yale Divinity School. Only when he began to study the history of his denomination did he discover that its recent patterns were an aberration. In the nineteenth century it had closely allied itself with abolitionist protests against slavery. Dayton's book retrieves the widespread social concern of many nineteenth-century Evangelicals, showing their involvement in civil disobedience, early feminism, and the Social Gospel, which stressed justice for the poor.

Other studies of evangelical history point to a similar conclusion. The turn to privatistic morality and support of the status quo only occurred in the 1920s, for a variety of reasons. Following the First World War, Americans generally engaged in great debates about the war's causes and implications. One result of these debates was an assault on orthodox Christianity. On many sides, the preeminent status of Protestant assumptions came under attack. At the same time, cities were growing and the rural era of American life was coming to an end. New immigrants were causing problems of assimilation, and the resources of philanthropists were sorely taxed. The result was that many Christians who had been reform-minded now lost heart. Retreating from social involvement, large numbers turned to private prayer and privatistic preaching about individual salvation. Others accepted the affluence that preceded the stockmarket crash of 1929 and lost any sense of identification with the poor.

When Evangelical spokesman William Jennings Bryan lost the symbolic battle of the Scopes Trial, a victim of the press as well as of opposing lawyer Clarence Darrow and the new science, the Evangelicals reached the pivotal point in what has been called their Great Reversal:

> More and more over the years after 1925, it became the habit to separate evangelism from social concern and to emphasize the individual and private at the expense of the corporate and public aspects of Christianity. Consequently and ironically, after dominating numerous aspects of American society and culture in the nineteenth century, evangelical Christians now took on many of the earmarks of an unimportant and despised subculture. Like blacks in America, they were given little notice in history textbooks and they virtually disappeared from the mass media's considerations during the generation following Bryan's death.[26]

Gradually the Evangelicals came out of this reversal, and during the 1960s whole groups had a social reawakening as well as an intellectual. For these, the Social Gospel, which had been abandoned as a liberal deviation, again became part of the evangelical heritage. Southern Baptists, Missouri Synod Lutherans, and other denominations supported new social agencies, and by 1973 a Chicago workshop on evangelical social concern could call for repentance and fellowship to confront the country's manifest social and political injustices.

Today there are perhaps 50 million Evangelicals in the U.S. Some espouse the cautious theology and politics of a Billy Graham, others espouse the aggressively conservative theology and politics of a Jerry Falwell; but an increasingly significant third group labor in programs like World Vision International and Bread for the World. Indeed, *Sojourners*, an interesting new journal, combines evangelical convictions with **radical politics**. This third group of Evangelicals seems indistinguishable from many of the delegates at the MIT conference, so before long evangelicalism, too, may be calling for a global society that is just, sustainable, and participatory.

Summary

As Latin American liberation theology shows Roman Catholicism to be alive and faithful, so the World Council of Churches' recent Conference on "Faith, Science, and the Future" shows Protestant Christianity to be alive and faithful. The MIT conference built on a distinguished history of WCC programs concerned with technology and justice, but it is doubtful that any previous Christian group had confronted the ecology of modern science and politics as thoroughly as MIT did. Using the stimuli of both scientists and theologians to think in process terms, the conference connected pollution, a nature increasingly found by science to be at core a series of mysteries, and a God made only more marvelous by these mysteries. Whether they accepted process theology's theses about God's finitude and limited responsibility for evil or not, most conference delegates affirmed the interconnectedness of cosmology, faith, and politics.

This interconnectedness appeared especially forcefully in consideration of ethical questions, such as how to design a sustainable economy, how to get food to the 450 million undernourished, how to bring about nuclear disarmament, and how to keep biological manipulation humane. First world delegates sometimes affirmed the detached quality of science, third world delegates often insisted that science means power (and so politics), but all delegates worked under the banner of pursuing a global society that is just, sustainable, and participatory. The popular image of evangelicalism as anti-intellectual and unconcerned about social change dovetailed with the relative absence of Evangelicals from the MIT conference, but a fair study of evangelicalism shows that both in its origins and in its future it can contest that image. If it wishes, evangelicalism, too, can promote a better ecology for faith.

Study Questions

1. How do the three adjectives prominent at MIT—just, sustainable, and participatory—interconnect?
2. How does process theology dovetail with a nonmechanistic view of nature?
3. Is the process theology notion of a finite God compatible with the biblical notion (Rev. 21:4) that God will wipe every tear from the eyes of the faithful? How so?
4. What are the principal arguments in favor of a steady-state economy?
5. In terms of priority, how would you rank nuclear disarmament and worldwide food distribution?
6. What basis has evangelicalism given for its image as anti-intellectual and unconcerned about social change?
7. What basis is there for evangelicalism to dispute this image?

Notes

1. Roger Shinn and Paul Abrecht, eds., *Faith and Science in an Unjust World* (Philadelphia: Fortress Press, 1980).
2. See Roger L. Shinn, "Introduction," ibid., vol. 1, pp. 5–6.
3. Whitehead's major work, quite difficult, is *Process and Reality* (New York: Harper Torchbooks, 1960).

4. Richard Dawkins, *The Selfish Gene* (London, Oxford University Press, 1976).
5. Birch, "Nature, Humanity, and God in Ecological Perspective," *Faith and Science in an Unjust World*, vol. 1, p. 64.
6. See ibid., p. 66.
7. See John B. Cobb, Jr. and David Ray Griffin, *Process Theology: An Introductory Exposition* (Philadelphia: Westminster, 1976).
8. See John Carmody, "A Note on the God-World Relation in Whitehead's *Process and Reality*," *Philosophy Today*, 15/4 (Winter 1971), pp. 302–312.
9. Langdon Gilkey, *Message and Existence* (New York: Seabury, 1979).
10. Lewis Ford, *The Lure of God* (Philadelphia: Fortress, 1978).
11. Harold K. Schilling, *The New Consciousness in Science and Religion* (Philadelphia: United Church Press, 1973).
12. See Herman E. Daly, ed., *Toward A Steady-State Economy* (San Francisco: W. H. Freeman, 1973). A more readable version of many of this book's themes is E. F. Schumacher's *Small is Beautiful* (New York: Harper & Row, 1973).
13. Herman E. Daly, "The Ecological and Moral Necessity for Limiting Economic Growth," *Faith and Science in an Unjust World*, vol. 1, p. 213.
14. Ibid., p. 221.
15. See ibid., p. 223.
16. See Jorgen Randers and Donella Meadows, "The Carrying Capacity of Our Global Environment," in Daly, *Toward a Steady-State Economy*, pp. 283–306.
17. Diogo de Gasper, "Economics and World Hunger," *Faith and Science in an Unjust World*, vol. 1, p. 227.
18. See ibid., p. 272.
19. Ibid., pp. 310–311.
20. See ibid, vol. 2, pp. 49–68.
21. Ibid., vol. 1, p. 282.
22. David F. Wells and John D. Woodbridge, in *The Evangelicals*, D. F. Wells and J. D. Woodbridge, eds. (Nashville: Abingdon, 1975), p. 9. Reprinted by permission.
23. John H. Gerstner, "The Theological Boundaries of Evangelical Faith," ibid., p. 25. Reprinted by permission.
24. Donald W. Dayton, *Discovering an Evangelical Heritage* (New York: Harper & Row, 1976).
25. Ibid., p. 2.
26. Robert D. Linder, "The Resurgence of Evangelical Social Concern," *The Evangelicals*, p. 199. Reprinted by permission.

CHAPTER 13

Eastern Orthodox Spirituality

Orthodox Faith and Science

Eastern Orthodox Christians have participated in the World Council of Churches since the First Assembly at Evanston, Illinois, in 1948, but not with complete satisfaction. Alexander Schmemann, a leading expatriate Russian Orthodox theologian, has expressed some reasons for this state of affairs. Speaking of the "failure" that has characterized the ecumenical contact between Orthodoxy and the West, he traces its roots to the experience "familiar to me since my first contacts with the ecumenical movement, of the Orthodox transplanted as it were into a spiritual and mental world radically different from his own; forced to use a theological language which, although he understands it, is not his language; and who, therefore, while agreeing on one level, experiences and realizes on another level the frustrating discrepancy between that formal agreement and the totality of the Orthodox *vision*."[1]

As an example of the misunderstanding the Orthodox have experienced in the WCC, Schmemann relates a conversation he had at Evanston with an ecumenical dignitary who explained that the Orthodox would be seated with representatives of the Western **high** (more formal) **churches**, such as the Swedish Lutherans, Old Catholics, and Polish Nationals, since they all shared a "horizontal" view of the Church. "To this I half jokingly remarked that in my studies of Orthodox theology I had never heard of such distinctions, and that without this information, had the choice been left to me, I might have selected a seat at the extreme left with the Quakers, whose emphasis on the Holy Spirit we Orthodox certainly share."[2]

An Orthodox view was present at the MIT conference through the contributions of Metropolitan (high ranking church leader) Paulos Gregorios of India, a theologian and bishop of the Syrian Orthodox Church of the East. As conference moderator, Gregorios preached two sermons and gave one plenary speech that illustrate some of the distinctive angles of the Orthodox vision.

In his plenary presentation, Gregorios set out to compare science and faith. This led him to press for the recovery of the ancient Semitic understanding of faith, which he considered all three branches of Christianity to have lost. Roman Catholicism has overemphasized intellectual aspects, he asserted, conceiving faith as an assent to dogmas proposed by the magisterium. Protestantism has fallen into the same trap, accepting Calvin's definition of faith as knowledge. Eastern Orthodoxy, said Gregorios, has been overly intellectual in regarding faith as the acceptance of the dogmatic definitions of the first seven ecumenical councils.[3]

By contrast, the ancient Semitic understanding of faith stressed nourishment, support, being carried in trust. It leaned on God as its rock, depended on God as its nurse or mother. Thus Semitic faith need not be seen as competing with science. It could deal directly with fundamental reality, complementing scientific hypotheses with a ground-level certitude: "In an apocalyptic age such as ours this kind of faith in a dependable, rock-like, reliable reality, takes on a new significance. To trust in God is not to panic, even in the midst of ecological catastrophe. This truth of faith, as contrasted with scientific truth, is not primarily propositional. Truth is reality, not statement. For faith, truth is not dogma, but reality—that which is and always will be—not a *description* of that which is."[4]

Many in the MIT audience probably found Gregorios's sense of faith hard to grasp. It is unusual for Westerners to speak directly of *reality*, of "that which is and always will be." Such speech is more typical of Hindus, who discourse on *sat*, the being of things, or of Buddhists, who deal in *tathata*, "suchness." It betrays an Eastern tendency toward the ontological, an Indo-European bent for metaphysics almost built into Sanskrit and Greek. Indeed, by exhibiting the contemplative character of the Indian and Greek traditions, Gregorios came close to showing himself a mystic. For the mystic loves unmediated communion, vision and indwelling that undercut the discursive mind.

Gregorios stayed in this mystical character during the Liturgy, when he chose to have those assembled meditate on Col. 1:15–20. For a conference on faith and science, this prime cosmological text probably commended itself to him spontaneously. Still, whether his choice was spontaneous or deliberate, it gave the lie to any dichotomy between Greek and Semitic approaches to God. In addition, it gave voice to the Orthodox conviction that the world rests in God, takes its inmost structure from the Logos.[5]

From this New Testament vision, Gregorios concluded that humanity and physical creation both subsist in God, in the Logos. Science and technology therefore both occur within the reality of God. Reversing the Western tendency to approach God from the particulars of creation, Gregorios implicitly reminded the conference that other Christians have approached the particulars of creation from the comprehensive reality of God. For them the Lord of All is the context of faithful science.

Gregorios's sermon to close the MIT conference was a third reflection of the Orthodox vision. Commenting on Rev. 12:1–6, he described the human race as in labor to bring forth a new humanity. Despite all the threats to its survival, this new humanity has its being in God.[6] For Orthodox theologians like Gregorios, the Logos has a priority over creation that Western theologians affirm but seldom take as their starting point.[7] One might say that the East tends to think from the One at the top to the many at the bottom, while the West tends to think from the many at the bottom to the One at the top.

Orthodox Spirituality and the Self

Another important difference, one on which we will dwell for the remainder of this chapter, between Orthodox and other Christianity is that Eastern Orthodoxy preserves more contemplative convictions about the self. One of the premises behind this book is that there are four primary dimensions to reality: nature, society, self, and divinity. All mature Christian theologians deal with these four realms, trying to illumine them from a center in Jesus Christ. However, all theologies or species of faith are not equally vital in all four dimensions. Latin American liberation theology, for example, burns with passion for social justice, but it has done relatively little with ecological issues. Protestant faith such as that shown at MIT is alert to both ecological and social issues, but it says little directly about the self. Eastern Orthodoxy has been more concerned with the self, ultimately because monasticism, which necessarily focuses on the self, is central to Orthodox faith (all bishops must be monks), and because the patristic age, in which analyses of Christ's self abounded, has remained the wellspring of Orthodox theology. Let us mine the Eastern spiritual tradition to focus our discussion of contemporary Christianity on the self.

For the rest of this chapter we will use as our main guide to Eastern Orthodox spirituality Sergius Bolshakoff, a Russian expatriate who has dedicated his life to working for Christian unity as a layman following the monastic Rule of Saint Benedict. For over fifty years Bolshakoff studied with numerous Russian spiritual fathers, bringing their teaching to bear on Western monastic practices. In recording the Russian traditions, and also those of monks on Mount Athos in Greece, he has preserved a centuries-old wisdom in danger of extinction under Communist rule. This wisdom continues in Orthodox circles, furnishing guidance back to practices that began with the desert fathers, in the earliest centuries of Christian faith. Expounding even a little of what Bolshakoff learned will take us close to the center of current Orthodox vitality. It will also show us the chasm that lies between traditional Orthodox views of the self and those of current Western culture.

Consider, first, a portion of the teaching that Bolshakoff received in 1926 from Father Theophan of the Pskovo-Petchersky Monastery in Estonia:

> We must be afraid of all daydreams, fantasies, and illusions and fill our heart with the invocation of the Divine Name. And yet we all dream, always waiting

> for something, even in our old age. The young dream all the time. They dream of having a prosperous life, full of pleasures, honors, riches, and power. And in order to attain such a life they resort to lies and flattery and become hard and cruel. There are, of course, many exceptions, but such is the rule. Do you know, Sergei Nikolaevich [Bolshakoff], that old age is better than youth? And why? Because it is wiser. In old age we realize at last that all is vanity. "Vanity of Vanities and all things are vanity," as the Ecclesiast says. Everything passes away: our youth, our health, our relatives and our friends, our foes, our wealth, and our honors. Only peace of mind, good deeds, and eternity remain.[8]

The Orthodox monastic tradition, like that of Western and Buddhist monasticism, has encouraged its adherents to pay careful attention to the contents of consciousness. Praying continuously, one learns that the self usually suffers a stream of preoccupations. To commune with God, one has to learn to control this stream, separating vain imaginings from solid contemplations. Most of what the world sets before human beings qualifies as vain imaginings. In terms that pre-Christian Greeks such as Heraclitus and Plato used, the world proposes a dream life. The first step on the road to wisdom therefore is to awaken from worldly assumptions, and the monastery provides an environment in which this becomes possible.

Unless we awaken from worldly assumptions, say the monks, we direct our energy to idols—false gods of power, pleasure, or status. Directed in such a false way, our energy distorts us: makes us liars, people hard and cruel. But the idols of worldly success always let us down, as though God and reality were bound finally to assert themselves. As time erodes what money can purchase, or shows the superficiality of carnal pleasure and worldly friendship, the vanity of their lives brings many to crisis. This is really a blessing, a chance to become sober and wise. If only at the threshold of death, it makes us ask the important questions the world tries to muffle: where can my soul find peace? Where is a joy that does not fail, a contentment simple and uncloying? Time and mortality are the religious person's friends, forcing her to contemplate eternity. Death, which most people flee, holds the key to living well. Thus the monk attempts continual dying to self, trusting Jesus's word that he who loses his life for Jesus's sake will find it.

This is but the first of numerous paradoxes Bolshakoff found in the oral tradition of the spiritual fathers. Where the world valued money, they chose poverty. Where the world exalted sexual pleasure, they pursued chastity. Autonomy, the watchword of modernity, was to them a deep pit, so they handed their will over to another. The preoccupations of city life—conversation, social intercourse, and entertainment—they found inimical to prayer, so they fled into solitude. As Father John of Petchenga, a community on the Russo-Norwegian border beyond the Arctic Circle, put it:

> Distractions and vain, wandering thoughts come because in our innermost selves we do not believe in the presence of God everywhere. He whose thoughts wander about even in church can hardly be called a devout Christian. All our troubles come about because of the absence within us of the fear of God. The Far North is a good teacher of the fear of God. In those endless snow-covered

> plains, where there is no town or village, we are confronted with eternal and unchangeable facts. The night sky, clear and dark, is lit up with myriads of stars and the mysterious aurora borealis.[9]

One can see a lovely ecology implicit in Father John's religious view of nature, but its first thrust is for silence to contemplate God.

Direction, Silence, and Mortification

To deal with the paradoxes of an intense spiritual life and the psychic dangers of solitude, Eastern Orthodoxy has structured its monastic life around spiritual direction. As the Hindu ascetic is counseled to follow the teaching of a wise guru, and the Zen Buddhist monk has regular conferences with a roshi, so the Orthodox monk follows a regime approved by a spiritual father or *staretz* who functions as a living interpreter of the monastic traditions. Above all, through the practice of *starchestvo* or "manifestation of conscience," the monk reveals his innermost thoughts, temptations, and aspirations to his spiritual father, for objective analysis and counsel. The idea is to nip problems in the bud and keep the novice from either excessive rigor or laxity. Since intense prayer approximates a psychoanalytic process of reforming the personality, it can activate all sorts of subconscious emotions, images, and energies. The *staretz* should be one who has been shown to have the gift of discerning the motions of the spirit, distinguishing healthy movements from destructive. The stakes are high in his work, because those who try intense spiritual exercise and fail can get discouraged, lose their balance, and even destroy their faith.

Father Nazary, a *staretz* Bolshakoff visited in Finland in 1954, assumed the tradition of spiritual direction when he commented that those practicing the Jesus Prayer (a special Orthodox devotion explained below) should see their spiritual father daily to confess their thoughts. After the evening meal they ought to go to him, bow, kneel, and open their souls, describing all they had done during the day. This included their deeds, their words, and even their thoughts: the way they had done their work, what they had said of other people, how they had been prideful or vain. The spiritual father ought to know even their most insignificant imaginings, so that both he and they could see any patterns in the disturbances of their peace of soul. Having made such a confession and received absolution for his offenses, the monk was to kiss the cross and icon, prostrate himself before the *staretz* again, and return to his cell, resolving to do better the next day.

This sort of self-examination depends on the regularity and helpful external conditions of monastic life. Most days monks follow an established daily order, rising early, spending time in private prayer, manual labor, and liturgical prayer, and maintaining silence as much as possible. Especially in the evening, a "great silence" ought to envelope them, assuring that they settle down interiorly, without distraction, for wholehearted communion with God. Indeed, monks have always considered silence, both external and internal, to be essential. The Russian monks who trekked to the northern wastes were pursuing silence—a quiet, peaceful life, far from the madding crowd. The early Egyptians who fled to the desert felt an intense hunger for undistracted concentration on God.

It is a peculiarity of contemplative prayer that feeding it silence only deepens its appetite. To be sure, from time to time monks can experience a distaste for silence, through **acedia** (boredom) or **desolation** (sadness). By and large, however, solitude and silence become more and more desirable. As a creative artist only deepens in her desire to work, or a loving spouse only strengthens in his desire to be with his partner, so the serious monk only increases in his love of silent communion. What happens in deepening prayer is so demanding and so fulfilling that it absorbs more and more of one's spirit. Partly through the monk's own efforts (sometimes called "acquired contemplation") and partly through God's free initiative (sometimes called "infused contemplation"), the loving communion becomes habitual. On the model of Paul's "I live, now not I, but Christ lives in me" (Gal. 2:20), an identification develops. Archimandrite Sophrony, another of the spiritual fathers Bolshakoff spoke to, described a monk who had not even realized this had happened to him:

> I once knew a postulant who had lived in this way [with confidence in the word of his spiritual father] for five years when his superior gave him a piece of intellectual work to do. He went to his cell to do what the superior had commanded, sat down at his desk, and then experienced a strange sensation, which he later described to me. He had the distinct impression that his mind rose up out of his heart, was transformed to his brain, and only then began to examine the matter at hand. At that moment he realized that for five or six years his intellect had never been separated from his heart. By this experience, which I would call negative, he understood the gift that the Lord had bestowed on him. And I think there are many monks, everywhere, whether in the East or the West, who live like this monk in the love of Christ and in fear, a great fear—even dread, for it is a dreadful thing to be separated from him.[10]

When they are healthy, Christian tradition says, monasteries sponsor austerities for the sake of such love of Christ. They do not discipline the flesh masochistically, but so that the spirit may thrive. Their only dread is a holy fear of losing communion with Christ, their great treasure. Thus monastic **mortification**, or dying to self, is not punitive or self-destructive. Monastic silence, fasting, and obedience attack only egotism, egocentricity. Egotism is the false proposition that the world revolves around my little "I." Some egotism falls away in any maturation, the casualty of the adult's move from seeking pleasure to accepting reality. But much egotism, pride, and self-serving remain in the typical adult, so genuine holiness must take aim at them. To commune with God, who is not sensible or under its control, the human spirit has to enter a dark night or a cloud of unknowing.[11] These images express the mortification necessary, according to Eastern Orthodox tradition, for divine life to flourish, for God to become utterly real. Then whatever *is* derives from God, whatever happens is God's providence. Then faith has flowered in spiritual marriage, love has reached mystical union.

The Jesus Prayer

The Jesus Prayer has been of central importance in Orthodox devotion. Also called the Prayer of the Heart, it centers on what Christians call the Holy Name. In full form it runs, "Lord Jesus Christ, Son of God, have mercy upon me, a sinner." In abbreviated form it may condense to the one word "Jesus." Orthodox Christians trace the Prayer back to the New Testament, citing a version of the publican's cry in Luke 18:13: "Lord Jesus, have mercy upon me." Saint Simeon the New Theologian (949–1022) championed the prayer, and Saint Gregory Palamas (1296–1359) defended it during his battles on behalf of the Hesychasts. The monks of Mount Sinai and Mount Athos have been ardent practitioners, and during the eighteenth century, when tsardom hampered monasticism in Russia and the Turks crushed Orthodoxy in Greece, the Neamtzu monastery in Romania kept its tradition alive. Many Westerners have learned the prayer from the Russian classic *The Way of a Pilgrim*.[12]

The Jesus Prayer is at the core of the instruction Mother Alexandra, Superior of the Monastery of the Holy Transfiguration in western Pennsylvania, gives young women who join her monastery. Mother Alexandra reflected ancient Orthodox conviction when she explained to Bolshakoff's collaborator, Basil Pennington, the beauty of the Jesus Prayer. For Mother Alexandra the great merit of the Jesus Prayer is its complete focus on Jesus: "All thoughts, striving, hope, faith, and love are outpoured in devotion to God the Son."[13] Further, it fulfills two basic injunctions of the New Testament: the command implicit in Jesus's assurance that whatever one asks in his name the Father will grant (John 16:23), and Paul's command to pray always (1 Thess. 5:17). It is in keeping with Jesus's instruction to pray in secret (Matt. 6:6), and since Jesus taught that both good and bad originate in the human heart (Luke 6:45), the Prayer aims at the seat of all morality.

Some of the ancient fathers developed the practice of correlating the prayer with one's breathing, the ideal being to make its recitation as rhythmic and unfailing as the intake and outflow of the breath. Although the beginner may find such recitation demanding, with time it becomes natural and easy. That is because the basic modality of the Jesus Prayer is an uncomplicated, affective love. One simply communes with Jesus through the prayer. The prayer helps to fix the mind, rivet the attention, but it is a medium more than a goal in itself. More important than any thoughts or images in the mind is spontaneous love in the heart: "When you are with someone you love, when you embrace him, you do not stop to reflect on how or why you love, or what you are doing; you just love and whisper his name as love draws you. That's all there is to it. Be quiet. Enter into the silence of love. Repeat the prayer quietly, unhurriedly, thoughtfully. Every thought is focused on Jesus. Everything else, however good, is left to drift away. The Prayer simplifies. We simply repeat the Name of the Beloved."[14]

Mother Alexandra sketches a fuller context for the Prayer by repeating the traditional Orthodox advice to have regular times and places for one's practice. She urges praying before an icon, out of traditional Orthodox conviction that the icon "is loaded with the objective presence of the One depicted." Further, many find it helpful to use a prayer cord (a sort of rosary) to fix the attention, but others prefer to close their eyes and focus inwardly. The Jesus Prayer can express praise, thanksgiving, petition, or simple love. It is a way of laying everything before God—work, worries, and ardent longings alike. With practice the Prayer becomes a sort of second heartbeat, continuing uninterruptedly through sleep and unconsciousness. Thus Mother Alexandra experienced waking from anesthesia after surgery with "Jesus" on her lips. The joy the Prayer gives her, its comfort and strength, lead her to recommend it to all who seek her advice about prayer.

It is worth remarking the simplicity of this popular Orthodox devotion, and its strangeness in worldly terms. All Christian faith and spiritual devotion come to focus in the repetition of "Lord Jesus Christ, Son of God, have mercy upon me, a sinner." Buddhist sects have developed similar practices of repeating a certain word or phrase, but the current Western mentality, whether religious or secular, is more external, attracted more to active works than to inner quiet. However, there have been parallel Western practices concerning the Bible, for instance the contemplative **lectio divina** (spiritual reading) of medieval Catholicism and the informal reflection of evangelical Protestantism. Both approximate the psychology of the Jesus Prayer, for like the Prayer both stress affective experience rather than practical work or speculative understanding. Despite all the tides of superficial education and religion, one leading the spiritual life realizes that one's way, one's calling, ought to bring an inner satisfaction. Unless it is a way of peace, a calling to joy, savor, and inner nourishment, it is not deeply wise, not what the spirit most needs. The spirit most needs something like the Jesus Prayer, some way of communing with deepest reality heart to heart.

Humility at Mount Athos

The traditions of spiritual direction, silence, mortification, and the Jesus Prayer live and flourish in the Monastic Republic of Mount Athos, a peninsula in the Aegean Sea southeast of Thessalonica, Greece, which has been for centuries the most revered site in Eastern Orthodox monasticism. Both Bolshakoff and Pennington have reported on their visits to monasteries on Mount Athos,[15] and by borrowing from these reports we can fill in something of the Greek side of the Orthodox spiritual tradition, which, though it largely agrees with the Russian, predates the Russian and so is more revered.

In 1954 Bolshakoff visited Mount Athos and was encouraged to meet one Father Euthemios, a "fool for Christ" living at the Greek monastery of Dionysiou. Father Euthemios was tall, ascetic, and spoke excellent Russian, having spent years in the Caucasus working as an accountant. When the Bolsheviks came to power, he left Russia and entered Dionysiou to spend his life as a monk. He was not a priest, but he had gained a reputation for insight, sanctity, and plain speech. One of his first words to Bolshakoff was a warning not to stay up late talking (on the evening of

Bolshakoff's arrival at Dionysiou), for that would make him oversleep and miss Morning Service. Bolshakoff did stay up late, and he did oversleep and miss Morning Service. When he went to the church, "the tall, dark figure of Father Euthemios appeared from nowhere. 'I told you yesterday,' he said to me quietly, 'to go to bed early so you would not oversleep, as you have done—but never mind; come with me.' "[16]

Later Bolshakoff had the opportunity to learn more about Father Euthemios's "foolishness." In Euthemios's opinion, the thing serious Christians most need is humility. Humility, however, only comes through much suffering. Most people love to be honored and made much of. Few people like to be humiliated. The one who must teach others humility therefore has a hard task, especially when they hold high station. Still, it is precisely those who hold high station that most need humility. Otherwise, God will teach them by their destruction, as he taught Hitler, Mussolini, and many others. "Even in the Church, even among bishops and abbots, there is far too much pomposity and intolerance. In Russia it disappeared, because the Bolsheviks taught such a lesson that it will take a long time for anyone to forget it. The Communists are the scourge of God, sent to teach us the path of virtue."[17]

If we pause momentarily to absorb this point of view, we sense again how distant the values of deep Christian spirituality are from the values of secular Western culture. To be sure, we are emphasizing this distance here, so as to set off something of the long Christian tradition that the self only prospers through a deep spirituality. Orthodoxy, like the rest of Christianity, has had to work out accommodations with secular society. It has had to contend with wealth, business, war, power, sex, work, and the rest of ordinary human life. But Orthodox monks like Father Euthemios have refused to patch over the conflict between the Gospel and the world. Recalling Christ's words about the impossibility of serving both God and mammon, they have insisted that mammon—all species of worldliness—is a plague upon the soul. On the way to holiness, one must root out such tawdry treasures as money, pride, honors, and prestige. God can only invade a poor, humble personality, for only a poor, humble personality offers God room, lives in the bedrock truth that it is nothing and God is all. Thus the "foolishness" of God that took Jesus to his cross is the highest wisdom on Mount Athos. The lowest station that the world despises is the place closest to the Lord. Like those blessed by Jesus's beatitudes, the odd, the marginal, and the eccentric can turn out to be those one should more revere.

Euthemios drove his paradoxes home with a story about a bishop ambitious to become a primate (the head of a larger territory). One day this bishop called on a holy monk. The monk ignored the bishop, going about his prescribed prayers and spiritual duties. The bishop, who was a proud man, broke out in fury, "Is this the way you treat a bishop?" The monk replied, "It is not good for a bishop to take a monk from his prayer in order to engage him in vain conversation. You should be humble and keep still. If you do, you may well become a primate. If you don't, but persist in trying to please people in high station, you will not only lose the primacy but your current diocese as well. Indeed, you will be sent to a monastery to do strict penance." And so it happened. The bishop had been told the monk was a fool for Christ and would speak plainly, but he could not abide such unvarnished truth. It turned out, though, that the penances he had to do in the monastery humbled the bishop. Thus he ended up with spiritual joys far more satisfying than any primacy.

This is clearly a teaching story, more myth than history. In straightforward speech, however, Euthemios explained that humiliations are far better for our spiritual health than praises. It is difficult, he agreed, to tell people the unvarnished truth, because few are able to bear it. Still, we must try, realizing the sinfulness our speech reveals: "All lie, some more, some less, some openly, some discreetly. Because we commit sins all the time, we must pray all the time. This is the reason for the Jesus Prayer. Remember also that the harder life is for you, the better. Nowadays everybody looks for comfort and easy living, but this is destructive to the soul and also to the body."[18]

There are questions one could raise about this view of humiliation, such as whether certain personalities don't suffer from a *lack* of pride, a self-image too low. Nonetheless, few people who have reflected on the speech of American society will disagree that all too often it is flattery, lies, and poison to the soul.

The Monastic Vocation

Visitors to Mount Athos who are able to penetrate the monasteries' inner life as Bolshakoff and Pennington did, come upon a number of remarkable personalities. By word of mouth, they learn that a Euthemios dramatically displays the "foolishness" of the Gospel, or that another monk has gifts of high prayer. In the ascetic and liturgical life that the monasteries foster these exceptional personalities have taken root and blossomed. Like precious gems dependent on a plain setting, they shine against the background of common Christian holiness to which tradition says asceticism and liturgy should conduce. By asceticism the Christian mortifies the flesh, the entire disposition of the human personality toward pride and self-indulgence. By liturgical prayer—the Eucharist and hours of the **office** (formal prayer throughout the day)—the Christian community sends up an unceasing chant of praise. Because it thinks itself an organ of Christ's mystical body, the monastic community serves not just itself but the whole Church at prayer. Thus monks do not pray merely for themselves, and monastic asceticism is not merely the pursuit of personal perfection. Both the Liturgy and personal asceticism are for the entire people of God. Orthodoxy insists that the Church or people of God is a **communion of saints**. It is a society, a family, an organic whole. If some members are called to active witness and ministry, others are called to silent, hidden prayer. Each member of the Church needs the gifts of the others. There are many rooms in God's household, many different vocations.

Father Vasileos of the monastery at Stavronikita on Mt. Athos put an Eastern edge on these common monastic convictions when he explained to Pennington, a Western Christian monk, his intuitions about East-West monastic differences.

> Father insisted that even though our lives are similar in their round of daily worship and work, the spirit with which we live them is quite different. His keen theological mind reached to a root of this difference. Father felt that the Western image of the Church, influenced so heavily by the philosophical concept of a perfect society, with its structures and laws, destroys the mystery. The constant communion with the heavenly realm as forming one Church with us radiates the whole life and space of the Orthodox monastery, and above all its katholicon [principal church] and the Services celebrated therein. The almost sensible presence, truly visible to the sensitive inner eyes of the faithful, of the awesome Divine Energies of the Transcendent Trinity and the Transfigured Christ bring about the deification of the devout and vigilant monk and of the holy community.[19]

Another way in which Eastern monastic spirituality may differ from Western is in the tendency of Eastern spirituality to allow the individual monk more freedom to work out an individual regime. Thus Father Paisios, the most revered spiritual father at Stavronikita, expressed the conviction that monasteries have to disorganize their life more than they tend to. They have to be more willing to let go of regimentation for the sake of spiritual freedom. Partly through Paisios's influence, Stavronikita leaves monks free from after Morning Service until evening **vespers** (office prayers). Each monk has certain assigned chores, but he can perform them when best suits his own rhythms. In consultation with his spiritual father, he works out the measures of private prayer, fasting, sleep, recreation, study, and the like that he needs. All monks retain an obligation to pray for the entire Church (especially through the daily office), but beyond that the Spirit deals with them as individuals. With inner tranquillity and freedom, each has to learn the mercy of God, to experience prayer not as a burden but a "resting." Such resting, reminiscent of the "abiding" of the Johannine writings, shows that contemplative prayer is a matter of being with God more than assaulting God with petitions or praises. It is a matter of holistic love more than performing particular devotions.

Father Vasileos meditated on several further aspects of monasticism and Eastern spirituality in a talk to the Pan-Orthodox Youth Congress held at Dijon, France, in November of 1974. He said that the monk is one who has been raised from the dead. His vocation makes no sense apart from the Resurrection of Christ, the transfiguration of the world by the uncreated **Divine Energies** (outflow of God). Alternately, the monk has the vocation to celebrate the sanctification of all things. Everything concerns him, since the Resurrection has touched all creation and the Liturgy uses all creation in its praise.

In a third figure, Vasileos spoke of the monk as one whose job is not to build houses, not to read or write, but to die in God, so that he can live and be moved by another Power. That is what gives him true freedom. Those who build for the sake of building, who write for the sake of writing, only enlarge their tombs and weave their shrouds. Those who live and breathe in search of divine mercy weave an incorruptible garment. Fourth, monks do not live this way for themselves but for the mystery of salvation. Not individual progress in sanctity but living for Christ, who died and rose for all humanity, justifies monastic life. Monastic life therefore must serve the universal, catholic will and tradition of the Church. It is not a place for individual virtuosity but for ecclesiastical service—the profound service of opening hearts to divine grace, the love-energy at the inmost center of creation.

Back and forth, in these rather mystical ways, Vasileos and other monks of Mount Athos turn over the multiple meanings of their life. Through their rapturous language one glimpses a romance, a quest for ravishing love.

Traditional Russian Faith under Fire

The rapturous language of Eastern Orthodox monasticism has long fed Russian spirituality and philosophy.[20] Since the Communist takeover of Russia in 1917, however, religion has been under assault. As an article in a philosophical dictionary published in Moscow in 1963 puts it:

> The Russian revolutionary democrats were militant, consistent atheists. Atheism in its most consistent form is found in Marxism-Leninism. . . . The philosophical basis of Marxist atheism is dialectical and historical materialism. Marxist atheism has a militant character. Throughout history it criticises religion from all sides, indicating by what paths and means it can be completely overcome. Marxist atheism has established that religion can be completely overcome only as a result of the destruction of its social roots through the process of building Communism. The experience of the USSR, where atheism has become a mass phenomenon, provides practical confirmation for the correctness of these theses.[21]

Since this dictionary was produced under Soviet auspices, we can take its views as representing the official government line.

What a government proposes, though, is not necessarily what a people disposes. Despite vigorous anti-religious propaganda, and even the persecution of the devout, in the last decade Christian faith has been on the upswing in Russia. One of the best documents on the recent situation is a collection of discussions led by a popular Russian priest named Dmitrii Dudko. Held during the mid-1970s, they show that not even a climate of heavy repression has snuffed out the religious longings of the Russian people. In addition, they show the ravages the Soviet regime has visited on its peoples' souls, for many of the questions put to Dudko reveal a sad state of religious or moral disarray.

The religious needs of the Russian people reveal themselves in simple human problems. For example, a woman aged forty had a son whom she had raised in the approved, atheistic spirit. In his teens the son began drinking and acting like a hooligan. The woman's husband, an atheist like herself, had left her for someone else, and she was close to despair. Suddenly things changed. Her son began going to church, stopped drinking, and left off his criminal behavior. The woman hesitated to ask him about this change, for they had agreed on little previously. She just marveled at the steady improvement in his character. Finally she couldn't contain herself, so she asked him what had happened. He told her that he had come to believe in God. This unexpected answer struck her like lightning. She began reflecting on her own mental state and concluded that she, too, ought to be baptized. Now she goes to church and proclaims her faith in Christ boldly, convinced that religion holds the answers contemporary people most need.

Father Dudko's discussions with the members of his parish outside Moscow contained a steady stream of such stories. At the time of the discussions he had had an active ministry of less than fifteen years and estimated that he personally had baptized more than 5000 adults, so simple division says that he averaged almost one baptism a day. The most frequent reason converts gave for coming to Christian faith was the joyless character of their atheistic lives. For many, depression was a daily companion. One man was so burdened by depression that he found himself on the brink of insanity. He had tried alcohol, immersing himself in work, civic projects, psychotherapy, and sleeping pills. He was about to commit himself to a mental institution when he happened on a copy of the New Testament. Reading it opened a new world to him, a joyous, happy world. "I read it and couldn't read it enough. Each word of that holy little book lay on my soul, and the greatest of all joys took place—the depression passed. Only one who has suffered from some degree of depression could understand me properly. The depression passed entirely! I believed in Christ and was baptized."[22]

Frequently those who profess their Christian faith openly in Russia suffer demotions at work, vilifications from their neighbors, or abuse from the Soviet authorities. At the Easter services of his church in 1973 Dudko had to confront a mob of anti-religionists, some of them in uniform, who formed a cordon to prevent people from entering the church. They would lead parishoners away, twisting their arms if they resisted. When Dudko protested to a policeman standing by, pointing out that this violated the law, he shrugged and turned away. At considerable risk to himself (he has since been arrested by the authorities), Dudko continued to hold services and conduct "dialogue" sermons in which people could ask any questions on their minds. No doubt his courage in face of the possibility of arrest, beating, and even death, stemmed from his having spent the years 1948–56 in a labor camp in Siberia, an inmate of the infamous Gulag Archipelago. At the time of his discussions he was married and had three young children. Like Solzhenitsyn, however, he was convinced that speaking the truth was more important even than the welfare of his family. In gospel imagery Dudko himself used, he was a shepherd commissioned to guard his sheep even at the cost of his life.

Though there are still churches in the Soviet Union where believers can worship openly, all who do so risk their freedom, if not their lives. The recent generations of Russian Orthodox Christians therefore have annealed their spirituality in the fire of strong opposition. Much of the fierce traditionalism one meets in Eastern Christianity owes its source to this fact. Like the fiercely traditional Roman Catholicism of Pope John Paul II, which has been annealed in the fires of Polish Communist opposition, it is faith too precious to be changed by modern notions—notions from a time when godlessness and cruelty have reached new heights. We may not be able to agree with all the instincts of Eastern spirituality, but we should be able to admire many of them.

Summary

Among the instincts of Eastern Orthodox spirituality that we might admire today is its search for a conception of faith that will overcome the excessively rational denotations faith has carried in the past and so prove more compatible with current ecological science. Metropolitan Paulos Gregorios's presentation on faith to the MIT conference illustrates this search, showing in addition the ontological accents in which Orthodoxy traditionally has read such scriptural passages as Col. 1:15–20 and Rev. 12:1–6.

Insofar as we press Eastern Orthodoxy into service to illumine the domain of the self, we discover that its traditional spirituality, both Russian and Greek, is rooted in monastic practices that contest current secular wisdom. As the reports of Sergius Bolshakoff and Basil Pennington on Eastern masters show, the monastic tradition has found much vanity in secular portraits of the self's prosperity. In place of money, power, and status, Orthodox monks and nuns have pursued poverty, humility, and seclusion. Taking direction from spiritual fathers and mothers, they have emphasized silence and mortification as prime avenues to spiritual prosperity. Such practices have not been ends in themselves; they have been means to loving absorption in Christ. As the Jesus Prayer especially assumes, true power and wisdom come from identifying with the Savior, the Lord who has mercy on selves that confess they are sinners.

From Mount Athos to current-day Moscow, this spirituality undergirds Orthodox holiness and survival. The monks of Mount Athos keep the traditions of foolishness for Christ, spiritual freedom, and religious paradox by intense devotion to the Liturgy, the Jesus Prayer, and deep silence. Beleaguered believers in the Soviet Union often have come back to their faith after finding Marxist atheism a cause of depression, alcoholism, or an inner void. Following a courageous priest like Dmitrii Dudko, they find they can endure much abuse from the government if it is the price of possessing the joy of New Testament faith.

Study Questions

1. Explain Metropolitan Gregorios's sentence, "Truth is reality, not statement."
2. What are the possible perils in the discovery at old age that all is vanity?
3. What are the advantages in the traditional monastic practice of *starchestvo*?
4. Give a brief reaction to Mother Alexandra's description of how to practice the Jesus Prayer.
5. Evaluate Father Euthemios's "foolishness."
6. How does an Orthodox monk or nun have a social function in the Church?
7. In what ways is traditional Russian Orthodoxy an antidote to Marxist atheistic views of the self?

Notes

1. Alexander Schmemann, "That East and West May Yet Meet," in *Against the World For the World*, Peter L. Berger and Richard John Neuhaus, eds. (New York: Seabury, 1976), p. 128.
2. Ibid., p. 129.
3. See Paulos Gregorios, "Science and Faith: Complementary or Contradictory?," in *Faith and Science in an Unjust World*, Roger L. Shinn, ed. (Philadelphia: Fortress, 1980), vol. 1, p. 47.
4. Ibid., p. 50.
5. See "Science and Technology within the Story of Redemption," ibid., p. 118.
6. "The Great Symbol," ibid., p. 379.
7. See also Nikos A. Nissiotis, "An Orthodox Contribution to Consensus," in *Consensus in Theology*, Leonard Swidler, ed. (Philadelphia: Westminster, 1980), pp. 100–109.
8. Sergius Bolshakoff and M. Basil Pennington, *In Search of True Wisdom*, p. 27. Copyright © 1979 by Cistercian Abbey of Spencer, Inc. Reprinted by permission of Doubleday & Company, Inc.
9. Ibid., p. 47. Reprinted by permission.
10. Ibid., p. 147. Reprinted by permission.
11. See Vladimir Lossky, *The Mystical Theology of the Eastern Church* (Crestwood, NY: St. Vladimir's Seminary Press, 1976), especially pp. 23–43.
12. See R. M. French, trans., *The Way of A Pilgrim* (New York: Seabury, 1965).
13. *In Search of True Wisdom*, p. 168.
14. Ibid., p. 164.
15. In addition to *In Search of True Wisdom*, see Pennington's *O Holy Mountain!* (Garden City, NY: Doubleday, 1978).
16. *In Search of True Wisdom*, p. 85.
17. Ibid., pp. 86–87.
18. Ibid., p. 88.
19. Ibid., p. 116.
20. See G. P. Fedotov, ed., *A Treasury of Russian Spirituality* (New York: Harper & Row, 1965), and Alexander Schmemann, ed., *Ultimate Questions* (Crestwood, New York: St. Vladimir's Seminary Press, 1977).
21. Quoted in *Our Hope*, by Dmitrii Dudko (Crestwood, NY: St. Vladimir's Seminary Press, 1977), p. 52. Reprinted by permission.
22. Ibid., p. 31. Reprinted by permission.

CHAPTER 14

Contemporary Black Theology

Afro-American Religious History[1]

Since the 1960s, black theology has been a powerful focus of liberation themes. The general story of black people in the United States is grim, full of a "mortification" less subject to illusion than that of Eastern Orthodox monks because blacks suffered unwillingly, as a result of physical slavery. The story begins in the earliest years of colonial America, with the arrival in 1619 of the first slave ship at Jamestown, Virginia. It was a Dutch vessel carrying at least 20 Africans who had been sold as indentured servants. By 1649 there were about 300 African slaves in Virginia (out of a population of about 15,000), most of them laboring on the tobacco plantations. Slaves arrived in Massachusetts as early as 1638, and the thirteen colonies finally came to contain about 427,000 indentured blacks. By 1800, there were 1 million blacks, representing about 20 percent of the population. Natural increase brought this figure to 4 million by the time of emancipation in 1863.

In the main, these American blacks came from West Africa or the region of Congo-Angola. Thus they derived from such tribal nations as the Mandinke, Yoruba, Ibo, Bakongo, Ewe, and Fon. Some of these tribal nations had converted to Islam, but others continued traditional African religious ways. In general, traditional African ways stressed the continuity between different aspects of life (animal, human, and spiritual), as well as the importance of tribal community. Kinship bonds were strong, rites of passage were elaborate, and divinity was associated with power or vitality. The West African high god usually was remote, but many intermediate gods were close and effective, working through diviners or ecstatics (people who went into trances). Most tribes celebrated sacrifices, often with exciting dances, and almost all were concerned with healing, which they associated with expelling evil spiritual influences. Africans did not have the Western sense of sin, nor the Western interest in a scriptural revelation. Their traditions stressed fertility for fields and families, gaining wisdom through ordeals and silences, and above all sharing tasks and pleasures with other members of their extended tribal family.

The slavers demoralized their African captives from the outset by breaking up families and separating people of the same tribe. Many captives died en route to the New World, for the conditions on board ship were unspeakable, and the law under which slave-trading proceeded in effect denied that the Africans were human persons. This condition of nonpersonhood, combined with their African heritage, determined the character of American blacks' Christianity. From their first contacts with Christian scripture, it made them identify with the Israelites who were enslaved under the pharaoh and the New Testament marginals whom Jesus blessed. The African heritage led to a rich mythology of **trickster** (anti-hero) tales, such as the stories of Brer Rabbit, and to a continued interest in healing rites, including those of voodoo, a half-Christian, half-tribal religion derived from Dahomey by way of Haiti.

While small numbers of blacks in Maryland and Louisiana became Roman Catholics, most who converted to Christianity became Protestants. However, white Christians were more than ambivalent about the conversion of their slaves to Christianity. On the one hand, baptism might seem to imply that slaves were children of God, and so equal to whites. The common-law tradition of England had reasoned this way, holding that baptism made a slave free. Thus by 1706 six colonial legislatures had passed statutes denying that baptism made a slave free. On the other hand, pious Christians thought that God wanted blacks to be his children, so they tried to persuade slaveholders that Christian faith would make blacks more humble and obedient—better slaves. The slaves themselves were slow to embrace the religion of their owners, greeting the efforts of such groups as the Society for the Propagation of the Gospel in Foreign Parts, an English organization that sent many missionaries in the early eighteenth century, with indifference. When Baptist and Methodist preachers employed down-to-earth sermons in the middle of the eighteenth century, however, quite a few blacks were moved to embrace Christianity. Before long these converts began to adapt Christian faith to their situation as slaves, joining it to what they had retained of their African heritage.

Much of this adaptation went on in secret, for slave revolts in the 1820s based on vengeful **apocalyptic** (that is, revealed) religious imagery had frightened white owners. Thus slaves often had to huddle at night in the woods at "hush harbors," praying and discussing only in whispers. They used what religious freedom they could gain to develop a distinctive style of preaching and singing, both of which emphasized being filled by the Spirit. With cadences reminiscent of African drums, the preacher would chant a repetitive message. The assembly would respond with shouts and affirmations, giving a sort of counterpoint. Songs based on favorite scriptural passages developed, and these "spirituals" sometimes led to shuffling choral dances. The result was a discernible black style calculated to help slaves vent their sorrows, express their angers, and keep their hopes alive. For special occasions like marriages and burials the community would but adapt its preaching, spirituals, and dances. Then the theme frequently was that those who suffered in the present would be happy in heaven, while those who gave pain in the present would suffer God's justice in hell.

Some black Christian congregations gained a measure of autonomy prior to emancipation, but after 1863 both black congregations in white churches, such as the Baptists and Methodists, and new black churches grew more rapidly. For example, black churches such as the African Methodist Episcopal Church and the African Methodist Episcopal Church Zion sent missionaries to the South after the Civil War and won many converts to their rolls. By 1900 about one-third of American blacks were church members, which meant about three million persons. Since only 4 or 5 percent of the black population had been church members in 1800, the nineteenth century was a time of considerable growth.

The twentieth century was a time of massive population shifts. Seventy-five percent of all blacks had lived in the rural South prior to 1900; 75 percent lived in cities (50 percent in Northern cities) in 1967. This caused great upheaval in black congregations, and major problems in black Americans' lives. The unemployment, poverty, and crime of the black urban ghetto became the daily adversary of black religion. Realizing the peculiar problems of their people, black religious leaders attempted a variety of solutions. Separationists such as Marcus Garvey preached a return to Africa. New Holiness and Pentecostal churches developed a vibrant spirituality focused on a black Jesus. Charismatic leaders like Father Divine and Daddy Grace extended this rising interest in blackness, preparing Afro-Americans for the preaching of Martin Luther King, Jr.

Civil Rights and Black Power

In the twentieth century two gifted religious leaders raised black consciousness to oppose the social structures strangling black people. Malcolm X (1925–65) was the most effective spokesman for the Black Muslims, and Martin Luther King, Jr. (1929–68) led Southern black Christians. King was the son of a prominent Southern preacher, nurtured on long years of American black experience with both slavery and freedom. He had studied at Boston University and in 1955, at the Montgomery, Alabama, bus boycott, he began a program of nonviolent resistance to segregation and other manifestations of racial injustice. At the head of marches in Birmingham, Selma, and Washington, D.C., King forced the United States to face the inferior treatment it was giving millions of its citizens. Legislation to improve the civil rights of blacks passed Congress in 1957, 1960, 1964, and 1965. Indeed, the Voting Rights Act of 1965 seemed to open the way for blacks to obtain political power, while King's reception of the Nobel Peace Prize in 1964 set his personal star high in the international firmament.

Nonetheless, events between 1965 and King's death in 1968 brought a strong challenge to his nonviolent style of leadership. Black churches had long identified with the ghettoes in which their people lived, and disturbances in such ghettoes as Harlem and Watts (Los Angeles) during the summers of the mid-60s were incubators for the concept of Black Power. King's initial reaction to Black Power was negative, for he thought it "a nihilistic philosophy born out of the conviction that the Negro can't win."[2] Many black preachers disagreed with him on this point, however, having become persuaded that unless blacks possessed political, economic, and perhaps even military clout they would make no significant progress in removing the causes of their ghetto woes. For many the theological validity of Black Power emerged only through bitter reflection on the violence of the eruptions in more than 128 cities during 1963–68. By 1968 perhaps a majority of black churchmen thought it clear that the Civil Rights Act of 1964 and the Voting Rights Act of 1965 were not going to alleviate hard-core urban suffering.

A series of statements by black church leaders in the years 1966 to 1968 gave public expression to this conviction, but before turning to one of those statements perhaps we should detail the sorts of experiences black church leaders had had. In Watts, black clergy had organized an armed guard of men from their congregations to repulse a white motorcycle gang trying to retaliate for the burnings. In Newark and Detroit they had cooperated with leaders of uprisings in ways that made them liable to prosecution (despite their yeoman efforts to turn their churches into shelters and centers of reconciliation). In almost all cities black clergy had had repeatedly to weigh the rights of police to truthful information against the rights of youngsters to protection against brutality and arbitrary arrest. In almost all cities they had had to temper their judgments about the destruction of property with close knowledge of the exploitation that banks, landlords, and municipal authorities inflicted on blacks each day. By 1968, the day had passed when most black clergy could still believe white America would acknowledge the wrongs of racial injustice and act in good will to remove them.

A statement by the National Committee of Negro Churchmen in the July 31, 1966 *New York Times* placed this conviction before the nation. Its main thesis was that the gross imbalance of power and conscience between blacks and whites obscured the controversy over Black Power, and that only righting this imbalance would deliver the nation from convulsive throes. To quote the fine rhetoric of the document itself, ". . . the power of white men and the conscience of black men have both been corrupted. The power of white men is corrupted because it meets little meaningful resistance from Negroes to temper it and keep white men from aping God. The conscience of black men is corrupted because, having no power to implement the demands of conscience, the concern for justice is transmuted into a distorted form of love, which, in the absence of justice, becomes chaotic self-surrender. Powerlessness breeds a race of beggars."[3]

To leaders of the country the churchmen argued that the true source of conflicts erupting in the ghettoes was the covert violence, often so smooth and smiling, with which white America pinned masses of blacks against the wall, leaving them without jobs, with a dilapidated educational system, with no chance for equal opportunity in *life* (despite advances in equal opportunity in law). They reminded such leaders that power itself is unexceptionable, and that at the heart of the Protestant Reformation lay the conviction that ultimate power belongs to God alone, with the correlative conviction that men become most inhuman when their concentrations of power lead them to try to rival God. Thus the churchmen pleaded that the country's leaders should hear in the cry for Black Power an effort to redress imbalances presently causing white Americans to act with signal inhumanity.

To white churchmen the black clergy offered reminders that integration was worthless unless it solved blacks' social inferiority, and that any discussion of love neglecting socio-economic justice was nugatory. The statement directed its most poignant reflections to black citizens themselves, trying to make them see how Black Power might heal some of their self-hatred, as well as solve their material problems. Black Power would entail cooperation with other blacks, and also a refusal to let the black Church concentrate unduly on *otherworldly* conceptions of God's power. It would set an agenda quite different from that of white America: "We must work with the remainder of the nation to organize whole cities for the task of making the rebuilding of our cities first priority in the use of our resources. This is more important than who gets to the moon first or the war in Vietnam."[4] With the media, finally, the churchmen pleaded for coverage of city problems, seeing there the future of the entire nation.

Black Theology

Two other documents from 1969 add to the impression that 1969 was the year when black theology really caught fire. The first is the Black Manifesto presented by activist James Forman to the National Black Economic Development Conference in Detroit. The second is a statement on black theology from the National Committee of Black Churchmen (previously Negro Churchmen). The Black Manifesto was adopted by the Conference on April 26, and Forman then presented it to the predominantly white congregation of Riverside Church in New York City on May 4. While certain features of the manifesto suggest it was more political than theological, the positive reception it received in many black churches showed it rang true to much black theological conviction.

The manifesto opened with an attack on American capitalism: ". . . the people must be educated to understand that any black man or Negro who is advocating a perpetuation of capitalism inside the United States is in fact seeking not only his ultimate destruction and death but is contributing to the continuous exploitation of black people all around the world."[5] Linking capitalism, racism, and imperialism, it went on to argue that only an armed, well-disciplined, black-controlled government could ensure the end of racism in the United States. As a concrete step in that direction, the manifesto demanded of the white Christian churches and Jewish synagogues $500 million in reparation for past injuries to blacks. The money would be spent to begin making blacks economically self-sufficient.

Specifically, the manifesto envisioned the $500 million going for a Southern land bank, to keep black farmers from being evicted from their lands; four major publishing and printing companies; four audio-visual networks; a research skills center; a training center to teach community organizing, photography, television repair, and other job skills; support of the National Welfare Rights Organization; a National Black Labor Strike and Defense Fund; an International Black Appeal to produce more capital for cooperative businesses in the United States and Africa; and a black university in the South. The Southern land bank and the black university would receive the largest amounts.

Forman and the other signers of the manifesto calculated that the half billion dollars they were demanding in reparation came to only fifteen dollars per black American. That seemed little enough redress for centuries of slavery. As the manifesto came to the attention of the American Christian churches, two of its assumptions dominated the discussion. First, it assumed that the white Christian churches and Jewish synagogues owed their financial prosperity to the racism of American socio-economic structures. The National Committee of Black Churchmen agreed. Responding to the manifesto it said:

> There is no question but that the American religious establishment, along with almost every other institution in the society, was the conscious beneficiary of the enforced labor of one of the most inhuman forms of chattel slavery the world has ever known. Some churches actually owned slaves and many others thrived on the tithes and offerings of both Northern and Southern churchmen who profited directly and indirectly from the uncompensated labor of slaves. The white churches and synagogues undeniably have been the moral cement of the structure of racism in this nation and the vast majority of them continue to play that role today.[6]

Second, the manifesto assumed that reparation was a time-honored way of repairing past injuries. In customary Christian moral teaching one who stole was obliged to make restitution; whites obviously had stolen more than they could repay, but $500 million would at least put their smooth words about reconciliation into practice.

The Black Manifesto catalyzed both individual black theologians and black clergy groups to clarify the notion of black theology itself. Thus theologian Gayraud Wilmore moved from a justification of reparations to an interpretation of the Black Manifesto as a moment of judgment (calling to account) and opportunity. In scriptural terms, James Forman reminded Wilmore of 1 Pet. 4:17—"The time has come for the judgment to begin; it is beginning with God's own household"—and Luke 12:22—"This night your soul is required of you; and the things you have prepared, whose will they be?" Pushing off from these texts, Wilmore reflected: "The theological meaning of the present crisis of race relations in the United States is that Black Power, the legal concept of reparations, and the appearance of James Forman as a stringent and arrogant critic of the American religious establishment may be seen, through the eyes of faith, to be redemptive."[7]

Reflecting similarly, the National Committee of Black Churchmen issued on June 13, 1969 a statement on black theology. It is the second document we offer in support of the view that in 1969 black theology became a distinctive distillate of black religious experience. The National Committee's statement first describes black theology as the appropriation black slaves made of the Gospel given them by their white oppressors. Thus black theology was essential to the survival of blacks as a people—present in their spirituals and slave songs, in the exhortations of their preachers and the dances in which they forgot their pain.

Second, the National Committee's statement describes black theology as a theology of liberation. "It seeks to plumb the black condition in the light of God's revelation in Jesus Christ, so that the black community can see that the gospel is commensurate with the achievement of black humanity."[8] Insofar as racism prevents whites from affirming their true humanity, black theology is also an affirmation of white people's humanity. Denying racism, it affirms what whites ought to be. As Luke 4:18 shows, Jesus came to preach deliverance to captives. Christ the Liberator therefore asks blacks to affirm their full dignity as persons just as he asks whites to surrender their presumptions of superiority. Black theology must press for the reparations that might begin this process, showing how reparation is part of the gospel message. It must also show the spuriousness of much of the Christianity imposed on blacks by whites. In any choice for *life*, that spurious Christianity will fall away. Significantly, the Black Churchmen conclude their statement on black theology with the words of Eldridge Cleaver: "We shall have our manhood. We shall have it or the earth will be leveled by our efforts to gain it."[9]

White Theological Reaction

Perhaps needless to say, the white churches and synagogues did not agree to the demands of the Black Manifesto that they pay $500 million in reparations. That was not surprising, for they had previously refused more modest demands. Indeed, the Black Manifesto came about largely as a result of the failure of the Interreligious Fund for Community Organization (IFCO) to gain black control over the inner-city projects of white denominations. When black churchmen came to the verge of dominating the IFCO, its white Christian and Jewish funding sources began to divert most of their allocations to "designated projects" they could continue to control. To blacks such tactics were but ecclesiastical colonialism. Prominent black clergymen like Albert B. Cleage, Jr., author of an influential book entitled *The Black Messiah*,[10] argued for the direct funding of ghetto organizations with no strings attached, but to no avail. The mainline white churches continued to support inner-city projects that in effect were missionary outposts of their own denominations. Keeping such projects mainly under the control of white "urban specialists," their actions shouted to the black community that the white church still considered it untrustworthy.

Nonetheless, some white theologians recognized the significance of black theology, and while they never dominated the white theological scene nor moved their churches to radical support of Black Power, they did mediate some of the central insights of the new movement to the white ecclesiastical community. A good example was John Coleman Bennett's book *The Radical Imperative*.[11] Bennett was president emeritus of Union Theological Seminary in New York City, one of the most prestigious mainline Protestant schools, and a well-respected writer on Christian ethics. His analysis of the views of James Cone, perhaps the most influential black theologian, shows both the affirmations that liberal Christian thinkers tended to make and their typical reservations.

First, Bennett could only agree with Cone that black theology was necessary because no white theology had ever taken the oppression of black people as the point of departure for analyzing God's activity in America. Indeed, until their first glimmerings of awareness in the 1950s, the white churches had seldom looked deeply into the wrongs blacks had suffered in this supposedly Christian nation. Even the proponents of the Social Gospel, who markedly heightened the churches' awareness of many social evils early in the twentieth century, had a blind spot regarding racism. White themselves, they overlooked the malformations racism had produced. Thus Walter Rauschenbusch, the greatest of the Social Gospel theologians, could write eloquently of the rapacity of untamed business, the powerlessness of industrial workers, and the poverty blighting Northern cities without noting their special destructiveness for blacks.

Second, Bennett defended Cone's attacks on whites with the sober denunciations of white indifference that Dr. Benjamin Mays, for many years president of Morehouse College, had laid out in his autobiography, *Born to Rebel*. Though not a militant, and probably not a proponent of black theology, Mays had written of the Christian churches: "I believe that throughout my lifetime, the local white church has been society's most conservative and hypocritical institution in the area of white-Negro relations."[12] Whatever their reservations about Black Power and black theology, men like Mays and Martin Luther King, Jr., knew just from having lived as blacks that racism was a sin staining the very center of American culture.

Third, Bennett added checks and balances to which Cone might have agreed (for example, ways in which whites had protested racism), and then offered some negative criticisms. These latter centered on Cone's use of the words *black* and *white*, which made them virtually synonymous with *good* and *evil*. Bennett admitted that Cone qualified this usage in several footnotes, but he worried that a narrowness of focus was keeping Cone from seeing racism in such other evils as the Vietnam War or the exploitation of American Indians. Single-mindedly, Cone had argued that Black Power was Christ's central message to twentieth-century America. Bennett could only accept the argument if it were made to illumine all instances of oppression.

Last, Bennett found Cone's vision of whites monolithic. In Bennett's own view, whites who were relative newcomers to the United States, having only arrived in the late nineteenth- and early twentieth-century immigrations, could not be expected to feel responsible for slavery, nor to hear calls for reparation with great sympathy. They were naive to argue that blacks ought to work hard and "make it" as they had, but it hurt the effectiveness of black theology not to distinguish them from the WASP establishment. Similarly, the tensions between blacks and Jews that resulted from quarrels about job quotas, Jews' being landlords in some ghettoes, and blacks' frequent identification with Arabs were not helped by a shotgun approach to all whites.

Cone showed himself respectful of Bennet's views,[13] but he did not retract his main tenets: Slavery and racism are such a potent symbol of human sinfulness, such a central specimen of the oppression the God of Exodus wants to overthrow, that black theologians have a privileged message. When the issue is God's action in the contemporary world, they are expert as no white theologians can be.

Openings to the Third World

An obvious alternative to black theologians as the privileged interpreters of God's action in the contemporary world are third world peoples, whose experiences of oppression often are as acute as those of ghetto blacks. Leading black theologians have been sensible enough to avoid any competition for the title "most wretched" and any appearance of pontificating about liberation. Increasingly, they have encouraged both a variety of black theologies and a variety of liberation theologies rooted in different racial, geographical, cultural, and sexual experiences. In meetings such as the 1975 Detroit Conference on Theology in the Americas,[14] black theologians have met with representatives of feminist, Asian, Chicano, Latin American, and other liberation schools. In international meetings of organizations such as the World Council of Churches, they have learned about other churches' efforts to develop indigenous theologies, liturgies, and modes of political expression. Probably their most acute encounters, however, have been with African theologians. Let us therefore concentrate on those.

A representative sampling of recent African theological preoccupations may be found in *African Theology en Route*, edited by Kofi Appiah-Kubi and Sergio Torres,[15] which is a collection of papers from the Pan-African Conference of Third World Theologians held at Accra, Ghana, in December 1977. While most of the delegates were Africans, fifteen came from North America. Several papers dwelt on the relation between American black theology and African theology, making it clear that they are likely to influence one another in the future.

For, first, there are historical connections between Afro-American and African Christians that bind them together ineluctably. The obvious connection is that black Americans derive from Africans carried away as slaves, but a less well-known connection runs in the other direction. Almost as soon as they accepted Christianity, black Americans dreamed of bringing it to Africa and the Caribbean. "For more than a hundred years, from the outbreak of the American Revolution to the dawn of the twentieth century, black people moved back and forth across the

Atlantic and the Caribbean to forge a bond between Africa and the New World that has been overlooked by most historians."[16] The major motivation in this moving back and forth was the propagation of Christian faith. Of the four earliest black American preachers historians can discuss, three went overseas to establish new churches. They went to Nova Scotia, Sierra Leone, Jamaica, and the Bahamas. Black Americans started foundations in West Africa as early as 1792 and 1811, and they continued throughout the nineteenth century to dream of missionizing their African brothers and sisters. Why? Because in their ecclesiology missionary activity was essential to Church life. The Gospel could not live fully unless a congregation was trying to hand it on to those who had not yet encountered salvation and liberation.

When Black Power and black theology emerged in the 1960s, they renewed this African connection. For instance, in 1969 two black theologians went uninvited to the Second Assembly of the All-Africa Conference of Churches at Abidjan, Ivory Coast. After some initial awkwardness, they established cordial relations with African clergy, making contacts that intensified through the 1970s. The differences between the two groups made for some strain, but on the whole they seemed to enjoy learning from one another. From the African side, the American stress on the political implications of the Gospel sometimes was problematic. Africans had enough bitter experience with colonialism to affirm many of American black theology's demands for liberation, but their context differed from that of a minority enslaved simply by their color. Interestingly, it is black South Africans who have been especially open to American political emphases, no doubt because of their own experiences with apartheid.

From the American side, there has been a need to hear Africans' insistence that their theology must have indigenous roots. At times this insistence has turned into a sharp criticism of American assumptions. Thus the Kenyan John Mbiti reproached American blacks for being "full of sorrow, bitterness, anger, and hatred."[17] For him black theology, American style, had no more relevance than European political theology or the liberation theology of Southeast Asia. Delicately, Afro-Americans such as James Cone[18] have admitted their incompetence in many areas of African theology without agreeing that their work has no special relevance for Africa. Quoting Africans who disagree with Mbiti's view, they have noted that much African theology may lack a "cutting edge"—a sufficiently political orientation. Insofar as colonialism was shot through with racism, and racism continues in South African countries to the present day, American reflections on Black Power might prove very instructive.

Regarding relations with other third world theologies, American black theology now seems to appreciate how much oppressed peoples everywhere have in common. Sometimes through the lens of biblical theology's predilection for the poor sometimes through socio-economic analyses of the collusion between capitalism and racism, black theologians are finding that their work crosses that of Latin Americans and Asians at many points. Within the United States, black theologian surely offer the best translation of the themes common to liberation theologie everywhere, because their experience, both past and present, assembles the most haunting instances of American sinfulness. Simply by being black, more than 10 percent of America's citizens have been fit to the lineaments of Isaiah's suffering servant: despised, rejected, people of sorrow acquainted with grief.[19]

The Spirituals and the Blues

Black theology uncovers the biblical message of liberation from the suffering side of American life. To a surrounding culture largely unsympathetic, it discloses the inhumanity of racism, the myriad ways sin can focus on something as accidental as color. These revelations are negative. From poverty and suffering, they suggest the healing a credible God would be longing to bring forth. Black religion has furnished more than negative revelations, however. Often it has furnished positive strength to best the oppressor. This strength has seeped into many black bones through soulful music. Thus even a brief look at black music will fill out our picture of black theology.

Fittingly enough, one of the best studies of black music comes from James Cone, the prominent black theologian. Cone distinguishes *spirituals* from *blues*, as religious songs from secular, but he denies that the two kinds of music differ radically in their functions. Spirituals have obvious roots in African songs and dances, and they probably began as soon as slaves settled in the colonies. Those who accepted Christianity strung biblical motifs into memorable refrains, so that convictions of faith could seep into black people's depths. Thus the slave spirituals sang of God's liberation, Jesus, and present sufferings. They sang of death, Satan, and sin. Perhaps their most important theme, though, was heaven, for by singing about heaven black slaves kept their hope for a better fate flickering.

Singing about heaven was a primary way slaves could take their pain and suffering seriously without rejecting God. When they interiorized biblical notions about heaven, they could admit present injustices without despairing of a greater justice before God. This does not mean that the spirituals made heaven entirely otherworldly. As many specific songs make plain, symbols for heaven (for instance, Canaan, Jordan, the Promised Land) could also signify the North, Canada, or Africa—quite this-worldly places to which slaves were trying to escape. Thus after reaching freedom Harriet Tubman said: "I looked at my hands to see if I was de same person now I was free. Dere was such glory ober everything, de sun came like gold trou de trees, and ober de fields, and I felt like I was in heaven."[20]

On the other hand, many slaves came to realize that they were not likely to reach Canada or Africa. For them heaven had to bring dignity and personhood to the wretched slave-holding South. It did this by symbolizing a transcendent now, as well as a hopeful future. If a God dwelling in heavenly perfection cared for them, slaves had a dignity no physical fetters could suppress. And if God promised them heaven after death, blacks could fail in their struggle for freedom without losing all basis for hope. Boarding the "gospel train," they could dissolve their second-class status and move toward better times:

Git on board, little chillen,
Git on board, little chillen,
Git on board, little chillen,
Dere's room for many a mo'.

De gospel train's a-comin',
I hear it jus' at han',
I hear de car wheels' movin',
An' rumblin' thro de lan'.

De fare is cheap, an' all can go,
De rich an' poor are dere,
No second class a-board dis train,
No difference in de fare.[21]

In hundreds of such verses, black slaves expressed their faith that God would see them through this dark, cold existence. After emanicipation, when conditions improved somewhat, but not as much as many had hoped, a new, more secular music came to the fore. It had antecedents among nonreligious blacks prior to emancipation, but it was bolder about worldly themes, especially sexual love. For Cone the blues are as quintessentially black as the spirituals, because they express oppressed black existence just as directly. Just as directly, they are living, organic music—music drawn from daily suffering, music insistent that body and soul belong together. Indeed, the continuity between the spirituals and the blues is quite apparent: "Nobody knows the trouble I've seen"; "I'm rollin' through an unfriendly world"; and "Sometimes I feel like a motherless child" are lines from spirituals, but they could come right from the "worried blues."[22] The seeming discontinuity stemming from the blues' profanity should not be exaggerated. For a sympathetic theologian, the blues simply underscore here-and-now troubles or joys that faith insists we can take to God.

Cone argues this thesis for such blues themes as suffering and humor. When they sing of prison or the spunk of the boll weevil, the blues prepare a sort of incarnationalism modern spirituals might attempt. Even regarding sex, where they have been more explicit than many churchgoing blacks like, the blues offer a helpful message. For blacks have experienced that human love is all the dearer when other comforts are slight. Thus when the blues sing, "Good lookin' woman make a mule kick his stable down," or "Woman without a man like a ship without a sail," or even "Peach Orchard Mama, you swore nobody'd pick your fruit but me, but I found three kid men shaking down your peaches free,"[23] they tell black theology, indeed all Christian theology, that it must baptize sexual love, take it to the table, wash it in the blood of the Lamb. Otherwise, the Word has not really become flesh and dwelt among us.

The Black Church

Through the black Church, Christian incarnationalism took hold of generations of slaves, and then generations of their nearly equally downtrodden descendants. Prominent black theologian J. Deotis Roberts has singled out the black Church and the black family as the two primary institutions of black culture. Prior to the Civil War, when slavery was the dominant feature of Afro-American life, black religious meetings often had an underground or invisible character, for slaves who met together without authorization usually were guilty of civil disobedience. For example, in 1819 South Carolina enacted a law against unapproved assemblies that made many black church meetings a matter of jeopardy.

Nonetheless, the African tradition of secret meetings of initiates inclined Christian slaves to risk assembling at night in "hush harbors." The earliest known black church was established in 1773 at Silver Bluff, South Carolina, and by 1794 there were two black churches in Philadelphia. In New York City the first assembly of the African Methodist Episcopal Zion Church was organized in 1796. Blacks protested discrimination in Northern mixed congregations as early as 1787, when Richard Allen walked out of St. George's Methodist Episcopal Church in Philadelphia.

After emancipation, the black Church could function more freely, and its history from that time is more certain. In historian Olin Moyd's schematization,[24] there was a formative period, from the Civil War through Reconstruction (1865–1877). This gave way to a maturation period, extending from Reconstruction to the Great Migration of blacks from the Southern plantations to the Northern cities (1877–1914). A third period, which Moyd labels "expansion-renaissance," lasted from 1914 to the beginning of the Second World War (1939). From 1939 to 1955 was a period of "passive protest," and from 1955 to the present has been a period of "radical reassertion." Let us look at these periods in more detail.

The formative period was a time of growth, excitement, and church influence. During Reconstruction, black churches were in the forefront of black political involvement. Blacks served in Congress. They were school superintendents, postmasters, state treasurers, state secretaries, and lieutenant governors. Out of the churches came social, educational, and political programs. In the churches blacks found a deepening theology and a solid spiritual comfort.

The maturation period was shaped by a disastrous compromise between the North and the South that set the black cause back dramatically. State legislatures passed laws stripping blacks of rights they had gained during Reconstruction; many Jim Crow (anti-black) statutes arose. Federal troops withdrew from Southern states, blacks lost political offices by fair means or foul, and such discriminatory measures as poll taxes and literacy tests disenfranchised most black voters. The 1896 Supreme Court separate-but-equal decree set a pattern of legal segregation that prevailed through most of the next century.

Still, the church matured in the sense that it held its own through such adversity. Segregation at least meant clearer lines of black power over the black church, and black ministers served their people's many needs forthrightly. By 1890 there were almost twenty-four thousand black churches in the country, with a total membership of about two-and-a-half million. That meant that more than a third of the nation's blacks were church-goers. In the South the figure was higher: 50 percent. Baptists and Methodists predominated, and overall there was one black church for every sixty black families. Theologically, there emerged the basic understanding of redemption that has characterized the black Church until recent times—applying the biblical good news to blacks' sorry temporal circumstances. Liturgically, preaching, music, and prayer-forms completed the transposition of African instincts to an American Christian situation.

During the Great Migration, white hostility and poor crop conditions forced hundreds of thousands of blacks to emigrate from the rural South to the urban North, boll weevil infestations and floods combining with racial enmity to produce a painful exodus. Prospects of better jobs in the industrialized North probably fell through more often than they were realized, but the exodus continued during World War I, as industrialization further increased. More than a half million blacks left the South in the war years, gravitating to cities such as Chicago, Cleveland, and New York. As a result, black Baptist and Methodist churches in the North experienced amazing growth, so much so that they were unable to handle all the newcomers' social and religious needs. Thus storefront churches and new cults arose, often with freer worship forms. On the other hand, Baptist and Pentecostal churches carried on the traditions of the South. In the "Harlem Renaissance" after World War I, black culture exploded in pride, only, however, to be deflated during the depression years of the 1930s.

Those years of passive protest saw the black Church (the only institution that blacks controlled) leading most efforts to help black people survive. For example, black churches regularly distributed the food the government provided. World War II brought some improvement in labor practices, which the black pulpit and black press supported vigorously, but few blacks controlled these industries or businesses, so most protests were easily blunted. Only in the recent period of radical reassertion, which we have studied in some detail, were Black Power and black theology able to arise, and from Martin Luther King, Jr, to James Cone and Gayraud Wilmore, sons of the black Church have led these movements. In sum, blacks made the Church the backbone of their culture, because it was their only autonomous institution.

Summary

Afro-American religious history begins with the arrival of the first boatload of slaves in 1619. By the time of emancipation in 1863, the number of Afro-Americans had reached four million, and of the nine million blacks living in the United States in 1900 about one-third were Christians. From their African tribes American blacks derived an optimistic view of the world as naturally a good place, an insistence on religious rites that celebrated *life*, and a strong sense of the group or extended family. With slavery and Bible-based Christianity, these African traditions have shaped black Christian Church life.

In the 1960s agitation for civil rights, and then discouragement over the paucity of their real gains, caused many black church leaders to endorse Black Power. In essence they were confessing that only economic and political leverage could bring their people equality. This spawned black theology, Christian reflection on the experiences of black people in a land that had enslaved and impoverished them. White Christianity and Judaism never acceded to the demands of blacks for reparations, but the political accents of black theology have made it a force for whites to reckon with. These political accents have divided African theologians as to the utility of American blacks' reflections, but they have tended to tie black theology to the liberation theologies emerging in Latin America, Asia, and the women's movement. Through common experiences of oppression, third world peoples feel united with black theologians against their first world oppressors.

Black music and black Church life have been the mainstays of black culture, and both exemplify the contribution that black theology makes to Christianity today. Black music has given feelings of enslavement, and desires for bodily fulfillment, extremely effective expression, while in the history of the black Church one can see a prime example of a Christian community struggling to preserve itself against the heaviest odds.

Study Questions

1. What pros and cons did white slave-owners have to face in allowing slaves to be baptized?
2. Why did black church leaders frequently endorse Black Power?
3. How was it possible for the Black Manifesto to catalyze black theology?
4. What is the main lesson white theology should have learned from early black theology?
5. Is it logical for black theologians to consider themselves part of the third world's theological reflection? Why?
6. How can the spirituals and the blues be considered kindred musical forms?
7. How has the black Church evolved since the Civil War?

Notes

1. This sketch depends principally on Catherine L. Albanese, *America: Religions and Religion* (Belmont, CA: Wadsworth, 1981), pp. 113–135.
2. Martin Luther King, Jr., *Where Do We Go From Here: Chaos or Community?* (New York: Harper & Row, 1967), p. 44. Quoted by Gayraud S. Wilmore and James H. Cone, eds., *Black Theology: A Documentary History, 1966–1979* (Maryknoll, NY: Orbis, 1979), p. 15. Reprinted by permission.
3. *Black Theology*, p. 23. Reprinted by permission.
4. Ibid., p. 28. Reprinted by permission.
5. Ibid., p. 80. Reprinted by permission.

6. Ibid., pp. 90–91. Reprinted by permission.
7. Ibid., p. 98. Reprinted by permission.
8. Ibid., p. 101. Reprinted by permission.
9. Ibid., p. 102. Reprinted by permission.
10. Albert B. Cleage, Jr., *The Black Messiah* (New York: Sheed & Ward, 1968).
11. John Coleman Bennett, *The Radical Imperative* (Philadelphia: Westminster, 1975).
12. Benjamin E. Mays, *Born to Rebel* (New York: Charles Scribner's Sons, 1971), p. 75.
13. See *Black Theology*, pp. 140–141.
14. See Sergio Torres and John Eagleson, eds., *Theology in the Americas* (Maryknoll, NY: Orbis, 1976).
15. Kofi Appiah-Kubi and Sergio Torres, eds., *African Theology en Route* (Maryknoll, NY: Orbis, 1979).
16. Gayraud S. Wilmore, "The Role of Afro-America in the Rise of Third World Theology: A Historical Reappraisal," *African Theology en Route*, p. 198.
17. See ibid., p. 205.
18. "A Black American Perspective on the Future of African Theology," ibid., pp. 176–186.
19. For the contribution black experience might make in reformulating American culture, see Vincent Harding, "Out of the Cauldron of Struggle: Black Religion and the Search for a New America," *Soundings*, 59/3 (Fall 1978), 339–354.
20. Quoted by James H. Cone, *The Spirituals & The Blues*, p. 89. Copyright © 1972 by James H. Cone. Used by permission of The Seabury Press, Inc.
21. Ibid., p. 94. Used by permission.
22. See ibid., p. 111.
23. See ibid., pp. 128–132.
24. See J. Deotis Roberts, *Roots of a Black Future: Family and Church* (Philadelphia: Westminster, 1980), pp. 64–72.

CHAPTER 15

Contemporary Feminist Theology

Black Women

The reflections of feminists interested in religion are among the most volatile contributions to the present-day consciousness of American Christianity. To bridge the way from the last chapter, we begin this survey of insights from current feminist theologians with a consideration of black women and the Church. Representing more than half the black population, black women are even more predominant statistically in the black Church, numbering about 75 percent of its membership. Through both slave times and post-emancipation, many have been models of strength and resistance. Sojourner Truth spoke for such women when, at a women's rights convention in the nineteenth century, she insisted on combining power, femininity and faith: "Look at me! Look at my arm! . . . I have plowed, and planted, and gathered into barns, and no man could head me—and ar'nt I a woman? I could work as much as a man (when I could get it), and bear de lash as well—and ar'nt I a woman? I have borne five chilern and I seen 'em mos' all sold off into slavery, and when I cried out with a mother's grief, none but Jesus heard—and ar'nt I a woman?"[1]

Sojourner's cry to Jesus fits an almost epic stereotype that has developed, in which her faith helps the black woman to be the rock of her family, much stronger than the black man. Recently that stereotype and many other aspects of the black woman's life have come up for reappraisal. As a shareholder in two important movements, Black Power and feminism, the black woman has had to assimilate an almost overwhelming amount of rhetoric, changed perception, and new philosophy. The only thing clear at present is that significant numbers of black women are likely to insist on *both* species of liberation. Refusing to trade off racism and sexism against one another, those who are Christians will force future Christian faith deeper, so that neither sex nor color is a cause for diminishment.

Black women have a grievance against black men, a grievance against both white men and white women, and a grievance against the Christian Church, insofar as it has formed both black men and whites badly. Against black men many black women bring the charge of having been blind to abuses and inequalities that have made the black woman liable to double jeopardy. Because of the oppressions to which white society has subjected him, the black man often has used the black woman badly, abandoning her (and his children) or refusing her emotional support. Because of his own machismo, the black activist or theologian often has failed to realize that he excludes women from Black Power or black theology. Black theologians such as James Cone and Gayraud Wilmore have accepted this latter accusation, admitting they have been slow to see women as equal partners and vowing to set black women's liberation high on their future agendas.

Black women's grievances against white society could make laundry lists without end. As feminist Frances Beale has summarized it, the black woman has been "the slave of a slave." The American system that reduced the black man to abject powerlessness gave the black woman no protector. Recently it has even tried to make her the scapegoat for the crime, family breakdown, and other evils to which black male powerlessness have led, as though she were the one who had castrated him. This is a classic instance of blaming the victim. The historical truth is that the black woman regularly was molested sexually by the white colonizer, and that she was exploited economically as the white woman's domestic servant and the white child's wet nurse. Simple statistics on the black working woman's income speak volumes about her oppression after emancipation. For example, in 1967 white males' average annual income was \$6704, nonwhite males' average annual income was \$4277, white females' average annual income was \$3991, and nonwhite females' average annual income was \$2861.[2]

Other melancholy figures shed more grim light on the black woman's condition. In a recent year, 79 percent of abortion deaths in New York occurred among nonwhites and Puerto Ricans.[3] In 1976 more than 50 percent of all black children were born out of wedlock.[4] Because of economic conditions, many black women have come to separate the roles of mother and wife. Where motherhood means maturity, and usually is accepted responsibly, marriage often signifies a very high risk. Many black women no longer are willing to play superwoman, trying to carry the whole burden of a family. As best-selling author and feminist Michelle Wallace has argued,[5] it is fallacious to assume that black mothers have been able to do without the love and companionship of husbands. Their vaunted self-sufficiency has been the product of dire necessity and no formula for happiness. Today black women need to stop oscillating between the image of the Amazon and that of the lady in white society. Black men would help them by not gravitating toward white women as soon as they become upwardly mobile.

Wallace is not loathe to criticize upwardly mobile black women, either. She has leveled broadsides at both Angela Davis, the political activist, and Nikki

Giovanni, the poet. Davis she criticizes for encouraging black women to give their lives to support politically radical black men. (In Wallace's view Davis did this herself, falling in love with a man, much her educational inferior, who thought black women enslaved black men.) At Riker's Island Penitentiary, Wallace thought she saw the logical consequences of Davis's advice to black women. The typical black woman prisoner at Riker's Island was there because she had supported a pimp, a dope supplier, or a thief. Female black political prisoners were there for the same reason: they had followed black political males.

Giovanni's advice in the '60s took much the same direction as Davis's, and produced much the same result. In Wallace's interpretation, Giovanni counseled black women to support black men returning to their roots and struggling for liberation. Shutting herself off from black women, Giovanni found herself largely ignored by black men, even by her fellow poets. Perhaps as a result, she began to speak positively of going to church and having children. She herself had a child, refusing to disclose the name of its father. She counseled others to bear children in order to "have something to love." Having an education and a career were secondary (although she herself had a good education and quite a successful career). Only later, as a tardy afterthought, did Giovanni get around to advising prospective black mothers to be sure they could support their love-children. "By the time she advised them later to first make sure they had enough income to support the child, a lot of women were already on welfare."[6]

We have no title to pass judgment on this debate within black feminist circles. Our reason for introducing it is simply to suggest, as vividly as we can, the complexity of the issues with which black women now struggle. Doubly oppressed, they, and other minority women, are the population women's liberation first must reach. In the perspective of the Christian faith that has formed so many black women, where God takes the side of the poor and marginalized, black and other minority women deserve special attention.

Mermaids and Minotaurs

The line of women deserving redress for the injustices of Western culture and Christianity stretches out of sight. By all economic, political, and social indices, women have been what Simone de Beauvoir called the "second sex." To this day, the average woman working full-time in the United States receives less than two-thirds the wages of her male counterpart.

The women's movement has mounted a wholesale campaign for equality, sending at least scouting parties to almost every front. Thus, the roles of women in education, business, the arts, the sciences, and religious institutions have all come in for scrutiny. On the whole, however, such scrutiny has remained relatively superficial. What a woman earns or how she is promoted is quite important, but is not at the root of the sexes' inequalities. Dorothy Dinnerstein's *The Mermaid and the Minotaur*,[7] subtitled *Sexual Arrangements and the Human Malaise*, looks deeper at the roots of sexual inequality. From her background in psychology, Dinnerstein probes child-rearing, one of our most elementary institutions. Her probing is so explosive in its implications that many feminists have seized on her book as a prime theoretical weapon. Insofar as Christianity has shaped many of our views of the sexes, the weapon often can be pointed at the Church.

Sexual arrangements are "the division of responsibility, opportunity, and privilege that prevails between male and female humans." By "human malaise" Dinnerstein means "our species' normal psychopathology, which has pervaded our cultural—and perhaps even the most recent stages of our physical—evolution, the maladaptive stance, chronically uncomfortable and at this point critically life-threatening, that humanity maintains toward itself and toward nature." Because she sees these two concepts (our current sex roles and our current malaise) linked in a relation of cause and effect, Dinnerstein says that "until we grow strong enough to renounce the pernicious prevailing forms of collaboration between the sexes, both man and woman will remain semi-human, monstrous."[8]

To symbolize this current semi-humanity or monstrosity, Dinnerstein employs the mythological figures of the mermaid and the minotaur. The mermaid stands for female treachery: the seductive, unfathomable female related to the dark, magic waters of life. Misusing her beauty, she lures voyagers to their doom. The minotaur, half-human and half-bull, stands for male animality. He is gigantic, eternally infantile, an offspring of unnatural lust. In his aberrant power, he conjures male force as mindless, destructive, devouring of human flesh. What is the source of this deformation to which social development has brought the sexes? Dinnerstein's hunch is that the main source is the fact that for virtually every one of us it has been a woman, usually our mother, who has provided our main initial contact with humanity and nature.

Now, certainly it is true that *any* adult, male or female, would exercise an enormous influence on a newborn wholly in its care, for a newborn is almost totally vulnerable in its first experiences. However, the fact that women have virtually monopolized this enormous influence has led, in Dinnerstein's view, to such vast consequences as a double standard for the sexes' behavior, women's and men's mutual views of one another as overgrown children, and a manifold antagonism toward women (much of it shared by women themselves). In other words, Dinnerstein places the core inferiority that women suffer in our culture back at the very beginnings of infant life. From almost her first breath, the tiny human being starts learning that women are more suspect than men, because women occasion almost all the first, emotionally most volatile, experiences of human finitude or imperfection. Just as the infant is most likely first to experience bliss with his mother, so is he most likely first to experience rage.

Perhaps the central analytic observation that Dinnerstein makes in elaborating the consequences of females' monopoly of early childcare is how this monopoly relates to a double standard of sexual behavior. In our culture (and in most other cultures, which also have had woman-dominated infant care), men have had a monopoly on making history. Colluding to keep women bound to child-rearing, both men and women have largely defined the public realm as a male preserve. Thus, in the main, only men have been free to go to war, work in laboratories, and stump the political trail. The interior implications of this exterior division of labor are vast: "Since it is he whose sexual impulsivity is legitimate, while she is expected to be receptive and undemanding, it is he, not she, at whose initiative erotic energy can with propriety be withdrawn from love and invested in worldly affairs: She, not he, is the one who must wait when the other turns away, and be sexually available when he comes back."[9]

In Dinnerstein's lexicon, "history-making" is shorthand for all the outer productivity to which human consciousness drives. It is all culture, technology, ideas, and material constructs. To remove women from such history-making has been to remove them from our specific humanity, for we are precisely the species that makes history. Neither men nor women have completely wanted this removal, so together they have devised subtle reinsertions of women. Thus, men have tended to ask their mothers' blessings on the history they have made, elevating women to a strange purity and native wisdom that might pass judgment on men's begrimed play with wars, machines, laws, and money piles. Woman has been a peculiar outsider, impotent yet able to debunk. Through all subsequent adult life she has kept something of the omnipotence the infant associates with the madonna countenance, making her both unduly revered and unduly resented. And her outsider status has also made woman contribute passively to the schizophrenic division between technical reason and humane intuition that lies at the base of our world's violence, ecological destruction, stupid warmaking, and ignorance of peace. We spawn feelingless men and mindless women because deep in our psyche minotaurs paw the ground, mermaids ripple the waters. Until we see that both sexes must work at the earliest parenting, making the raising of the next generation their joint first responsibility, we will continue to suffer a dreadful malaise.

Feminist Spiritual Quests

Some of the most effective portraits of women's share in the current human malaise occur in feminist novels. Carol Christ is a feminist religious scholar who has studied such novels carefully, paying special attention to the ways they reformulate women's spiritual quests—women's searches for new visions and lifestyles. Christ's *Diving Deep and Surfacing*[10] discusses the work of authors such as Kate Chopin, Margaret Atwood, Doris Lessing, Adrienne Rich, and Ntozake Shange, who furnish vivid portraits of women awakening in the depths of their souls and reevaluating their position in society or even the universe. Christ weaves her autobiography into her discussion of these portraits. She herself has found that physical nature affords her the best grounding for her life and that male-dominated culture is inadequate to meet her needs as a woman.

The novels that Christ studies spotlight women finding a new "self-naming," a new identification of who they are. This new self-naming is rooted in nature and returns the protagonists to wholeness, allowing them to regain communion with the world. Opposed to masculine naming that excludes or denigrates women, it brings the protagonists alive to their own dignity and creativity. The heroines who model such new self-naming pass through experiences of nothingness, awakening, and insight, in order finally to gain fresh conceptions of themselves. The negativities of an inadequate culture force them into spiritual journeys that painfully but surely bring a solid hope and fulfillment. Moving away from negative self-images is progress, so the spiritual quest is a very positive experience in which traveling can be as therapeutic as arriving.

Kate Chopin's novel *The Awakening*, published in 1899, is a pioneering depiction of a woman trying to affirm the creative parts of herself against strong social opposition. The division that this inflicts on the protagonist, Edna Pontellier, culminates in her suicide, an ambiguous final symbol. While suicide gives her a way out of her terrible conflict, and so is a mode of liberation, it shows the awful power of social pressure, and so also is a mode of defeat. The protagonist of Margaret Atwood's novel *Surfacing*, published in 1972, overcomes a similar sort of division and breaks through to a new lifestyle. She does this by returning to an intimacy, almost an identification, with nature much like that which archaic women probably enjoyed. The effect of such an identification with nature is to connect the woman with great powers—powers more venerable and healing than the ones modern culture can command. In Carol Christ's judgment, "By naming anew such great powers and women's grounding in them, such novels provide women with alternatives to patriarchal notions of power that can aid their struggle to change the social world."[11]

In Doris Lessing's *Children of Violence* series, and especially in the culminating volume *The Four Gated City*, Christ finds the naming of women's experience that had eluded her personally. Martha Quest, the heroine of the series, rejects the negative role models society offers her and strikes out after the insight that would make her a real, independent person. At the end of a mystic journey along the edge of madness, in which she has to face the destructiveness at the core of current culture, she finds a pool of power. It turns out to be the power generated when one connects with the center of her self. Lessing's vision in the *Children of Violence* novels is more apocalyptic than Carol Christ's view, but Lessing's great gift for naming women's struggles has made her a prime resource for feminist theoreticians.

It is the poet Adrienne Rich whom Christ thinks provides the clearest vision of how to transform feminist insight into social reality. Rich shows how female nurturing and inclusiveness could remove much male destructiveness and dichotomizing (cutting apart, as a habit of mind). In a poem called "Natural Resources,"[12] Rich symbolizes women's traditional services as a fraying blanket, pulled across a sick child's shoulder or wrapped around a warrior's maimed legs. Much like Dinnerstein, she is furious that history should have become so distorted because of men's arrogance and women's weakness. Black feminist writer Ntozake Shange expresses similar feelings in accents developed by black women's sufferings. Her theatrical "choreopoem" *For Colored Girls Who Have Considered Suicide/ When the Rainbow is Enuf* ends by affirming womanhood and again rooting it in greater powers: "i found god in myself//and I loved her//i loved her fiercely."

All the authors whom Christ employs work at a new naming of woman's self and world, stimulated by experiences of awakening. All reject the negative images of the female body that society has taught them, and their new namings tend to blur the boundaries between this body and nature, between feminist rituals and feminist literature, and between the body and the spirit. By preference, they gravitate to holistic attitudes and forms. Developing this line, some religious feminists have focused their awakening sense of nature, their bodies, and the new powers available to them in a spiritual practice focused on a Great Goddess figure. The Great Goddess has historical and symbolic ties with the female divinity (often called "Mother Earth") of many archaic and traditional religions, but current feminists like Christ tend to see her more as a personification of female power. Dedicating themselves to a positive species of witchcraft, these feminists have devised rituals and organizations that celebrate female power. As we shall show, feminists more traditionally Christian tend to prefer Jesus Christ to the Goddess as a spiritual focus, but, in our view, the more astute among them recognize that the new witchcraft movement has many valid aims. We will discuss it further in the section after next.

Radical Feminist Rejection of Christianity

Radical feminists have been saying a great deal to Christianity by their rejection of Christian tradition and their development of counter-Christian alternatives. Among the radical feminists who have rejected traditional Christianity, Mary Daly holds a prominent place. She is a close friend of Adrienne Rich's, and her passage from reformist Roman Catholic Christianity to radical feminism shows many of the most serious obstacles to faith that women's reflections have unveiled.[13] *Gyn/Ecology*, Daly's most recent work, is subtitled *The Metaethics of Radical Feminism*, and it documents in considerable detail the injuries that various religious traditions have inflicted on women. Hinduism has burned widows, Chinese religion has imposed footbinding, African tribal religion and Islam have sponsored genital mutilation, Christian Europe burned hundreds of thousands of witches. In each case, Daly argues that the abuse is not accidental to the prevailing religion but a logical extension of its inherent patriarchal bias. Reformers in each of these traditions can dispute this last thesis, arguing that the patriarchal biases are not at the core, but Daly's evidence depicts a series of formidable scandals. If half of what she presents occurred as she says, the traditional religions have a great burden of proof to show today that they support women's dignity.

For our purposes, Daly's charges against Christianity, which come into clearest focus in her chapter on European witchburning, are most pertinent. First, she notes that those considered witches were regularly accused of sexual impurity. As the authors of the *Malleus Maleficarum* (1486), the most important catechism of demonology, put it: "All witchcraft comes from carnal lust which is in women insatiable."[14] Women accused as witches regularly were tortured until they confessed to having had intercourse with Satan, killed little children, raised tempests, and the like. Usually those accused as witches were social deviants—spinsters and widows who fell somewhat outside the patriarchal authority of the church, the state, and the family.

Second, the rituals of witchburning regularly relieved men of responsibility for the atrocities inflicted on women. This abdication of responsibility is a psychological constant that Daly also finds in widow-burning, foot-binding, genital mutilation, and current gynecological medicine. Here let us use Daly's own language, for her language is both carefully crafted and especially important to the overall evaluation of her book:

> Since the demonologies accused the witches of lewd acts, their male persecutors were perfectly "justified" in destroying them. To this end, the good sons of the holy father projected their fantasies upon the accused women. It was believed that at the Sabbat the witches kissed the devil in homage, under the tail if he appeared as a stinking goat, on the lips if he were a toad. After this they allegedly threw themselves into promiscuous sexual orgies. It was clear, therefore, that they *should* be tortured. Since their obscene "acts" were performed with the devil, god's enemy, their christian killers could feel totally religious and righteous.[15]

The papacy of Innocent VIII supported the Dominican inquisitors Sprenger and Kramer, authors of the *Malleus Maleficarum*, threatening harsh ecclesiastical penalties for all who opposed their work.

Witchburning spread like wildfire during the years 1500–1650, with the years 1600–1650 the worst period. Estimates of the number of witches put to death vary enormously, from two hundred thousand to more than nine million, but there is no doubt they comprised a great multitude. Geographically the craze spread from the mountainous regions of Germany and Italy to Spain, France, and the countries of northern Europe. All sorts of Europeans participated: Catholics and Protestants, learned and ignorant, divines and laity. Daly thinks that the deepest motivation of the witchburnings was a desire to destroy "female-identified goodness"—the strength, wisdom, and learning that won women respect as healers, counselors, and teachers. Unable to abide this competition, the male leaders of European society, religious and secular alike, turned on deviant women furiously. There may have been more superficial motives, such as the sugar industry's hatred of witches for counseling people not to eat sugar, but in Daly's analysis the heart of the matter was male misogyny—hatred of females.

Daly's data and analyses are hard to evaluate. On the one hand, she marshal figures, historical quotations, and other scholars' opinions that outline an incon-trovertible case that European Christianity lost its balance and projected onto socia deviants—a great many of them women—inordinate fears of the demonic. Perhap social pressures such as the plagues, wars, and massive changes (religious, eco-nomic, and political), caused an acute anxiety to pervade the mid-fifteenth t mid-seventeenth centuries, but these circumstances fail to explain, let alone exon erate, the hostility that deviant women suffered. Probably there is something solid in Daly's charge of misogyny, and surely it should lead current-day Christians to examine carefully the patriarchy at their historical origins. If such patriarchy is intrinsically hateful toward women, it has to be excised, as a malignancy incompatible with Christ's love. The most modest surgery would be formulating ecclesiastical laws and programs to protect women from abuse and afford them full equality in Church rights and opportunities.

On the other hand, Daly's rhetoric mottles her credibility and tries the reader's sympathies. In the following paragraph, for example, one doesn't know whether Daly is proposing a conclusion from historical evidence or injecting a personal conviction that has colored her very interpretation of such historical evidence:

> It is important to note here an essential pattern in the maze of the witchcraze. On the symbolic level, the emphasis centers around god-the-son, "The Second Person of the Divine Trinity," who "became incarnate." Dogmatically speaking, "the Word became Flesh." Thus in christian doctrine, the "fact" that god-the-son became man (male), assuming a human—that is, male—body, enabled males to become gods. It prepared the way for the Brotherhood representing/replacing Yahweh & Son. Thus the original christian divine model for Big Brother in Orwell's *1984* is the godman, Jesus. It is significant that in this "futuristic"—that is, patriarchally past and contemporary—novel it is not Big Father who is the Head. For everyone knows on some level that this "divine" father is omni-absent, a figurehead as blatant as Archie Bunker, Idi Amin (Dada), Tricky Dick Nixon, or Pope Paul the Sicksth [VI: *sic*]. Rather it is Big Brother who is omni-present—seeing/knowing/controlling all, constantly purifying the body politic of deviants. Male (and male-identified) professionals and aspirants to political power have identified with this more accessible and "real" symbol.[16]

The New Witchcraft

Carol Christ and Mary Daly share a desire to participate in a new witchcraft, one that would celebrate feminine power and escape the negativities of patriarchal religions such as Christianity. Naomi Goldenberg also shares this desire, but she comes to it more explicitly from psychology. Goldenberg's book *Changing of the Gods*[17] is subtitled *Feminism and the End of Traditional Religions*. At least as far as Judaism and Christianity are concerned, her feminism gives license to kill: "The feminist movement in Western culture is engaged in the slow execution of Christ and Yahweh."[18] The view of Christ and Yahweh as male Gods has led to the denigration of women. Since women have not been able to identify with the prime symbols for divinity, they have fallen to an estate lower than men's. As the historical scholarship of many feminists shows, "Judaism and Christianity have always been chiefly concerned with the welfare of males and the exaltation of a male god."[19] Jesus surely cannot symbolize the liberation of women, radical feminists say, so women who want liberation will have to find an ultimate symbol other than Jesus.

To Goldenberg, religion's power has always lain in its mediation, through rites and symbols, of the psyche's searches for meaning and fulfillment. Feminist theology is on the way to becoming psychology, helping women outgrow an Oedipal dependence on paternalistic authority and find fulfillment in the Goddess.

Goldenberg has a colorful chapter on contemporary feminist witchcraft that offers a positive example of how this new psychological religion is trying to effect great meaning and fulfillment. Reporting on the coven (witchcraft group) activities of such American witches as Starhawk and Z. Budapest, she portrays the new witchcraft as creative, nature-oriented, spontaneous, and life-affirming. For instance, at the winter solstice Starhawk's coven meets to celebrate the birthday of the sun. In the large, high-ceilinged room a fire burns. Two snakeskins, shed by the witch's pet boa constrictors, hang from a chandelier. The twenty celebrants, more women than men, stand naked in a circle, chanting to the Goddess and the Horned God. Invoking these gods' presences, they affirm that each member of the coven is herself a goddess or is himself a god.

Such new witchcraft draws many self-affirmations from the celebrants, but above all it aims at freeing them to enjoy their bodies, their time, and the natural world. A symbolism to which many women respond enthusiastically is the three phases of the Goddess. As Maiden, Mother, and Crone, she stands for the young woman free of male domination, the mature woman creative and fruitful, and the aged woman rich with wisdom. The covens tend to conceive time as periodic and cyclic, gearing their calendars and self-understandings to the phases of the moon. This periodicity allows them to incorporate all types of experience, depressing as well as exhilarating, making all times serve a sense of growth, of growing weighty. By fixing their vision on the cyclic earth, and refusing to lose themselves in world-transcending abstractions, they oppose divisions of body and spirit, time and eternity, and the like. Death and life both have their seasons. It is natural to give birth and natural to die. A viable religion must affirm the goodness of such a mortal, cyclic human span. It must be a way to joy, peace, and fulfillment, not something ascetic, morbid, or life-denying. Using tarot cards and other imagery, the witches try to help their coven members better understand their current needs, fears, projections, and hopes. Their rituals encourage self-assertion and strength, uninhibited enjoyment of sex, and a sense that only hurting someone or something else is illegitimate.

Goldenberg summarizes her discussion of the new witchcraft with an interesting table of twelve of its principal attributes. The twelve attributes can serve us as a handy resumé. First, female deities dominate the craft. Second, it resists the body/soul dualism to which Western religions have conditioned us. Third, it views nature as sacred, rather than as subordinate to human beings. Fourth, it places a high value on the human will, instead of urging surrender to God's will. Fifth, the craft usually has a spiral, upward circling, rather than a linear notion of time and, sixth, a cyclic notion of bodily growth and decay. Seventh, witches reject the notion of original sin and, eighth, they tend to resist divisions of things or ideas into "good" and "evil." Ninth, the craft seldom has a sacred text and, tenth, it seldom has rigid disciplinary laws. This leads to pluralism and diversity. Eleventh, the craft is relaxed about spontaneous sexual expression. Twelfth, it places a high premium on play.

Goldenberg writes with high spirit, playfully and provocatively. No doubt she shares the anger at injustice that drives Mary Daly, but she gives the reader less occasion for thinking it has turned her bitter. Stressing creative, healing, and fulfilling projections of the psyche, she offers a positive counterpoint to the negative critique of patriarchy that she and others have accumulated. We shall come to some of the problems that the radical feminist program poses, but at this juncture it seems well to underscore the new vision that witches and seekers are discovering. Most of their rituals entail self-affirmations that a sex long suppressed badly needs. Most of their depictions of the social and natural orders are nurturing and egalitarian. One finds little in their thoughts or actions that would encourage war, racial prejudice, ecological devastation, or dehumanizing work. One finds much in their Goddess that fills out the received portrait of the Western God.

Reformist Feminist Christianity

Radical feminist religion attacks Christianity as misogynistic, a powerful force in women's oppression, and calls for new rites that would celebrate the feminine. What we are calling reformist feminist Christianity admits that Christianity has abused women in the past but insists that the essence of Christianity, its core love of God and love of neighbor, is an unparalleled liberation. Reformist feminist Christianity also makes the debate a two-way street, by not hesitating to attack inadequacies in radical feminist interpretations of Christianity or the religious programs of the new witchcraft. In these last two sections we hope to indicate the rich potential in this debate, even though our own sympathies are clearly with the reformists.

Let us begin with queries critics have raised about the new witchcraft. Paula Fredriksen Landes is a critic with impeccable academic credentials who, in reviewing five recent works by feminists on religion (including those by Christ and Goldenberg) comes away dissatisfied.[20] First, she thinks that the tension between the academic nature of these feminists' criticisms of traditional religion and the nonacademic nature of their prescriptions for a new religion confuses their project. They are trying to work on two different levels whose relation they fail adequately to clarify. For example, they never define the capital terms "religion" and "experience" lucidly. Second, in advocating the Goddess cult these writers tend to proceed as though one could generate religious symbols self-consciously. Their stress on psychology makes them admirably sensitive to the power of religious symbols, but they seem to forget the analyses of such prime theoreticians as Carl Jung and Clifford Geertz. These analyses show that truly forceful symbols (1) rise up from the unconscious, and (2) occur within the historical context of a given culture and so are received as something traditional.

Third, and most disturbing to Landes, "in their efforts to repudiate male religiosity these women paradoxically recapitulate patterns they condemn in men."[21]

For example, they claim that male spirituality is hierarchical and female egalitarian, but they also claim that divinity is more appropriately symbolized in female terms than in male. They emphasize the nurturing character of women, yet the heroines of the novels they laud turn their backs on their own children. "Christ views . . . the role of the male in the act of love and conception as 'incidental.' . . . Goldenberg argues . . . that the correct position for men in the cult of the Goddess is prone. This hardly strikes a blow against sexism."[22] Last, Landes thinks it both too late and too empty to worship "a recycled agricultural Earth goddess."

Landes is not especially disturbed by the radical feminists' psychologizing of religion (reducing it to needs of the psyche) perhaps because for her the "father God" and the debate between atheists and theists are intellectually marginal. She has only brief space at her disposal, so she does not clarify this thesis, but one could infer from it that transcendence is not a pressing matter. By transcendence we mean the objective, independent reality of the divine, and so the outgoing, ego-exceeding reference of religion. Judith Plaskow is a prominent feminist on the border between the radical and reformist camps who is concerned about transcendence. In a thoughtful article entitled "The Feminist Transformation of Theology,"[23] she recalls that monotheistic theology calls all persons to transcend their own limited experience. Whether this theology be a traditional sort, like that of her own Jewish tradition, or a new ontological sort, like the focus of the Mary Daly of *Beyond God the Father* on God-the-verb (God as action), it takes the theologian and believer in a universalizing direction, toward an intuition of Being. Just as an intuition of liberation tends to stretch the intuitor toward *all* persons' freeing, so the thrust of traditional theology, for all the imperfection of its realization, is toward something total, in-finite, much more than the self's projection. Against this horizon, the restriction of theology to psychology is a diminishment, a jacket small and straitening. Realizing this, the new discipline of transpersonal psychology opens the self to a larger universe.

The transcendent thrust of traditional theology and religion illumines another defect in much radical feminism, in our view. By stressing the universal expansion of God toward Being, traditional theology gave some prominence to the parts of human nature that are neither male nor female. If God transcended sexual delimitation, then God's image somewhat transcended sexual delimitation. A radical feminist such as Goldenberg seems so preoccupied with the (admittedly powerful) psychological aspects of religion that she misses the whole tradition of negative theology that stresses God's otherness. From patristic times, Christian theologians spoke of the divine immensity as being so overwhelming to the human mind that it renders all our symbolisms inadequate. To restrict religion to the symbolic is to truncate human nature and human experience.

Further, Goldenberg does not take seriously the Christian theology of the Trinity or the Incarnation. She speaks of Christ as though he were God *simply*, without the qualifications that the divinity of the Father and the Spirit and his own humanity impose. The millions of faithful who have attended Christian liturgies regularly may not have learned the sophisticated aspects of the Trinity and the

Incarnation, but those liturgies, like their catechisms, drive home the main lines of trinitarian and incarnational doctrine. Thus the average Christian thinks of God as more than a male, and thinks of Jesus as less than directly convertible with God. Such thought had considerable effect. In the case at hand, few Christians would recognize the God radical feminists claim Christians have worshiped. Almost all would insist on more nuance.

Retrieving the Feminine in Christianity

If reformist feminist Christians are pointing to inadequacies in radical feminist programs for a new religion, they are also putting forth positive reasons for laboring to refurbish their tradition. As there is a retrieval being practiced by historians of religion who are showing that the history of women's experiences in all religions has included positive as well as negative elements,[24] so there is a retrieval being practiced by historians of Christianity that is offering present-day feminists positive as well as negative role models from the past. From the viewpoint of social psychiatry, Robert and Jane Coles' *Women of Crisis*[25] shows that even supposedly marginal, little-educated women are coming to impressive measures of wisdom about their struggles today, and that much of this wisdom is clarified through a reflection nourished by their Christian faith. From the viewpoint of theology and church history, two collections of studies, *Womanspirit Rising* and *Women of Spirit*,[26] describe many forebears in faith who invite contemporary feminists to mine their traditions rather than reject them out of hand.

Introducing *Women of Spirit*, Rosemary Ruether and Eleanor McLaughlin provide a careful orientation to the complexities that any retrieval of past Christian women's exemplary accomplishments entails. Women have been marginal to the main blocs of the history of institutional Christianity, normally cut off from official power and status. Even sources written by women themselves tend to have internalized a patriarchal point of view. Although early Christianity gave women some teaching and missionary roles, the Fathers assumed that women could not be public teachers and the medieval universities locked women out. Women could write on spirituality but not scholastic theology. The Protestant emphasis on academic theological training further minimized the female teaching tradition, so most Protestant women teachers appeared either as heretics or in left-wing traditions such as Quakerism. Today women have to make a special effort to see through this past marginality to the influence Christian women *did* exercise—"to see that women have played surprisingly varied and authoritative roles in Western religion."[27]

First, there was the significant place that early heretical groups, such as the Gnostics, afforded women and feminine symbolism.[28] Second, there was the ministerial power exercised by Christian women in the New Testament era.[29] Third, there were women throughout the later periods of Christian history—patristic, medieval, reformation, and modern—who found ascetic, mystical, prophetic, and ministerial modes for developing a profound faith and serving it to the world. Although such women frequently found official church office closed to them, the Christian community often remained sufficiently alert to charismatic authority—the power of those manifestly filled by the Spirit—to enable them to exert great influence.

In the traditions such as the Roman Catholic where celibacy and monastic separateness had a place, women could escape some of the limitations secular society imposed on their sex. Among the left-wing Protestant churches, which stressed lay leadership and charismatic inspiration, many women came to the fore. By holiness and charismatic power a gifted woman could transcend normal boundaries, pointing to a deity mysteriously male-female. Therefore Ruether and McLaughlin counsel feminists not to lose sight of the gains their predecessors won despite segregationist social structures. As women's educational institutions today can gain as well as lose by admitting men, so women's marginality in the past often was several-sided.

Although the nineteenth century privatized religion as a feminine preserve, making it unseemly for "ladies" or the clergy to deal with the dirty world of work and politics, that was not always the case in prior centuries. One has to develop an eye for the subtle, complicated ways that power and fulfillment actually go forward in a given era. Ruether and McLaughlin imply that a feminism knowledgeable about its sources would make more measured judgments than do many radicals.

That is not to say that reformist feminist Christians are not calling for the wholesale overhaul of the Church. Until women get strict equality of right and opportunity, reformist feminists will call the Church guilty of sexist injustice. As such, they feel, the Church sinfully fails its founder and palpably diminishes its credibility. Sexist authority commands little respect. Where the institutional Church blocks the way to life, we believe, one must circumvent the institutional Church. *Primum est vivere*, the tradition said: the first thing is to stay alive. In more explicitly theological translation, the first thing is the Spirit, the downpayment on Christ's victory. The letters and the laws are secondary.

It is the Spirit of Christ, the life of love, that knowing reformist Christians treasure, and that treasure is their answer both to unreformed fellow Christians, who continue to oppress women, and to radical feminists who would execute Christ. For all the vitality they see in radical feminism, and all the just anger and creative hope they feel for the Church, reformers still see Jesus as the liberator without peer. If one loves God with whole mind, heart, soul, and strength, as Jesus commanded, she is soon free of all idols and ideologies. If one loves her neighbor as herself, she has found the golden rule, the map for community. A sister helping a sister to love this way is like a strong city. A person helping a person to live this way is a little church, a microcosm of the people of God.[30]

Summary

Feminist theology focuses on the liberation of women, as black theology focuses on the liberation of blacks. Perhaps black women suffer the most acute oppressions of our society, for they often experience double jeopardy. Thus the struggles of black women to overcome the effects of centuries of slavery, and to sensitize black men to feminism, place them at the front lines of liberation theology.

Throughout American society, men and women inflict much inhumanity on one another. Dorothy Dinnerstein places the roots of this inhumanity in our child-rearing arrangements, arguing that men's absence from child-raising produces mermaids and minotaurs. In feminist literature, one finds quests to escape such inter-sexual malaise. The heroines of authors like Margaret Atwood and Doris Lessing awaken to new possibilities. Egalitarian, inclusive, and nature-oriented, these possibilities are the building blocks of a new social theory.

Feminists interested in tearing up the roots of social oppression often look to the overthrow of traditional Western religion. Whether through historical atrocities like the witchburnings, or symbol systems that have denied women's imaging of God, traditional Christianity often has abetted oppression. Through new witchcraft rituals, many radical feminists are rejecting Christianity and affirming female sacrality through worship of the Goddess.

Reformist feminist Christians accept many of the criticisms leveled against traditional Christianity, without judging it irredeemable. In their eyes its abuses of women neither spring from nor vitiate the core. While pressing strongly for institutional and cultural changes that would advance women to strict equality, they argue that the core of Christian religion—Christ's love—remains the most powerful human liberation. In addition, they argue that the wisdom accumulated through the Christian centuries, and the accomplishments of many marvelous female leaders, should be appropriated rather than jettisoned.

Study Questions

1. How are black women's oppressions reflected in black family life?
2. What is the relation between women's predominance in child-rearing and their exclusion from history-making?
3. Explicate Adrienne Rich's symbol of the fraying blanket.
4. Comment on the proposition, "All witchcraft comes from carnal lust which is in women insatiable."
5. What aspects of the new witchcraft would a Christianity open to feminism appropriate?
6. How injurious to radical feminist religion is Landes's charge that it seems sexist toward men?
7. How supportive of reformist feminist Christianity is the evidence of effective women leaders one can document in the Christian past?

Notes

1. Quoted by Frances Beale, "Double Jeopardy: To Be Black and Female," in *Black Theology*, Gayraud S. Wilmore and James H. Cone, eds. (Maryknoll, NY: Orbis, 1979), p. 369.
2. Ibid., p. 371.
3. Ibid., p. 374.
4. J. Deotis Roberts, *Roots of a Black Future* (Philadelphia: Westminster, 1980), p. 123.
5. See Michelle Wallace, *Black Macho and the Myth of the Superwoman* (New York: Dial Press, 1979), especially Chapter 3.
6. Ibid., pp. 167–168.
7. Dorothy Dinnerstein, *The Mermaid and the Minotaur* (New York: Harper Colophon, 1977).
8. Ibid., pp. 4–5.
9. Ibid., p. 208.
10. Carol Christ, *Diving Deep and Surfacing* (Boston: Beacon Press, 1980).
11. Ibid., p. 50.
12. See Adrienne Rich, *The Dream of a Common Language* (New York: W. W. Norton, 1978), p. 66.
13. Daly's writings expressing this passage are *The Church and the Second Sex* (New York: Harper & Row, 1968); *Beyond God the Father* (Boston: Beacon, 1973); *Gyn/Ecology* (Boston: Beacon, 1979).
14. *Gyn/Ecology*, p. 180.
15. From *Gyn/Ecology: The Metaethics of Radical Feminism* by Mary Daly, pp. 187–188. Copyright © 1978 by Mary Daly. Reprinted by permission of Beacon Press.
16. Ibid., p. 187. Reprinted by permission.
17. Naomi Goldenberg, *Changing of the Gods* (Boston: Beacon, 1979).
18. Ibid., p. 4.
19. Ibid., p. 17.
20. Paula Fredriksen Landes, *Signs* 6/2 (Winter 1980), 328–334.
21. Ibid., p. 333.
22. Ibid.
23. Rita M. Gross, ed., *Beyond Androcentrism* (Missoula, MT: Scholars Press, 1977), pp. 23–31.
24. See Nancy A. Falk and Rita M. Gross, eds., *Unspoken Worlds: Women's Religious Lives in Non-Western Cultures* (San Francisco: Harper & Row, 1980); Denise Lardner Carmody, *Women & World Religions* (Nashville: Abingdon, 1979).

25. Robert and Jane Coles, *Women of Crisis* (New York: Delta/Seymour Lawrence, 1978).
26. Carol P. Christ and Judith Plaskow, eds. *Womanspirit Rising* (San Francisco: Harper & Row, 1979); Rosemary Ruether and Eleanor McLaughlin, eds., *Women of Spirit* (New York: Simon & Schuster, 1979).
27. *Women of Spirit*, p. 18.
28. See Elaine Pagels, *The Gnostic Gospels* (New York: Random House, 1979), pp. 48–69.
29. Elisabeth Schüssler Fiorenza, "Word, Spirit, and Power: Women in Early Christian Communities," *Women of Spirit*, pp. 29–70; "Women in the Early Christian Movement," *Womanspirit Rising*, pp. 84–92.
30. For a full discussion of the debate between radical feminism and Christianity, see Denise Lardner Carmody, *Feminism and Christianity: A Two-Way Reflection* (Nashville: Abingdon, 1982).

Conclusion

Chapter 16, in which we attempt a conclusion, is entitled "Angles of Repose." We call it this because in each of its sections we try to place Christianity in a larger perspective to illumine the path we have surveyed throughout the book. Thus, in considering Jesus's relation to non-Christians our goal is not so much new information, news of still another aspect of current Christian reflection, as evoking the living center of current Christian faith in relation to a problem you have not hitherto studied. The same holds for the sections on Christian-Jewish relations, the essence of Christian history, the problem of evil, and the rest. Having taken you through the whole, we offer you several exercises that should help evoke that whole. The result, we hope, will be a final sketch of Christian religion that reminds you of its worldview, history, and current expressions.

Dead Christ with Angels, by Edouard Manet, French, 1832–1883. Nelson Gallery–Atkins Museum, Kansas City, Missouri (Gift of Mr. and Mrs. Milton McGreevy through the Westport Fund).

CHAPTER 16

Angles of Repose

Jesus and Non-Christians

Christianity is the religion that derives from Jesus of Nazareth. According to traditional Christian orthodoxy, Jesus is different from the founders of other religions. Where Moses was God's lawgiver, Muhammad was God's prophet, or the Buddha was the exemplar of enlightenment, Jesus was the divine Logos incarnate. Fully human, he was affected by all the historical and psychological dynamics that other initiators of religion experienced, but in him there was something more: the intrinsic self-expression of the divine ultimacy, the Word of the Father. As such, the question arises, how does Jesus relate to non-Christians?

Let us angle into this question by noting, first, that many non-Christians admire Jesus and place him in their gallery of heroes. For example, Muhammad and the Koran value Jesus highly, calling him a prophet and the Messiah. British scholar Geoffrey Parrinder shows the problematic situation in which this leaves Islam regarding Jesus:

> In Islam there is clearly a mystery about Jesus. It was accepted generally that his birth was unusual, comparable only with that of Adam. On the common interpretation of sura [a chapter in the Koran] 4, 156/157 Jesus would be the only man in history who had not died. But if it felt after the mystery this interpretation did not grasp it. The stark tragedy of the crucifixion reveals depths of the human and divine natures that remain unapprehended. Yet the challenge remains, to search for the truth of the revelation of love and the relationship of God to man which appeared in the person of Christ. 'What think ye of Christ?' is still a question to be answered.[1]

For the Christian dialogue with Islam, and the more than a billion and a half persons Islam represents, a peaceful discussion of Jesus clearly is capital. Insofar as

Muslims can respect Jesus, they can offer a hand of friendship to Christians. Insofar as Christians can understand Jesus's divinity in ways that do not denigrate Muhammad's prophecy, they can offer a hand of friendship back.

One could suggest similarly positive possibilities for the Christian-Buddhist dialogue,[2] the dialogue of Christians with atheists, the Christian-Hindu dialogue, and so on. In each case, Jesus's signal humanity lays a bridge before the non-Christian, while a modest view of Jesus's divinity lays a bridge before the Christian. Is such a nonimperialist view possible? Can the Christian maintain that Jesus Christ is the divine Logos incarnate and not by that very fact depreciate other paths to ultimate meaning?

There are various reasons for thinking that the Christian can. For example, Karl Rahner, the influential Roman Catholic theologian, has spoken of "anonymous Christians," meaning those who live the substance of Christian faith without explicitly professing themselves to be Christians. His notion is that, for Christian faith, Jesus is the sacrament of all human authenticity, the human being whose yes to the mystery of life and death, whose love of God and neighbor, illumines all the cultural varieties of human goodness. As a recent expositor of Rahner's Christology has put it: "Instead of regarding non-Christian religions, and even atheistic humanism, in a totally negative fashion, the Christian can truly learn from them, since the grace of God in Christ is or can be operative in these traditions, as it is in the hearts of all men and women."[3]

There are those who think that the term "anonymous Christian" is bound to offend non-Christians, and those who think that theocentrism (focusing mainly on God), rather than Christocentrism, is the way to improve dialogue with non-Christians.[4] Even they, however, usually employ a version of the Logos doctrine to show that the atheist's, or Buddhist's, or Muslim's manifestation of human wisdom and goodness is not in conflict with God's Word. Taking Jesus's humanity seriously, they point out that, as finite, it could not exhaust all the possible manifestations of divine wisdom and goodness. As Jesus was limited in the language he commanded, the history and culture he knew, so he was limited by his biblical and Jewish background in explicitly religious matters. Thus, a Buddhist insight into ultimacy expressed in terms of "nothingness," or an atheistic insight expressed by attacking religious hypocrisy, might not occur explicitly in Jesus's teaching. But the apostle Paul certainly felt that faith in Jesus Christ ought to develop a largemindedness that could embrace these insights, for he told the Philippians (4:8): "Fill your minds with everything that is true, everything that is noble, everything that can be thought virtuous or worthy of praise." The obvious inference is that deep adherence to Jesus Christ ought to make one rejoice in all human sanctity, wisdom, and goodness, wherever found. By an instinct ultimately owed to Christ's Spirit, the mature Christian senses that true, noble, good, pure, loveable, honorable, virtuous, and praiseworthy things take her toward Christ, not away.

To be sure, there remain problems of terminology and conceptual conflict, which scholars, especially, are never slow to find. For the real encounter of the different deep positions, however, these problems matter less than the bedrock accord the positions can achieve. Looking less to human words than to human performance, the mature Christian is mainly concerned with the honesty and love that a person manifests or fails to manifest. What that person calls himself, how he names his ultimate allegiance, is secondary. True, names and allegiances play a part, for they come from traditions and histories that mold us somewhat. But even traditions and histories finally are forms through which the human spirit strives for meaning and fulfillment.

When the spirit is reaching out to ultimate reality, passing beyond limited goods in search of Goodness itself, its tradition and history are more instrumental than determinative. In other words, a Thai Buddhist and a Lithuanian Christian may hold more in common than apart. Despite vast differences in language and history, they both may be seeking the same center, the same sanctuary that the poet T. S. Eliot called "the still point of the turning world." From the Christian's point of view, Jesus Christ is God's decisive sign toward that still point. From the Buddhist's point of view, Gautama is such a sign. However, if we let the Logos really inform all creation (Col. 1:16), and we let Jesus's humanity show that God takes history and culture fully seriously, we can let both signs be saving revelations.

Christians and Jews

If serious reflection on Jesus's function in a pluralistic world leads toward the conclusion that, without detracting from Jesus's essential adequacy, God can use other signs for saving revelation, then there is all the more hope for better dialogue between Christians and Jews in the future, based on Christians' better appreciation of Jewish revelation. In the past, as all sober students of history admit, there has been enmity and hurt ill-befitting both groups who call themselves God's children. Because Christians usually had the greater political power, they were able to give more damaging vent to their spleen, through pogroms, expulsions, and diverse forms of discrimination against Jews. But reflection on the Nazi Holocaust that claimed the lives of six million Jews in the middle of the twentieth century has brought the two parties to a new phase of conversation, as has reflection on the emergence of the state of Israel.

In this new situation, Christians can be especially grateful for Jews like Martin Buber, who went out of his way to embrace Jesus as a blood brother. Responding, they might go out of their way to express gratitude to the people from whom they have derived, the people who have given them their Christ, much of their Bible, and much of their religious vocabulary. Numerous Christian theologians are realizing this, and their preliminary work suggests that Jewish-Christian relations could improve significantly in the years ahead. For example, Daniel J. Harrington, a Roman Catholic biblical scholar, has suggested that Christians reaffirm the faith of Abraham, remembering the New Testament's use of Abraham as a paradigm for deep fidelity to God. Harrington notes also that recent attention to the historical settings of the gospels of Matthew and John (the gospels most apparently anti-Jewish) shows that the harshest sayings against Jews come from Jewish Christians who were addressing predominantly Jewish-Christian churches engaged in conflict with synagogues. In other words, the harshest sayings should be taken with more than a grain of salt, as the sort of bile only a family quarrel can generate. As Harrington sees the current situation, "The positive significance of Judaism is a topic just beginning to surface in discussions between Christian theologians and their Jewish counterparts. For Christians, the question is this: What positive contribution to Christian faith today can be made by Judaism as an independent group that carries on the heritage of ancient Israel?"[5]

Paul Van Buren is a Protestant philosophical theologian who has embarked on a full-scale answer to this question. His *Discerning the Way* is subtitled *A Theology of the Jewish-Christian Reality*. Insisting that all human beings must find their way and walk it with their own feet, Van Buren proposes a conversation among Christians and other walkers. Almost immediately, however, he runs into the horrors that give any serious conversationalist pause: "Given the horrors of this century, we can walk at best by faith, not by sight. We must proceed today under thin but endless clouds of burned children, mostly Jewish children. Under that cloud it is hard to strike up a conversation."[6] Though Van Buren postpones his full-scale examination of Judaism to Volume 2, *The Way of Israel*, he tips his hand somewhat in Volume 1: "Forgetting about the Jews has contributed to our forgetfulness of the fact that we are Gentiles who have been called to walk the Way of Israel's God in a new way. With our back turned on God's first witnesses, no wonder that we have become confused about our own witness, to the point of thinking we were supposed to persuade them to abandon their calling from God and join us!"[7]

Insofar as they center in Jesus, a son of Israel, future Christologies may well make more of the permanent validity that Judaism retains in divine revelation than did past Christologies. They may well extend the "way of Israel" to the time after the early Jewish-Christian conflict, when Judaism lost the Temple and became centered on Torah and Talmud. With lessons to learn as well as lessons to offer, Christians could approach Talmudic Judaism as something germane to their own heritage. Asking themselves how the Logos is manifest in moving portions of Talmud (for instance, the beloved section called the *Pirke Avot*, "The Sayings of the Fathers"), they could gain a better sense of the wisdom tradition of Israel, both after Jesus and before. Asking themselves how the humanity of Jesus and Paul limited their appreciation of the Law, Christians could seek instruction in the religious utilities of kosher observance, sabbath observance, and the like. The result might be a deeper penetration of the dialectic between freedom and constraint—a clearer sense of the utilities and the dangers of each.

There are only 15 million Jews (contrasted with about 550 million Muslims and 470 million Hindus), so the stress in this dialogue has to be qualitative rather than quantitative. It is the depth of Israel's way, and its centrality to the revelation of the Western God, that Christians should expect better to appreciate. The God of the Bible surely desires all persons' salvation (1 Tim. 2:4), not just that of Christians and Jews, but Christians and Jews have family business to be settled that is important to the whole scheme of things.

The Essence of Christian History

As our first two angles of repose suggest, one cannot put in focus current questions about such matters as Jesus's relation to non-Christians or the relation of Christians and Jews without stepping back to reflect on the whole scheme of things. One cannot understand the present in isolation from the past. How, then, are we to understand the Christian past? What is the epitomizing, essentialist view of Christian history that a conclusion such as this one ought to offer?

A rather traditional view of Church history, not very different from the fivefold division that we have employed in this book, divides it into four basic periods: (1) the Church within Graeco-Roman civilization (30–700); (2) the Church as the dominant factor in the Western community of nations (700–1300); (3) the disintegration of the Church and the transition to a worldwide mission (1300–1750); and (4) the Church in the period of industrialization (1750–present).

The first period was foundational, as the Church established its basic identity and structure. Working with their Jewish heritage and adapting to Hellenistic forms, the Christians of the foundational era developed a full theology, spirituality, polity, and so forth. The second period welded antiquity and Christianity to Germanic culture. "A profound grasp of the Christian ethos and naive openness to the world produced in time a genuine organic union of Church and State and, in the early medieval German and French kingdoms, an impressive unified religio-political culture."[8]

The third period had a transitional character, marked by the Church's new self-awareness and struggle for reform. Subdividing it, we should note that the years 1300–1500 were no longer medieval (having a relatively unified culture), while the years 1500–1750 were not yet modern (focused by "enlightened" human reason). Since what was going forward was nothing less than the disintegration of the two universally recognized authorities of the unified civilization of the West, the empire and the papacy, great disorder and confusion prevailed. Obviously disorder and confusion can cause much pain, but they can also occasion growth, providing the chaos that precedes a new creation. "Whenever an era comes to an end, the Church is summoned to detach itself from the previous environment in which it has made itself at home, and to open itself to new peoples and cultures. For the sake of its divine commission it must not identify itself with any civilization but must 'accommodate' itself to the new order in order to assimilate it to itself, i.e., in order to make possible Christ's incorporation into it."[9]

That held for the fourth period, the Church's encounter with industrialization. From the watershed event of the French Revolution (1789), the Church derived a long-needed modification of its traditional forms and its intellectual rigidity. On the other hand, in the same event it saw the power of militant secularism, the form its enemy was to take in the modern age. Today the various faiths contest for the increasingly unified culture of the whole world. On the one side are the Marxist and capitalist secularisms. On the other side are the species of religion that confess something transcendent, something that makes all power and money but passing idols. The struggle between these two sets of faiths is as old as the fight between God and mammon, and as portentous.

Karl Rahner has recently proposed a more radical epitome of Christian history that schematizes it in terms of three epochs, the last of which is just dawning.[10] First, there was the short period of Jewish Christianity. Second, there were the nineteen-hundred years or so when the Church basically lived in one distinct cultural region, that of Hellenism and European civilization. Third, only recently has Christianity started to be—close to its core—a worldwide faith and community.

For Rahner the first epoch, of Jewish Christianity, was distinguished by the fact that "its human historical situation was that of the fundamental Christian salvation event, the death and resurrection of Jesus himself; the event was proclaimed *within* its *own* historical situation and not in one different from it; it was proclamation precisely in Israel and to it."[11] For those with eyes to see, such an interpretation of Christianity's foundational period holds the seeds of a rich gratitude toward Israel.

The second epoch grew from Paul's Gentile mission, transposing Christianity onto pagan soil. This transposition played through all the complexities of European history, including the missions to non-European lands. But essentially it was the story of proclaiming the Gospel in the new, non-Jewish idioms of Greece and Europe. Today Christians face a third epoch, a second transposition. Today Christians have to rethink the Church, reproclaim the Gospel, in the many idioms of a worldwide community. Especially, Christians have to take the cultures of Africa and Asia as seriously as the first Jewish adherents to Jesus took the culture of the Gentiles to whom they offered the good news of Jesus.

Rahner thinks that Vatican II made the beginnings of such a move within the Roman Catholic orbit, and he links the significance of that move to questions such as those we brought forward in the first section of this chapter: with ". . . some minor exceptions, modern missionary history shows that Christianity as a Western export actually succeeded neither with the high cultures of the East nor in the world of Islam, precisely because it was Western Christianity and sought in that way to establish itself in the rest of the world, without risking a really new beginning or breaking with many continuities that seem self-evident to us."[12]

A Short Formula of Christian Faith

As efforts to understand current problems such as Jesus's relation to non-Christians force us to search for the main lines of Christian history, so searching for the main lines of Christian history forces us back to decisions about what Christianity itself essentially is. In other words, what is the subject of the history we call Christian? What ideas, institutions, persons, or commitments should we track through the centuries we label A.D.? The current section is an effort to answer such questions.

Karl Rahner, who seems to be dominating this conclusion, has pioneered the use of "short formulas" of Christian faith. In the midst of the complexity of current culture, he says, people need a brief exposition of the heart of the matter, one that cuts to the core. Rahner's own *Foundations of Christian Faith* presents three such brief creedal statements. One he describes as theological, one as anthropological, and one as future-oriented. Because it best advances the line we have been pursuing thus far, we present the future-oriented creed: "Christianity is the religion which keeps open the question about the absolute future which wills to give itself in its own reality by self-communication, and which has established this will as eschatologically irreversible in Jesus Christ, and this future is called God."[13]

To interpret, let us begin from the end. For Rahner God is the absolute future. If we take seriously human temporality, we have to ask about the future, as well as the present and the past. Where are we going? What end gives us a final explanation? If life is merely a succession of moments, just today and today and today, we are close to absurdity. Faith says there is more than today and today and today. One future today, one tomorrow, ushers us into the presence of something absolute, something outside the flux. God is that absolute something, the finalizing reality that takes our succession up into something consummating. In that sense, God is the absolute—the unconditioned—future.

Christianity says three things about God the absolute future. First, the question of what God is, how God draws us, in what mode God exists—this summary question about that toward which our temporality orients us remains open. God is for us intrinsically mysterious, bound always to exceed our comprehension. Second, God wills to give herself, to communicate the divine reality to creation. Third, the warrant for saying that God wills to communicate herself, and for adding that God has achieved her will once and for all, irreversibly, is Jesus Christ. In the incarnation, life, death, and resurrection of Jesus, the absolute future accomplished the desire of its heart, the intent of its will, and both gave its love and had that love accepted. Jesus Christ, the Logos incarnate, the victim who died and Lord who was raised, is the embodied offer of God's love and its successful human reception. As such, he is the axis of history, the revelation of what all the eons were in labor to bring forth.

One can see, then, why Rahner has to relate all human goodness to Jesus, why he has drawn so heavily on the Greek theme that grace is deification, and why he is primed to see the Church as on the verge of a new, worldwide era of self-reconstitution. At core Christianity is but an explicit form for God's worldwide offer of love, God's worldwide accomplishment of his love's acceptance.

We ourselves have composed a short formula of Christian faith. It runs as follows: "Moved by the strange fit between our human experience and the life, death, and resurrection of Jesus of Nazareth, we confess that the prime treasure and first command of human existence is to love God with our whole minds, hearts, souls, and strength, and to love our neighbors as ourselves."[14] "Strange fit" originally was "paradoxical congruence." With either phrase, we mean to point up the alluring, intriguing way that Jesus both fulfills our intuitions of what we are called to be and challenges them. He is a truth-teller, no respecter of persons, a mind quick and poetic, a heart coopted by nothing less than the absolute future, the eternal present. He stands with the poor, stands against mammon, says the Sabbath was made for human beings.

However, we also find that Jesus tells us our lusts are foolish, our vanities are folly, our love of the earth is impure. To live beautifully, deeply, we must die, like seed falling in the earth. To save our lives we must lose them. Ultimately, we must carry a cross, as Jesus ultimately had to carry a cross. But Jesus was raised, the victor over death, so the paradox keeps turning. Thus, though he fulfills the Christian as can no one else, his fulfillment is hard, paradoxical, more than we handle gladly.

Condensed, Jesus's prescriptions to his followers were to love God utterly (set their hearts on nothing finite) and to love other people as they loved themselves. Theologians of our persuasion think that the first command can give capacious freedom, slaying the idols that often enslave us. The second command is a positive golden rule, as fecund in community, friendship, marriage, and the like as our wit and goodness allow.

Christian Worship

Worship is the place where Jesus's twofold command, and the rest of the Christian vision, has come home to most Christians. Formally, regularly, the Sunday liturgy has, through the ages, been Christian faith's most important expression. And while the different groups within the Christian family have worshiped with different emphases, all have tried to go back in memory to Jesus, in order to set the present and the future in the lines of his teaching and power.

The main ingredients of the Christian Sunday worship have been Scripture and sacraments. Reading the Bible aloud, and preaching about its current applications, has been a staple of almost all traditions' services. For the Bible becomes God's word in a special sense when it is read out to a solemn assembly of the faithful, who believe their convening enjoys the presence and assistance of the Holy Spirit. To be sure, not all readers and preachers know how to let the Spirit bring the scriptural words to life. In our experience, today's expositors often give the text insufficient space in which to grow impressive, because they often neglect to blend silence with their reading and speech. Another defect frequently hampering the scriptural part of Christian worship is the expositors' failure to appreciate the cultural distance separating their audiences from Jesus's time. Not only did many of Jesus's parables assume an agricultural setting, but also all his teachings assumed a Jewish faith. Thus a large part of the teaching function of the Christian ministry, throughout all ages, has been to translate across gaps such as these.

The scriptural portion of Christian worship tends to predominate in Protestant churches. In Orthodox and Catholic churches, the sacrament of the Eucharist is more to the fore. The Eucharist is a memorial of Jesus's last supper, the meal that Scripture (like Matt. 26, Luke 22) portrays him taking with his disciples before his arrest, trial, and death. The word *eucharist* itself means "thanksgiving."

Traditionally, Christians have gathered for Sunday worship in a spirit of thanksgiving. The cause of this thanksgiving has been the great deeds they believe God has done for them, above all the deed of salvation that God has wrought in Jesus's death and resurrection. Orthodox and Catholic Christians have tended to wrap the Eucharist in solemn ceremony. Using music (which Protestants also have stressed), incense, vestments, and ritualized gestures, they have tried to dramatize the meaning of the eucharistic memorial in such a way that it might affect all the human senses. In addition to having scripture readings and a sermon, they have reenacted Jesus's own reported actions at the Last Supper, emphasizing especially his giving himself to his disciples in the guise of bread and wine. Indeed, these two foods have come to stand for the new life that God is thought to nourish in the faithful.

Perhaps it would concretize this angle of repose to describe a synthesis of the traditional Christian Eucharist made by a small ecumenical group of Christians with whom we ourselves have been associated. The group gathers every other Sunday in a member's home. They begin with a prayer, or sometimes with a song from a record or of their own inspiration. Then they listen to one or two scriptural selections, from either the Old or New Testament. Following this they share a brief period of silence, so that the selection, which ideally has been read slowly, can further resonate in their hearts. When the leader for the evening thinks sufficient time has passed, he or she offers a few words of interpretation or application, which the group knows are simply meant to initiate a discussion.

The discussion may range from the theology of the text to its implications for daily living. When the discussion has run its course, the leader invites the people to express the things for which they want especially to pray. These blend into the offering of the gifts of bread and wine to God the Father in thanksgiving for all the good things of creation and in petition for all the helps that humanity needs. The offering asks the Holy Spirit to move over the gifts and in the group's hearts, so that they may find Jesus Christ in this breaking of the bread.

The leader then reads a canon, a version of the central liturgical prayer that summarizes what Jesus did (in the context of biblical history as a whole), especially what he did at his Last Supper. The canon peaks in a repetition of Jesus's words giving himself through the bread and wine, and then concludes with a remembrance of Jesus's death and resurrection. Following this the group says the Lord's Prayer ("Our Father") and then shares the (transformed) bread and wine. There follows a period of silence, and then a final prayer and song. Usually the evening continues as a relaxed social affair, with good food and good talk.

In small scope, this group tries to make less formal (and perhaps more effective) the basic worship experience that goes on in larger church groups each Sunday. It tries to renew its faith again by hearing the story of what God has done in Jesus and communing with the God it believes is present through Jesus. Well or poorly, artistically or distractedly, Christian worship through the centuries has labored at this central task. Coming together to reassert their bonds with God and one another, worshiping Christians have experienced enough peace and joy to keep their faith alive for almost two thousand years.

A Christian View of the Life Cycle

Whether we worship as Christians or not, we age toward a confrontation with the absolute future. Psychologists such as Erik Erikson have studied the typical stages of the human life cycle, and theologians have started to apply such findings to study of the development of Christian faith.[15] Although there are rich fields to mine in the work of child psychologists on the early human personality, perhaps especially in the work of Jean Piaget, our space limits us to concentrating on the crises of adulthood. In Erikson's broad schema they are three: the conflict between intimacy and isolation that should find resolution in love, the conflict between generativity and self-absorption that should find resolution in care, and the conflict between integrity and despair that should find resolution in wisdom.

Having come through adolescence to some sense of identity, the typical person struggles to apply the fidelity (the ability to pledge herself) that identity connotes to something or someone worthy of it. To take an obvious application, she struggles to make intimacy overbalance isolation in a romantic, bonding relationship with another person. Intimacy is what thrills Romeo and Juliet, what makes their *eros* escape sterile imagination and reach a concrete other who can anchor it in the real world. It is what can transmute isolation into clear relationship, keeping Romeo and Juliet from drowning in hopeless frustration. Love is what works such balances, what fosters such intimacy and grows in its heart. Love makes the beloved another self, yet it keeps one singing *vive la difference*. In love, Romeo and Juliet no longer are children or adolescents. They are adults, having to shoulder family conflicts, sex, and even mortality.

Love ought to show itself in care. Overbalancing isolation with intimacy, young lovers, bonded adults, have to face a further conflict, between generativity and self-absorption. Through children, work, social assignments, and the like, they seek production, accomplishment. The mature human personality needs to beget, to make, to lead, to contribute. It needs to be needed—by children, customers, students, colleagues. Unless generativity overbalances self-absorption, the fine objectivity, dependability, and weightiness that we associate with mature adulthood never will arrive. Narcissism or selfishness will ruin the fruit that should have been. Careless, in flight from responsibility, the person will remain somewhat childish. He will cheat the next generation, to whom he owes at least the measure of care he himself received from parents, teachers, and other elders. Without care, the generations gap dangerously. Without care, the whole enterprise of the race comes to crisis.

Old age knows these things in its bones, brittle though they may be. These things lead into the last crisis, between integrity and despair. At the end of her span, the human person should have become integral, a rounded "one," something complete and whole. But physical decay, and long exposure to human frailty (ignorance, sinfulness, and more), tempt the aged person to think life all sound and fury, a tale told by an idiot. Wisdom is the ability so to see things in the round, under the aspect of eternity, that integrity triumphs over despair, that one can love life in face of his death. Looking back in wisdom, the completed human person sees the necessity of care, love, fidelity, and the other virtues, and the necessity of the conflicts in which they were annealed. If a Bible reader, such a person approaches Luke's view of divine necessity, of the fact that *it had to be* that the Christ should suffer and so enter his glory (Luke 24:26). Our lives, with all their mistakes and follies, are an impenetrable blend of freedom and necessity.

Believing that God shares such a life cycle, that the Spirit groans in the depths of all her crises and anoints all her virtues, the Christian can view human temporality as an adventure. We are given time to grow wise. We have life as a set of inchoate talents we are to work for rich yield. Ultimately, we have life in order to give it over: to intimate friends in love, to children and clients in care, to the absolute future itself in wise, faithful hope. There is nothing we can do, throughout the process, that will separate us from God's love. There is no stone we can throw against the absolute future that will stop God from being God: eternal, faithful, loving because of himself, his own inalienable goodness.

The Problem of Evil

"All well and good, Professors Carmody," you may say, "but we, the presumptive objects of your love, care, and wisdom, put you one not so small question. Why don't we see this splendid vision incarnate in our world? Why doesn't the abounding of grace over sin, the victory of faith over death, flash forth more obviously? In short, why doesn't God solve the problem of evil?" A good question. The capital issue, before which all sane **theodicy** grows pale.

We have no answer to the problem of evil, no solution. At best, we can draw responses from the Christian tradition that keep the problem somewhat at bay, letting God and Christ remain responsible options. First, there is a helpful but ultimately inadequate observation that some evils turn out to be goods. Take the case of a person who loses a job and goes down in the dumps. It was a good job, well-paying and quite satisfying. But the person's co-workers were nasty, envious, backbiting. They finally convinced the boss that this goody-goody didn't fit, so the boss fired him. Came then the dark night: visits to the unemployment office, visions of the kids trudging off to school in rags, nightmares of a career badly derailed. Six months later, though, the person is singing ragtime. A new job has appeared, with better pay and better fellow workers. Having endured the dark night, the person, his wife, and their kids find themselves stronger. They now live day by day, trying just to do good work and make a family circle of love twenty-four hours at a time.

One could write parallel scenarios for the sickness that first makes a woman reflective, the broken engagement that leads to a much better lover, even the handicapped child who becomes a special treasure. In each case, an apparent evil turns out to bring much good. Having apparent evils turn out to bring much good does not make evil itself something good. The sickness that brings the woman to the hospital, the anger that breaks the engagement, the crippling that makes the child handicapped are things that should not be. But they can so lead on to growth or benefit that we think we can see in them some higher purpose. We think we may discern the finger of God.

It is not the same with evils more massive, poignant, or acute. Who would dare to point to God's positive will in the camps of Dachau, the Gulag Archipelago? What greater good appears for the little black child, his afro as big as the rest of him, whom we see dragging himself to second grade each morning, already heavily burdened by racism? What is there to say to the colleague who loses two children to death, at ages four and thirteen?[16] The breath catches, the mouth stops. Words are almost sacrilegious. In the concrete, present to persons suffering such evils, one does well to lighten their pain a trifle simply by being there, by not fleeing the crushing reality.

Back in the study, where one composes formulas or analyses on the understanding that only prudence can mediate them to concrete situations well, two observations from Christian tradition come to mind. They are (1) the heritage from Job and Paul to the effect that we are the pots, not the potter, and (2) Jesus's cross. The heritage from Job and Paul does not suggest that we avert our gaze from evil. It simply reminds us that the ultimate order of things lies outside our grasp. We are creatures, not the Creator. We can, probably should, rage at the evils that we encounter, rage even at the Creator ultimately responsible for them. If God is as the Bible depicts her, she encourages absolute honesty, she likes it when Job tries to make his case and when Abraham haggles for Sodom. But God's final answer to Job, out of the whirlwind, reminds him of bedrock reality. Unless he was at the founding of the world—can measure the mystery of things—Job cannot judge where his suffering finally fits in. So too with the rest of us, skeptics and atheists quite included. It is simply not the case that any of us can pass judgment on the ultimate meaning of a historical event, evil or good. As process theology has reminded us recently, all things historical interconnect. Therefore, only he who knows the whole knows the full significance of the part. None of us knows the whole. Each of us, therefore, should preserve a decent silence, even before cancer, war, or nazism.

Theologizing further, we find that Jesus's cross but deepens the wise person's silence. Paul called it a stumbling block to Jews and to Gentiles foolishness, but to faith the power and wisdom of God (1 Cor. 1:23–25). Jews have had good cause to stumble: the cross is repellent, and Christians have pressed it upon Jews hatefully. Gentiles have been human to think the Christian reverence for the crucifixion foolish: most of us do not spontaneously picture divinity or highly developed humanity in terms of a criminal hanging from a cross. Only in an orbit of faith, akin to the mother-love that does not give up on even the criminal child, does the Spirit whisper that, yes, God could be so good he would suffer that way for his people. Yes, he could assume our evil to show that evil is not the last word.

Toward an Education for Wisdom[17]

It has never been easy to determine what evil is, what evil signifies when one stands at the end of the life cycle, trying to love life in face of death. The evils in today's world should prompt serious reflection about American culture, as the evils of recent events in Cambodia apparently prompted Jerry Falwell, leader of the Moral Majority, to reflect seriously.[18] For all that our full reflection might differ from Falwell's—not accepting his fundamentalist interpretation of the Bible or his strong advocacy of American capitalism—we agree that the reflection is extremely urgent.

Now, push reflection far enough and you come to the domain of religion, the domain of ultimate concerns. Education ought to provide us tools for reflecting wisely on this domain, but as it is presently constituted in America, it does not. The love of learning does not seem to dominate American education, as the love of God and the love of neighbor do not seem to dominate American religion. Neither institution knows what is necessary for its prosperity and peace. Neither institution has many who know the good taste of wisdom, the savor of solid food for the mind, the heart, the soul, the mature personality's strengths.

To be sure, this has always been so, to some degree. The university, the church, the synagogue, the military, the government have always been all too human. One need not take up the burden of proving that current institutions are worse than they used to be to argue that our institutions are not serving us well in any of the four prime facets of reality. Our energy crises and ecological crises demonstrate that we are not wise about nature. The injustices in our worldwide economic system, its starvations and wars, demonstrate that we are not wise about society. Our sufferings worldwide in the areas of work and love (the two areas Freud made capital for psychological health) demonstrate that we are not wise about the self. Our confusion about ultimate goals, and our pervasive joylessness, demonstrates that we are not wise about God.

Doris Lessing gives many evidences of being a wise woman, a **wicca**, with a vision adequate to the great span of our problems, including those in the domain of ultimate concern. In the third volume of her *Canopus in Argos: Chronicles*,[19] she shows the essential problem: we can hear neither the right questions nor the answers that they evoke. Because of distortions in our selves, the basic instruments we must use, we receive as static or a foreign language the wisdom nature would teach us and the wisdom of the human past. Lessing herself sensed very early that she would have to listen carefully from the heart if she were to learn wisdom. Almost accidentally, she avoided most of the bad listening others would have inflicted on her in the name of critical interpretation. By dropping out of school at fourteen, Lessing chose to search out wisdom for herself, judging ideas in terms of whether or not they rang true in her depths.[20]

If we point Lessing's stance toward the question of how we are to educate for wisdom, it discloses the importance of what one sensitive theologian recently has called "the way of the heart."[21] Information and intellect have their important places, but the crux of solid, satisfying, effective education is the exercise of deep judgment and decision[22]—the learning that connects us with what so many peoples, biblical and nonbiblical alike, spontaneously have called "the heart." Philosopher Blaise Pascal said, "The heart has its reasons, which reason knows nothing of." If education were to help the mind learn even a few of the reasons of the heart, it would take a giant step toward enabling us to resolve our deepest problems.

Summary

Our first angle of repose was the currently bruited question of Jesus's relation to non-Christians. The realities of a pluralistic world force this question as previous centuries did not, and the most adequate of the preliminary answers gravitate toward the core of the central Christian dogma, the mystery of Jesus's finite humanity and infinite divinity. A second angle, both less acute than the first and more, was the relation of Jews and Christians. Here the pressures forcing the question stemmed from the Holocaust and the establishment of the state of Israel, and the inchoate answers both take Christianity back to its Jewish heritage and help it better esteem the wisdoms of Judaism since 70 C.E.

After considering these two contemporary issues, we moved to a deeper level, attempting an essentialist history that might provide the issue a clearer framework. What, after all, has Christianity been over time? Exposing both a traditional and a brand new periodization, we noted the exfoliation of the Gospel and the Church, their branching from the seed of Jesus's life, death, and resurrection to a good news meant for a very vast world. In short formulas of Christian faith, we tried to encapsulate the book's first section, where we delved into the Christian worldview. Our section on worship showed how Christians have regularly expressed this worldview through Scripture and the sacraments. Angling into the life cycle, we focused on a faithful vision of adult crises and virtues, only to be brought up short by the problem of evil, of so many things that should not be. Silence, a sense of creaturely limitation, and the cross of Christ were the only responses we could muster. However, in the context of an education pointed toward wisdom such response would not seem eccentric, for an education pointed toward wisdom would teach the way of the heart, the listening for a word that breathes forth honesty and love.

Study Questions

1. How does the question of Jesus's relation to non-Christians function as an angle of repose?
2. What might it mean for Jewish-Christian relations to focus on Jesus as a son of Israel?
3. What is Karl Rahner's radical epitome of Christian history?
4. Explain how God is the absolute future.

5. Why must love show itself in care?
6. What does it matter, for the problem of evil, that we are the pots, not the potter?
7. Why would you like, or not like, an education conceived as a way of the heart?

Notes

1. Geoffrey Parrinder, *Jesus in the Qur'an* (New York: Oxford, 1977), p. 173.
2. See Hans Waldenfels, *Absolute Nothingness* (New York: Paulist, 1980). Also John Carmody, "A Next Step for Roman Catholic Theology," *Theology Today*, 32 (1976), 371–381.
3. J. Peter Schineller, "Discovering Jesus Christ: A History We Share," in *A World of Grace*, Leo J. O'Donovan, ed. (New York: Seabury, 1980), p. 102.
4. See Paul Knitter, "Christianity As Religion: True and Absolute? A Roman Catholic Perspective," in *What is Religion: An Enquiry for Christian Theology*, Mircea Eliade and David Tracy, eds. (New York: Seabury, 1980), pp. 12–21.
5. Daniel J. Harrington, *God's People in Christ* (Philadelphia: Fortress, 1980), p. 114.
6. Paul Van Buren, *Discerning the Way* (New York: Seabury, 1980), p. 2.
7. Ibid, p. 44.
8. August Franzen, "Church History," in *Sacramentum Mundi*, ed. Karl Rahner et al. (New York: Herder & Herder, 1968), vol. 1, p. 368.
9. Ibid., p. 366.
10. "Towards a Fundamental Theological Interpretation of Vatican II," *Theological Studies*, 40/4 (Dec. 1979), 716–727.
11. Ibid., p. 721.
12. Ibid., p. 724.
13. Karl Rahner, *Foundations of Christian Faith* (New York: Seabury, 1978), p. 457.
14. For a book-length elaboration, see John Carmody, *The Heart of the Christian Matter* (Nashville: Abingdon, 1983).
15. See Erik H. Erikson, "Reflections on Dr. Borg's Life Cycle," in *Adulthood*, Erik H. Erikson, ed. (New York: Norton, 1978), pp. 1–31; James W. Fowler, Robin W. Lovin, et al., *Trajectories in Faith* (Nashville: Abingdon, 1980); John Carmody, *Theology for the 1980s* (Philadelphia: Westminster, 1980), pp. 87–97.
16. See Jerry A. Irish, *A Boy Thirteen* (Philadelphia: Westminster, 1976).
17. For further elaboration, see John Carmody, *The Progressive Pilgrim* (Notre Dame, IN: Fides/Claretian, 1980), pp. 60–84.
18. See his *Listen, America!* (Garden City, NY: Doubleday, 1980), pp. 3–23.
19. Doris Lessing, *The Sirian Experiments* (New York: Knopf, 1981).

20. See Doris Lessing, *The Golden Notebook* (New York: Bantam, 1973), p. xviii.
21. Henri Nouwen, *The Way of the Heart* (New York: Seabury, 1981).
22. See Frederick Crowe, *The Lonergan Enterprise* (Cambridge, MA: Cowley, 1980).

APPENDIX A

Membership Data on Major American Religious Groups (1979)

Adventists, Seventh Day 525,000
Baptists 26,000,000
Buddhists 60,000
Christian Church (Disciples of Christ) 1,260,000
Christian Churches and Churches of Christ 1,050,000
Church of the Nazarene 455,000
Churches of Christ 2,500,000
Eastern Churches (Orthodox) 4,050,000
Episcopal Church 2,820,000
Friends United Meeting (Quakers) 65,000
Jehovah's Witnesses 555,000
Jewish Congregations 5,775,000
Latter Day Saints (Mormons) 2,670,000
Lutherans 8,500,000
Mennonites 100,000
Methodists 13,500,000
Pentecostals 3,300,000
Presbyterians 3,600,000
Roman Catholics 50,000,000
Salvation Army 400,000
Unitarian Universalist Association 200,000
United Churches of Christ 1,800,000

Glossary

acedia: spiritual sadness, sloth, or torpor; a prime manifestation of **desolation**.

Albigensians: a heretical sect that appeared in southern France in the eleventh century and taught a form of Manichean dualism along with implacable hatred of the Church.

alienation: the process of estrangement, of being made foreign.

allegorical interpretation: exegesis of scripture that purports to go beneath the literal meaning to find symbols and analogies that unlock spiritual meanings.

apocalyptic: purportedly deriving from a revelation, and usually pertaining to the approach of the "end."

apologetics: argumentation to defend faith or demonstrate its reasonableness, usually to those outside the believing community.

ascetic: stressing self-denial.

atonement: overcoming the distance between human beings and God, satisfying for sin, and restoring communion.

beatific vision: the direct enjoyment of God that fulfills the mind and heart.

being: reality taken with an emphasis on its "isness," its standing forth from nothingness and existing.

canonization: (a) the process by which certain writings become normative or scriptural; (b) the process that declares the certain holiness of a person and so makes official his or her sanctity.

catholic: universal, worldwide, all-embracing.

Christ: synonym for Messiah (anointed one)—the Savior-King of Jewish expectation. His followers gave Jesus this title in the belief that he had fulfilled Jewish prophecy.

Christology: the study of Jesus, especially as resurrected and divine.

circumincession: the mutual indwelling of the three persons of the Trinity.

civil religion: the consecration of one's city or country, in such a way that the local way of life and set of values seem inseparable from divinity.

communion of saints: the society of all Christian believers, past and present.

concursus: God's coaction with creatures or undergirding of their active being.

confessor: (a) one who testifies publicly to his or her Christian faith; (b) one who administers the sacrament of penance and religious advice.

conscience: human awareness in its moral capacity to weigh right and wrong.

conservation: God's preservation of creatures in being; creation as ongoing.

contemplation: careful attention that tries to engage the core of one's reason an may well bear fruit in affective prayer.

conversion: a radical reorientation of the personality, usually in the sense of from sin to grace or God.

cosmological myth: the worldview in which the physical universe is a single continuum, often considered to be alive, and the various beings that compose it are considered to be consubstantial—of the same ultimate stuff.

cosmology: the study of nature or the physical world, especially regarding its ultimate causes.

covenant: a compact or contract, usually between God and a people, especially between God and Israel.

creation: (a) the act of making something freshly; (b) the product or products of such an act.

culture: the sum of a people's self-expressions and meanings.

deification: the process of coming to share God's nature.

Deists: seventeenth- and eighteenth-century Europeans who believed in a remote, inactive Creator.

desolation: the depressed state of feeling bereft of the Spirit, carnal, out of sorts, disgusted with oneself and the world. The opposite of consolation.

determinism: a control that excludes human freedom.

dialectic: a clash of judgments, worldviews, or faiths, for the sake of clarifying their respective truths.

discernment of spirits: the effort to read the signs of grace, in the context of traditional Christian wisdom.

Divine Energies: the Orthodox characterization of the exterior manifestations of God that work human deification and operate in the realm of the economy of salvation.

Docetism: a heresy from the first centuries of Church history that considered the body and sufferings of Jesus only apparently, not actually, real.

dogma: doctrine that has been taught by proper Church authority decisively.

dogmatism: rigid insistence on a given point of view.

Donatism: a fourth century African heresy that refused apostates readmission to the church and required personal sanctity of the ministers if sacraments were to be accounted valid.

ecclesiology: the study of the Church.

economy: Greek term for order or dispensation, usually used of salvation or grace to stress God's actions in relation to the world and human beings.

ecumenical: worldwide, pertaining to the entire inhabited world; now used mainly to signify the Christian movement for the separated churches' reunion.

empiricism: the philosophical conviction that facts or data are what primarily, if not exclusively, determine reality.

encyclical: a public letter in which a pope expresses his view of current events.

eschatological: pertaining to "last things"—either the final age, when the Kingdom of God has arrived, or death, judgment, heaven, and hell.

Eucharist ("thanksgiving"): the Lord's Supper or Mass, which is the prime Christian sacrament.

Evangelical: (a) related to the Gospel; (b) Church groups, often fundamentalist, that base themselves wholly on the Gospel.

exegesis: study that works out the meaning of a text, especially one of Scripture.

existentialist: one who stresses human beings' responsibility for what they are or become.

faith: committing oneself beyond the strict warrant of evidence because of a trustworthy authority.

filioque: the notion of Western trinitarian theology that the Holy Spirit proceeds from the Son as well as the Father. The East has regarded it as a heretical addition to the Nicene Creed.

fundamentalism: a literalist mentality that tends to read documents, especially Scripture, without attention to the historical and literary mentalities of their authors.

fundamental option: the basic choice, basic yes or no to Mystery, that sets the deepest orientation of personal morality.

Gnosticism: a family of heresies that flourished in the first three centuries and had in common the notion of a secret teaching about a cosmic fall and a subsequent path of redemption. Gnosticism tended to be anti-material and anti-sexual.

grace: (a) favor with God; (b) a share in the divine life; (c) help from God toward right action.

heaven: the state of complete fulfillment that comes from permanent union with God.

hell: the state of self-ruin that comes from permanent deprivation of God.

heresy: deviance from accepted teaching.

Hesychasm: an Eastern Orthodox school of spirituality stressing inner silence rhythmic breathing, and the Jesus Prayer.

high churches: groups that have a hierarchical structure (that is, an episcopacy and a solemn liturgy.

holy: pure, really real, most ultimate, most unsullied, and most powerful.

Holy Spirit: the third "Person" of the Trinity; God as Divine Love given to human beings and effectively received by them.

hope: opening oneself to the future in trust.

humanist: one concerned with human affairs, sometimes in the sense of to the exclusion of divine affairs.

hypostatic union: the mysterious union of Jesus's divinity and humanity in the person (*hypostatis*) of the Logos.

icon: a holy image; usually meaning the Eastern Christian religious portraits of Jesus, Mary, and the saints.

iconoclast: one who would destroy icons.

iconodule: one who reveres icons.

idealism: the philosophical conviction that reality is essentially mental, consisting of spirit or ideas.

ideology: (a) a distorting set of assumptions or orientations that filters out things not to one's advantage; (b) the set of ideas by which one organizes the world.

Incarnation: the enfleshment of the Logos.

incarnationalism: the positive evaluation of embodiedness that Christians derive from the Word's having taken flesh.

indulgence: the remission by the Church of the temporal punishment due to sin (even after its forgiveness), based on the merits of Christ and the saints. In the early sixteenth century one could gain an indulgence by almsgiving, which led to the abuses that Luther castigated.

inspiration: the notion that Scripture derives from authors illumined by God. In crude versions it amounts to God's having dictated Scripture. In sophisticated versions it amounts to sensitivity to the Holy Spirit.

intellectualist: stressing reason.

Johannine: related to the writings of John the Evangelist (the Gospel of John, Epistles of John, and sometimes the book of Revelation).

judgment: God's rendering justice to both sinners and the just after their deaths.

lectio divina: a medieval devotional form in which one read a text (usually Scripture) slowly and ruminatively, for its religious savor more than its intellectual content.

liturgy: the "work of the people" that is official worship.

Logos: the Divine Word or Second Person of the Trinity.

love: the core act of the human person, combining light and warmth, that culminates in self-giving.

magisterium: the authoritative teaching office of the Church, especially as expressed through the upper clergy; used mainly by Roman Catholics.

mammon: worldly prosperity.

Manicheanism: a third- and fourth-century C.E. heresy that taught that matter is evil.

Marcionism: a second- and third-century heresy that rejected the Old Testament, conceived of the Gospel as wholly a message of love, and reduced the New Testament mainly to the Pauline and Lucan portions.

mechanism: the view that nature operates basically like a machine, with few mysteries and little need for holistic approaches on the part of cosmologists.

Messiah: Hebrew for "the anointed one" or "king" who was to give Israel a golden age. Christians confess Jesus to be the *Christ* ("anointed one" in Greek), and interpret his kingdom in spiritual terms.

metropolitan: a bishop who is in charge not merely of a diocese but also of the province or geographical unit which that diocese is the center of.

millennium: the coming thousand-year period during which Christ will reign on earth.

miracle: an extraordinary happening, often in apparent violation of the laws of nature, that testifies to God's action and supports faith.

Monarchists: those who stressed God's unity.

monasticism: the withdrawal from the world to live a common religious life under vows of poverty, chastity, and obedience.

monophysites: heretics who taught that Christ only had one nature.

Montanism: an apocalyptic movement of the latter half of the second century that expected a speedy outpouring of the Holy Spirit on the Church.

mortification: disciplining the flesh so that the spirit may flourish.

mystagogy: the evocation of divine mystery and religious truths, often through sacraments or liturgical ceremonies.

mystery: the fullness of being and intelligibility onto which human experience opens.

mystical: concerned with the experience of ultimate reality.

myth: an explanation of ultimate reality in terms of a story.

natural law: the inbuilt patterns that things have or ought to have insofar as they possess essences created by a purposeful God.

Neoplatonism: the development of Plato's philosophy that was influential in the early centuries of the Common Era.

Nestorianism: the fifth century heresy that said there were two persons in the incarnate Logos, one divine and one human.

nominalism: the philosophy greatly concerned with the way we name realities.

noosphere: the evolutionary layer of thought; a term often associated with the theories of Roman Catholic evolutionist Pierre Teilhard de Chardin.

office: the obligatory prayer to which religious and priests have been bound. Often it is communal and consists of psalms, scripture readings, and selections from the Fathers, set to music and spaced throughout the day.

ontology: the study of being, sometimes synonymous with metaphysics.

Original Sin: the state of division and alienation that affects humanity so radically that it suggests a Fall at the beginning.

orthodox: (a) traditionally regarded as correct; (b) (*cap.*) Eastern Christians, distinguished from Catholics and Protestants.

pagan: those not Christian or Jewish.

pantheism: the view that everything is God.

patristic: referring to the era dominated by the Church Fathers (ca. 200–500).

Paulicians: members of a medieval Byzantine sect that taught matter is evil.

Pauline: pertaining to the apostle Paul.

Pelagianism: a fourth-century C.E. heresy that overstressed human freedom.

Pietists: descendants of a seventeenth-century movement in the German Lutheran church that tried to vivify the rather stodgy official Protestantism of the day by developing a more devotional faith.

pragmatism: (a) a school of philosophy associated with Americans such as James, Peirce, and Dewey, that stresses the primacy of action; (b) crass evaluation in terms only of results.

predestination: the decree of God that coincides with a person's eternal destiny.

problem of evil: the tension between a good Creator and an unjust or cruel creation. Classical Christian theology (like Augustine's) approached it by analyzing evil as a privation of good, and so as non-being. Process thought approaches it by conceiving of God as finite.

process theology: a school that stresses the interrelatedness and development of all realities, including God.

prophecy: expressing judgments on a time in the name of divine standards.

psychological analogy: the imagery for the Trinity drawn from the human spiritual acts of knowing and loving.

purgatory: a state of purification that virtuous but not wholly saintly persons must endure before entering heaven. Held by Roman Catholics, disputed by Protestants and Orthodox as unbiblical.

radical politics: work for social arrangements that honor the root conditions of human prosperity. Although the term can have connotations of violence, it need not have them. Many Christian radical politicians lean toward pacifist positions. Almost all, however, are deeply critical of Christians' alliances with capitalism.

rationalism: the philosophy or outlook in which reason so passes judgment on reality that other ways to truth, beauty, or value are slighted.

redeemer: the one who "buys back" humanity from alienation and sin.

Reformation: the sixteenth-century upheavals and renovations in Western Christianity.

reformer: (a) one who attempts to renovate a tradition; (b) (*cap.*) a significant figure in the sixteenth-century Protestant renovation.

religion: human dealings with Mystery or the Sacred, depreciated by some theologians (such as Karl Barth) as opposed to revelation and faith.

revelation: the Ultimate Mystery "removing the veil" and disclosing itself.

sacrament: (a) an outward and visible sign of an inward and spiritual grace; (b) alternately and more precisely, the official acts in which the Church expresses its nature as the eschatological community of salvation.

sacrifice: making over to God something of special worth, to honor the deity and petition forgiveness of sins.

salvation: making whole, returning to communion with God.

schism: separation due to political or organizational differences rather than doctrinal ones.

Scholasticism: the medieval philosophy and theology that perhaps overstressed careful analyses and distinctions.

scripture: writing that is privileged because considered to be God's Word; the Old and New Testaments are Christian scripture.

secularism: a horizon limited to this world of space and time.

secularization: the process by which the world appears to become less divine, even emptied of divinity.

shaman: the prime religious figure in archaic cultures; a specialist in archaic techniques of ecstasy.

Shema: the confession of faith recorded in Deut. 6.

sin: culpable moral failure, "missing the mark."

socialism: political theory that stresses the importance of the group, sometimes to the detriment of the individual.

steady-state economy: one that would not postulate constant growth, as most capitalist and Communist models do, but would pivot on a balance between renewable resources and limited consumption.

sublation: the way that grace takes nature up into a higher order that both preserves and perfects nature.

supernatural: beyond what is owed or required by a being's essence.

supernatural existential: the theory that all persons inhabit an order of grace, so that there is no purely "natural" struggle for human authenticity.

synoptic: the first three Gospels: Matthew, Mark, and Luke.

theodicy: the justification or defense of God's ways, especially in face of the problem of evil.

theological virtue: a power coming from God by grace that enables the believer to live the Christian life (or the good life that leads to salvation). Faith, hope, and love are the prime theological virtues.

Torah: Jewish Law or Teaching, sometimes taken as the Pentateuch (Genesis, Exodus, Leviticus, Numbers, Deuteronomy) attributed to Moses, and sometimes taken as the full range of both oral and written (Talmudic) tradition.

transcendent: going beyond the secular world and so ultimate or divine.

transubstantiation: the eucharistic doctrine that the elements of bread and wine become changed into the substance of Jesus, his literal body and blood.

trickster: a mythological figure, common in Native American and African lore, who is both cunning and a dupe. He usually has wild adventures that give vent to tabooed desires and so represents something of the psychoanalytic id. In Afro-American mythology Brer Rabbit shows many trickster features.

Trinity: God as Father, Son, and Holy Spirit.

uncreated grace: the favor of God's self-communication, equivalent to deification.

utopia: the ideal state of affairs that ought to exist, according to human reason and conscience at their most healthy.

vespers: the portion of the office that occurs around sunset.

voluntarist: one who greatly stresses the human will.

wicca: a wise woman—used by the new witchcraft to venerate feminine experience and sagacity.

Annotated Bibliography

Ahlstrom, Sydney E. A *Religious History of the American People*. New Haven: Yale University Press, 1972. A massive study, winner of the National Book Award in philosophy and religion for 1973, which has become the first reference on the topic.

Albanese, Catherine L. *America: Religions and Religion*. Belmont, CA: Wadsworth, 1981. A solid single-volume introduction to the varieties of American religious experience.

Appiah-Kubi, Kofi and Torres, Sergio, eds. *African Theology en Route*. Maryknoll, NY: Orbis, 1979. Papers from the 1977 Pan-African Conference of Third World Theologians that give a good indication both of recent African theological reflection and of African theologians' relations to American black theology.

Atwood, Margaret. *Life Before Man*. New York: Simon & Schuster, 1979. An effective novel that displays the confusion of secular Western urbanites about life's meaning and their own personal morality.

Berger, Peter L. and Neuhaus, Richard John, eds. *Against The World for the World*. New York: Seabury, 1976. Papers from the conference that issued the 1975 Hartford Appeal against the inroads of secularism into Western civil and church life.

Bolshakoff, Sergius and Pennington, M. Basil. *In Search of True Wisdom*. Garden City, NY: Doubleday, 1979. Reports of interviews with Russian and Greek Orthodox masters of the spiritual life.

Brown, Raymond E. *The Community of the Beloved Disciple*. New York: Paulist, 1979. A semi-technical study of the sociological forces behind the Johannine literature.

Brown, Robert McAfee. *Creative Dislocation—The Movement of Grace*. Nashville: Abingdon, 1980. A very readable account of Brown's personal changes in the past two decades that recapitulates and analyzes some of the major items on faith's agenda.

Brown, Robert McAfee. *The Spirit of Protestantism*. New York: Oxford University Press, 1965. A clear presentation of the central concerns of Protestantism and its style.

Burrell, David B. *Exercises in Religious Understanding*. Notre Dame, IN: University of Notre Dame Press, 1974. Studies of five important religious thinkers: Augustine, Anselm, Aquinas, Kierkegaard, and Jung.

Callenbach, Ernest. *Ecotopia*. New York: Bantam, 1977. An imaginative utopian solution to the ecological crisis.

Cardenal, Ernesto. *The Gospel in Solentiname*. Maryknoll, NY: Orbis, 1976, 1978, 1979. Three volumes of discussions on the Gospel by the Solentiname community that express the grass roots implications of liberation theology winsomely.

Carmody, Denise Lardner. *Feminism and Christianity: A Two-Way Reflection*. Nashville: Abingdon, 1982. A dialectical analysis of the strengths and weaknesses that the debate between radical feminism and Christianity reveals on both sides.

Carmody, Denise Lardner. *The Oldest God: Archaic Religion Yesterday and Today*. Nashville: Abingdon, 1981. A survey of the archaic religious mind in prehistoric, early historic, and modern cases (Amerindian, African, and Australian).

Carmody, Denise Lardner. *Women and World Religions*. Nashville: Abingdon, 1979. An overview of women's experience and status in the major religious traditions.

Carmody, Denise Lardner and Carmody, John Tully. *Ways to the Center: An Introduction to the World Religions*. Belmont, CA: Wadsworth, 1981. A comprehensive text that treats ancient, Eastern, and Western religions in terms of their appearances, histories, and worldviews.

Carmody, John. *Theology for the 1980s*. Philadelphia: Westminster, 1980. A survey of recent trends in Christian theology that prescribes future tasks under the five headings of nature, society, self, divinity, and Christology.

Chadwick, Henry. *The Early Church*. Baltimore: Penguin, 1967. A clear overview of the first four centuries or so.

Chadwick, Owen. *The Reformation*. Baltimore: Penguin, 1964. A readable overview of the Reformation that provides both historical information and doctrinal interpretation.

Chadwick, Owen. *The Secularization of the European Mind in the Nineteenth Century*. New York: Cambridge University Press, 1975. Chadwick gave the substance of this book as the 1973–74 Gifford Lectures at Edinburgh, and it indicates how a learned, somewhat demanding historian approaches an assignment in intellectual history.

Childs, Brevard S. *Introduction to the Old Testament as Scripture*. Philadelphia: Fortress, 1979. A fine but quite technical survey and adjudication of recent Old Testament scholarship.

Christ, Carol P. *Diving Deep and Surfacing*. Boston: Beacon Press, 1980. A study of women's spiritual quest, as illustrated in recent feminist literature.

Christ, Carol P. and Plaskow, Judith, eds. *Womanspirit Rising*. San Francisco: Harper & Row, 1979. A reader that gives a good illustration of recent feminist work at recasting Jewish and Christian theologies.

Clebsch, William A. *Christianity in European History*. New York: Oxford University Press, 1979. An overview of the topic in terms of the religious types (for example, monk, martyr, moralist) that dominated in each of five historical periods.

Cobb, John B., Jr. and Griffin, David Ray. *Process Theology: An Introductory Exposition*. Philadelphia: Westminster, 1976. A book of medium-range difficulty that gives the process view on most of the traditional concerns of Christian theology.

Cone, James H. *The Spirituals and the Blues*. New York: Seabury, 1972. An insightful study of the religious themes expressed in the slave spirituals and the secular blues.

Cooke, Bernard. *Ministry to Word and Sacrament*. Philadelphia: Fortress, 1976. A large study of Christian ministry that does full justice to both its history (in the West) and its current theology.

Cragg, Gerald R. *The Church and the Age of Reason 1648–1789*. Grand Rapids, MI: Eerdmans, 1960. A good survey of developments in Europe, with emphasis on the Church's responses to the challenges of the age.

Crowe, Frederick. *The Lonergan Enterprise*. Cambridge, MA: Cowley, 1980. A readable introduction to the work of the Roman Catholic theologian who has proposed perhaps the most far-reaching reform of Christian theology.

Cunliffe-Jones, Hubert, ed. *A History of Christian Doctrine*. Philadelphia: Fortress, 1980. A fine one-volume survey with contributions by experts on the different periods in the history of Christian doctrine.

Daly, Mary. *Gyn/Ecology*. Boston: Beacon, 1979. A powerful study of the abuses the traditional religions have worked on women, with a call to women to remove themselves from male influence.

Dayton, Donald W. *Discovering an Evangelical Heritage.* New York: Harper & Row, 1976. Portraits of influential figures and causes in evangelical history that give the lie to recent Evangelicals' claims that Christian faith need not concern itself with social issues.

Dinnerstein, Dorothy. *The Mermaid and the Minotaur.* New York: Harper Colophon, 1977. A psychoanalytic study of the malaise between the sexes that focuses on female dominance of child-rearing.

Dudko, Dmitrii. *Our Hope.* Crestwood, NY: St. Vladimir's Seminary Press, 1977. Dialogues between a Russian Orthodox priest and current Soviet citizens that offer a stark window onto the religious scene in the USSR.

Eagleson, John, and Scharper, Philip, eds. *Puebla and Beyond.* Maryknoll, NY: Orbis, 1979. The text of CELAM III's main document and John Paul II's opening address, plus helpful commentaries.

Erikson, Erik H., ed. *Adulthood.* New York: Norton, 1978. Essays by distinguished scholars from several different fields that treat various models of human maturation, many of them with direct religious reference.

Evans, Robert and Parker, Thomas, eds. *Christian Theology: A Case Method Approach.* New York: Harper & Row, 1976. A presentation of Christian doctrine through studies in the style of the Harvard Business School's case method—interesting pedagogically.

Falwell, Jerry. *Listen, America!* Garden City, NJ: Doubleday, 1980. A full statement by the leader of the Moral Majority that shows that group's understanding of biblical faith and its application to many aspects of American culture.

Fedotov, G. P. *A Treasury of Russian Spirituality.* New York: Harper & Row, 1965. A good collection of selections from the writings of relatively recent Russian saints on spiritual topics such as prayer and mortification.

Fowler, James W., Lovin, Robin W., et al. *Trajectories in Faith.* Nashville: Abingdon, 1980. Life stories of Malcolm X, Anne Hutchinson, Blaise Pascal, Ludwig Wittgenstein, and Dietrich Bonhoeffer that illumine the Christian life cycle.

Frankfurt, Henri, et al. *Before Philosophy.* Baltimore: Penguin, 1949. A classic popular presentation of the ancient Middle Eastern worldviews that furnished the broad milieu for the Genesis story.

French, R. M., trans. *The Way of a Pilgrim.* New York: Seabury, 1965. Autobiographical narrations of an unknown nineteenth-century Russian pilgrim that reveal much of the Hesychast spirit.

Geertz, Clifford, ed. *Myth, Symbol, and Culture.* New York: Norton, 1974. Essays by distinguished scholars from several different fields that focus on the symbolic aspect of such diverse phenomena as a Balinese cockfight and the poetic function of Neptune.

Gilkey, Langdon. *Message and Existence.* New York: Seabury, 1979. An exposition of the Christian creed by a leading Protestant theologian with process sympathies.

Goldenberg, Naomi. *Changing of the Gods.* Boston: Beacon, 1979. A provocative study arguing that feminism will slay traditional religion.

Griffin, Emilie. *Turning: Reflections on the Experience of Conversion.* Garden City, NY: Doubleday, 1980. A lucid evocation and analysis of the stages in shifting one's life onto a new religious path.

Grollenberg, Lucas. *Jesus.* Philadelphia: Westminster, 1978. A simple, affecting portrait of Jesus that stresses his humanity and extraordinary reliance on God.

Grollenberg, Lucas. *Paul.* Philadelphia: Westminster, 1978. A nontechnical study of Paul's theological development through the letters thought most surely authentic.

Gutierrez, Gustavo. *A Theology of Liberation.* Maryknoll, NY: Orbis, 1973. The pioneer work of Latin American liberation theology.

Heilbroner, Robert L. *Marxism: For and Against.* New York: W. W. Norton, 1980. An illuminating introduction whose strongest suit is the author's economic background.

Hollenbach, David. *Claims in Conflict.* New York: Paulist, 1979. A fine survey of recent Roman Catholic social thought with thoughtful suggestions for its further development.

Jaki, Stanley L. *The Road of Science and the Ways to God.* Chicago: University of Chicago Press, 1978. The Gifford Lectures for 1974–75 and 1975–76, amounting to a heavily documented argument that the assumptions of Western science do not reject but rather assume the basic reality of God.

Jung, C. G., ed. *Man and His Symbols.* New York: Dell, 1964. Essays by several Jungians that clarify the role of the subconscious in many areas of life, including religion.

Kee, Howard Clark. *Christian Origins in Sociological Perspective.* Philadelphia: Westminster, 1980. A clear presentation of some of the implications that recent socio-historical studies of the worldviews of the early Christian environment are suggesting to New Testament scholars.

Leon-Dufour, Xavier. *Dictionary of the New Testament.* New York: Harper & Row, 1980. A useful treatment of major New Testament terms, with a helpful historical introduction.

Lessing, Doris. *Canopus in Argos: Archives.* New York: Alfred A. Knopf, 1979 ff. A profound meditation on humanity's current ills in the genre of science fiction.

Lonergan, Bernard J. F. *Method in Theology.* New York: Herder and Herder, 1972. Lonergan has studied the dynamics of human understanding and applied them to the study of theology, deriving eight "functional specialities" that could collaborate across disciplines.

Lossky, Vladimir. *The Mystical Theology of the Eastern Church.* Crestwood, NY: St. Vladimir's Seminary Press, 1976. A solid presentation of Orthodox theology with special attention to its roots in deep religious experience.

Lynch, William F. *Images of Hope.* New York: Mentor, 1965. A rich but demanding study of the natural basis for this theological virtue.

Mead, Sidney E. *The Lively Experiment.* New York: Harper & Row, 1963. A series of essays on the shaping of Christianity in America that stress the creativity of American pluralism.

Merton, Thomas. *The Wisdom of the Desert.* New York: New Directions, 1960. A brief collection of sayings from the desert fathers that renders well their laconic style and milieu of silence.

Miranda, José. *Being and the Messiah.* Maryknoll, NY: Orbis, 1977. A penetrating study of Johannine thought as a theology of liberation.

Miranda, José. *Marx and the Bible.* Maryknoll, NY: Orbis, 1974. A difficult but rewarding study of the affinities between Marxist humanism and Old Testament faith.

Neill, Stephen. *A History of Christian Missions.* Baltimore: Penguin, 1964. An informative one-volume view of the whole, distinguished by the sympathies deriving from the author's own missionary experience.

Nouwen, Henri. *The Way of the Heart*. New York: Seabury, 1981. A lyric adaptation of the spirituality of the desert fathers to the needs of contemporary Westerners, especially Christian ministers.

Nygren, Anders. *Agape and Eros*. Philadelphia: Westminster, 1953. An influential treatment by a prominent Protestant theologian of the past generation.

O'Donovan, Leo J., ed. *A World of Grace*. New York: Seabury, 1980. Essays on Christian theology that treat central topics from the standpoint of Karl Rahner's *Foundations of Christian Faith*.

Pagels, Elaine. *The Gnostic Gospels*. New York: Random House, 1979. A readable treatment that stresses the political factors in the struggle of the early Church with Gnosticism and emphasizes the liberalizing forces the Gnostics might have contributed.

Pelikan, Jaroslav. *The Christian Tradition: A History of the Development of Christian Doctrine*. Chicago: University of Chicago Press, 1971 ff. A multi-volume history of doctrine distinguished by its clarity and attention to Eastern Christian movements.

Perkins, Pheme. *The Gnostic Dialogue*. New York: Paulist, 1980. A solid study of the main body of Gnostic writings that delineates both their beliefs and their connections with orthodoxy.

Piaget, Jean. *The Child's Conception of The World*. Totowa, NJ: Littlefield, Adams, & Co., 1967. One of the numerous studies by the great investigator of children's intelligence that shows the structures in terms of which we first shape our meanings.

Pieper, Josef. *Guide to Thomas Aquinas*. New York: Mentor-Omega, 1962. A clear introduction that stresses Aquinas's intellectual biography.

Rahner, Karl. *Foundations of Christian Faith*. New York: Seabury, 1978. A summary statement of the whole by the most influential Roman Catholic theologian of the twentieth century.

Rahner, Karl. *Nature and Grace*. New York: Sheed and Ward, 1964. A study that represents Rahner's earlier views and reflects the problems of updating the traditional tension between nature and grace.

Rahner, Karl. *On The Theology of Death*. New York: Herder and Herder, 1961. A brilliant analysis of death, difficult but very rewarding.

Ricoeur, Paul. *The Symbolism of Evil*. Boston: Beacon, 1969. A difficult but rewarding analysis by a leading Protestant philosopher.

Roberts, J. Deotis. *Roots of a Black Future: Family and Church*. Philadelphia: Westminster, 1980. Theological reflections on the black Church and family by a leading black theologian that obliquely convey much black history as well as the author's position on topics currently debated within the black theology camp.

Ruether, Rosemary and McLaughlin, Eleanor, eds. *Women of Spirit*. New York: Simon & Schuster, 1979. Historical studies that show how Christian women have exercised leadership in the past.

Schilling, Harold K. *The New Consciousness in Science and Religion*. Philadelphia: Pilgrim Press, 1973. An encouraging report on the possible rapprochement of science and religion in terms of mystery.

Schmemann, Alexander. *The Historical Road of Eastern Orthodoxy*. Crestwood, NY: St. Vladimir's Seminary Press, 1977. A somewhat sketchy view of the whole, written primarily for Russian Orthodox believers.

Schmemann, Alexander, ed. *Ultimate Questions: An Anthology of Modern Russian Religious Thought*. Crestwood, NY: St. Vladimir's Seminary Press, 1977. Selections from leading thinkers that show the suffusion of Christian humanism through modern non-Communist Russian reflection.

Segundo, Juan Luis. *The Liberation of Theology*. Maryknoll, NY: Orbis, 1976. The work of liberation theology most reflective about methodology.

Shinn, Roger L. and Abrecht, Paul, eds. *Faith and Science in an Unjust Age: Report of the World Council of Churches' Conference on Faith, Science and the Future*. Plenary Presentations, vol. 1; Reports and Recommendations, vol. 2. Philadelphia: Fortress, 1980. A window onto some of the best features of the current Protestant churches.

Sobrino, Jon. *Christology at the Crossroads*. Maryknoll, NY: Orbis, 1978. The best Christological work yet to come from Latin American liberation theology.

Solzhenitsyn, Aleksandr I. *East and West*. New York: Harper & Row, 1980. A short work collecting Solzhenitsyn's Nobel Prize address, 1978 commencement address at Harvard, 1973 letter to the Soviet leaders, and 1979 interview on the fifth anniversary of his deportation.

Solzhenitsyn, Aleksandr I. *Lenin in Zürich*. New York: Farrar, Straus & Giroux, 1976. An imaginative reconstruction of Lenin's time in Zürich prior to the 1917 Russian Revolution. It develops Solzhenitsyn's grounds for hating Marxism-Leninism and seeing the abuses of the Soviet regime as its inevitable fruit.

Spicq, Ceslaus. *Agape in the New Testament*. St. Louis: B. Herder, 1963–66. A several-volume treatment by a respected Roman Catholic scripture scholar that shows the richness of this central New Testament concept.

Terrien, Samuel. *The Elusive Presence*. New York: Harper & Row, 1978. A rich presentation of biblical theology by a mature Protestant scholar.

Tillich, Paul. *The Courage to Be*. New Haven: Yale, 1952. A good statement of Tillich's existential interests, pregnant with implications for religion, faith, and theology.

Tillich, Paul. *Dynamics of Faith*. New York: Harper & Row, 1957. A fairly readable short work on faith by one of the giants of the past theological generation.

Tillich, Paul. *Systematic Theology*. Chicago: The University of Chicago Press, 1967. A three-volume work of philosophical reflection on Christian faith out of the Protestant tradition—one of the most influential theological visions of the twentieth century.

Torres, Sergio and Eagleson, John, eds. *Theology in the Americas*. Maryknoll, NY: Orbis, 1976. Papers from the 1975 Detroit conference that show the various liberation theologies—black, Latin American, Asian, feminist, Chicano, Native American—in one of their first, most conflict-ridden encounters with one another and with white theology.

Van Buren, Paul. *Discerning the Way*. New York: Seabury, 1980. The first volume of what may prove to be the major effort, from Christianity, to converse deeply with Jewish faith.

Vidler, Alec R. *The Church in an Age of Revolution*. Baltimore: Penguin, 1961. A good source of basic information on the trends and movements since 1789.

Ward, Barbara. *Progress for a Small Planet*. New York: W. W. Norton, 1979. A fine survey of the economic and environmental problems facing the global community.

Ware, Kallistos (Timothy). *The Orthodox Way*. Crestwood, NY: St. Vladimir's Seminary Press, 1979. A relatively simple presentation of the Orthodox view of God using figures for divinity such as spirit and prayer.

Ware, Timothy. *The Orthodox Church*. Baltimore: Penguin, 1964. A good introduction that combines historical and doctrinal information.

Wells, David F. and Woodbridge, John D. *The Evangelicals: What They Believe, Who They Are, Where They Are Changing*. Nashville: Abingdon, 1975. A collection of essays that gives a good overview of evangelicalism.

Wilmore, Gayraud S. and Cone, James H., eds. *Black Theology: A Documentary History, 1966–1979*. Maryknoll, NY: Orbis, 1979. An excellent source of primary documents on the recent developments and tensions in black theology.

Index